PENGUIN REFERENCE

The Penguin Dictionary of Media Studies

Nicholas Abercrombie retired in 2004 from the University of Lancaster, where he was deputy vice-chancellor and professor of sociology. His academic interests include the mass media, the sociology of culture and the sociology of money. He has also published extensively in introductory sociology, most recently in *Contemporary British Society* (2000), *Readings in Contemporary British Society* (2000) and *Sociology* (2004).

Brian Longhurst is Professor of Sociology and Dean of the Faculty of Arts, Media and Social Sciences at the University of Salford. He has longstanding interests in media studies, cultural studies and the sociology of culture. His books include *Popular Music and Society* (1995, 2007). His co-authored books include *Globalization and Belonging* (2005), *Introducing Cultural Studies* (1999, 2004) and, with Nicholas Abercrombie, *Audiences: A Sociological Theory of Performance and Imagination* (1998).

The Penguin Dictionary of

MEDIA STUDIES

Nicholas Abercrombie
Brian Longhurst

PENGUIN BOOKS

PENGUIN BOOKS

Published by the Penguin Group
Penguin Books Ltd, 80 Strand, London WC2R 0RL, England
Penguin Group (USA) Inc., 375 Hudson Street, New York, New York 10014, USA
Penguin Group (Canada), 90 Eglinton Avenue East, Suite 700, Toronto, Ontario, Canada M4P 2Y3
(a division of Pearson Penguin Canada Inc.)
Penguin Ireland, 25 St Stephen's Green, Dublin 2, Ireland
(a division of Penguin Books Ltd)
Penguin Group (Australia), 250 Camberwell Road, Camberwell, Victoria 3124, Australia
(a division of Pearson Australia Group Pty Ltd)
Penguin Books India Pvt Ltd, 11 Community Centre, Panchsheel Park, New Delhi – 110 017, India
Penguin Group (NZ), 67 Apollo Drive, Rosedale, North Shore 0632, New Zealand
(a division of Pearson New Zealand Ltd)
Penguin Books (South Africa) (Pty) Ltd, 24 Sturdee Avenue, Rosebank, Johannesburg 2196, South Africa

Penguin Books Ltd, Registered Offices: 80 Strand, London WC2R 0RL, England

www.penguin.com

First published 2007
1

Copyright © Nicholas Abercrombie and Brian Longhurst, 2007
All rights reserved

The moral right of the authors has been asserted

Set in 8.5/11.4 pt ITC Stone
Typeset by Rowland Phototypesetting Ltd, Bury St Edmunds, Suffolk
Printed in England by Clays Ltd, St Ives plc

ISBN 978–0–141–01427–2

Contents

Acknowledgements

N A is very grateful to Louise and Joe Abercrombie for help and advice on more technical aspects of television production and post-production. Bren Abercrombie not only answered obscure questions on the media but also used her editorial pen with great effect. As always, this book could not have been written without her help and support.

BL would like to thank all the students who have contributed to his understanding of the media over the years. Much of this book was written during the period when he was Head of the School of English, Sociology, Politics and Contemporary History at the University of Salford. That he was able to conduct any academic work at all during this period of managerial responsibility is in no small measure due to the professional excellence of his colleagues in the School. He would like to thank them all, but to extend special thanks to Paul Callick, Liz Dew, Rob Flynn, Linda Jones, Kate Marritt, Beryl Pluples, Greg Smith, Nicola Toole and Sue Vaughan. In this role he was also indebted to colleagues in the Faculty of Arts, Media and Social Sciences, especially Chris Bryant and Richard Towell as successive Deans of Faculty and Jackie Flynn as Faculty Administrator. The final thanks are the most important. Bernadette, James and Tim continue to make Brian's life special in all sorts of ways. The sharing of TV, cinema and music is only a part of it, but it has contributed to this book significantly.

NA and BL are very grateful to staff at Penguin Books: Martin Toseland, who commissioned the book, Georgina Laycock and Nigel Wilcockson, who provided very helpful editorial input, Kristen Harrison, who has taken over editorial responsibility, David Watson, who, in the course of copy-editing, made very many welcome suggestions for improvement and Ellie Smith, who calmly and skilfully guided the book through the production process.

How to Use This Dictionary

The discipline of media studies does not have a good press. Its practitioners have no need to feel defensive, however. This is a new field of study, and academic innovations of this kind are often greeted by criticism, especially when they deal with phenomena that people come across in their daily life.

Like any other new field of study, the boundaries of media studies are sometimes difficult to establish. In our choice of entries we have tried not to define the subject too narrowly. Besides reflecting the content of work on television, radio, popular music, advertising, the press, book publishing and new media, we also have entries from cultural studies because that discipline has provided much of the theoretical underpinning of media studies.

This book is intended for students and teachers of media studies and practitioners in the various branches of the media. Each entry is designed to stand on its own to provide an account – brief or lengthy depending on its importance – of a topic. Entries also have links to other entries, rather in the manner of a website, to give further information. These links are at three levels of relevance. First, words appearing in small capitals in the body of an entry are important for a full understanding of the topic. Second, other words are printed in bold preceded by 'SEE:', again in the text itself. These, we believe, are helpful in taking the subject further. The third level of link terms, in italics, are preceded by 'SEE ALSO:' and are found at the end of an entry. These indicate other relevant topics. For example, the entry on **Advertising Standards Authority (ASA)** has OFCOM and the PRESS COMPLAINTS COMMISSION printed in small capitals within it. We believe that you will need to refer to these two entries for a full understanding of how the ASA works. The entry also has 'SEE: **advertising ethics**'. This is useful in providing a context for the ASA's work. The last line in the entry is 'SEE ALSO: **regulation**'. This entry is relevant and provides general context but is not critical for a narrower understanding of the ASA.

There is a need for a generic term for the products of media organizations such as television programmes, films or books. We have adopted the word 'text' to serve this purpose. Similarly, there is a need to refer generally to the act of appropriation of media texts. We have chosen the word 'consume' for this purpose. We apologize to any readers who find these usages infelicitous.

In early editions of this book, we realize that there will be mistakes and omissions of useful terms and some entries will be less clear than they should be. We welcome comments and suggestions from our readers and these should be addressed to: Penguin Press, Reference, Penguin Group (UK), 80 Strand, London WC2R ORL.

A & R (Artist and Repertoire)   The part of a music company that has primary responsibility for the signing and development of artists. A & R staff will seek to spot talent and to collaborate with other sections of the company, for example the PRODUCER and the MARKETING department, to steer the career of an artist. In the rock parts of the music industry, A & R has been important in contributing to the value placed on 'live performance' and for scouting bands with potential when they are playing live. Negus (1992) argues that A & R departments have set the music industry along lines that reinforce ideas that rock is authentic, in that artists are original in creating their own music and are motivated by personal commitment.

SEE ALSO: **authenticity; music industry**.

ABC (American Broadcasting Corporation)   One of the four big American television networks and currently owned by the DISNEY Corporation, ABC was founded in the early 1940s (SEE: **CBS; Fox Network; NBC**).

SEE ALSO: **television network**.

ABC   See: AUDIT BUREAU OF CIRCULATIONS.

aberrant decoding   An audience interpretation or reading of a media text that is not the PREFERRED READING. For example, in a television documentary or drama about domestic violence, it may be clear that the writer, producer, director and actors take the view that physical violence against women is wrong and expect the audience to take that view also; that is the preferred reading. However, some members of the audience may believe, for religious reasons perhaps, that the physical chastisement of women by their husbands is perfectly acceptable; that would be an aberrant decoding.

SEE ALSO: **encoding/decoding; *Nationwide* study**.

access   The ways in which people have access to the media, either as producers or consumers, are important to the manner in which the media reinforce distributions of power and equality. For example, the INTERNET is often celebrated as a way in which citizens can have power. Yet many people in the UK, let alone the world as a whole, do not have internet access (SEE: **digital divide**). Again, particular individuals, politicians for example, have access to journalists in ways denied to ordinary people, and this allows them to exercise influence. As the ownership of the media becomes more concentrated and remote, ordinary citizens may feel increasingly cut off from its provision. One solution to this problem is the provision of locally based media which allow the active participation of ordinary citizens. An example of that is access or community television. This takes different forms in different countries. Commonly, however, the local community owns and runs a TV production facility which allows local people to express their views and provides a focus for community life. Community programmes of this type can then be transmitted locally (or even further afield) by cable, the internet or microwave. In the United States, cable companies have provided equipment and training, and subsequent access to cable broadcast, to allow local people access to television.

SEE ALSO: **concentration of ownership; domination**.

access television See: ACCESS.

accountability To be held responsible for the consequences of actions. It is often felt that the media have considerable power, which they ought to wield responsibly. If they fail in that responsibility, it is argued, then there should be some means by which they are held accountable and make reparation of some kind. From time to time, various ways of ensuring press responsibility have been proposed, ranging from legislation to protect the right to privacy to a formal right of reply to press comment.

SEE ALSO: **Press Complaints Commission; regulation; responsibility**.

acculturation The process by which cultures interact with, and influence, one another. Acculturation may involve direct contact between people, by immigration or invasion or indirectly, for example, by the exposure of one cultural group to the mass media of another. Either of these may result in the assimilation by one powerful group of the culture of the other. In this process, however, it is unlikely that the more dominant culture will remain entirely unchanged. There has always been cultural change stemming from contacts between cultures. In the contemporary world, however, there are fears that one culture, in essence American culture, will obliterate others because of American domination of the media and the importance of the English language.

SEE ALSO: **media imperialism**.

ACORN A system for classifying neighbourhoods, in which people with similar income, tastes, lifestyles and spending patterns live near one another. The ACORN system produces some fifty different types of consumer, differentiated by such factors as income, size of house and car ownership. This information is very useful to advertisers, who can then target particular types of consumers with mailshots, telephone marketing or even personal calling.

SEE ALSO: **geodemographics**.

action **1** The activity in a film, as generated by the director's call of 'action' at the beginning of a take.

2 A GENRE of cinema, which has become very popular with audiences since the 1980s and formed an increasingly important part of the output of the film industry. The action genre usually revolves around the exploits of a male hero who possesses (almost) superhuman powers (though is not a superhero like Batman or Superman) and who is in conflict with a powerful villain or group of villains. As a genre, the action movie developed from the 1980s onwards, with examples being the *Rambo* series, the *Die Hard* trilogy, the *Terminator* series and the *Lethal Weapon* series. The development of the genre was facilitated by the increased technological sophistication of special effects, which involved greater use of computer graphics. Part of the appeal of the genre comes from the appreciation of what can now be done technically. In addition, the development of the genre has been seen as espousing a right-wing politics. This is because the male hero saves a world from the villains by acting outside the law and in a vigilante fashion. Ideologically (SEE: **ideology**) the genre can be seen as suggesting that the world can be saved only by the intervention of the exceptional male individual who needs 'freedom' to act in confronting the forces of evil. The effects in action movies have sometimes been compared to those in computer games.

SEE ALSO: **police series; western**.

action code The parts of a narrative that are concerned with actions or things that happen. Thus, a simple narrative like 'The police, who were in a black car, chased after the villain, who was in a red car' is concerned with action. However, another possible and subsequent narrative sentence such as 'The villain was worried that the police might catch him' introduces a different code concerned with feelings. The action code is sometimes referred to as the proairetic code, from the work of ROLAND BARTHES.

SEE ALSO: **code**.

active audience Audiences that, rather than sitting passively in front of a television, positively interact with what they are seeing and hearing.

The proposition is that, rather than television doing things to audiences, audiences do things with television. Audience activity is of different kinds. For example, households use television to avoid each other, to provide moments of family warmth or as a way of regulating the behaviour of children. Most important of all, however, audience members actively interpret television programmes using their own experiences and backgrounds (SEE: **television talk**). It is also important to remember that, even if the set is switched on, nobody may be paying it any kind of attention (SEE: **regimes of watching**).

SEE ALSO: **gaze; household**.

actor 1 Someone who practises the profession of performing. Thus, one of the ways of evaluating texts (such as films, plays or television drama) is by the quality of the performance in terms of the technical accomplishments of the actors. Actors themselves can gain CELEBRITY or star-like status, though it is only a small minority who manage to achieve this. There has been significant attention to this phenomenon in media studies.

2 An individual or group that is involved in social action. For example, a media corporation is said to be an actor in global media markets.

One of the common features of both meanings is the implication that such action involves a degree of performance. The actor performs for an audience, while the media corporation performs in the economic system. A view expressed by much media and cultural theory is that, rather than aspects of life being simply given or learned, they are performed in our relations and interactions with other people. For example, men are not simply naturally masculine, or learn to be masculine, but they perform masculinity in their relationships with other people in a variety of ways on a day-to-day basis. The media can be resources for these performances as they provide material for the performance. For example, television police series can provide ideas of how a man should behave when interacting.

SEE ALSO: **star; star system; star text**.

actuality 1 Film that is shot of real life, using real people rather than actors. Fictional films may make use of actuality as part of the narrative. The term captures the idea that this is actual life, which is different from the rest of the film in the sense that it is not performed for the camera by paid actors. For example, footage of cars being driven along a motorway or the crowd at a football match may be cut into a film using actors in specific scenes.

SEE ALSO: **docudrama; documentary; docusoap**.

2 In radio and television the sound or sound and pictures of actual activities, which may be recorded or broadcast live.

adaptation Process of changing a text originally produced within one medium for use in another, as well as the text that results from this process. The most well-known process of adaptation is from a novel (often a 'classic' literary text) to film, radio or television. Some novels have been adapted in this way many times. Adaptations of this form tend to be popular with audiences but are often also seen as conveying distinction or quality to the medium to which they have been adapted. Thus, in the early days of new media such as the cinema, radio and television, the status of the medium was enhanced by its ability to display that it could convey the 'high culture' associated with literature. This is a continuing process, and examples that are given of quality TV will often include literary adaptations. It is significant that the process does not operate to the same effect when the process goes in the opposite direction. Thus, 'novelizations' of hit films and TV series are often treated with critical disdain, or are seen as rather degraded fan texts.

ad-ed ratio The ratio of advertising to editorial matter in a magazine or newspaper.

Adorno, T. W. (1903–69) Theodor Adorno was a member of the so-called FRANKFURT SCHOOL of social and cultural theory founded at the University of Frankfurt in 1923. Adorno, like other members of the School, criticized what he regarded as capitalist control over social and cultural life and the inequalities, oppression and injustice that this caused. Adorno, in work with Max Horkheimer, maintained that the operation of the culture industry was crucial in contemporary forms of oppression. According to Adorno and Horkheimer, the culture industry produces commodities like other industries: that is, culture, which is produced to be bought and sold on a capitalist market. This process has led to a standardization of cultural products. The clearest example of this process comes in Adorno's analysis of popular music. In Adorno's view, popular music as the product of the culture industry exists in a limited number of standardized forms – the parts of which are essentially interchangeable. This contrasts with what Adorno refers to as serious music, where the parts are not interchangeable in this way. Adorno thought that listeners to popular music also respond in standardized ways. The listener tends to be inattentive and distracted – not giving the music the whole of their attention. In this view the pleasures of popular music are superficial and false. There are many criticisms that can be made of Adorno: he neglects the variation in popular music; does not fully understand how it is produced; does not consider how audiences actually respond to popular music; writes from an elitist perspective constrained by the traditions of German philosophy.

Despite such criticisms, his account and the wider work with Hork-heimer remain an important starting point for many analyses of popular music (and other media). His work draws attention to how the cultural industries, which produce films, TV and music, work in an industrialized way, seek to standardize products in genres and channel audiences so that they will consume these genres.

SEE ALSO: **cultural industries; music industry**.

ADSL (asymmetric digital subscriber line) A BROADBAND system which can work over existing telephone lines and hence does not need new and specialized cabling installing.

advance Payment made to a recording artist or author in anticipation of future earnings through ROYALTIES. The size of an advance is often seen as indication of the market value of an artist. Advances to celebrities, such as footballers Wayne Rooney and David Beckham or model Jordan, for their 'ghost-written' memoirs have been increasing significantly, re-flecting both the sales potential of the resulting product and the preva-lence of a celebrity culture fed by magazines such as *Hello!* and *OK!* It may be the case that royalties earned from sales of the book do not match the advance paid.

advertisement An image or a text that attempts to persuade people to buy something. They may achieve this by treating the consumer as a rational purchaser who simply wishes to buy the product that best serves his or her needs. The advertisement will stress the reliability of the prod-uct, its value for money or its efficiency. To do that, typically there will be an amount of text that presents an argument for the product. Or the advertisement may aim to appeal to a set of feelings or desires – a wish to be liked, to be beautiful, to belong to some favoured group or to be looked up to, for example. Advertisements aiming to persuade in this second way may make do with very little, or no, text but rely instead on evocative or suggestive images. They are attempting to suggest, rather than argue, that, if you buy this product, you will achieve your heart's desire. To a great extent, the history of advertising in the twentieth century is a movement from the first type of advertising to the second. In no small measure, this is a function of the change in the media available to advertisers. Until the middle of the century, advertisers were largely drawing on the experience of the medium of print with its conventions of text accompanied by pictures. Television, however, gives new visual possibilities and its conventions have fed back into print advertising, which, in its turn, has become more visual.

Advertisements must do two things. First, they must establish a clear *difference* between the product being advertised and its competitors. This is often described as establishing the UNIQUE SELLING PROPOSITION (USP). A USP can be established through a variety of means: the product itself, its packaging or the advantages claimed for it. Second, advertisements have to associate the product with some other desirable quality. Again, that association can be managed in many different ways. For example, the language used or references to cultural objects in the advertisement can imply that a cultured elite will buy the product; green fields and streams will suggest purity; or the involvement of a celebrity connotes high status.

The use of BRAND image is one way of achieving both difference and association. Brands are built up over time and identify the distinctiveness of the products involved. At the same time, the whole idea of a brand is that consumers, or the interested consumers at any rate, think of it as possessing features that they value.

advertising agency A company that provides services for those wishing to advertise. Although most large companies will have marketing departments of their own, as a rule, when an ADVERTISING CAMPAIGN is needed, they turn to advertising agencies. Agencies carry out a number of functions for clients. They will have someone who is the main point of contact and is responsible for overseeing the client's campaign. That person is sometimes called an account manager. The agency will then provide research evidence that will inform the campaign. That research is not usually carried out in-house but is more commonly obtained from a standard source (for example, SEE: **target group index**). Armed with the appropriate research data, the client's wants and needs and the budget, the MEDIA PLANNER designs the campaign, deciding such issues as the type of media to be used and the timing and frequency of advertisements. The creative personnel in the agency – the copywriter and the art director – then actually design the advertisements. Some larger agencies not only provide these services, they also offer other forms of marketing, e.g. direct mailing.

As in other branches of the media, advertising agencies are undergoing a process of CONCENTRATION OF OWNERSHIP. There has also been a tendency to hive off processes into specialist companies. For example, there is an advantage in buying advertising space in newspapers in bulk and thereby lowering costs. Specialist companies have appeared which effectively pool the demands for such space from many advertising agencies.

SEE ALSO: **advertisement**.

advertising campaign The planned sequence of operations involved in promoting a product in the market. When an ADVERTISING AGENCY and its client decide on the promotion of a particular product or service, the production of an advertisement or sequence of advertisements is not a random or unplanned process. To be effective, a campaign is needed which integrates the client's needs with creative input for the design of the advertisements themselves, MEDIA PLANNING and subsequent evaluation of the effectiveness of the campaign.

advertising ethics Codes of practice governing the moral or potentially harmful/beneficial consequences of advertising. If advertising and other forms of product promotion and marketing have the persuasive effects that are often claimed for them, advertisers clearly have an ethical responsibility. In recognition of this, the industry regulates itself through the ADVERTISING STANDARDS AUTHORITY (ASA) which issues a code of conduct which specifies that non-broadcast advertisements, sales promotions and direct marketing should be legal, decent, honest and truthful. Although the ASA has probably been successful in regulating the content and methods of advertising, its remit illustrates the limitations of self-regulation for it cannot be held responsible for the ethical implications of the advertised products themselves. This is particularly clear in questions of public health. Governments have had to intervene directly to control advertisements for products deemed harmful to public health. Tobacco is the obvious example, but more recently in the UK there has been a debate about the regulation of advertisements for foods high in fat, sugar and salt content.

Ethical concerns of another type have also surfaced within the last twenty years or so. MERCHANDISING, PRODUCT PLACEMENT, SPONSORSHIP and ADVERTORIALS are all marketing techniques that may hide the fact that someone is trying to persuade us to buy something. Sponsorship has caused particular difficulties when companies sponsor an event or an activity in order to counter unfavourable publicity for their products. Some tobacco companies have sought to associate themselves with sport in this way.

Lastly, there are those who take a more extreme ethical position, arguing that advertising persuades people to buy products that they neither need nor can afford. As an extended variant of this argument, some critics will suggest that advertising is a form of communication that celebrates a consumer and capitalist society and helps to perpetuate it (SEE: **consumer society; domination**). Both these arguments exaggerate the persuasive power of advertising.

SEE ALSO: **regulation**.

Advertising Standards Authority (ASA) The independent self-regulatory agency for non-broadcast advertisements, sales promotions and direct marketing in the UK. It regulates the content of advertisements through its application of the BRITISH CODE OF ADVERTISING, SALES PRO-MOTION AND DIRECT MARKETING (CAP) to ensure that they are legal, decent, honest and truthful. Television and radio advertisements are regu-lated by OFCOM. The ASA is controlled by a council, and its work is funded by a levy on advertising and direct-mail expenditure. All the main trade and professional bodies representing advertisers, advertising agencies and media owners, e.g. the Direct Marketing Association, sub-scribe to the CAP, and their members are required to abide by it. If any member refuses to comply, sanctions can be applied, including the loss of reputation through adverse publicity or reference to the Office of Fair Trading. The ASA responds to complaints from the public and also con-ducts its own spot checks on advertisements. Although the ASA was originally set up in 1962 to fend off statutory regulation, it is fair to say that it is a form of self-regulation in the media that is a good deal less controversial than the PRESS COMPLAINTS COMMISSION. Critics, however, complain that this misses the point. They argue that the ethical issues in advertising are really to do with the harmful properties of the products being advertised, e.g. tobacco and fatty foods (SEE: **advertising ethics**), rather than in the manner in which they are advertised.

SEE ALSO: **regulation**.

advertorial Material in newspapers and magazines that is attempting to persuade readers to buy a product but which is written to look like the non-advertisement material in the rest of the publication. Clearly news-papers and magazines carry advertisements which help them to survive. Sometimes, it is not entirely clear what is advertising and what is editorial content. Some advertisements, especially in magazines, are written in such a way that they look as if they are the magazine's opinion. Similarly, some editorial matter contains comments on products or brand names and comes close to advertising them. The reader is at risk of being confused and assuming that a magazine is endorsing one product rather than another.

SEE ALSO: **advertising ethics; puff**.

aesthetic code A CODE that is concerned with the aesthetics of a text, such as colour or lighting in film. These effects convey particular meanings to the audience. For example, shadows and contrasts between light and dark were used in FILM NOIR to convey meanings of moral ambiguity; contemporary films shot in black and white tend to convey the sense that life is hard and tough; the use of brown tones conveys 'earthiness'; and so on.

SEE ALSO: **aesthetics; lighting.**

aestheticization of everyday life The view that the routines of EVERY-DAY LIFE have become more an object of SPECTACLE than they once were and that they have thus acquired an aesthetic or artistic slant. Examples that might illustrate this process are the way in which occasions like birthdays are increasingly performed in public in Britain by the display of posters on houses (celebrating that a resident is now fifty and the like), how football fans will wear a team shirt while watching their team on TV in the home or in a public house or the interest in the design and style of ordinary household objects.

SEE ALSO: **Debord; postmodernism.**

aesthetics The study and appreciation of beauty, usually beauty in art. While this has been one of the classic disciplines of the humanities and has formed a key branch of philosophy concerned with how value can be judged, it has been less of a direct concern in media studies, which has tended to suspend judgements about the value of a text in favour of its systematic study in a social and cultural context. One consequence of this approach is that all texts, irrespective of judgements about aesthetic value, are open to analysis. In practice this has meant that forms of POPULAR CULTURE have been opened to similar analysis as serious or HIGH CULTURE. This has been controversial as some critics maintain than this implies that popular texts have equal worth to serious ones and that media studies is therefore a symptom of cultural decline. It has been argued in response that this view conflates analysis with the judgement of worth. Moreover, media studies has been a key mover in the further opening up of the judgement of value to wider debate in the context of POLITICS and social change. This has led to questions being asked about why some forms of culture are seen to be better than others. One development has been that some writers from within media studies have argued that media and cultural studies now needs to pay far greater attention to such issues and to the way in which judgements of aesthetic worth are made, especially as, in everyday life, members of the audience are making judgements about standards all the time. For example, young people routinely talk about why they like the music of one band rather than another.

Agence France-Presse The first NEWS AGENCY, AFP was founded in 1832. Although originally a private company, it is now a public body located in Paris. It offers television and photograph services as well as print and has a turnover of about £140 million. The bulk of the business is French and the majority of clients are state organizations.

agenda setting The determination of the terms in which public discussion takes place by concealing items of public interest or failing to provide complete information. There have long been worries that the media have the power to mould opinion and belief. One of the ways in which this is said to happen is that the media set the agenda and hence ensure that particular issues do not emerge at all and audiences do not consider them. The GLASGOW UNIVERSITY MEDIA GROUP, for example, argues that television decides what is important and provides only certain information about those items. It includes certain views and information and excludes other, perhaps contrary, opinions and makes them invisible to the viewer. In a detailed content analysis of television coverage of high rates of inflation during the 1970s, the Group concluded that statements saying that rising wages were the main cause of inflation outnumbered by eight to one those reports that contradicted that view. The agenda was constructed so that some views were especially prominent.

Even if one accepts the conclusion that the media do set an agenda (and there is substantial disagreement with the Glasgow University Media Group's work), that still does not show that there is an effect on the audience. There is evidence that the order of importance given in the media to issues of the day is much the same as that given by the public. But one cannot draw from that the conclusion that the agenda adopted by the media *causes* a similar ordering of priorities in the audience.

It may well be that particular segments of the audience are influenced by the agenda-setting capacities of the media. Politicians, for example, may be swayed by comment and opinion expressed in newspapers, as is alleged to have happened to members of the third Blair administration in the UK in formulating a law and order policy.

SEE ALSO: **bias; effects; framing; news values**.

agent An intermediary between creative people and media organizations. For the best part of the twentieth century, creative personnel in the media, especially actors and writers and, more recently, musicians, have had agents to represent their interests. One of the intriguing features of the media industries is that creative people, while absolutely critical to the industry, are not usually directly employed by an organization for long periods but instead work freelance for several organizations. Agents fill the gap between such people and media organizations. On the one side, they act for the writer, musician or actor by finding jobs or placing work. In many cases, this will extend to managing a whole career. On the other side, they increasingly function to relieve the media organization of some of their tasks, in particular, the management of their clients – their support, planning their next projects and making sure that they complete existing work well and on time (SEE: **outsourcing**). In some areas, this will go further still. LITERARY AGENTS, for example, effectively are finding suitable books for publishers.

Al-Jazeera A broadcasting station based in Qatar, Al-Jazeera achieved fame during 2002–4. The station has made very good use of its contacts in the Muslim world and has had a number of scoops. In particular, videotapes made by Osama bin Laden and his associates or Saddam Hussein had their first airing on Al-Jazeera. The station has been accused of bias by the Western media, and particularly by the government of the United States, but replies that it upholds standards of journalistic integrity and objectivity.

alternative media/alternative press See: RADICAL MEDIA/RADICAL PRESS.

alternative rock A form of rock music that defines itself, or is defined by the audience, as outside of the MAINSTREAM genres of rock music. There are many similarities to the term 'indie', which is used as an abbreviation for independent. While in one sense this captures the way in which some groups and artists seek to be critical of mainstream values and practices, in another the boundaries between mainstream and alternative are often blurred. There is a process where bands often CROSS OVER rapidly between the forms – for example, REM. The term has been shortened to 'alt' as in alt-country, which is music that defines itself as outside the Nashville-based mainstream country music, as represented by bands like Uncle Tupelo and the Jayhawks and artists like Bonnie Prince Billy. Despite the definition of these artists as 'alt', it is actually sometimes very difficult to state clearly what the features of such 'alt' musics are, as they change over time and may reflect the nature of the mainstream against which they are defining themselves. However, it can at least be suggested that 'alt' rock forms will be likely to be less lavishly produced than the mainstream, to attempt to be more 'authentic' in some way, and to attempt to capture 'real life'.

SEE ALSO: **independent company.**

Althusser, Louis (1918–90) A French Marxist structuralist philosopher, Althusser was influential in media and cultural studies in three main ways, especially in the 1960s and 1970s. First, he reformulated MARXISM to accord more weight to the ideological rather than the economic, which influenced the work of the CENTRE FOR CONTEMPORARY CULTURAL STUDIES in the 1970s. Second, he argued for the integration of a psychoanalytic approach in his theory of IDEOLOGY, which proposed that subjects are created (or interpellated) through a hailing process. This was an influence on those studies of film texts that drew attention to the mechanisms by which members of an audience are placed in particular subject positions, e.g. as a woman. Third, through his theory of the importance of the IDEOLOGICAL STATE APPARATUSES (ISAs) he emphasized the role of the state in reproducing social inequality. In his view, the ISAs operate in combination with the Repressive State Apparatus (RSA) to ensure the survival of an unequal capitalist society, based on class. This led to further attention to how the education system ensures that some people end up in low-paid jobs (Willis, 1977). It also influenced attention on the role of non-commercial broadcasting systems in producing social cohesion, in the work of the GLASGOW UNIVERSITY MEDIA GROUP and Brunsdon and Morley (1978).

In these ways, Althusser's work, especially as interpreted and filtered through the cultural studies developed at Birmingham and in the work of STUART HALL, has become part of media studies currency, even though his specific influence declined rapidly from the 1980s onwards. This was most importantly due in theoretical terms to the structural determinism in his work that increasingly came under attack from POSTSTRUCTURALIST and POSTMODERNIST directions.

SEE ALSO: **structuralism.**

AM/FM (amplitude modulation and frequency modulation) Techniques for the transmission of information in a signal, either by varying the amplitude of the cycle (AM) or the frequency with which the cycle is repeated (FM). Amplitude modulation is where the amplitude of the wave is altered; in frequency modulation the frequency of the carrier wave is altered, while the amplitude is kept constant. The most significant aspect of this in non-technical terms is that the development of FM radio led to a higher quality of signal and clarity of reception. At first, like many innovations in the technical reproduction of music, this was used in the transmission of classical music, but as FM progressed in the 1960s it was increasingly used to broadcast the developing rock music that was album- rather than singles-based. In turn, this was connected to the aesthetic of this form as something to be appreciated and listened to rather than to be danced to and contributed to the increasing divide between pop (AM) stations devoted to the top singles and rock (FM) stations concerned with album tracks.

amplification of deviance The way in which the press feeds off television and television in turn responds to the press can lead to a spiral of concern in which the various elements of the media create public interest in a deviant act. The media thus amplify the initial deviant act. This can create a MORAL PANIC – a surge of social anxiety about some problem. The classic study of this phenomenon is STANLEY COHEN'S *Folk Devils and Moral Panics: The Creation of Mods and Rockers* (1973). Cohen argued that, at certain times of social stress, societies get into moral panics about a social issue, during which a great deal of attention, especially media attention, is focused on particular social groups who are in some way deviating from the norms of society. His study concentrated on conflicts between mods and rockers in British seaside towns in the 1960s, but its conclusions could apply equally well to asylum-seekers, travellers or young people in the street. The media amplify the panic because they report it extensively and selectively and, because of this media attention, the authorities – government, police and courts – believe that they have to do something to control it. Those acts of control in turn receive more media attention, giving another twist to the spiral, further fuelling the sense of anxiety or panic. Any unorthodox behaviour or minor criminal conduct can become therefore an act of deviance amplified by the media.

analogue The manner in which electronic devices use a continuously varying voltage to represent what is being transmitted. Analogue television and broadcasting systems are gradually being replaced by DIGITAL ones.

anamorphic Process in film-making where images are compressed verti- cally and then projected via an anamorphic lens to produce WIDESCREEN effects.

SEE ALSO: **aspect ratio**.

anchorage The restricting of the meaning of an image or a text, making them more CLOSED by constraining alternative interpretations. For example, a television newsreader or correspondent will comment on the images that are being shown to us, thus potentially restricting the range of interpretations that we can place on them.

Anderson, Benedict (b. 1936)   Emeritus Professor in the Department of Government at Cornell University, USA. He is most widely known, and influential, in media studies for coining the term IMAGINED COMMUNITY in his work on nationalism.

Ang, Ien (b. 1954)   Professor of Cultural Studies at the University of Western Sydney, Australia. Ang's work has been particularly influential in audience studies, especially her analysis (1985) of the audience for the very popular American soap opera *Dallas*. This developed the idea of emotional realism and identified a particular STRUCTURE OF FEELING. Ang argued that the female audience response to *Dallas* identified with the text in terms of the reality of the emotions, rather than the 'objective' reality of the action or the setting. She developed her analysis of AUDIENCE issues in subsequent books and has more recently considered a range of issues concerning GLOBALIZATION, migration and ethnicity and the representation of Asia and Australia.

SEE ALSO: *Dallas*.

animation   Technique of using drawings or, increasingly, computer-generated images to create moving-action films. Animation has tended to develop along two broad directions in the history of the cinema. First, there is a commercial strand, of which the best example is DISNEY. The second strand has been consciously experimental and AVANT-GARDE, using the form to depart from established realist narrative cinema. This can break established conventions of time and space. At points, this more experimental genre can 'cross over' to the mainstream, as in *Spirited Away* (which is set in a 'magical' bath house) and *Belleville Rendezvous* (where characters cross the Atlantic Ocean with great speed). The former also shows the importance of the Japanese animation industry and style, which has influenced contemporary techniques.

SEE ALSO: comic; graphic novel.

Annan Report   The Annan Committee on the Future of Broadcasting (1977) felt that the then duopoly of BBC and INDEPENDENT TELEVISION excluded minorities within the population. The recommendations of the Committee led directly to the creation in 1982 of CHANNEL FOUR, which was required to produce programming that would appeal to minorities. Another of Annan's ideas was also adopted in the design of Channel Four in that the new channel does not make its own programmes but instead operates rather like a publishing house and commissions programmes from others, including independent producers, a model now widely adopted by other television networks.

anti-narrative Textual strategies that seek to break with more conventional or orthodox forms of NARRATIVE and storytelling. This may be done from the desire to be artistically innovative and to show the inadequacy of REALIST narrative in artistic terms and/or from a concern to make the point that alternative political expression requires new artistic forms which disrupt the dominant conventions of narrative. For example, the films of the Russian director Sergei Eisenstein or the French 'New Wave' of the 1950s and 1960s used techniques of juxtaposed images or JUMP CUTS to work against narrative coherence.

SEE ALSO: **art cinema; avant-garde**.

AOL Time Warner A very large media company with a turnover in 2005 of over £20 billion. It was formed in 2000 by a merger between America Online and Time Warner. In that this was a merger of an internet service-provider with a supplier of media content, it was widely hailed as the media company of the future. Things have not turned out so well so far. The share price of the company has declined and there has even been talk of demerging. The company is now known as TIME WARNER.

apparatus In critical film theory a term used to characterize the technology and practices of cinema. This is not simply a descriptive term but is used to address the idea that the whole cinematic apparatus produces spectators who are constructed through the cinematic experience. Spectators are positioned in an ideological fashion through this process.

SEE ALSO: **film theory; ideology**.

appreciation index (AI) A measurement of the opinions that television viewers have of the programmes that they have watched. For television producers the size of an audience is important, but so also are the opinions of the audience on the merits of what they watch. To construct an appreciation index, a large panel of viewers are asked to score programmes that they watch on a scale from 1 (not at all enjoyable) to 6 (extremely enjoyable). The scores are then averaged and presented as a percentage (where an average of 6 would be 100 per cent). The majority of programmes score between 65 and 75. It is important to note that the appreciation index is not necessarily related to audience size. Thus, some programmes may attract only small audiences which, nevertheless, rate them very highly.

SEE ALSO: **audience measurement; audience ratings; audience research**.

A-roll Camera shots in television that are taken directly for the purpose of the programme, e.g. interviews. B-roll shots, on the other hand, are more general shots used to provide context and background, e.g. a building or streetscape. These can be taken for the purpose, as is the case in news programmes, or they can come from an archive.

art and commerce There is an extensive story to be told of the intricate relationships between art and commerce. One position is to suggest that the two activities are completely separate and that any commercial interruption in artistic endeavour will lead to the corruption of the pursuit of art for art's sake. Rock fans often talk of bands 'selling out' which suggests that artistic purity has been sacrificed to financial gain. It can be argued that such a view neglects the intimate relationship between the two activities. While it is the case that the state and governments have sponsored art, often to preserve or develop forms of artistic activity that would otherwise wither from the lack of commercial funding, the main funding of the arts has come from commercial activity in one form or another. This is despite the fact that artists themselves often have anti-commercial views. These complex dynamics are particularly prevalent in popular music. Here, there is often a strong anti-commercial set of feelings among musicians, who may in their minds be faced with 'selling-out' by playing commercial music, or not making a living at all. This is reinforced by the views of those audience members who also seek a form of artistic purity from the band that they follow. Thus, a band signing with a major label will often be interpreted as the death knell of their artistic achievement. The adoption by a band or singer of anti-authority views, or a critique of the record industry, will only tend to mask for a while the relations between art and commerce. The further irony is that an anti-commercial line will often be very saleable and lucrative.

SEE ALSO: **artist**; **author**.

art cinema A type of cinema that consciously offers an alternative to MAINSTREAM commercial cinema. In general, such films will have relatively small budgets, will tend to offer an alternative look at everyday life (perhaps being critical of what are perceived to be established or dominant values) and will use 'alternative' cinematic techniques (such as breaking from conventional narrative). However, despite this relative separation from the mainstream (SEE: **Hollywood**), art cinema can cross over into the commercial, and boundaries between art cinema and mainstream are blurred. While art cinema may seek to be outside the mainstream it may still need to be commercially successful in its own terms. And some Hollywood films, like *Sideways* (dir. Alexander Payne, 2004), have been shown in ART-HOUSE cinemas and been seen as art cinema.

SEE ALSO: **anti-narrative**; **avant-garde**.

art-house Sometimes used as an alternative to ART CINEMA, this also refers to the type of cinema that screens art or AVANT-GARDE films. Most centres of large population will have such a cinema (perhaps attached to a university or film society), which may also show MAINSTREAM commercial films.

articulation The contingent linkage between cultural or social phenomena. The easiest way to think of the idea is through the analogy of the articulated truck or lorry (a semi-truck in the USA). Here, the cab section and the container or box section are directly connected but can also be separated and joined up to different parts. Such links can be changed as a box can be connected with a different cab at different times. For example, in the late 1960s reggae music was particularly popular with skinheads in the UK, but by the 1970s it had become liked by a wider audience of rock fans who previously had disparaged the genre.

artist A term with a long history but most particularly connected to the development of Romanticism, a movement in the arts that developed from the late eighteenth century onwards and which emphasized imagination, emotion and artistic rebellion. Consequently, an artist was defined to be the true creator of a piece of work through the application of his/her talent or genius. The term was significantly developed in the tradition of European oil painting (Berger, 1972) and has since been applied in a range of different fields. It is now commonplace to draw attention to artistic genius and to see the artist as possessing special qualities. The term is now equally often applied in those fields that value live performance in theatre, film, music, and even where recording is the norm.

SEE ALSO: **auteur; author**.

artwork Graphic or other illustrative material that is prepared separately but is then married to text before printing.

aspect ratio Relationship between width and height in frame of film or television screen. The long-established main standard was 4:3 (or 1.33:1), which mean that the picture was four measures long to three measures in height. This was established in the early days of the cinema due to the ability of the Edison Company to determine standardization of technology. This ratio was also adopted by television. As television developed in popularity in the 1950s film companies experimented with a range of widescreen ratios, and now different aspect ratios are used in the cinema including 2.2:1 and 1.66:1. The standard for HDTV is 1.76:1. Consequently, there is now much variation in aspect ratios. As TV in the home has become more cinema-like (SEE: **media convergence**), it has become possible on contemporary digital televisions to alter the aspect ratio at the push of the remote control button.

SEE ALSO: **widescreen**.

assembly edit See: ROUGH CUT.

Associated Newspapers Publishers of the *Mail*, the *Mail on Sunday*, the *Evening Standard* and a group of regional newspapers. Associated News-papers belongs to a larger group, the Daily Mail and General Trust, which has wider media interests.

SEE ALSO: **newspaper; Northcliffe**.

Associated Press A not-for-profit news agency run as a cooperative and owned by a large group of newspapers in the United States. Turnover in 2004 was about £600 million. Although a much smaller company than REUTERS, it is about the same size in its provision of non-domestic news.

Astra satellite See: BSKYB.

asymmetic digital subscriber line See: ADSL.

asynchronization Where sound is out of step with images in cinema and television. Thus, if when we are watching TV or a film and a person's lips move and the voice comes along later, we will read this as a mistake or error in the technological process. However, experimental film-makers have used such techniques to disrupt the REALISM of texts, by showing how they are put together.

atmosphere In radio, noise or sound that is the background to the main voices. For example, a radio commentary on a football match might include the sound of the crowd shouting out or chanting, or a story about fell-walking might include the sound of the wind in the background.

SEE ALSO: **bed**.

attitude A relatively stable system of belief concerning some object and resulting in an evaluation of that object. Research into the media, whether conducted by the industry in search of information useful for sales or by academics, often consists of surveys, which ask for attitudes of one kind or another. People might be asked, for example, about their attitudes to the portrayal of violence in the media. On the whole, these attitudes are stable over time and they consist in evaluations, such as that such portray-als are harmful to children. In surveys of attitudes, it is often assumed that relatively superficial attitudes are a good guide to more deeply held values and to behaviour. Neither of these assumptions is necessarily true. Expressed attitudes may not relate to deeper feelings because, for example, people may respond to questions about their attitudes in ways that they believe are acceptable to the questioner. Similarly, expressed attitudes have often been shown to be inconsistent with subsequent behaviour.

SEE ALSO: **audience measurement; values.**

audience Groups of people before whom a performance of one kind or another takes place. Critical to what it means to be a member of an audience is the idea of performance. A routine distinction is made between the simple and direct audience experience of the theatre, a rock concert or a football match, on the one hand, and the experience of being a member of the audience for a performance mediated through television, radio, film or records, on the other. The mass media, in other words, make a difference to audience experience. By comparison with direct audience events, the experience of mass-media events is not restricted to a particular space, the communication is not so direct, the experience is more of an everyday one and is not so invested with ceremony and ritual, less attention is paid to the performance, which is typically received in private rather than in public, and there is a much greater social and physical distance between performers and audience.

These features of the mass-media audience have prompted anxieties of various kinds. Critics from the left have argued that audiences are encouraged to participate in consumer society and to accept their lot in life (SEE: **domination**). Critics from the right argue that the mass media promulgate materialistic values and immoral ways of behaving and encourage violence and sexual deviance. Common to both these perspectives are the assumptions that the content of the mass media is trivial and undemanding and that the audience is essentially passive, simply taking in what is offered. While it may be true that the mass media, especially television, film and radio, do not demand concentrated attention all of the time from their audience, it is not so true that the audience is passive. Many media theorists now argue that audiences do make active use of what they see on television or cinema (SEE: **active audience**).

Most mass-media organizations clearly have a commercial interest in finding out about their audience (SEE: **audience measurement**). Detailed academic study of audiences has developed rather late on, however, and until relatively recently, analysis focused on content of the media or on the way in which media organizations worked to produce that content.

SEE ALSO: **effects; television audience.**

audience classification See: AUDIENCE DIFFERENTIATION; DEMOGRAPHICS.

audience demographics See: DEMOGRAPHICS.

audience differentiation The separation of the audience for the media into segments each of which has different tastes and concerns. There is often a tendency in public discussions of the media to think of the audience as a single block responding to the media in more or less the same way. Actually, the audience is highly differentiated by such factors as age, gender, social class, ethnicity and taste. For example, an older woman employed as a Health Service manager and an unemployed young man may want to watch very different television programmes and may have very different responses to them. Furthermore, it can be argued that changes in society are fragmenting the audience still further. As a result, it is no longer possible to produce magazines or television channels that will suit most people. Instead, media products have to be differentiated to appeal to particular groups within the audience. Hence the proliferation of specialized magazine titles and television channels. Even with increasing audience differentiation it is worth remembering that audiences often still do behave in a coherent fashion. For example, in the UK many television programmes, e.g. soap operas, can command a large proportion of the television audience. Again, some television can have a global reach, e.g. the Live Eight concerts or Princess Diana's funeral. Some books, the Harry Potter series for example, have very large sales, both domestically and globally, and can cross sectors of the audience otherwise rather separate.

SEE ALSO: **individualization; market segmentation/differentiation**.

audience fragmentation See: AUDIENCE DIFFERENTIATION.

audience measurement Those who work in the media industries, whether they are newspaper editors, broadcast schedulers, advertisers or television producers, naturally want to know as much as possible about those who are, effectively, buying their products – their audiences. Television producers, advertisers and schedulers, for example, will want to know, amongst other things, what programmes are preferred by what sections of the audience, when they are watched in company with whom, what advertisements are watched, and how much the television is on.

Audience measurement, however, is not quite so straightforward as it may appear. Even defining the act of reading, watching or listening is problematic. If the radio is on in the background, for instance, can people be said to be listening? Furthermore, the audience itself is changing as it becomes less of a mass and breaks up more into different segments demanding more sophistication of measurement and analysis (SEE: **audience differentiation**).

A variety of means are used to measure audiences. Favoured methods are diaries kept by audience members, questionnaires and various electronic devices, largely used for measuring television audiences (SEE: **People-meter**). Sometimes these methods are applied to the same sample of people over time (a panel) while for other purposes a different sample will be chosen each time. Whatever the means, however, usually the aim is to produce valid and reliable quantitative data by using large enough samples.

Most audience measurement is carried out by independent industry-wide bodies, which helps to reduce cost and gives confidence in the results (SEE: **BARB**; **JICRAR**; **National Readership Surveys**).

SEE ALSO: **appreciation index**; **audience rating**; **audience research**; **market research**.

audience needs See: USES AND GRATIFICATIONS.

audience rating A term used, confusingly, in two senses. **1** The size of the audience in relation to the potential audience. Television and radio producers are clearly interested in the size of audience for programmes. This can be expressed in simple numerical terms. However, it is more common for a rating to be presented as a proportion of a relevant population. That could be all those with television or radio sets or it could be a more specialized audience – all those with television sets in Scotland, for example.

2 The judgement made by an audience on the quality of a media product. Audience size will be determined by a number of factors including time of day, advance publicity and whether or not they like the programme. However, there is no necessary relationship between size and audience appreciation (SEE: **appreciation index**). For example, small audiences for cult programmes may record higher levels of appreciation than much larger audiences for more mainstream programmes.

SEE ALSO: **audience measurement**; **audience research**.

audience reach The size of the relevant audience for the output of a given medium. Although apparently simple, the concept of audience reach is actually quite complex, and those working in different media have different notions of how to describe the size of the audience for their product. In the newspaper industry, for example, the audience may be defined as those who buy a newspaper or those who read it. Those who buy may not read and there may be several readers of any copy bought.

Furthermore, there is a larger potential audience, composed of those who *could* buy and read, but do not. For television, there is an audience that comprises all those who have access to a televison set. For any one television channel or programme, that is the potential audience. However, clearly, only a proportion of that potential audience will switch on to see a particular programme. What is more, not all those whose television set *is* switched on will be paying attention to the programme being transmitted. In sum, the audience and audience size can be defined in different ways for dfferent purposes. For example, advertisers are, in the end, interested in those who read newspapers or those who are not only watching a television programme, but who are also actually paying attention to it.

The simple size of an audience is not the only characteristic of audiences that interests media producers and advertisers. Also important is the AUDIENCE SHARE – the relationship between the audience reached, however it is defined, and the potential audience for that media product – and the AUDIENCE RATING – the quality of the media product in the eyes of the audience.

SEE ALSO: **audience measurement; audience research**.

audience research Research into what audiences do with media messages and what they might want from media products is of interest both to the industry (SEE: **audience measurement**) and to academics (SEE: **audience**). Methods of audience research are conventionally divided into the quantitative and the qualitative. In the former, the aim is to produce valid and reliable data by asking questions of a sample of people. That sample has to be large enough to justify coming to conclusions that will validly apply to the whole population from which the sample is drawn. Instruments like questionnaires or electronic recording devices (SEE: **Peoplemeter**) have to be used which can be applied to fairly large numbers of people. They have to be simple, unambiguous, easy to administer and capable of yielding numerical conclusions. For many research purposes, quantitative techniques of this kind are essential. For others, they may not be appropriate. They do not lend themselves, for example, to a detailed exploration of what a television programme means to an audience. For these purposes qualitative techniques are better suited. There are a great range of such techniques varying from simple observation to group discussions in focus groups. They are not designed to produce valid and reliable numerical conclusions but they do produce data of a different kind and are in widespread use in media research.

SEE ALSO: **attitude; market research**.

audience share The proportion of the total potential audience taken by any media product. The difficulty lies in defining the potential audience. For example, the potential audience for the soap opera *Coronation Street* could be defined as all those who have their television set switched on at the relevant time. *Coronation Street*'s audience share is then simply the proportion of that audience that actually does watch the show. But the potential audience could be alternatively defined as all those who watch soap opera. The idea of audience share is often extended to media companies rather than particular media products and is usually known as market share.

SEE ALSO: **audience rating; audience reach**.

audio clip See: NEWS CUT.

Audit Bureau of Circulations (ABC) Set up in 1931 and governed and financed by advertisers, advertising agencies and publishers, the ABC sets standards in the provision of circulation figures by the newspaper and magazine industry. This is important since advertisers will want to know that the circulation figures claimed are accurate. The ABC verifies claims about circulation made by publishers by an inspection (audit) of the means by which those claims are made and by the training of newspaper and magazine staff. Originally set up to deal with print media, the ABC now also audits electronic media.

SEE ALSO: **circulation; National Readership Survey**.

auteur Used to denote the director of a movie as its 'AUTHOR', who determines the form and content of the film. The French term is still used as French film theorists and practitioners originally developed the idea.

auteur theory Theory that has its origins in the work of a group of film theorists (later directors) who wrote for the French film journal *Cahiers du Cinéma* (1951–). In criticizing much established French film-making as routine and unexceptional in comparison with the superior aesthetic qualities of some American and a small number of French directors, the idea was developed that films could essentially be seen as the product of a presiding artistic genius or AUTHOR. The skill of the director would integrate the contradictory and complex aspects of the production process of a film. The idea was taken up and developed to become one of the staples of film criticism in both academic and popular modes. It is now commonplace for discussions of film to see the movie as the product of the overall control of the DIRECTOR, who is the author or auteur. This is despite criticism of the idea from two broad directions. First, there is a sociological view that the production of a film is actually a collective, rather than individual, process involving the creative input of a number of people in different roles. Second, there is a more theoretical approach that contests the idea that any one single author can be seen as the creator of any cultural product. In this view, authors tend to act as vehicles through which a DISCOURSE or discourses flow, or are themselves representations of structural forces in a culture. This trend is particularly associated with structuralist and post-structuralist thought, which also tends to argue in its more psychoanalytic versions that the individual does not have a unified consciousness or subjectivity. Given, in this view, that subjectivity is always in process, it is difficult to see how the unified vision of the author or auteur can result.

SEE ALSO: **structuralism; poststructuralism.**

authenticity To be true to a set of principles or to an essence of a human being or social group. In media studies, the idea is most used in the popular-music field, where it is often seen as a badge of particular value. For example, 'good' music is that which most commonly reflects the personality and/or the social circumstances of the artist. 'Black' (African-American) musicians, who can communicate the experience of living in a ghetto (or 'hood), in this view, do so in performing rap music. A white artist from the suburbs would be in danger of producing inauthentic rap music. Discussions of this sort are common in popular music and led in the 1960s to arguments over whether it was possible for white people to play blues music, arguments that were satirized by the Bonzo Dog Do Dah Band in 'Can Blue Men Sing the Whites?' Moreover, the ability to sing and play 'live' is another key component of authenticity in rock music. This situation is complicated by the complex relationship between ART AND COMMERCE.

author The idea of the author as the single individual creator of a text is now a commonplace. However, it actually emerged as part of the Romantic movement in European thought and culture, which emphasized the role of the ARTIST. Here the text is essentially seen as the creation of the individual genius of the author. This idea fed into film studies through the development of AUTEUR THEORY in the second part of the twentieth century in France. The idea that the text is the product of the guiding hand of the single artistic genius has been criticized from a sociological direction, which recognizes the complex social processes that contribute to textual production, and from a theoretical direction, especially in currents associated with STRUCTURALIST, POSTSTRUCTURALIST and POSTMODERNIST thought. Thus, ROLAND BARTHES saw the text as a site where discourses clash and famously proclaimed the 'death of the author'. Texts would not be analysed to find a single meaning put there by the author, but as a place where many ideas come together outside the intention of the author. Such a view was itself subsequently criticized as the theory of the analysis of texts advanced. However, while this leaves space for different conceptions of authorship, it has not led to a restatement in simple terms of the power of the author.

autocue Device that enables presenters to speak directly to a camera without appearing to read from a script. The autocue is placed near the camera and read accordingly. Similar devices are now used in much public speaking, especially by politicians.

avant-garde An art movement that is at the leading edge of development. The avant-garde of any movement or in any period is often the subject of intense debate and criticism for more conservative defenders of established artistic forms, who often have a livelihood to protect. The passage of time tends to turn yesterday's avant-garde into today's establishment. Perhaps the most telling example of this can be found in Impressionist painting, which was very controversial at its inception, but prints of which now adorn the walls of houses the world over.

avatar The manifestation of a human being in a virtual world. For example, in many COMPUTER GAMES, players each take on a personality and a physical appearance in the game.

SEE ALSO: **virtual reality**.

Avid A manufacturer of the industry-standard computer equipment and software for NON-LINEAR EDITING.

back catalogue The previous recordings made by a popular music artist. Exploitation of the back catalogue became an important source of revenue for the MUSIC INDUSTRY, especially during the period when vinyl record collections were replaced by CDs during the 1990s. The rights to a back catalogue of successful artists such as The Beatles are often a highly prized asset because of the revenue that can be generated from them. For successful and critically acclaimed artists the recycling of the back catalogue as recordings are repackaged with alternative versions of songs and additional live tracks has become more prominent. In part, this is an attempt by the music industry to continue to resell the back catalogue even after vinyl has been replaced by CD. It also contributes to the construction of a canon of valued recordings that are seen to represent key moments in popular music history. Many artists are now having their earlier albums expanded and released in this way. Examples include bands like The Stooges, Can and The Cure.

SEE ALSO: **copyright**.

backing In music-making refers to the background music, behind the dominant voice of the singer. The extent to which the music is referred to in this way to some degree reflects the power of the singer and his or her popularity. Thus the history of many pop and rock groups charts a movement where the singer becomes more prominent, and the rest of the members are seen to be backing him or her. This also happened in earlier musical history. Thus the big bands of the 1930s and 1940s would often include a singer who performed on some of the numbers. They would be seen as secondary to the musicians. However, as they became popular in their own right, the band or orchestra would become backing for their voice. Good examples of this are Bing Crosby and Frank Sinatra.

back projection Technique in film-making that projects an image on to a screen from behind which enables other action to be filmed in front of the screen. A good example of this would be a film narrative that involves action that is being filmed in a studio using back projection of the countryside to produce the filmic effect or illusion that the action is actually taking place outside.

SEE ALSO: **front projection**.

Bad News studies The GLASGOW UNIVERSITY MEDIA GROUP conducted a very well-known series of studies of the way that the media – chiefly television but also newspapers – report the news. The first book was published in 1976, and the studies have continued ever since, although from the early 1990s they have had a declining impact. The Group's overall conclusion is that television news is biased in that it violates the formal obligation to give a balanced account (Glasgow University Media Group, 1976, 1980, 1982, 1985, 1993).

The *Bad News* studies are based on a detailed CONTENT ANALYSIS of news reports on a variety of topics including industrial relations, the behaviour of the economy and war and peace. Television news is essentially agenda-setting, including certain views and information and excluding other opinions which are, therefore, invisible to the television viewer. This process happens in a number of ways. Most importantly, the news defines the issue, decides what is important and organizes its presentation in terms of those news values. For example, in the late 1970s, there was extensive public discussion of the poor financial performance of British Leyland, a company then manufacturing Austin, Morris, Triumph and Jaguar motor cars. There were two competing explanations of this – low investment and poor management by the company and disruptive behaviour, particularly strikes, by the workers. Television news preferred the latter explanation, mentioning it far more frequently than the alternative. This form of presentation was supported further by the people interviewed and the way in which they are treated. Official figures, whether they be company directors or politicians, are given more space and time to air their views and are treated with more respect by interviewers than, say, employees or union officials. Dissenting or oppositional views do not get such exposure at least partly because journalists are often dependent on official sources for information. For example, in coverage of an industrial dispute involving dustcart drivers in Glasgow, which left a great deal of rubbish uncollected in the street, not one striker was interviewed although ten others were, some of them several times. The presentation of items can also lead to bias. Figures of authority tend to be interviewed in authoritative situations, in offices for instance, while strikers might be interviewed in a noisy street. Language can be distorting. For example, strikers are characterized by television news as making 'demands', while the management makes (the milder) 'offers'.

The *Bad News* studies have been much criticized, not least by media organizations. First, the authors of the studies are accused of not making clear what the standards of judgement are. Second, other studies of the same or comparable material conclude that there is at least not such extreme bias as that found by the Glasgow University Media Group. For example, they have not found disapproving or approving language used any more frequently for strikers than for officials. Lastly, and most importantly, they concentrate on the content of the news rather than on its effect on the audience. Other studies have found that viewers gave a quite different priority to issues from that which the news did. The original studies were also criticized because they did not look at audience reaction but concentrated instead on the way in which the news was presented. Later publications by members of the Glasgow University Media Group have attempted to correct this emphasis (Philo, 1990).

SEE ALSO: **audience; bias; news; objectivity; television news**.

Bakhtin, M. M. (1895–1975) A Russian analyst of literary texts. Bakhtin was the leading figure of the so-called Bakhtin circle, which produced a number of analyses of language and literature during the 1920s. His best-known work is concerned with the analysis of carnival and the transgressive nature of popular culture (Bakhtin, 1984) and with the nature of clashing DISCOURSES in the middle-class novel (Bakhtin, 1981). These works have been influential in contemporary literary and cultural studies, especially in the context of the development of POSTSTRUCTURALISM, where the text is viewed as a site of discursive struggle.

bandwidth The capacity of a medium of transmission to carry information. The greater the bandwidth, the greater the amount of information that can be carried.

banner headlines Headlines in a newspaper that are printed in large type and extend across a page in order to give emphasis to the story printed underneath.

BARB (Broadcasters' Audience Research Board) An organization providing, on behalf of the industry, detailed data on television audiences. This includes which channels and programmes are being watched, the number of people watching, and the audience composition – the type of people who are watching. The viewing figures are obtained from panels of television-owning households designed to be representative of all television households in the UK. Panel members have all their television sets and video-recorders electronically monitored by a meter (SEE: **People-meter**), and all household members and their guests register their presence when they are in a room with a television set on. Data from the People-meter are then automatically downloaded and analysed.

SEE ALSO: **audience measurement**.

Barthes, Roland (1915–80) A French literary critic and cultural analyst, whose development of STRUCTURALIST and POSTSTRUCTURALIST ideas in the context of writing on literature and EVERYDAY LIFE was particularly influential on the early development of cultural and media studies. He identified hemeneutic (or ENIGMA), proairetic (or ACTION), REFERENTIAL, semic and symbolic CODES from a structuralist and semiotic perspective. He is now best known in media and cultural studies for his application of the ideas of SEMIOLOGY to the nature of everyday life. These short analyses were collected in his book *Mythologies* (Barthes, 1973, first published 1957). Here Barthes dug below the surface of everyday life and representation for deeper meaning to show the operation of power. He criticized a number of forms and activities as being, in his view, part of ideological mystification. Barthes' analysis of a photograph of a young black soldier saluting the French flag, which he sees as connoting the benefits of French imperialism, is one of the best-known examples of this semiological approach. His latter work was increasingly concerned with his own identity and subjectivity, under the influence of poststructuralism.

base and superstructure Karl Marx argued that upon the economic base of society there arose a political and ideological superstructure that had the effect of concealing the exploitative social class relationships that existed in the economic base. While this idea was used in often sophisticated and complex ways by Marx and Engels, some later Marxists used it in a much more mechanical manner to suggest that culture simply reflected what was happening in the base. This was later criticized by different variations of Western MARXISM, which argued for the greater significance of the cultural. This movement was influential in the development of media studies. Here an emphasis has been on the ideological role of the media (as part of the superstructure) in the concealment of the exploitative nature of the capitalist economic system. For example, it has been argued that television news reports events in a way that systematically emphasizes versions that favour dominant groups, or use sources that favour governments.

SEE ALSO: **Althusser; Bad News studies; hegemony; ideology; political economy**.

bastard measure A print character that is of a different size or weight from others on the page.

Baudrillard, Jean (b. 1929) A French sociologist, Baudrillard has analysed the production, exchange and consumption of signs and symbols in consumer society. He argues that the electronic media of communication falsify social relations, which become merely simulations of social reality. He has been concerned to understand the way in which mass communications impact on society. Because social reality is a simulation, he claims that society becomes HYPERREAL. Critics disagree sharply as to the importance of Baudrillard's work. This is especially the case in the controversy over his analysis of the first Gulf War. Baudrillard's suggestion that, because of the nature of media representation, the war was not a real event seems absurd in the context where people are being killed. However, it does draw attention to the way that events and their representation on television are inseparable in contemporary societies.

BBC (British Broadcasting Corporation) Probably the best-known and most widely respected broadcasting organization in the world, the BBC has its origin in an agreement between manufacturers of radio receiving sets after the First World War. This consortium set up the BBC as a private company in 1922 to provide a national network of radio transmitters and a broadcasting service. JOHN REITH was appointed the managing director of the company in 1923. It became clear that broadcasting was to be a major force in national life, and the government decided to investigate options for the regulation of the BBC by setting up two committees (SEE: **Crawford Committee; Sykes Committee**). The outcome of the deliberations of these committees was the formation of the BBC as a PUBLIC SERVICE BROADCASTER and it was granted a Royal Charter of incorporation in 1927. Direct government control over broadcasting was rejected, and the BBC remained an autonomous corporation. But, at the same time, the BBC was guaranteed as a public service by requiring it to have a licence which specified the responsibilities of the corporation which was therefore ultimately responsible to the government. In its deliberations about what kind of entity the BBC was to be, the government and its committees were much influenced by the views of John Reith, who became Director-General of the new Corporation in 1927 and stayed in that role until 1938. Reith believed that every household in the UK should have equal access to broadcasting, which therefore had a democratic function. Further, the content of broadcasting should not be driven by market considerations, but should be the best available, reflecting the highest cultural standards. Broadcasting, in other words, should not only be used for entertainment, but should also educate and inform. He felt that the achievement of these two objectives would only be possible if there was a single provider of broadcasting which could ensure that programming of the required quality was delivered to every citizen.

The BBC stayed in this form until after the Second World War. At that point, the BBC's monopoly came under pressure and finally, in the mid-1950s, competition from commercial television, funded by advertising, was permitted (SEE: **Independent Television**). This was an important change and, once any competition was permitted, it became very difficult to resist the introduction of more commercial broadcasters. The BBC now faces competition from terrestrial broadcasters like ITV, Channel Four and Channel Five, but also from broadcasters using other technologies, especially SATELLITE. The effect on the BBC has been profound in that it has started to behave like any other competitor in the broadcasting marketplace. The corporation has retreated from its Reithian mission to educate and inform. Instead, it competes by offering programmes that will attract the highest viewing figures possible, and critics have complained that this produces a DUMBING DOWN. It has broadened out its activities to attract additional funds. For example, it is substantially involved in MERCHANDISING, especially in books and magazines. It has invested in DIGITAL TV and has created a multiplicity of channels. It has moved into the internet. These activities have created an uneasy situation. On the one hand, it is unclear whether, and in what way, the public service ideal to which the BBC is wedded can be sustained. On the other, commercial competitors complain routinely that the BBC competes unfairly. This latter argument often focuses around the funding of the corporation.

In the 1920s, anyone who wanted to have a radio set had to buy a licence in order to use it to receive broadcasts. With the formation of the BBC, these licence fees became its principal means of funding. It has remained so ever since, although now the licence is for television reception. The level of the fee is set by government. Although the licence fee remains the largest source of income for the corporation, there are also earnings from other sources. The Foreign and Commonwealth Office funds the BBC World Service directly, for example. In addition, as indicated above, there is a growing commercial income from merchandising and from the exploitation of the corporation's back catalogue of past programmes. For the BBC's competitors, the difficulty with this method of funding is that it conveys an unfair advantage in that it, in effect, gives a guaranteed source of money while allowing the BBC to compete directly. Successive governments are therefore lobbied to end the licence fee system.

If the BBC occupies an uneasy position in the competitive broadcasting market, it also has an ambiguous relationship with government. On the one hand, it is an autonomous corporation. On the other, governments have control to an extent, not least because of their setting of the licence fee. The BBC has a long history of conflict with governments, which frequently feel that the corporation is not balanced in its treatment of government actions. The most recent example was the Labour government's claim in 2004 that the BBC reported inaccurately on its case for going to war in Iraq. The upshot was the resignations of both the Director-General of the BBC and its Chairman. The ambiguities in the BBC's position are unlikely to diminish. Digital broadcasting will mean a large increase in the number of television channels on offer. It does not seem to make sense that a few of these channels will offer comprehensive programming appealing to everybody. It is likely, rather, that each channel will provide specialized programmes. This seems to undermine the ideals of public service broadcasting in that viewers, by not watching the same programmes, are not participating in a shared public experience. In addition, if viewers have to pay separate subscriptions for individual channels why should all viewers pay via the licence fee for BBC channels which they may not watch?

SEE ALSO: **government and the media; regulation**.

beat Pulse or rhythm of music. The emphasis on beat led to the development of a particular type of music in the early 1960s, especially in the UK. Derived from American origins, especially rhythm and blues (R 'n' B), the beat was emphasized in the guitar and drums music that was most effectively popularized by The Beatles in their earlier work. This definition also drew on the idea of 'beat' in the Beat literature movement of the 1950s as exemplified by writers such as Jack Kerouac and Allen Ginsberg, where the writer was seen as outside the orthodox patterns of everyday life and lived as a bohemian. Beat music thus had a particular style of music and attitude to conventional everyday life.

Beaverbrook, Viscount (1879–1964) An early MEDIA MOGUL, William Maxwell Aitken, Viscount Beaverbrook, built up a substantial portfolio of publications, most importantly the *Daily Express*, but also the London *Evening Standard* and the *Sunday Express*. An active Conservative politician occupying cabinet posts during the Second World War, Beaverbrook made unashamed use of his newspapers as vehicles for his own political views.

bed In radio, the sound that is under the main voices or other dominant sound. For example, it provides a base for the voices of the participants in an interview or the narration of a news story. The bed could be ATMOSPHERE.

behaviourism A school of social science that deals with observable behaviour and disregards the subjective aspects of human activity such as consciousness, meaning or intention. Many social scientists think that it is impossible to come to valid conclusions about human activity without consideration of the subjective side. Some critics argue that much audience research, in that it depends on obtaining quantitative data from questionnaires, is behaviourist.

SEE ALSO: **audience research; effects.**

Benjamin, Walter (1892–1940) A social theorist and philosopher born in Germany, who was associated with the writers of the FRANKFURT SCHOOL in debates around CRITICAL THEORY. He made a major contribution to cultural and media studies through his concern to understand the impact of new technologies, in particular photography and film, on cultural representation. He is probably best known in media studies for his argument that the aura which surrounds art in pre-modern societies is destroyed by its reproduction in modern mass media. For example, a painting such as the *Mona Lisa* conveys a sense of awe by its scale, setting, texture and reputation that is lost in the millions of reproductions that have been made of it. However, there is some value to be gained from such mass circulation which is not seen in straightforwardly negative terms.

Berliner A size of newspaper intermediate between TABLOID and BROADSHEET. In the UK, it has been adopted by the *Guardian* newspaper.

Berlusconi, Silvio (b. 1936) Berlusconi started his business career in property development. From that position, he has built up a very large business empire comprising interests in football, insurance, banking, food and construction as well as in the media. His companies dominate Italian media provision, and he is invested in television, newspapers, advertising, film and book and magazine publishing. He has made less successful forays into the wider European media market. From the early 1990s, he started to develop a political career and became prime minister of Italy in 1994. His government was very short-lived, however, and it collapsed in a few months. Nonetheless, he returned as prime minister in 2001. His career has been dogged by scandal and he has been accused of using his control of the media to enhance his political career and his political position to further his business interests.

SEE ALSO: **media companies.**

Bertelsmann A large, global media company based in Germany with sales in 2004 of almost £10 billion. Its interests include music, e.g. RCA records, books, e.g. Random House and Knopf, newspaper and magazine publishing, television, e.g. Channel Five, and film.

SEE ALSO: **media companies**.

bias A prejudice, sometimes acknowledged, but sometimes hidden or unconscious, that distorts the way in which the world is seen or reported. OBJECTIVITY is an important journalistic ideal. For various reasons, much of what is presented in the media falls short of that ideal (SEE: **news**). One may say that the media are biased when such failures amount to a persistent espousal of one point of view, which is distorting the presentation of events. For example, for much of 2002, the media were very concerned with the issue of Eastern European asylum-seekers. Newspapers such as the *Daily Mail* printed stories about the ever greater numbers of such people waiting to cross to the UK, their involvement in crime once there and their dependence on the welfare state. These accounts fall short of the standards of objectivity in that journalists did not investigate alternative accounts of criminal activity or of the actual numbers involved. It also is biased in that it represents a persistent statement of only one point of view. Bias is not always a question of words. Pictures may be a more potent source and, indeed, photographs may be deliberately altered to make a point.

Bias is not necessarily deliberate. As commonly, it may simply be the unconscious expression of the views of a journalist, editor or proprietor, and newspapers generally try, sometimes unsuccessfully, to separate reporting from advocacy or opinion.

SEE ALSO: *Bad News* **studies; objectivity; truth**.

binary opposition Opposition of two ideas in the narrative of a text. STRUCTURALIST thought focuses on the binary oppositions which, it suggests, constitute human culture. The analysis of a text will concern itself with how meaning is created through such oppositions as good and evil, the individual and society, the rural and the urban, the hero and the villain. The idea derives in some respects from the 0,1 binary code of computer science. Binary oppositions structure the basic aspects of texts and are a tool to analyse them. Thus, the WESTERN centres on the opposition between a hero and the villains and involves the opposition between wilderness and civilization, and the SOAP OPERA partly works on that between the inside and the outside. Specific aspects of the narrative are built upon these broad foundations. For example, in a western like *Shane* (dir. George Stevens, 1953), the hero (played by Audie Murphy) confronts a group of evil ranchers while in *Unforgiven* (dir. Clint Eastwood, 1992), Will Munny, played by Clint Eastwood, faces a different set of villains, but has many similar traits as a hero. Likewise, in *Coronation Street*, the inside of the street itself is contrasted with the outside of all other places, and characters are often in danger when they go outside of the street. The characters may also be put at risk in the street by people coming from outside.

SEE ALSO: **semiology**.

binding The means by which the pages in a magazine or book are held together. Several varieties may be distinguished. Perfect binding uses glue to attach pages at one edge, while stapling simply inserts staples through the middle of the centre pages. These two methods are used for magazine binding, although perfect binding is also commonly employed for paperback books. Hardback books, and some paperbacks, usually have the pages sewn together. Spiral bindings are used for specialist books, e.g. atlases, for which it is important that the book can lie flat when open.

Birt, John (b. 1944) Director-General of the BBC from 1992 to 2000. Though his management style was widely criticized within the corporation, he is credited with taking the BBC into the age of digital broadcasting. Since his resignation as Director-General, he has continued to have an influence on broadcasting policy from his position in the House of Lords.

SEE ALSO: **producer choice**.

black cinema Film produced or performed by black people. As with the similar idea of BLACK MUSIC, this is more complicated than might be thought. A number of issues are significant. First, there is the definition of black, a definition that is typically vague and shifting. Thus, there is a tendency to define 'black' as people of African or Caribbean descent, though it can also include other forms of ethnic lineage and identity, especially in the UK, e.g. people of South Asian descent. Second, there is this idea that in addition to being produced by 'black' people, such cinema will address the black 'community' or its concerns. An important issue here is whether there is such a community or whether it is fragmented by for example, class, space, age and gender. This also has implications for a third issue concerning the politics of black cinema. There tends to be an assumption that such cinema will oppose oppression and the way in which black people are treated in a white-dominated society. However, the problem can arise that, in seeking to address some modes of oppression, others are reinforced. Thus, in a film like *Do the Right Thing* (1989), the black director (Spike Lee) explores the condition of African-Americans through contrasts to Italian-Americans, who might also be seen as oppressed. Indeed, part of Lee's intention could be to show how all oppressed groups are turned on each other by dominant powers, but there still remains an issue of differential treatment. Other films by Lee have caused debate around gender issues, as for example in hooks' (1996) critique of *She's Got to Have It* (1986). A further issue concerns the extent to which black cinema should involve different institutions and practices from those used in the mainstream. Thus, is a black film director who works in Hollywood, like Spike Lee, producing black cinema if he works with 'white' people? There is often an implication that forms of cinema that are by oppressed groups should be more collectively produced and seek to further the careers of others who form minorities.

black music Music associated with, or performed by, black people. This simple definition is more problematic than may initially appear. First, some commentators have suggested that there is a problem where a black person is performing music that would not normally be thought to have any 'black' connections, such as a piece from the European classical music tradition. Second, attention has been drawn to the immense problem of defining what a black person is. In the United States, for example, the legal definition of black used to vary between states, meaning that a person could move from being black to white by crossing a state line (Hatch and Millward, 1987). It has also been argued that, despite there being a number of contenders, there are no musical features that are inherently black. For example, Tagg (1989) rejects the idea of black music as predicated on the idea that some essence to black music can be found. However, other writers have suggested that the term black music can be used in a more circumspect way that does entail a return to essentialism. For example, writers such as P. Gilroy (1987, 1993) recognize that the idea of black music identifies important political and social connections between black people and articulates key concerns of black expressive culture. This facilitates linkages between black people who live scattered across the world, and shows how forms of music such as R 'n' B, blues, soul, gospel, reggae, hip-hop and rap articulate issues that are debated within black communities, such as the representation of women and criminality. Such issues concerning the difficulty of a clear definition of black music have been taken into account in the development of the idea of Music of Black Origin (MOBO), which is now used in such as the MOBO awards in the UK.

SEE ALSO: **black cinema; Gilroy; politics**.

bleed Where printed text extends outside its standard margins and spreads to the edge of the paper or close to images or other graphic material.

blog A regular publication appearing on the WORLD WIDE WEB. The word itself is a shortened version of weblog. Blogs vary widely in content. Some are simply online personal diaries while others are commentaries on politics, culture, enthusiasms, science or education. Some are single-authored, while others rely on a team of authors or allow other people to express views on the contents of the blog. Most blogs give a list (the so-called blogroll) of other blog sites that the author recommends, a practice which effectively creates an online community of those with similar views or activities.

Blogging has become a popular activity very quickly. From very small beginnings in the 1990s the number of blogs has grown to an estimated 25 million in 2006. Many of these sites will have very small numbers of readers, perhaps deliberately so. Others, however, have regular readers numbered in the thousands and can be very influential as a result.

There are various views on the significance of blogging in very much the same way as there is an active debate on the social and political implications of the INTERNET more generally. For many, blogging represents the personal freedom to say what one likes and to engage in untrammelled debate with opponents and allies alike, while functioning as an intensely social activity. For others, many blogs give currency to vicious opinions or ill-informed rumour and may actually isolate citizens from wider debate by confining them within a circle of those with similar views and tastes.

The activity has probably come to public prominence mostly because of its uncertain relationship to the conventional mass media, although it is also important to note its significance as a medium of personal communication. Many blogs have begun to rival conventional journalism as sources of opinion and comment. And they are a good deal cheaper and easier to access. They have broken stories that newspapers and tele-vision have not dared to touch. The best-known example of this to date is the way that blogs reported remarks made by Trent Lott, the majority leader in the US Senate, and started a process that led to his resignation. Both television and newspapers have responded by reporting the activities of influential blogs. It is too early to tell how blogging, and the use of the internet in general, will finally impact on the conventional mass media and the business model on which it works.

SEE ALSO: **instant messaging; MySpace.**

body The body may be thought to be a natural phenomenon, in that we all have bodies that differ naturally and are subject to the ageing process, but it also has important social and cultural dimensions. We learn to move in particular ways that are socially sanctioned and constructed, especially by GENDER. Media studies has tended to focus its attention on how the body and bodies are represented. An example would be in discussions of the portrayal of women in the media and specifically in the representation of female bodies in women's magazines. There have also been extensive debates on PORNOGRAPHY and the exploitation of women. More recently, a different sort of approach has begun to pay more attention to the physicality of the body in relation to performance, by producers and the audience. Thus, performers use their bodies to convey particular meanings (such as sexual desire) and the audience may move their bodies in time to music. There is a developing literature on dance that reflects these trends.

SEE ALSO: **identity**.

body copy The main block of printed text in a newspaper or magazine as opposed to such other material as illustrations or captions.

bold See: TYPEFACE.

Bollywood The main Hindi centre of the very large Indian film industry is in Mumbai (Bombay). The Indian film industry is the world's largest national cinema and also has a strong export performance. The term Bollywood has been coined to demonstrate the importance of the type of movie made in Mumbai in a way akin to the dominance of HOLLYWOOD. In 1985, for example, 905 feature films were made in India, of which 185 were produced in Hindi in Bombay (Banker, 2001). Bollywood is often used to stand for the whole of the Indian film industry, which is actually much more diverse. Like Hollywood, Bollywood therefore refers to a real place (if only through the first letter of the old name), a mode of film-making (highly industrialized with a strong STAR system) and a style of output (with emphasis on music and romance). The latter is increasingly well known and satirized, through the influence of the Indian Diaspora in the Western world. The films often feature exaggerated acting and performance styles, a glossy look and are reliant on music and conventionalized (often romantic) narratives. Recent successful examples include *Mohabbatein* (dir. Aditya Chopra, 2000) and *Kaho Na Pyar Hai* (dir. Rakesh Roshan, 2000).

book With a fair claim to be the first mass medium, the book could only attain that status with the advent of Guttenberg's printing press using moveable metal type (SEE: **print**). Before that, the availability of books was limited by the need to copy them by hand or by using carved wooden printing blocks.

Religion dominated the content of early books. Religious subjects accounted for about half of the output from the invention of the printing press in the mid-fifteenth century to the eighteenth century. In that period, the remaining books dealt with such topics as the law and occupational knowledge, farming for instance. In the eighteenth century, however, the population had a greater disposable income, and books became cheaper. Above all, literacy and the habit of reading were becoming more widespread. It is estimated that, by the mid-eighteenth century in the United Kingdom, some 40 per cent of men and a rather lower proportion of women were able to read. The result of these trends was that the output of the growing publishing industry became more diverse and more focused on entertainment. In particular, novels made their appearance at this time (SEE: **reading public**).

During the first 300 years or so, the printing of books was fairly closely controlled (SEE: **government and the media**). Governments were nervous about the subversive potentialities of printed media and sought to limit any damage that they might do. In the sixteenth and seventeenth centuries, this was achieved by royal censorship and the granting of royal patents – monopolies in certain kinds of books – to favoured publishers who would be less likely to support dissident views. The use of these powers was supported by the trade itself since it reduced competition. In the eighteenth century, however, direct censorship of this kind became less common. Although some kind of government control was effectively exercised via taxation of various kinds, a much freer market developed as new kinds of book, and of customer, made their appearance.

The organizational structure of book publishing was also changed by the development of a reading public and a market in books in the eighteenth century. In the first two or three centuries of the book, the activity of publishing was closely attached to the means of production, namely printing. Printers, often under the patronage of the Court, an aristocrat or the Church, would take responsibility, not only for the printing, but also for the selling and distribution of books. By the late seventeenth century, however, booksellers, who were much closer to the growing market, began to take on the publishing role and, significantly, commissioned new books from authors that they thought they might be able to sell. By the late eighteenth century, companies recognizable as modern publishing companies had evolved out of bookselling (SEE: **book publishing**).

The book has been a critical element in the democratization of all societies. Even so, it has been widely predicted that it will disappear under pressure from other media. There is no sign that this is happening and, if anything, the production and reading of books is as significant an activity as it has always been (SEE: **reading public**).

SEE ALSO: **binding**.

book publishing Book publishers are typically, though not invariably, profit-making companies. They find authors for books that they believe will sell or respond to manuscripts sent in to them by authors or their agents. Once the author has submitted a manuscript, the publisher then arranges for the printing of the book, usually with a separate company. The publisher will also take responsibility for advertising and marketing and for the sale and distribution of copies to booksellers. In the modern book publishing industry, therefore, the authorship, publishing, printing and retail sale of books are separate processes carried out in separate organizations. In the early days of publishing, publishers would simply buy a book from an author for a set fee. Although this kind of arrangement is still found today, it is much more common for the author to retain COPYRIGHT and for the publisher to buy the right to reproduce and sell copies of the work.

The history of the book publishing industry may be divided into three phases. In the early history of publishing, the commissioning and production of books was largely in the hands of printers; the issuing of books was a natural outgrowth of their manufacture (SEE: **book**). However, from the late seventeenth to the early nineteenth centuries, the publishing function became increasingly closely connected with bookselling (See: READING PUBLIC). Booksellers were close to their customers and took a very commercial attitude to publishing, commissioning books to fill specific market gaps and controlling their authors closely. From the middle of the nineteenth century to the middle of the twentieth, book publishing entered what many regard as its golden age, separating out the commissioning and marketing of books from their manufacture and retail selling. Book publishing became a distinctive enterprise in its own right and, at its centre, was the figure of the COMMISSIONING EDITOR, who was responsible for finding authors and books for the company to publish. Commissioning editors were expected to be multi-skilled, combining expertise in finance, rights, contracts and production with a knowledge of books, art and literature. As a result, they tended to be highly educated and of a particular cultural disposition. They prided themselves on not being driven solely by commercial considerations, but also publishing books that deserved a readership for their artistic, literary or intellectual merits.

A third phase in the history of publishing starts in about 1950. There is greater concentration of ownership as large companies buy up the smaller independent ones. Although the names and, to some extent, the organization of very long-established publishing houses (e.g. Collins or Hutchinson) are still kept, the companies themselves are owned by conglomerates. For example, Collins is owned by HarperCollins, in turn owned by NEWS INTERNATIONAL, while Hutchinson belongs to Random House, which is part of BERTELSMANN, a very large conglomerate with interests across the media. At the same time, publishing companies are changing in their structure. The commissioning editor is no longer all-powerful; the marketing and rights functions are correspondingly more important. LITERARY AGENTS are taking over much of the commissioning function. There has also been a dramatic change in bookselling as large booksellers (e.g. Waterstones) have appeared, and many small, local independent shops have gone out of business. In turn, these booksellers are facing competition from potentially even larger internet booksellers like Amazon. The existence of large bookshop chains changes the economics of publishing and has led to the demise of the NET BOOK AGREEMENT.

Since the end of the Second World War commentators have been predicting the collapse of the book publishing industry. Partly this has been because of concerns about the book as a means of providing information and entertainment. It has been thought that the computer would replace the book as a provider of information and film and television would replace the entertainment function. At the same time, there have been anxieties about the economics and structure of the industry. There were widespread fears that the increasing concentration of ownership of book publishing but also of bookshops would restrict the range of books being published to a relatively few best-sellers. At the same time, it seemed very difficult for the industry to continue to produce a large number of new titles when so few of them even covered their costs. As is the case in much of the media, the music recording industry for example, relatively few products are responsible for much of the profit. In fact, at least at present, these fears have not been realized. The number of titles published in the UK continues to grow and currently stands at almost 100,000 per year, about fifteen times the number published at the beginning of the twentieth century. The industry continues to be sustained by the importance of the English language globally and by the way in which film and television actually promote the sales of books (SEE: **cross over**). At the same time, there is no indication that demanding or difficult books fail to find a publisher to a greater extent than fifty years ago.

SEE ALSO: **book; print.**

boom A tool used to extend other devices (especially microphones) during the process of film-making. Thus, a microphone placed on a boom can capture sound over the heads of actors, while remaining out of camera shot.

SEE ALSO: **microphone**.

Bordwell, David (b. 1947) Jacques Ledoux Professor of Film Studies at the University of Wisconsin-Madison, USA. He is one of the most prominent academic writers on film, having covered a wide range of topics such as film history and different national cinemas. He is co-author, with Kristin Thompson, of one of the most successful and comprehensive texts on film in *Film Art: An Introduction* (7th edition 2005, first published 1979).

Bourdieu, Pierre (1930–2002) French sociologist who was originally best known in the English-speaking world in the sociology of education, Bourdieu's work on culture has become hugely influential since the 1980s. Bourdieu's key contribution has been to introduce and examine the idea of CULTURAL CAPITAL, which he distinguishes from economic (e.g. money and shares) and social capital (social connections or networks). In his work *Distinction* (1984) Bourdieu examines how social classes are differentiated from each other through both economic and cultural processes and the possession of economic and cultural capital. For example, the manager of a company may be high in economic capital in that he or she is highly paid and may own shares, but relatively low in cultural capital in that he or she is not able to appreciate classical music or AVANT-GARDE painting. The extent to which these capitals are 'useful' depends on their recognition and value in a context. To take account of this, Bourdieu developed the idea of FIELD. Thus, the lack of appreciation of classical music may not hinder the progress of the manager, as within the field in which he/she operates this may not be highly valued. However, for the person seeking advancement in the field of French academia this may be a significant disadvantage. Bourdieu was also responsible for development of the idea of HABITUS. The habitus of a group or individual refers to the way in which they have developed ways of classifying or understanding the world around them, which have become habitual. Thus, our initial response to a new phenomenon will be conditioned by our habitus. Habitus does not just refer to the ways in which we think about things, but also references our modes of speech, bodily movements and so on in the world which we inhabit.

B picture or **B movie** Type of film produced in Hollywood that was shorter and cheaper to make than the more prestigious A picture. As

HOLLYWOOD cinema developed, it evolved a highly industrialized system of film production. With the popularity of film booming, a category of film developed to fill demand. The B picture was less aesthetically sophisticated and more often produced within clear generic constraints, especially as WESTERNS and detective films. B pictures were usually shown as part of the same bill as A pictures, when cinemas used to show an entire programme of films, which might also include a newsreel. As the classic Hollywood system declined, partly as a consequence of anti-trust legislation and the rise in importance of television from the late 1940s onwards in the USA, the need and demand for the B picture declined.

brainwashing A process whereby an interrogator persuades a prisoner to renounce all previous beliefs, values and even identity, and adopt a new set provided by the interrogator. It is often claimed that brainwashing techniques were employed, for example, on American servicemen captured in the wars in Korea and Vietnam in that the prisoners did publicly renounce their past. The idea has been extended to converts of new religious sects and, further still, to whole populations who, it is claimed, have been brainwashed by the media. If it works at all, brainwashing is effective only in limited circumstances – on individuals who are kept in close confinement with their captors. The media may misinform the public of modern societies, but the idea that they brainwash them is an exaggeration.

SEE ALSO: **active audience; democracy; domination**.

brand A marketing device that links a range of different products and/ or services into a saleable form by giving them a distinctive common identity. Armani, Coca-Cola and Audi are all brands and, as such, are associated with particular feelings or ideas in the minds of consumers. Armani, for example, conjures up style, luxury and status. The relationship between a brand and its customers is an emotional one. Brands establish a product or group of products as distinctive and different from competitors. In buying a brand, people are therefore not only buying an image, they are also rejecting other brands and images that are not consonant with the image that they are expressing. Branding is not simply a marketing issue; it is also a cultural phenomenon. Brands, therefore, are increasingly important to IDENTITY as people define themselves through the brands that they adopt. From the point of view of the companies, brands produce loyalty in customers and manage market uncertainty. Branding is used increasingly for media products. This is probably most obvious in popular music but writers (e.g. J. K. Rowling) and films (e.g. *Star Wars*) also have the attributes of brands.

In recent years advertising has been very much directed towards the projection of these brand values, and a great deal of care goes into managing the brand so that a consistent image is projected. If the management of the brand is successful, then it will have a substantial commercial value. It may, for example, attract a premium price or simply eliminate competitors.

Brands have tended in the past to link similar sorts of products but in recent times have included an increasingly diverse array of products and services within one particular brand. A good example of this is Virgin, which covers record shops, radio, trains, aeroplanes and insurance services. Brands are also increasingly mobile across products; it is possible to buy a Timberland watch as well as shoes. In popular music there has been increased attention on the part of record companies to the branding of particular artists, a process which can be used to sell a range of commodities under the shell of a brand. An early example of this came with the development of the characteristic Rolling Stones logo.

SEE ALSO: **advertisement; consumer society**.

breakfast TV Originally simply television programming based around studio interviewing and put on in the morning, Breakfast TV (started in the early 1980s) is now used by some critics as a term of abuse for undemanding and trivial television for those who have nothing better to do in the morning. This form of abuse is often extended to daytime television in general.

breaking news The reporting of events that have only just occurred. Typically, media organizations, in their construction of news, give importance to recent events.

SEE ALSO: **news values**.

Brecht, Bertolt (1898–1956) German Marxist playwright and poet who developed alternative forms in the theatre (in plays such as *Mother Courage* and *The Caucasian Chalk Circle*), seeking to disrupt what he saw as the conventional, passive theatre audience experience. He thought that such passivity served to maintain the established and unjust class order in that it did not lead to radical questioning on the part of the audience. These ideas became influential beyond the theatre and have informed radical artists and film-makers who have sought to produce an 'alienation effect' through the disruption of conventional narrative forms.

SEE ALSO: **avant-garde; Marxism**.

bricolage The transformation of the meaning of objects by using them in quite a different manner from established practice or by associating them with other objects in novel ways. The most extensive application of the idea in cultural studies is by Hebdige (1979), who argued that members of youth subcultures engaged in this process by giving everyday objects (such as a safety pin) new meanings (such as punk style). The way that rockers and mods invested 'conventional' smart clothing with new meanings is another example. The word comes from the French, and those that engage in the process are called bricoleurs.

SEE ALSO: **Centre for Contemporary Cultural Studies; semiology; youth culture**.

British Board of Film Classification The organization that classifies films in Britain. It was established by the cinema industry in 1912 and it was given the responsibility for classifying videos in 1985. All films and videos on release carry a classification that refers to their suitability for different age groups. The current classifications that apply in Britain are Uc (video only), U, PG, 12A (cinema only), 12, 15, 18 and R18 (licensed sex shops and cinemas only). The decisions of the Board can cause controversy and can be overruled by local authorities, which still have the statutory responsibility for licensing films.

SEE ALSO: **censorship**.

British Code of Advertising, Sales Promotion and Direct Marketing (CAP) The code of behaviour applied by the ADVERTISING STANDARDS AUTHORITY (ASA) to advertisers to regulate the content of advertisements. The code is written by members of the industry and was updated recently: the latest edition was published in 2003. The basic principles of the code are that advertisements, sales promotions and direct marketing should be legal, decent, honest and truthful, prepared with a sense of responsibility to consumers and to society, and in line with the principles of fair competition generally accepted in business. The ASA claims that its own research shows that 96 per cent of press advertisements, 99 per cent of posters and 91 per cent of direct marketing comply with the CAP.

British Film Institute (BFI) An organization in Britain that promotes the study of film and film education. The BFI was established in 1933 and now runs the National Film Theatre and an IMAX cinema in London and has responsibility for a National Film and Television Archive and a National Library of material on film and television. It has available a range of resources and training packs, engages in publishing, releases films, videos and DVDs and runs the London Film Festival.

British Market Research Bureau A large and long-established MARKET RESEARCH bureau owned by J. Walter Thompson. It originated the TARGET

GROUP INDEX and is also involved in public interest research such as the British Crime Survey.

British Satellite Broadcasting (BSB) See: BSKYB.

broadband A medium of communication that can carry relatively large volumes of data, allowing the transmission of both audio and video signals and a large number of separate channels of communication.

broadcasting Much of the media is broadcast in the sense that identical products, whether those be films, television or books, are delivered to as wide an audience as possible. The broadcast technology of radio and television reinforced that tendency. However, more recently, the media have become more interested in appealing, not to a mass audience, but to particular segments of the audience (SEE: **audience differentiation; mass audience**). Again, the technology has developed to permit and encourage this tendency. For example, print costs have fallen, allowing short runs of books, appealing to smaller audiences. Cable and satellite systems, using digital technology, have enabled the proliferation of television channels, each of which serves a specialized audience. Broadcasting is gradually being replaced by 'narrowcasting'.

SEE ALSO: **broadcast television; digital broadcasting**.

Broadcasting Act 1990 An important piece of legislation that accelerated the deregulation of the British broadcasting industry. In particular, it introduced competitive bidding for the allocation of independent television licences, insisted that all terrestrial television broadcasters should commission a minimum of a quarter of their programming from independent production companies, provided for a light-touch regulator, replacing the Independent Broadcasting Authority with the Independent Television Commission, and created conditions which allowed satellite broadcasters an entry into the market. The Act, however, also retained elements of public service broadcasting. The BBC was untouched, there were continued restrictions on cross-media ownership (relaxed later), and an insistence on impartiality was maintained.

SEE ALSO: **Broadcasting Act 1996; deregulation; public service broadcasting**.

Broadcasting Act 1996 This legislation continued a process of deregulation of the media industry in the UK that had been accelerated by the 1990 Act. In particular, it relaxed the controls on multiple ownerships and cross-media ownership. Thus, television companies were permitted to own more than two licences as long as they did not thereby own more than 15 per cent of the sector. Similarly, newspapers were for the first time permitted to own television channels, although newspapers with more than 20 per cent of newspaper sales were still not allowed to do so.

SEE ALSO: **concentration of ownership; deregulation.**

Broadcasting Standards Commission This body, originally responsible for monitoring standards in broadcasting, ceased to exist in 2003 and its powers and responsibilities were transferred to OFCOM.

broadcast spectrum See: RADIO SPECTRUM.

broadcast television In the earlier days of television, all programmes were broadcast utilizing radio technology. In the UK at least, television was seen as PUBLIC SERVICE BROADCASTING which assumed a mass audience comprising the majority of the population, receiving more or less the same programmes. Changes in the industry, technology and means of regulation, however, have altered methods of programme delivery. As well as being broadcast, television programmes can be made available via satellite or cable to smaller sections of the audience.

SEE ALSO: **broadcasting.**

broadsheet Typically contrasted with TABLOID newspapers, broadsheet newspapers originally were simply of a greater size. Confusingly, more recently, some broadsheets, *The Times* and the *Independent*, for example, have been published simultaneously in both formats with a view to becoming tabloid in time. One former broadsheet, the *Guardian*, has adopted a format in between the tabloid and the broadsheet, the BERLINER. However, the term is also used to refer to content. Broadsheets are said to be more 'serious' and they have a better-educated readership and concentrate more on hard news.

B-roll See: A-ROLL.

BSkyB Formed in 1990 by a merger between BSB and Sky TV, BSkyB is carried on the Astra satellite. The launch of more Astra satellites in 1997 enabled an all-digital service with the potential to carry hundreds of television and radio channels. NEWS CORPORATION has a 40 per cent stake in the company.

SEE ALSO: **satellite.**

bulletin board A storage area in a computer system in which users can exchange messages with each other or have active discussions. Bulletin boards therefore function rather like electronic versions of the bulletin boards fixed to walls in public places. They are typically used by people who have similar interests which they wish to pursue together.

business-to-business publications Those publications that are addressed to business readers rather than general ones and deal with topics concerned with work.

Butler, Judith (b. 1956) Maxine Elliot Professor in the Departments of Rhetoric and Comparative Literature at the University of California at Berkeley. Butler is best known for her highly influential book *Gender Trouble* (1990), which radicalized discussions of sex and GENDER. Arguing against biologically determined notions of sex and gender, she considers the way in which sex and gender are performed and hence socially malleable. This is important in promoting the ideas of performance and perfomativity, which have grown in significance in media and cultural studies in recent years.

by-line Much of what appears in newspapers and magazines is written anonymously. However, when a piece appears under a journalist's name, it is said to be appearing with his or her by-line.

C

cable television Originally a means of supplying television programmes by cables buried in the ground, cable technology is now used for other purposes. At first, television programmes were supplied by broadcasting using the radio spectrum. From the 1970s onwards, however, this traditional technology was challenged by other methods of supply, one of which was cable. Early cable systems, installed for households that could not receive microwave transmission from towers, were unreliable and had an uncertain picture quality. Technological advances, particularly the use of fibre-optical cable and digital signals, have improved matters greatly. Cable systems now combine cable with terrestrial and satellite microwave transmission.

Transmission via cable laid underground permits a much greater number of channels than broadcasting and has the potential to be used for purposes other than television. At first, cable was used to relay broadcast television to homes that could not receive radio transmissions directly. Over time material that could not be received via broadcast television was added, mostly films but also community programming. Cable is also exploited to provide more sophisticated communications facilities such as internet access, telephone, burglar alarm systems and teleshopping.

Cable has proved popular in the United States. More than half of the population has chosen to pay for cable services. The position in Europe is more mixed. In some countries the penetration is very high indeed. In Belgium, for example, some 90 per cent of homes that have television are subscribers to cable. In Britain, on the other hand, the proportion is less than 20 per cent.

Cahiers du Cinéma An influential journal of film analysis and criticism in France. Founded in 1951, it was most prominent in the 1950s when it was the site of activity for a new wave of French writers who subsequently became important film-makers in their own right (for example, François Truffaut and Jean-Luc Godard). The journal was influential in the development of AUTEUR THEORY and in the systematic theoretical investigation of commercial, especially HOLLYWOOD, cinema.

Calcutt Committee In the late 1980s, the government, worried about intrusion by the press into the private lives of individuals, set up a committee to make proposals. The Calcutt Committee reported in 1990. It concluded that fierce competition amongst the tabloid newspapers had forced them into trying to raise sales by investigating the private lives of celebrities and politicians. While conceding that newspapers had indeed become unpleasantly intrusive, Calcutt nevertheless argued against further government regulation including the introduction of a statutory RIGHT OF REPLY. Instead, the committee proposed strengthening the system of self-regulation. The press should adopt a code of practice which would be policed by a new body, the PRESS COMPLAINTS COMMISSION. However, if the press did not abide by the stronger self-regulation, the committee recommended that the government should step in and introduce statutory regulation.

SEE ALSO: **government and the media; privacy**.

camcorder Combined video camera and sound recording device that has become increasingly small as video recording technology has developed. Its development facilitated the recording of the events of everyday life (parties, concerts and so on) in an enhanced way.

camera See: PHOTOGRAPHY.

camera angle The angle at which a camera is placed relative to the action that it is recording. Through our familiarity with the 'meaning' of different camera angles, we can understand how the way in which a film is shot is part of the meaning of the action. For example, a close-up may signal heightened emotion and a wide-shot may signal how action is to be located in a place.

camera movement While unplanned movement of a camera violates the conventions and techniques of realist film-making, planned movement is a core part of the creation of meaning in a film. The extent and nature of, for example, a tracking shot, can often be one of the most discussed and significant parts of a movie – a good example is the opening of *Touch of Evil* (dir. Orson Welles, 1958).

SEE ALSO: **realism**.

camera obscura An ancient way of producing a visual image. Light enters a small box or room through an opening, which creates an image on a back wall or screen. The image is inverted. The camera obscura was used as a drawing and painting aid, as represented, for example, in the novel *Girl with a Pearl Earring* (Tracy Chevalier, 1999) and its film version.

The camera obscura is sometimes built in a high point of a town or city to enable sightseers to see the view.

campaign See: ADVERTISING CAMPAIGN.

Campaign for Press and Broadcasting Freedom A well-established and active organization that campaigns against censorship, the concentration of ownership in the media and interference by owners of press and broadcasting organizations in the journalistic freedoms of their employees.

CAP See: BRITISH CODE OF ADVERTISING, SALES PROMOTION AND DIRECT MARKETING.

caption The description used at the bottom of, or in association with, a visual image such as a photograph.

caricature Drawing or image of a person or animal that accentuates particular features. This is most often used by political cartoonists in the interests of satire, for example in the common depiction of Tony Blair with staring eyes or Prince Charles with enlarged ears.

SEE ALSO: **animation; cartoon**.

Carlton A large UK-based media group with global sales in the early 2000s of more than £1.5 billion. Primarily involved in television production and broadcasting, Carlton also has interests in book publishing, film libraries and advertising. Although mainly operating in the UK, the company has operating units in the US, South America, Continental Europe and Canada.

Carlton started in the 1960s by providing technical services to the film and television industries. The company went public in the early 1980s and then expanded rapidly. Their first move was into television post-production in both the US and the UK, and within ten years, Carlton had established itself as one of the world's largest suppliers of pre-recorded cassettes and of general post-production services. By the end of the 1980s, it was also the UK's largest independent maker of TV programmes. In the early 1990s, Carlton finally became a television broadcaster by acquiring the London weekday franchise. That acquisition was followed by others, giving it television broadcasting coverage of some 40 per cent of the UK population. In 2003, Carlton merged with GRANADA to form ITV plc.

SEE ALSO: **independent television**.

carnival Period of celebration outside routine and ordered social relations. M. M. BAKHTIN analysed the significance of canivalesque moments in culture when, for short periods of time, established social roles are inverted and normal boundaries broken. These moments can be seen as a kind of cultural and social 'safety valve' in which, for a period of time, power relations are overturned or repudiated, and which enables them to continue outside the carnival period.

cartoon Commonly used to refer to a single-image drawing, using CARI-CATURE, in a newspaper or magazine, which has comic and/or satirical intent. Also used to refer to animated films, which have used drawings in the past and which are now more likely to be computer-generated. While there are a number of antecedents, cartoons in the modern sense became popular from the 1840s onwards, especially with the development in Britain of *Punch* magazine, which was founded in 1841.

SEE ALSO: **animation; comic.**

case study The detailed examination of a single example of a class of phenomena. A case study cannot provide reliable information about the broader class. For example, a study of a single news organization will shed light on the way that journalists work in that case. Although it would be illegitimate to infer that all journalists work in that way from that solitary case study, it may nonetheless provide hypotheses which can be tested on a wider range of cases.

casting director Person in charge of the casting of a film, radio or television programme. This can be a very important aspect of the production of a film. Thus, the presence of a star name can 'brand' the film in important ways and even determine if the film gets made at all, but even choices and decisions about who should play more minor roles can have significant effects on how an audience might view a film.

SEE ALSO: **celebrity; star; star system; star text.**

casualization The process by which full-time, permanently employed workers are replaced by those who work freelance, part-time or on short contracts. The media have always employed casual workers. Even in the nineteenth century, press journalists would be paid by their contributions rather than as full-time employees. As competition amongst media organizations has increased in the latter part of the twentieth century, they have looked at ways of reducing their costs. One of the results of this process is OUTSOURCING. Another is the growing casualization of the workforce. Even when media workers had previously been full-time employees, their positions have been made into freelance ones so that they become self-employed. So, for example, in television production many roles – including producers, directors, cameramen, editors, writers – will now be taken by freelancers when previously they would have been occupied by the permanently employed. Trades unions contest casualization because they believe that workers are thereby made a great deal more insecure.

SEE ALSO: **Fordism/post-Fordism**.

catchline See: SLUG.

CBS (Columbia Broadcasting System) Founded in the late 1920s as a radio network and starting television broadcasting in 1939, CBS is now owned by Viacom. An early association with Columbia Records came to an end in 1988 when that label was sold to Sony. For a long period after the Second World War, CBS was the dominant network in the United States but has now been displaced by others.

SEE ALSO: **ABC; Fox Network; NBC**.

CCTV (Closed Circuit Television) A technology usually used to keep places or people under observation, as for example in prison security systems. CCTV utilizes a camera that feeds directly to a screen and a recording device. The images are therefore available only to a small (closed) number of viewers.

SEE ALSO: **surveillance society**.

CD (compact disc) Format used for storing digital information, especially music, where it has effectively replaced vinyl and audiotape as the dominant format in advanced Western societies.

SEE ALSO: **digital broadcasting**.

ceefax The oldest TELETEXT service in the world, ceefax was launched by the BBC in 1974.

cel A single plastic sheet used in animation. Cels can be placed over each other to produce a more complex image. The term is derived from cellulose.

celebrity 'The attribution of glamorous or notorious status to an individual within the public sphere' (Rojek, 2001: 10). While fame and celebrity have long histories, this is increasingly a situation where a person, David Beckham, for example, takes on special status due to significant media attention. Connected with the STAR SYSTEM, celebrity, it is often suggested, is becoming increasingly divorced from any special achievement beyond the appearance in the media. Thus, the media create celebrities through their own processes, such as through programmes like *Big Brother,* rather than representing those who have achieved fame elsewhere. The increased attention to celebrity is sometimes seen as an aspect of a POST-

MODERNIST or consumer culture in that society has become obsessed with the superficial pleasures of fame and the possession of objects. Thus for Rojek (2001) there are three types of celebrity: ascribed, achieved and attributed (p. 17). 'Ascribed status concerns lineage' (p. 17), 'achieved celebrity derives from the perceived accomplishments of the individual in open competition' (p. 18) and attributed celebrity 'is largely the result of the concentrated representation of an individual as noteworthy or exceptional by cultural intermediaries' (p. 18). Thus, David Beckham's celebrity does not derive from his lineage, as he is not for example a member of the royal family. He has gained celebrity through his footballing achievements, which has been a base for his attributed celebrity through media appearances outside football such as in celebrity magazines and the tabloid press.

SEE ALSO: **actor; consumer society; star text**.

celluloid Material used to carry film images invented by John Hyatt in New York State in 1869.

censorship The control of the content of the media. Any medium is liable to censorship. The spoken word has the longest history of censorship, but print media – newspapers and books – attracted attention from those who wished to regulate their content from the moment of their appearance because of their capacity to convey information and opinion to large numbers of people (SEE: **book; newspaper**). More recently, the appearance of other media of mass communication, most recently the INTERNET, has been greeted with a debate about the extent of control.

A variety of agencies have been responsible for censorship. Historically the most important is government. There are three main reasons for government censorship – political, cultural and economic. Governments have always been tempted to try to control what citizens say and write. They can be very sensitive to criticism, not least because, if that criticism is widespread, they can lose political power. Even if censorship is in the interests of particular regimes, it usually is not presented as such. Governments are more inclined to propose controls over the written word on the grounds that social order might be threatened by unfettered free speech. In the UK (and other European countries), battles over political censorship were to some extent resolved in the late eighteenth and early nineteenth centuries by the passage of legislation concerning free speech and the growth of the view that debate was actually a condition of a healthy society. In the twenty-first century there are still governments – in China, Saudi Arabia, Burma or North Korea, for example – that exercise political censorship over the expression of opinions that they consider dangerous. However, in European or North American societies, governments may introduce censorship, even if it is hidden, in times of national crisis, such as war or terrorist attack. Furthermore, governments may contribute to a national mood which is intimidatory. It is often said, for example, that the political atmosphere in the United States, encouraged by President Bush's government, has effectively stifled the expression of dissenting opinions.

Governments have also censored for cultural reasons, chiefly that some sections of the population may be offended by something said or written. In the recent past, most controversy has been caused by books, films or television programmes that have been alleged to offend against current sexual morality or which depict excessive violence. There have also been debates about the need to legislate against material which offends against religious sensibilities. Government economic regulation and deregulation may also be related to freedom of expression. For example, one of the reasons advanced for government promotion of greater competition in the media marketplace is that it will encourage a wider diversity of opinion (although it is not at all clear that, for example, the proliferation of television channels has produced such a diversity).

Governments are not the only agents of censorship. Importantly, organizations and individuals may censor themselves for fear of offending someone or of acquiring an undesirable reputation. Many argue that this is a far more insidious form of censorship because it is not so obvious.

SEE ALSO: **government and the media; pornography; press freedom; regulation; self-regulation.**

Centre for Contemporary Cultural Studies (CCCS) Often known as the Birmingham Centre for Contemporary Cultural Studies or the Birmingham School, the Centre was the key site for the development of cultural studies in the 1960s and 1970s and its work has been influential on the subsequent expansion of media studies. RICHARD HOGGART, who founded the Centre in 1964, was succeeded as Director from 1968 to 1979 by STUART HALL. Subsequently the Centre became a department at Birmingham University. Founded to develop the ideas formulated by Hoggart in *The Uses of Literacy* (1957), the Centre rapidly became influential through its stencilled Occasional Papers Series, which included papers on a diverse range of cultural and media topics. It also produced its own journal, *Working Papers in Cultural Studies*. In the 1970s the work of the Centre was heavily influenced by forms of cultural MARXISM, especially that associated with ANTONIO GRAMSCI. This emphasized the role of culture in hegemonic domination and the resistance to power and informed the analysis in key collectively written texts such as *Resistance Through Rituals* (Hall and Jefferson, 1976), *Policing the Crisis* (Hall et. al., 1978), *On Ideology* (Centre for Contemporary Cultural Studies, 1977) and *Working Class Culture* (Clarke et al., 1979). The emphasis on class in such books was contested by feminists at the Centre in *Women Take Issue* (Women's Studies Group, 1978) and the relative inattention to race in *The Empire Strikes Back* (Centre for Contemporary Cultural Studies, 1982). Writers associated with the Centre in its most productive period have become some of the most important figures in contemporary cultural and media studies. These include Stuart Hall, Paul Willis, Dick Hebdige, Angela McRobbie, David Morley, Larry Grossberg and Paul Gilroy. The Centre's work on YOUTH CULTURE, news and IDEOLOGY has been of particular influence in media studies.

SEE ALSO: **hegemony**.

centre-spread A two-page SPREAD occupying the centre pages of a newspaper or magazine and therefore taking a very prominent position. Also known as a gatefold.

certification See: BRITISH BOARD OF FILM CLASSIFICATION; CENSORSHIP.

channel Used to refer to stations on TV. Recent years have seen increased channel proliferation due to the further development of satellite and digital TV.

Channel Four Founded in 1982, the organization is unusual because it is a mixture of a public institution and a commercial entity. It is a non-profit-making public corporation with a public service remit but is funded by advertising. In its first decade, it was managed by the Independent Broadcasting Authority, which collected subscriptions from the commercial television franchise holders (SEE: **Independent Television**). These companies, in turn, managed the advertising shown on Channel Four. These arrangements were changed by the BROADCASTING ACT 1990 and the channel now manages its own advertising and is constituted as a public corporation.

From its beginnings, Channel Four was intended to offer innovative programmes which might appeal to minorities, which were not well served by the existing channels, public and commercial. As a way of stimulating such innovation, the channel made few of its own programmes, instead commissioning content from independent production companies (the publishing model). Although criticized in recent years for offering undemanding and routine television, Channel Four has had a considerable impact on British television. Other channels have been encouraged to broaden the limits of what counts as acceptable programming by Four's innovations, and all channels now commission programmes from independents.

SEE ALSO: **BBC; television**.

channel hopping The practice among some sections of the television audience of moving between channels in any one period of viewing rather than staying with one.

SEE ALSO: **audience; channel loyalty; regimes of watching**.

channel loyalty In countries in which audiences can choose between several television channels, programme-producers try to ensure that viewers stay with their channel. Such loyalty can be encouraged by giving a channel a distinctive character or BRAND and using such SCHEDULING devices as 'hammocking', that is, sandwiching a less popular programme between two popular ones. Despite the best efforts of television producers, audiences are not very loyal. For example, although the audience for a soap opera such as *Coronation Street* is much the same size from week to week, actually that audience is not composed of the same people. Only about half of the audience in one week will watch the programme in the following week. Audience members are, in effect, dipping in and out of their soaps, and the programme-makers have to take this into account.

SEE ALSO: **audience; channel hopping; zapping**.

charisma A type of authority deriving from extraordinary personal gifts rather than the nature of the position held. The term has come into ordinary speech and is used to describe people in the public eye who have strong personalities and the ability to persuade people of the rightness of their cause.

SEE ALSO: **persuasion; star**.

chat room The use of computer networks to provide opportunities for people to exchange text-based messages in real time. The technique has been welcomed in that it appears to permit and encourage real interactivity. In education, for example, chat rooms are used for interactions between students and between teachers and students to supplement classroom teaching and learning. There have also been extensive public worries about the uncontrolled use of chat rooms and BULLETIN BOARDS because they may be used by those who wish to encourage others to illegal, anti-social or harmful acts, e.g. child abuse or sucide pacts.

chat show A genre of television and, to some extent, radio, chat shows consist of a host – often a PERSONALITY – and one or more invited partici-pants who are usually celebrities or would-be celebrities. The aim is to have an interesting and revealing conversation, and, occasionally, this aim is achieved. The genre further demonstrates the domestic quality of television. The ideal of chat shows seems to be to simulate the kind of conversation – only involving celebrities – that might take place around the kitchen table.

chequebook journalism In an increasingly competitive market, media organizations are tending to pay more and more for scandalous stories which they believe will increase sales or audiences. While this is widely true of the TABLOID press, it is a practice that is becoming more widespread in BROADSHEETS and television. Politicians and others have expressed worries about this tendency when it involves payments to criminals.

children and television Ever since the introduction of television there have been worries about the relationship of the medium to children and adolescents. These worries cover a variety of areas: children watch too much television to the point of addiction and therefore neglect other activities such as physical exercise or homework; they become solitary and fail to develop social skills; they are exposed to behaviour which parents may think is undesirable – swearing, sex or the wrong accent, for instance; and they will be made more violent by seeing violence on the screen. Television is not the only medium to have attracted attention in this way. Comics and rock music have both been accused of fostering undesirable behaviour in children.

Worries such as these are a reflection of more general anxieties about children in contemporary society. They receive public expression in media stories themselves. Thus, violent behaviour on the part of children and young people is often attributed by newspapers to exposure to television or video. Politicians respond by making speeches and perhaps try to legislate, lobbying organizations are set up, and broadcasters introduce policies – generally unsuccessful – like the WATERSHED, designed to reduce the exposure of children to material deemed unsuitable.

Children between 4 and 12 watch an average of about 3 hours television per day. They are by no means the heaviest viewers. Adults between 25 and 45 watch about 3.5 hours and the retired spend over 5 hours in front of the set. Young people between 16 and 25 are the least inclined to watch. While it is clear that television watching will displace some other activities, it is less clear what those activities are. It is not obvious, for example, that the decline in physical fitness can be attributed to television viewing. Indeed, some researchers have argued that those children who watch a lot of television also participate heavily in other socially approved activities.

Many of the earlier studies of the impact of television and video on violent behaviour in children were based on laboratory studies. Fundamentally, these consisted in showing children violent scenes and trying to measure subsequent behaviour. Although some studies did indeed show some effect, others did not. In any event, even if children were more violent immediately after exposure to violent scenes, it is also clear that the great majority of them could tell the difference between real and pretended violence. However, the main difficulties with laboratory studies of this kind is that they tend to measure only short-term effect and they do not necessarily indicate what happens in real-life situations. Again, those studies that do attempt to measure long-term effect come to inconsistent conclusions. At the very best, the connection between violence on television and violent behaviour is unproven. At worst, there isn't one. This makes the persistent public belief that there is one a little difficult to understand.

In discussing the relationship between children and the media, it is important to realize that violence is not the only issue. Many media researchers take a more positive view of the relationship. There is the obvious point that television can be educational, and it is worth reminding ourselves that children might actually enjoy watching television. Researchers have focused recently, not on what television does to children, but, rather, on what children do with television (SEE: **active audience**). Thus, children may use television programmes to investigate and discuss the secrets of the adult world. Within certain communities, television watching may be used to manage tensions of various kinds. For example, young people in a Punjabi community in London used their watching of *Neighbours* to understand the relationship of their community to the surrounding white society. Such uses of television can also be playful. For example, one study investigated a group of children who used the series *Prisoner: Cell Block H* as the basis for games in the playground. As a matter of routine, they would re-enact or invent episodes of the programme, sometimes involving a teacher in playing the role of prison officer. Perhaps the similarities between school and prison are not entirely coincidental!

SEE ALSO: **censorship; effects; violence**.

Chomsky, Noam (b. 1928) Institute Professor of Linguistics at the Massachusetts Institute of Technology, Cambridge, USA. Chomsky is one of the leading authorities in the study of language and mind. He contributed to the development of STRUCTURALISM and to the wider understanding of linguistic structures in the wider academic community. He has also been a radical critic of American foreign policy, paying attention to the role of media representations in this respect.

SEE ALSO: **manufacture of consent**.

cinema The technology of cinema dates from the late nineteenth century and is related to the development of photography. CELLULOID film was invented in 1887, and in 1891 Thomas Edison took out patents on the Kinetograph and the Kinetoscope (to exhibit the films). A company to manufacture Kinetoscopes was set up 1893. The films shown in Kineto-scope parlours, the first of which opened in New York City in 1894, lasted less than a minute and featured, for example, the movements of animals or dancers. In 1895, which is commonly used as the marker year of the birth of cinema, the Skladanowsky brothers exhibited a cinema process in Berlin, and the Lumière brothers demonstrated their Cinémato-graphe in Paris. The Cinématographe was then demonstrated in New York City in 1896. The exhibition of these technologies for the showing of films led to the inclusion of films in vaudeville shows in the USA and the development of nickleodeons. The making of, and demand for, films grew rapidly from this point on.

In France the Pathé company quickly established itself as an important supplier to this new market and was very important in the US market. After struggles over the US market, Pathé turned its attention more to Europe, and the American film industry developed rapidly. This was quickly concentrated in HOLLYWOOD, which has dominated concepts and practices of cinema since. However, it is important to recognize that cinema industries developed in other industrialized countries rapidly, and that there are separate traditions that have been explored by historians and analysts of cinema. The national cinemas of, for example, India (SEE: **Bollywood**), Japan, Britain, France, Italy, Germany and Russia have been much written about.

Hollywood led the way in a number of subsequent technological inno-vations. The arrival of sound is usually dated to the production of *The Jazz Singer* by Warner Brothers in 1927, though live sound had been used to accompany silent films previously, and Warner Brothers had also pro-duced short sound films and *Don Juan* in 1926. Colour film production was experimented with during the early part of the twentieth century, and the first colour features were produced by Warner Brothers in 1929, in partnership with Technicolor. Despite this, colour was not rapidly taken up due to the expense of production relative to the returns that could be generated. Thus, in 1940, only a tiny fraction of films in the US were in colour. 'By 1951 this figure had risen to 51 per cent but in 1958 had fallen to 25 per cent as a result of shrinking budgets and the emergence of the black-and-white television market. By 1967, however, the television networks having turned to colour broadcasting, the percentage rose once more to 75 per cent, and in 1976, to 94 per cent' (Cook and Bernink, 1999: 51).

Widescreen technologies have been experimented with and used at various points in cinema history including the recent IMAX technology. There have been many advances in lighting and camera technologies. Since the late 1980s rapid advances in computer and digital technologies have facilitated the greater use of sophisticated special effects in ACTION films like *Terminator 2: Judgment Day* (dir. James Cameron, 1991).

The development of the technologies of cinema is only one part of the story. Attention has also been paid to a range of production processes, such as the role of the large companies in the development of the Hollywood film industries. Companies of this type sought not only to make films but also to control their DISTRIBUTION and hence exhibition. It is important, therefore, to recognize that cinema also refers to a place where films are shown, and there are studies of the meaning of the architecture and design of cinemas and the pleasure that audiences have derived from these places as well as the films shown in them (for example, Stacey, 1994). There are also a range of roles in the production of films like that of PRODUCER or DIRECTOR that have been the subject of much attention, with the later often being examined through the lens of AUTEUR THEORY.

Cinema texts have also been considered in a variety of ways. A range of GENRES have been examined such as ACTION, COMEDY, CRIME, HORROR, FILM NOIR, MELODRAMA, MUSICAL and the WESTERN. Genres group together the particular NARRATIVES that make up the individual films. An important further focus of attention has been on the STARS and the STAR SYSTEM.

Cinema AUDIENCES have also been the subject of academic study. Much attention has been given to how audiences are affected by the viewing of films, for example by the screening of violent or pornographic images (SEE: **pornography; violence**). Another approach, informed by psychoanalysis and MARXISM, has examined how films construct particular positions from which they are viewed, and produce a SPECTATOR who is determined by IDEOLOGY. An important example of this is the consideration of how classic narrative cinema constructs a MALE GAZE. In addition to these approaches that focus on what films do to the audience, there is another approach that pays more attention to what audiences do with films. Much informed by more recent studies of the audience, emphasis has been placed on the active way in which audience members interpret films in different ways and how they may want to adopt, for example, styles of dress of the stars in everyday life (Stacey, 1994).

cinemascope WIDESCREEN cinema effect that was developed in the 1950s.

SEE ALSO: **anamorphic; aspect ratio; IMAX**.

cinematographer See: CINEMATOGRAPHY.

cinematography Process of decision-making about cameras and lighting in the shooting of a film. The cinematographer (also known as the director of photography or the lighting cameraman) plays an important role in supporting the DIRECTOR of a film and has charge of other roles in the shooting of a film that are concerned with cameras (for example, the camera operator, the camera assistant, the clapper loader and the grip) and lighting (for example the gaffer). The director has overall control of the film-making but relies significantly on the cinematographer to realize those views, through the cinematographer's direction of those on his/her team who are responsible for the specific operation of the cameras and the adjustment of lighting and so on.

cinéma vérité See: DOCUMENTARY.

circulation The numbers of copies that newspapers and magazines sell. Clearly, circulation will directly affect the income of publishers via the COVER PRICE, but it also indirectly affects it in that advertisers will place advertisements in publications that reach the largest number of readers of the right kind. Estimates of readership are formed by the NATIONAL READERSHIP SURVEY and are audited by the AUDIT BUREAU OF CIRCULATIONS.

It is worth remembering that circulation – the numbers sold – is not the same as readership – the numbers who actually read the publication. If a newspaper is delivered to a house, for example, it will be read by several people even if it only represents one copy sold.

SEE ALSO: **magazine; newspaper**.

clip Excerpt from a recording, used in radio and television. Also sometimes referred to as a CUT.

closed-ended questions The sort of questions used in questionnaires where the respondent is asked to choose from a limited number of replies. An example is a question on age which presents the respondent with a set of age-ranges, one of which is to be ticked or circled. These are useful in securing clear responses that can then be analysed statistically but are less successful in gaining a sense of the meaning of the response for the individual.

closed text A text where meaning appears to be open to one, or a very limited number of, interpretations. An example would be a children's nursery rhyme or a top-twenty popular song, where a narrative is relatively simple, one action follows another and the ending ties up the issues raised by the narrative. It must be stressed that this is relative in the sense that even texts which appear to be closed can contain a multiplicity of meanings.

SEE ALSO: **closure; open text.**

close-up Type of shot that is framed closely on a person (for example, their face or head) or an aspect of action. It tends to convey emotion or concentrates attention on the individual. This is especially important in film and television and contributes to the distinctive style of acting required in these media by comparison with the theatre.

SEE ALSO: **camera angle.**

closure Process by which the possible multiple meanings that are generated in a text are brought to a conclusion that restricts further interpretations. For example, closure in a murder mystery almost without exception revolves around the explanation of who did it and how. Closure also has a more ideological dimension as it may involve the closing down of ideas and issues that have been brought into play during the development of a narrative or text. Thus, in FILM NOIR, for example, the woman who is 'out of place' by being active will be 'destroyed' in some way during closure, perhaps through her death or imprisonment. Nineteenth-century realist novels often used devices that explain the fates of key characters at the end of the novel to bring about and reinforce narrative and ideological/discursive closure. In a romance, the male and female central characters, despite being separated and arguing during the narrative, may get married at the end, potentially closing off issues of female independence.

SEE ALSO: **closed text; open text.**

CNN Launched in 1980 by Ted Turner and now owned by Time Warner, CNN pioneered the idea of 24-hour news coverage. The second-most-watched news channel in the United States (behind Fox News), CNN has expanded its news service globally and now claims to reach more than one billion people in over 200 countries. This global reach was enhanced by the network's prominence in the reporting of the first Gulf War in the early 1990s. Although it has tried to produce more localized news for its worldwide audience, CNN is often accused of giving a very American view of world events.

SEE ALSO: **news**.

coated paper A heavy paper of high quality traditionally coated with clay and used because it gives sharper and better-defined images.

code According to STRUCTURALIST thought sets of signs are organized into systems that convey meaning. These systems are often called codes. Structuralist writers developed the idea of code to suggest that there are within texts a number of different basic codes that are independent of the author's intention. One well-known and influential example of this is ROLAND BARTHES' conceptualization of hermeneutic (or ENIGMA), pro-airetic (or ACTION), REFERENTIAL, semic and symbolic codes. Codes have been identified in a variety of cultural and media forms in addition to literature. Thus, Middleton (1990) discusses levels of musical code from the most general, such as the code of Western music, to the particular ones associated with specific composers. Codes have also been identified in popular cultural forms such as WESTERN films (Wright, 1975) and the novels of James Bond (Eco, 1982). An influential development of the idea of code in media studies can be found in STUART HALL'S ENCODING/DECODING theory.

SEE ALSO: **discourse**.

cognitive How things are known in ways that do not depend upon emotion. Analysts point to the way in which the media provide opportunities for cognitive learning (through, for example, DOCUMENTARY) and which help in the rational understanding of the world (through, for example, NEWS).

cognitive dissonance Leon Festinger's theory of cognitive dissonance is that people find dissonance or lack of fit between attitudes, or between attitudes and behaviour, unacceptable because they have a need for consistency and harmony. They will therefore try to reduce the dissonance. For example, if the members of a cult expecting the arrival of aliens by flying saucers find that the saucers do not arrive on the appointed day, the inconsistency will force them either to revise their beliefs in the cult or to reinterpret the prediction so that they can go on believing in the cult.

Cohen, Stanley (b. 1942) Martin White Professor of Sociology at the

London School of Economics. Cohen has had an influential career as a radical sociologist of deviance. His best-known book, *Folk Devils and Moral Panics* (1973), made an important contribution to understandings of how the media (in particular the popular press) amplify events such as relatively minor skirmishes between groups of young people at British seaside resorts in the 1960s. The media therefore demonize particular groups and produce a MORAL PANIC.

SEE ALSO: **amplification of deviance**.

cold media See: HOT MEDIA.

colonization Over a number of centuries, some European countries colonized parts of Africa, Asia, Australasia and South America by invading them and installing a government. Although such physical colonization has largely stopped, it is argued that a more subtle form now prevails in which powerful countries such as the United States dominate the society and culture of other countries through the spread of Western media throughout the world.

SEE ALSO: **cultural imperialism; media imperialism**.

comedy A very popular GENRE in film, television and radio. The boundaries of comedy between these different media and live performance have tended to be fluid. Thus, in the early days of cinema and radio, performers often moved from live performance in variety shows into the new media. This also happened to some extent with television. In cinema Bob Hope (a comedian) and Bing Crosby (a singer and actor) appeared in the very successful 'Road' series of comedy films, as well as performing live and appearing on radio and TV. These boundaries are still porous in that comedians will appear in live performance and in mediated form. Recordings of live performances often sell well on video and DVD. Here some performers will be able to deal with topics and use 'bad' language that would not be allowed on broadcast TV or radio. Some performers who very rarely appear on TV sustain the mediated aspects of their careers in this way. In these ways and others comedy as a genre crosses media types and boundaries. Some forms have been more successful on particular media. Thus, SITUATION COMEDY has been an important genre on TV, teen comedies have been more successful in the cinema, and review programmes and panel games have tended to be best suited to radio.

A key issue with respect to the analysis of comedy in media studies has been the use of STEREOTYPES. There has been much debate about the use of racist stereotypes in British TV comedy. The character of Alf Garnett in the very popular *Till Death Us Do Part* in the 1960s and 1970s was envisioned by his creator (Johnny Speight) and the actor who played the part (Warren Mitchell) as a vehicle to expose racist stereotypes, though there was no guarantee that the audience was not laughing with Alf rather than at him. Other programmes of the time were even cruder in racial stereotyping. These programmes and those that employed gender stereotypes were criticized by 'alternative' comedy from the 1980s onwards, though this arguably used its own stereotypes. More recent comedy has tended to use stereotypes in an ironic way, playing in a 'knowing' fashion on previous comedy formats. This, again, has happened across all media, but most markedly on TV.

comic A media form that uses drawings to tell a story. A more sophisticated definition is 'Juxtaposed pictorial and other images in deliberate sequence' (McCloud, 1994: 9). The form can be found in the story of the Norman Conquest in the Bayeux Tapestry and the narratives of Egyptian hieroglyphics, but the invention of printing provided the opportunity for it to become a mass form. The work of William Hogarth (in the eighteenth century) and that of Rudolphe Topffer (in the nineteenth century) are more modern examples (McCloud, 1994). There are many different variations on the comic form that have developed since the late nineteenth century. In Britain publications such as the *Dandy* (started in 1937) and the *Beano* (started in 1938) from the D. C. Thomson company based in Dundee in Scotland have been part of the childhood of successive generations. In the USA Superman was launched in *Action Comics* in 1938 and Batman followed the year after.

Different types of comic will appeal to different audiences. Comics are often aimed at children, but there are also very large adult markets, especially for the American action comic (or comic book), which has spawned some of the most internationally recognizable cultural heroes, such as Superman, Batman, Spider-Man and the X-Men. Such superheroes have been reinvented in numerous ways, and much analysis has been undertaken of Batman (see, for example, Pearson and Uricchio, 1991), who is the subject of one of the best known GRAPHIC NOVELS. The Japanese Manga form of comic has also been a key development; it has secured a strong base in popular culture and has become more widely influential. There are also connections to the development of computer gaming.

SEE ALSO: **animation; cartoon**.

comic book See: COMIC.

commercial radio See: RADIO.

commercialization When profit-making companies take over activities either not organized at all or previously carried out by public or not-for-profit organizations, it is loosely referred to as commercialization. For example, until the 1950s, the BBC, a not-for-profit organization, enjoyed a monopoly in television broadcasting guaranteed by the government. Since then, it has faced competition from commercial broadcasters which has itself forced the BBC to become more commercial in its attitudes and conduct. The history of other forms of the media, newspapers and books, for example, is a history of gradual commercialization and relaxation of government control. Commercial organizations usually argue for dismantling government controls and encouraging a market for the media to develop. Besides being in their economic interests, a free and competitive media environment, such companies argue, is the best guarantee of free speech. While this argument has merit in a society which really does have many media organizations, it is much less convincing when companies start to grow by taking each other over, so reducing competition.

SEE ALSO: **art and commerce; concentration of ownership; consumer society; government and the media**.

commercial television   In the UK, though not in other countries, television was, in its early days, provided by a quasi-governmental organization, the BBC, and was funded by income from the licences that viewers were required to purchase. In the 1950s, however, successive Conservative governments became convinced that commercial organizations ought to be allowed to broadcast television in competition with the BBC and be funded by the revenue from advertising. In 1955, ITV began broadcasting via a system of regional franchises. Worldwide, the bulk of television is now provided by private commercial organizations.

SEE ALSO: **BBC; Independent Television; regulation**.

commissioning editor   The person who, in most media organizations, has the ability and authority to buy or commission a piece of work, whether it is a television programme or a book. The term is most commonly used in book publishing, and more rarely in other branches of the media (SEE: **producer**). A commissioning editor usually specializes in a part of the publisher's list, in cookery or dictionaries, for example. She or he has to keep up with developments in the market, trying to sense what books customers are buying or will be buying. Authors, or authors' agents, will be sending her manuscripts or ideas for books and she will be making a judgement about whether or not to publish. At the same time, she will be having ideas for suitable books and approaching potential authors for them. Having agreed to publish a particular book, the commissioning editor will arrange for a contract to be drawn up and will then stay in contact with the author while the book is being written. If the book is a success, the commissioning editor may want to commission further books from the same author.

Traditionally, the commissioning editor is the critical point of contact between the author and the publishing house. The role is the bridge between the commercial requirements of a business, which needs books to sell, and the author, who may well have a mixture of motives – commercial, artistic or academic. As such, commissioning editors have been important to the success of publishing houses and many have acquired reputations for building up a strongly selling list as well as finding and nurturing new authors. However, this traditional role is being eroded partly by changes in the book publishing industry and partly by the growing importance of LITERARY AGENTS, who have taken over some of the functions of commissioning editors.

Commissioning editors should not be confused with COPY EDITORS.
SEE ALSO: **book publishing**.

commodification In Marxist theory, the production of goods or services specifically for sale in a market. Such goods are commodities that possess use values (that is they are useful for human beings to do things with) but more significantly they also possess exchange value as they can be exchanged for other goods or for money. In media studies, some commentators, such as T. W. ADORNO, see commodification as producing standardized products which are consumed by passive audiences. Critics of commodification suggest that goods and practices that were originally produced in local communities in response to real needs are now produced by cultural industries to satisfy desires that have been bred by, for example, advertising. In this view, commodification and the marketing of culture is less concerned with real human feelings and experience than with satisfying the need of cultural industries to generate profit. Thus, PORNOGRAPHY in the representation of human sexuality in magazines, DVDs and on the internet offers for sale on a market that which is an intimate human experience and, for the critic, devalues it through the commodification process.

SEE ALSO: **Marxism**.

communication The transfer of MESSAGES from one party to another. Those who study communication are interested in such questions as: 'Who communicates to whom by what means, with what content and with what effect?' Communication processes can take place at a number of different levels – between individuals, between social groups, within a society or between societies, and the study of communication can therefore range from the consideration of two individuals engaged in a conversation to the way in which a television programme is understood by an audience of millions. Different academic disciplines study different aspects of communication at different levels. Psychology, for instance, is primarily interested in the interpersonal level. Media studies, in the UK at least, has tended to move away from a psychological approach towards more large-scale and sociological studies.

SEE ALSO: **communication science**.

Communications Act 2003 This legislation set up OFCOM and removed some restrictions on media ownership.

communication science The study of the process of COMMUNICATION – or at least one approach to the study. Classical communications science tends to see the process as a linear one; messages are seen as flowing simply from the sender to the receiver in a transfer of information. In constructing models of how this process works, and in order to explain how miscommunication can occur, communication scientists have introduced complexities into the simple linear model. For example, they introduced the idea of noise in the channel down which messages are sent. That idea, originating in the crackling to which telephone lines are subject occasionally, can be extended to any interference in the channel of communication which prevents a message being received in the manner intended. Or, to incorporate the obvious idea that the receiver's response to a message will have an effect on the sender, they proposed the concept of feedback.

Communication scientists of this kind are adopting a view of human communication which is rather mechanical for some critics. Their linear approach is contested by those who see communication as an interplay of *meaning*. For such an approach, the issue is not so much what the effect and accuracy of the message is but rather how the message is read so as to give it meaning. For this school, the success or failure of an act of communication in giving information is not the point, for all meanings are fluid.

SEE ALSO: **semiology**.

compassion fatigue The process whereby the population begins to lose sympathy with those who are subject to adverse circumstances so that they become tired and their compassion is exhausted. It is sometimes thought that the media (and especially television) have made a significant contribution to such a process. For example, it is suggested that images of famine or natural disaster have become so familiar to those viewing in advanced Western societies that they have lost the power to shock. However, the events around Band Aid and Live Aid in the mid-1980s or the response to the Tsunami of 2004 might suggest otherwise.

competence The capacity of an audience or section of an audience to deploy skills in the interpretation of a text. These skills may be learned formally, as in the way that the appreciation of classical music is taught, or more informally, as in the way that understandings of popular music are developed. Media studies has contributed greatly to the understanding of such popular competences, with the recognition that forms like popular music, popular novels and films and television SOAP OPERA are rule-governed and thus need skills and competence to understand their intricacies. For example, fully to appreciate British soap opera, the viewer needs to have an understanding of patterns and narratives of romance. This sort of consideration of popular competences has been controversial with those authors who do not appreciate such rules and skills and who seek to confine competence to 'high' cultural forms.

SEE ALSO: **Bourdieu; cultural capital; habitus**.

competition Process where groups seek advantage. Competition between social groups and social institutions is a key feature of capitalist economies, where the market is central. Media studies will most often consider competition between different media companies and the social effects of the outcomes of such processes. For example, competition between TABLOID newspapers for greater circulations or share of markets might lead to increased payments for photographs of celebrities and more intrusion into 'private' lives. This has also led to price-cutting 'wars', where newspapers seek to gain greater market share through reduction of COVER PRICE. The absence of competition, or MONOPOLY, tends to restrict the range of information sources to which an informed public should have access. For some commentators and politicians competition is held to lead to improvement of media output as programme-makers seek to please the audience. This is especially the case in commercial media systems. Such rationales have also been used to justify a movement away from public service media dominance. An example of this is the introduction of commercial TV as competition to the BBC in Britain in 1955.

SEE ALSO: **commodification; consumer society**.

composer In music the person who is credited with the authorship of a particular piece of music. This is important as the rights and therefore income that accrues to this identification can be very significant, a point which has led to much dispute in popular music. It can be difficult to disentangle who the composer (or author) of a particular piece of music is, especially when this has existed for a long period without being written down. For example, some rock musicians in the 1960s and 1970s appeared to be claiming composers' rights to music that seemed very similar to that in earlier blues recordings (Led Zeppelin were much criticized in this respect). This can be even more complex when the creation of a piece of music is in some sense a collective process. At some point in practice or recording, a member of a band may chip in with a suggestion that they might think is an aspect of composing, whereas the main author may have a different view.

SEE ALSO: **auteur theory; author; copyright.**

compression A software technique that compresses data so that it takes up less storage space on a disk. The data can then be uncompressed later.

computer games Although simple games were available on mainframe computers in the years after the Second World War, their widespread adoption had to wait until the emergence of microchips and then personal computers. Currently there are five main platforms available for playing computer games. First, game consoles can be attached to television sets. This method is largely preferred by teenagers. Second, the new generation of handheld machines has been used for gaming and attracts pre-teens who play, for example, *Pokémon*. Third, gaming software is written for personal computers which have other uses. This platform is largely used by adults. Fourth, computer games have taken their place in amusement arcades, which are mainly patronized by older teenagers. Fifth, ONLINE GAMES are now available to internet users, who tend to be young adults.

There are obvious overlaps with other media – comics, animated film and film – especially in visual aspects. Computer games also come in many of the GENRES common in other media forms, including horror, fantasy and science fiction. The difference, of course, lies in the fact that computer games are *games*.

The traditional image of the computer gamer is of a young man addicted to sitting in the dark in front of a screen. Actually, an increasing proportion of users and buyers of computer games (more than one-third in the United States, one-quarter in Western Europe and no less than three-quarters in Korea) are women, who are thought to be attracted by the appearance of sophisticated simulation games such as *Sim City*, or by online puzzles, rather than by the fast-action games. Furthermore, it is no longer quite so clear that computer gamers are young. According to industry sources, the average age of players is twenty-nine, and some two-fifths of the most frequent players are over thirty-five (Carr et al., 2006).

As with many new forms of popular culture, computer games have attracted substantial criticism and anxiety (SEE: **moral panic**). Besides fears about addiction, they have been blamed for violent acts. The Columbine school shootings, for example, were attributed to the perpetrators' liking for the game *Doom*. There is no serious evidence to support such assertions (SEE: **children and television**). Computer games have also been seen more positively. It has been argued, for example, that, unlike film or television, they permit greater interactivity with the medium. They can, moreover, encourage creativity as players adopt different identities. Lastly, many games are social, a conclusion at variance with the more negative image of computers as encouraging young people to be solitary. As Carr et al. (2006) found, players can transform even one-player computer games into multi-player events.

Computer gaming is undoubtedly popular and it is a rapidly expanding sector of the media. The worldwide market is estimated at more than £13 billion, and, in the UK, the games industry is twice the size of the market for video rentals. It is estimated that, at the height of the popularity of the game *Pokémon*, fully one-half of all Japenese children between seven and twelve years old were regular players. Computer games also illustrate the importance of cross-media developments. Several computer games have been made into films and vice versa. *Pokémon* itself generated a substantial MERCHANDISING business worth some £3 billion in 2005.

SEE ALSO: **media convergence**.

computer-generated image Increasingly, cinema employs images produced through the use of computer technology in addition to live action and animated drawings. The greater sophistication of computer technology has fuelled this process and has contributed to the success of ACTION films and the spectacular cinema of the early twenty-first century.

SEE ALSO: **action**; **animation**; **spectacle**.

computer-mediated communication The use of computers that permits direct communication between users, e.g. BULLETIN BOARDS, CHAT ROOMS, EMAIL, INSTANT MESSAGING, WEBSITES.

concentration See: CONCENTRATION OF OWNERSHIP.

concentration of ownership Although there is a multitude of commercial companies operating in various fields of the media, there has been an increasing tendency for a concentration of ownership as companies merge or are taken over. The result is that relatively few companies dominate the market, even if they do so via different brand names. Initially, this kind of growth takes place by HORIZONTAL INTEGRATION and VERTICAL

INTEGRATION. Thus, with respect to horizontal integration music companies operate with a number of different labels, and a company like Bertelsmann is horizontally integrated.

Within the last two decades or so, concentration in a different form has excited interest. This is known as DIAGONAL INTEGRATION. Large media companies have begun to acquire other businesses in quite different branches of the media, a process much helped by the use of digital technology in all aspects of the media (SEE: **media convergence**). Furthermore, this has become a global phenomenon as very large companies operate enterprises in many different countries (SEE: **global media**). The result is that relatively few companies now dominate the global media landscape, and five are particularly large and influential: BERTELSMANN, DISNEY, NEWS CORPORATION, TIME WARNER and VIACOM.

What are the advantages to companies in merger and acquisition? First, there are ECONOMIES OF SCALE. Companies are driven to grow in order to compete, and the fastest way of doing this is by acquiring other companies, or, at least, forming alliances with them. This tendency is compounded by the cost of new technology and of the necessary marketing and promotion, all of which require the resources of a large company. This is underpinned by the particular economics of the media. Most of the cost lies in the production of the first copy. Showing that to an audience or making subsequent copies cost little or nothing. Hence the incentive to have as large an audience or sales as possible to generate as much revenue as possible to cover the relatively high initial cost. Second, media companies believe that there are substantial economies to be made in owning several branches of the media (SEE: **economies of scope**). It is possible for one branch to promote the products of another, for television to advertise the appearance of a film or book, for instance. More important than these economies of marketing, however, are the potential economies in creative activity. Companies will argue that it is the same kind of resource that goes into producing a film, a television programme or a book, and they might as well make the best use of that resource. So novels can be used as the basis for television programmes (which in turn can be used as video-cassettes or DVDs), for audio-tapes, and have extracts used in magazines. It is also important to note that the concentration of ownership by horizontal, vertical and diagonal integration has been much helped by the deregulation of industry and commerce in the past two or three decades (SEE: **regulation**). In particular, barriers to cross-media ownership have been relaxed.

The tendency to concentration of ownership, and particularly cross-media ownership, has been accompanied by a great deal of public anxiety.

Any concentration produces a decline in competition, but it can be argued that concentration in the media industries is especially concerning. The major reason for this is that newspapers, television, radio, books and magazines represent the main ways by which citizens can be informed about the issues of the day and can have access to reasoned debate. Competitive media are part of the democratic process itself. The anxieties will be all the more justified to the extent that proprietors use the media to promote their own political and social beliefs (SEE: **Berlusconi; Murdoch**). It has also been argued that there is an inverse relationship between the concentration of a market and the creativity exemplified by the products that it contains. So the more concentration the less the creativity and innovation that will occur. An influential argument concerning the cyclical nature of this process in the music industry was made by Peterson and Berger (1990).

SEE ALSO: **global media; media companies; media imperialism.**

conglomerate A large company that has grown typically by buying other companies not necessarily in the same field (SEE: **diagonal integration**). An example is NEWS CORPORATION, which has interests in many countries in radio, newspapers, television, film, and book and magazine publishing. Conglomeration is an important strategy for companies because it diversifies their products and therefore manages the risk involved in any downturn in the demand for any one of them.

SEE ALSO: **concentration of ownership; media companies.**

conglomeration See: CONCENTRATION OF OWNERSHIP.

connotation See: DENOTATION/CONNOTATION.

SEE ALSO: **Barthes; code; structuralism.**

consensus An agreement, explicit or not, between several parties. The word is used in everyday speech when relatively small groups of people come to an agreement. However, in social science the term is used for a condition of society in which there is widespread agreement in the population on basic values. The questions for social scientists are then: is there consensus and, if there is, how is it produced? As to the first, many social scientists argue that there are substantial value conflicts in society, and they are more likely to be deepening than anything else. Students of media studies are more likely to be interested in the second question, however. There are two schools of thought as to how consensus might arise. The first emphasizes the power of institutions of society, especially the media, to mould opinion and belief. By exposure to press, television, radio, magazines, it is argued, people come to acquire a particular view of the world that they find in those sources. The alternative is to argue that people acquire common values because they learn them in the process of socialization (upbringing). Both these positions are only partially true. The first is limited because the media are simply not that effective. The second overemphasizes the degree to which socialization processes are similar across society. The critical point for both arguments is that there is not nearly the degree of consensus in societies that is often assumed.

SEE ALSO: **domination**.

consent An abiding problem in social theory is how social order is achieved and how people do or do not give their consent to the way that their society is organized. To put it very crudely, the issue is whether societies are orderly because, on the whole, people believe in the basic values of society or because they are effectively coerced by the threat of punishment if they break the rules – or both of these. In any theory which stresses the importance of consent, the media play a substantial role. For many people, the media are the most important source of information about what is going on around them and of opinion and debate about contemporary events. They are therefore an important influence on whether consent is given – or withheld. It is important, however, not to overemphasize the influence of the media.

SEE ALSO: **consensus; domination; effects**.

conspiracy theory From time to time, the public imagination is gripped by an account of a public event that attributes that event to a conspiracy. Examples include the death of Princess Diana, which some believe to be the work of the secret services, and the claim that President Kennedy was not shot by a lone assassin but was the victim of a carefully organized conspiracy. These conspiracy theories concern the sudden and unexpected deaths of public figures but they can occur in different circumstances. Governments and politicians are often the focus. For example, conspiracy theories about the attacks on the Twin Towers surfaced immediately after 9/11, variously attributing the incident to the American secret service and the Israelis. It has been argued that there is a strongly paranoid streak in American culture and politics which means that conspiracy theories are common in the United States.

There are similarities between the manner in which conspiracy theories arise and the way in which MORAL PANICS spread through society in that both are driven through a spiral of media attention, public interest and government action. People who have access to the media ('moral entrepreneurs') advance the theory. It is then taken up by the media, which need stories, especially scandalous or arresting ones. This is usually led by the press, but television and radio follow. Books appear which give credibility, and other public figures become involved. A movement develops, and the government becomes involved because it needs to counter the allegations being made. That may become so serious that a formal investigation or public inquiry is required. Such investigations almost always find against the conspiracy theory, and that may stop the spiral of media attention and public interest.

constructionism See: SOCIAL CONSTRUCTIONISM.

consumer behaviour The manner in which consumers come to choose what goods and services to buy. The study of such conduct is clearly of crucial interest to advertisers, who are, after all, attempting to persuade consumers to buy one product rather than another. A variety of theories are on offer to explain consumer behaviour, ranging from those that suggest that the most important factor is the social environment in which the consumer is placed to those which stress the significance of fundamental human needs and drives.

SEE ALSO: **consumer society**.

consumer culture See: CONSUMER SOCIETY.

consumer magazine A magazine that is bought directly from a shop by consumers, or obtained on subscription, and is aimed largely at leisure pursuits. The contrast is with trade magazines aimed at particular kinds of business or occupations and which are almost invariably bought by subscription.

consumer society It is frequently argued that modern societies, especially in the West, are increasingly organized around the consumption of goods and services and therefore give prominence to advertising and other forms of product promotion. Although there is an active debate about the characteristics of consumer society, the following are often cited. First, over the twentieth century as a whole, and following the Second World War in particular, the inhabitants of many Western countries have simply had a good deal more money to spend on consumer goods and leisure pursuits. It is estimated that over the course of the twentieth century, consumption expenditure worldwide increased almost twenty-fold. Second, over the same period, working hours have gradually fallen, allowing more time for leisure pursuits. Third, and more controversially, people now take their very identity from their activities as consumers and from their leisure pursuits rather than from their work. There is more interest in the construction of a lifestyle and in the presentation of an image, which involve the purchase of commodities of various kinds. Acts of consumption, the development of a lifestyle and the acquisition of certain goods are increasingly used as markers of social position (SEE: **positional goods**). Fourth, while for much of the twentieth century, social class or gender were the main sources of social division, these are being replaced by divisions based on patterns of consumption. Fifth, in consumer societies consumers gain power at the expense of producers, whether these are producers of goods or professionals offering a service, such as doctors, teachers or lawyers. In some respects the economic position of the consumer is substituting for political rights and duties; the consumer replaces the citizen. This is related to a gradual extension of the market into more aspects of human life. More and more goods and services are being offered for sale.

Although modern societies do indeed have some of these characteristics, it is by no means clear that they have all of them, or what their significance might be, or whether they are to be welcomed. For example, it is argued that social class, gender and ethnicity continue to be important sources of social differentiation.

SEE ALSO: **advertisement; brand**.

contagion The process by which a phenomenon spreads. Derived from consideration of how diseases spread and processes of influence, the term has been used with respect to the media to describe how ideas or practices are spread out from a media message to others rapidly. This is one of the ideas behind some uses of the concept of MORAL PANIC, where the public react on the basis of restricted or misleading information supplied by the media. The idea may also be used to consider how one medium affects another. For example, the reporting of a story by a newspaper will often be picked up by radio and television and developed further. In turn, this will be reported by the newspapers, and a spiral of influence develops. In this sense, media are parasitic upon each other.

content analysis A method for the study of texts. Ball and Smith (1992: 21–2) identify six steps in the method. First, 'selecting a topic and determining a research problem'; second, 'selecting a documentary source'; third, 'devising a set of analytic categories'; fourth, 'formulating an explicit set of instructions for using the categories to code the material'; fifth, 'establishing a principled basis for sampling the documents'; and sixth, 'counting the frequency of a given category or theme in the documents sampled'. A good example of content analysis can be found in Laing's (1985) comparison of the lyrical content of punk songs with that of top-fifty songs. This systematically shows the difference in content between the two genres. Thus punk songs were less concerned with romantic and heterosexual relations than are pop songs and were more concerned to explore issues raised by sexuality. Punk songs also contained more political and social comment. However, and this is a general limitation of content analysis, in concentrating on textual material, it is not able to examine other ways in which the lyrics make meaning. For example, the vocalist can make a difference to meaning by variations in the tone of voice. Moreover, content analysis abstracts the analysis of content from context or FORM. Thus, similar content in a comedy (for example, *Austin Powers*) may have different meanings from that in an action film (for example, James Bond films).

continuity Process in film and television that ensures that details are consistent through the narrative. For example, the continuity person will make sure that the actor's hairstyle does not change from shot to shot.

contrast In film and television the difference between the darkest and lightest visual tones in a scene.

control Power to determine the outcome of a social process. Used with respect to the media in two main ways. First, to describe how media corporations or companies are controlled by those who own or manage them. This is important as control of this kind gives significant power over the content of the texts that media companies produce. The clearest examples of this come from consideration of the ownership of NEWS-PAPERS. Second, control over production is thought to give a measure of influence over how the audience therefore thinks about issues. In cruder versions of these ideas, control of an organization leads to direct control over media texts, which then influence the audience directly. The history of media studies is partly about subjecting such crude claims to empirical and theoretical scrutiny.

SEE ALSO: **effects; media mogul.**

convention Established rules or understandings that are deployed in texts. The conventions of a text are usually related to the nature of a particular GENRE. For example, in the detective story, it was conventional for the detective to be a man, who tended to operate outside of a set of rules (even if employed by an organization) but in the pursuit of justice. The breaking of such conventions is a way to innovate. Thus, making the hero of the detective story female means that a new set of possibilities for a narrative are opened up. Innovation also occurs when conventions from one genre are combined with another to produce new forms and new genres. Thus, a television text like *The Sopranos* combines aspects of the gangster genre with soap opera to produce an innovative new hybrid. Here the male hero is exceptionally strong in some aspects (as a gang leader) but dominated by his mother (in the first season) in other ways. A DOCUSOAP combines the conventions of DOCUMENTARY and SOAP OPERA and so on.

convergence See: MEDIA CONVERGENCE.

conversational analysis A form of analysis which attempts to record patterns of conversation in order to uncover the rules that permit communication to proceed in an orderly and meaningful fashion. The use of language in conversations provides order and management of the social settings in which talking takes place. Conversational analysis provides descriptions of the way in which conversations achieve this order. It is not concerned with the actual subject matter of conversations but with the rules that organize them. Actual studies include the way in which the first five seconds of telephone conversations are structured and the manner in which courtroom conversational interaction is ordered.

co-production A form of production and financing of television programmes and films which involves two or more organizations working in partnership. Although television companies are often accused of making cheap programmes, some are very expensive to make. The most obvious examples are drama serials using exotic locations, famous actors or complex historical reconstructions. In order to help to finance such programmes, television companies sometimes enter into co-production deals whereby two or more companies share the costs and revenues and transmit in several countries. These arrangements are frequently international, as English-language programmes can be shown worldwide. As a consequence, co-productions often have actors from different countries and may use a diversity of international locations.

copy The material provided by a journalist for an edition of a newspaper or by an advertising copywriter for an advertisement. The copy will usually then be edited by a sub-editor before inclusion.

SEE ALSO: **copywriter**.

copy editor In most forms of the media, there is someone who is responsible for editing the product – preparing it for final release. In book publishing, this person is called a copy editor, a term sometimes also applied in print journalism, though the term sub-editor is more commonly used. When an author finally submits a manuscript to a publisher, after the commissioning editor has decided that it is suitable, the copy editor prepares it – raising queries with the author about style, consistency, omissions and illustration and marking up the manuscript so that it can be typeset.

SEE ALSO: **book publishing; commissioning editor; editor; typesetter.**

copyright The legal ownership of a text – that is, the content of the work, rather than any physical manifestation of it. The copyright holder of a text controls who can reproduce it or sell copies. In media industries, copyright is based on intellectual property right, which is the 'right given to the creators of original literary, dramatic, musical and artistic works, and which also extends to the creators of original sound recordings, films, broadcasts, cable programmes and the typographic arrangement of published editions' (*Cultural Trends*, 1993: 56). The owner of a copyright may let others use it for a payment. For example, in the music industry there are three main types of right: performing, public performance and mechanical. The first two concern the rights due to the performance of a song or the playing of a recording. Mechanical rights are paid for the recording of a song or piece of music. Rights payments have to be collected. Income from rights is collected on the behalf of the owner by collecting societies, such as the PERFORMING RIGHTS SOCIETY. Exploitation of rights has become increasingly important as a source of income for all media owners. It has also become a source of angry debate and legal action (SEE: **intellectual property**), such as around file-sharing and downloading of music. Media companies are also concerned about the circulation of pirate copies of the texts to which they own the rights, as this can affect their profitability in significant ways.

SEE ALSO: **author; book publishing; music industry; piracy.**

copywriter The person who is responsible for thinking up the text that goes with advertisements. Although much of this may be simply writing the words that are persuasive, copywriters have been responsible for slogans or catchphrases that become strongly associated with the product in the public's mind. One famous example is: 'Go to work on an egg.' Text of this kind is therefore of importance in the creation of a BRAND image.

SEE ALSO: **advertisement.**

Corporation for Public Broadcasting (CPB) See: PUBLIC BROADCAST-ING SERVICE.

costume design Production role in TV, film and theatre responsible for the clothes of actors. The costume design can add much to the look of any production. It is also an aspect of the text that audiences may comment on. This suggests that approaches that focus exclusively on narrative would miss the significance of the look of a text or image and thus overlook an important way in which meaning is conveyed and understood. For example, the communication of REALISM in the cinema and TV has much to do with how characters are dressed. The costume designer will need to research the right mode of dress for a particular historical period or place. In forms which rely more on spectacular visual appeal, such as MUSICALS in the cinema and theatre, a key aspect of the enjoyment of the production on the part of the audience may come from the costumes of the performers. There is a tendency for media studies to neglect these aspects by concentrating on the narrative of the text.

costume drama In film and television, a GENRE set in the past, which is signified through period costume, language and setting. There is a tendency for the term to have some negative connotations, which can be related ideologically to the appeal of the genre to women and to the fact that it arguably appeals to a sanitized, 'heritage' view of culture. The genre is related to MELODRAMA and ROMANCE.

couch potato A term of abuse for someone who will watch anything on television and who watches a great deal but does so totally uncritically and without any degree of attention.
    SEE ALSO: **active audience**.

counter cinema Films that seek to oppose the conventions, the politics or social ideas of what is seen as mainstream, dominant or Hollywood cinema. It may thus use different conventions (SEE: **art cinema** or **avant-garde**), or more established conventions but use under-represented groups (e.g. black people, women) or address political and social exclusion and oppression.

counter culture The culture of opposition and resistance to mainstream or dominant culture that developed in the advanced Western world during the 1960s particularly among young people. It incorporated a range of cultural forms (such as rock music), cultural practices (such as 'be-ins' and 'love-ins'), forms of reorganization of everyday life (such as communal living) and overt political practices (demonstrations and occupations). An analytic discussion of the counter culture can be found in *Resistance through Rituals* (Hall and Jefferson, 1976) from the Birmingham Centre for Contemporary Cultural Studies and in the work of Martin (1981), where its development is related systematically to contextual changes in society and culture more widely. The term has also been used more recently in the study of consumption (SEE: **consumer society**) to denote the way in which everyday culture has become more centred on shopping (i.e. trade over a counter). There is a degree of play with the earlier meaning here, as it is suggested that the culture of opposition and hedonism released in the 1960s has been transformed into the activity of shopping and acquisition.

SEE ALSO: **youth culture**.

cover lines The text on a magazine cover that conveys detail about the most important stories and articles inside the publication.

cover price The full retail price as declared on the cover or front page of a newspaper, magazine or book. From time to time, price wars break out and newspaper and magazine proprietors will effectively give discounts on the cover price in order to win customers. Generally speaking, they return to the original price, or a higher one, in time. The same principle applies to books. Publishers put a cover price on their books, but book-shops frequently discount that price.

SEE ALSO: **Net Book Agreement**.

crane Platform for mounting a camera, which can then be moved up and down.

Crawford Committee Following on rapidly from the SYKES COMMITTEE, the Crawford Committee reported in 1925. It recommended that the BBC should be constituted as an autonomous corporation, established by Royal Charter, run by a board of governors appointed by the government and run by a Director-General appointed by the governors.

SEE ALSO: **BBC**.

creative industries A term with an imprecise meaning: creative indus-tries are those companies and other organizations which produce or use knowledge. Included in this category are organizations utilizing advanced scientific knowledge, in pharmaceuticals or information technology for example, the media, arts and design organizations and universities. Governments over the last two or three decades have become increasingly interested in the economic benefits of the creative industries, attracted partly by the argument that advanced industrial countries will keep a competitive advantage by specializing in science and design rather than manufacture. The term 'creative industries' overlaps considerably with CULTURAL INDUSTRIES.

creativity The process of creation of new forms and new texts involving innovation. While much media production is routine and conventional, there is still scope for creativity on the part of media producers in seeking to innovate in such contexts. Thus, it may be that, for the audience, one of the pleasures of the contemporary media is the recognition that such creativity has been applied to produce new forms. It has also been suggested that media audiences are creative in the way that they consume and deal with media texts. Thus, the process of understanding a text at all involves creativity on the part of the audience member. Furthermore, audience members may use their COMPETENCE or CULTURAL CAPITAL to manipulate the text in various ways. One of the more extreme forms of such creativity is the way in which female *Star Trek* fans have written new *Star Trek* stories that put the main characters into new relationships (such as Kirk and Spock being sexually involved with each other) and new situations (see Bacon-Smith, 1992; Jenkins, 1992; and Penley, 1992).

SEE ALSO: **fan.**

crime Behaviour or act that breaks the law. Crime is of significance with respect to the media in a number of ways. First, fictional media texts are often concerned with crime and its policing. It has been suggested that such representations systematically distort the actual occurrence of crime and the way in which it can be controlled. This is due to the overrepresentation of violent crime and the suggestion that the police solve all the crimes that they are confronted with. This has led to the second broad area of concern. Many analysts argue that the representation of the nature of crime in the media (and most importantly on television) has led to an increased fear of crime which is out of proportion to the actual likelihood of being a victim. The evidence suggests that such a fear is more prevalent among heavy users of television. Third, the reporting of crimes forms a significant part of the content of factual media such as news programmes or newspapers. Again, there have been studies that argue that the media are selective in the sorts of crimes that are focused upon – for example, significantly neglecting corporate or white-collar crime. Analyses of this sort of selectivity can be found in S. Cohen's (1973) discussion of MORAL PANICS and the work of the CENTRE FOR CONTEMPORARY CULTURAL STUDIES on 'mugging' and the 'invention' by the media of a 'crime' that does not actually exist in law (Hall et al., 1978). This 'crime' was represented as being mainly carried out by a particular social group – young black men – a representation that effectively demonized that group as a whole.

SEE ALSO: **cultivation theory; police series.**

critical framing See: FRAMING; TELEVISION TALK.

critical reading See: NATIONWIDE STUDY.

critical theory The form of social and cultural theory associated with the writers of the FRANKFURT SCHOOL. Critical theory is concerned to critique and supersede traditional or descriptive ways of theorizing and to promote social and cultural change. For example, some forms of audience study simply count the numbers of people that watch a programme or ask the audience what they think of the programme in terms of how much they appreciate it. Critical theorists would find fault with such an approach. First, they see this as an essentially descriptive approach in that the number of people watching is counted in a mechanical way, without considering the assumptions behind the calculations and the social processes involved. Second, appreciation is condensed into a limited index. A critical theory would want to consider why the audience are watching in the way that they do and would criticize the nature of the reasons given for their responses by the audience as not reaching deeper levels of understanding of the motivation of the audience. In particular, audience responses would likely be seen as rationalized and standardized into particular forms by the control of people's minds and behaviour by the cultural industries. For example, in his discussions of popular music audiences and radio listeners, T. W. ADORNO sees the audience as acting in standardized and conformist ways in response to the commodified and standardized products of the music industry. His approach rests on a critique of these responses on the basis of how people respond to the serious music that is complex and not commodified. A problem with this sort of approach is that it rests on the acceptance of the characterization of society provided by the Frankfurt School authors. However, much research into audiences shows that audience responses are not standardized but are instead remarkably diverse.

SEE ALSO: **audience; ideology**.

cropping The process of reducing a larger image to a smaller one by the removal of parts of the larger image. It is a very significant practice in PHOTOGRAPHY, where it has been used to convey meanings through the reproduction of a particular part of an image, which might even be contradicted by the whole. For example, a picture of two people shaking hands might suggest friendship between them, but if the bigger picture showed that one of the people had a gun at his/her head it would change the meaning to suggest that the gesture of friendship had been rather forced. The connotation of friendship of the first picture would be changed to that of threat or duress in the second through the process of cropping (SEE: **denotation/connotation**).

cross-cutting Switching between different actions or streams of narrative in a film.

SEE ALSO: **parallel action**.

cross-media ownership Many media enterprises started life as independent companies. However, over time, those companies have grown larger by acquiring others. More recently still, companies are buying into other branches of the media, giving cross-media ownership. Companies do this partly to grow larger in related fields and achieve ECONOMIES OF SCALE and ECONOMIES OF SCOPE and partly because the skills that are employed in one branch of the media can be transferred to others. Companies contemplating merger or acquisition often make use of the notion of synergy. The claim is that because media fields overlap, it is possible to use products in one field in another. For example, in a company like NEWS CORPORATION that owns both television stations and newspapers, journalists and news stories can appear in both media. In other companies novels can be made into film scripts or popular music can be used as a soundtrack for films or TV programmes. The result of this process is that the largest media companies tend to be invested in several media fields (SEE: **Bertelsmann; Time Warner; Viacom**).

Cross-ownership of the media has given rise to substantial concerns about lack of competition and anxieties that a few large media companies will control access to information.

SEE ALSO: **concentration of ownership; media imperialism; newspaper**.

cross over 1 Different branches of the media are coming closer together, partly because of the DIGITAL REVOLUTION and partly because of CROSS-MEDIA OWNERSHIP, and, as a result, ideas and techniques are crossing over from one branch to another (SEE: **media convergence**).

2 The boundaries between different GENRES of television are not as clear as they were, and the conventions of one genre are crossing over into another (SEE: **docusoap**).

3 Forms of popular music also cross over when, for example, a specialist music becomes part of the mainstream and more commercially successful.

cue Introduction to a written item or a performance.

cult In its anthropological usage, the beliefs and practices of a particular group in relation to a god or gods. In media studies, the term has mostly been applied to particular texts (cult media) and to the practices of audiences in relation to such texts (see Hills, 2002). Particular texts thus function almost as objects of worship (though not uncritically) for certain audience members. These may be science-fiction-derived (e.g. *Star Trek*,

Blake's 7, *Doctor Who*), variants on a horror genre (e.g. *Buffy the Vampire Slayer*) or concerned with stylistic violence (kung fu movies). Such intense interaction with media has tended to be denigrated, but media studies has taken the investigation of these forms and attachments seriously, most importantly in the burgeoning area of studies of fandom and FANS.

cultivation theory The idea that prolonged and heavy exposure to television develops (or cultivates) in viewers a view of the world consistent with the dominant or majority view expounded by TV. This may replace views that were more based in the everyday experience of the viewer. There are two aspects of the research on which this theory is based (SEE: **Gerbner**). First, over some thirty years, researchers studied the content of television and concluded that, in certain respects, particularly for violence, crime and family matters, television systematically distorts reality. Second, long-term surveys of audiences concluded that the attitudes and beliefs held by heavy users of television were consistent with those provided by television. Television cultivates a view of society that is essentially mainstream and which tends to marginalize beliefs and groups which do not fit that view (Morgan and Signorelli, 1990). The difficulty with cultivation theory lies in establishing the *causal* relationship between heavy television viewing and the adoption of particular views. Thus, it might be the case that people that take mainstream views of society are also those who choose to watch a great deal of television.
SEE ALSO: **effects; uses and gratifications**.

cultural apparatus Term derived from MARXISM to denote the way in which cultural institutions and organizations effectively operating together convey IDEOLOGY to the benefit of those in power. For example, the media and the education system may form an apparatus that promotes similar messages about competing with others to advance oneself, thus reinforcing ideas of individualism and masculinity.
SEE ALSO: **Althusser**.

cultural capital Concept deployed by the French sociologist PIERRE BOURDIEU to denote cultural resources such as knowledge and qualifications acquired through the education system, understanding of valued artefacts and practices such as classical music and fine art, and customs, practices and manners that are seen as legitimate. He used the idea in tandem with the more familiar idea of economic capital. Thus, in discussing the ways in which classes seek to distinguish themselves from each other, Bourdieu pointed out that some groups, while high in economic capital, are low in cultural capital. Hence, businesspeople may be well paid and own shares in their company but they may not be able to understand fine art or classical literature, or know the correct way to behave with members of the aristocracy. On the other hand, there are some groups that tend to be high in cultural capital but relatively low in economic capital – university lecturers, for example. Cultural capital, like economic capital (and social capital, which describes the resources provided by social networks), is a resource to be drawn upon in the pursuit of power. Cultural capital, as developed through the education system, may be very significant in advancing people to powerful positions in the education system itself or the state bureaucracy. Cultural capital and economic capital may be useful in different contexts. Bourdieu's most famous book, *Distinction* (1984, first published 1979), used survey data to map some of the complexities of the relations between different sectors of the French middle class, such as business and academic. This has inspired theoretical refinement of the concept of cultural capital, as well as further empirical work in a number of countries. In media studies the idea of cultural capital can be used to understand the COMPETENCES of different audience sections. The concept has been developed into the idea of subcultural capital: the means whereby subcultural groups create distinction. Thus, with dance and rave culture it was important to be in possession of (or know) the hip record or to have the correct style (Thornton, 1995).

SEE ALSO: **field; habitus.**

cultural imperialism The imposition of the culture of one country on others which may have very different indigenous cultures. Before the twentieth century, it happened most commonly as a result of war, conquest or occupation. The means by which it occurred could be varied. It might be the conqueror's language, religion, system of law or customs and manners which were imposed. For example, the global spread of the English language in Africa, North America, Australasia and, to some extent, Asia, is mostly attributable to centuries of empire-building by Britain. At the same time, missionary activity, especially in the nineteenth century and in Africa, was responsible for much of the indigenous population becoming Christian.

More recently, however, cultural imperialism, to the extent that it exists, is an outcome more of global trading and economic power than military occupation, although the latter helps. And it is the cultural dominance of the United States rather than European countries that is the issue. Although the global availability of American goods and brands clearly is important in cultural imperialism, the pervasiveness of American-dominated media is even more so. Film, television and popular music bring the English (or American) language and American culture, customs and practices to a worldwide audience (SEE: **media imperialism**). However, it is important not to overstate the case for cultural imperialism. Because local populations buy Coca-Cola, listen to American pop music and watch American television does not mean that they adopt American culture wholesale. Audiences are not sponges (SEE: **active audience**). Furthermore, the resilience of local cultures should not be underestimated. Cultural differences persist, encouraged by local initiatives such as indigenous film industries and local recording industries for popular music.

SEE ALSO: **global media; transculture**.

cultural industries A rather vague term which overlaps both with CRE-ATIVE INDUSTRIES and with 'media industries'. Cultural industries include advertising, TELEVISION, RADIO, NEWSPAPERS, INTERNET publishing, MAGAZINES, BOOK PUBLISHING, FILM and theatre. On the margins of the category are educational organizations, particularly universities. Cultural industries have attracted attention from government partly because of their economic significance in developed societies. In the UK in 2004, this sector generated about 5 per cent of gross domestic product, earns over £10 billion in exports and employs 1.3 million people. In addition, it has also played a role in regional policy especially in regenerating city centres.

Despite their apparent differences, the various cultural industries do have common features. Thus, they all involve the management of creativity. The production of the material that they ultimately distribute is dependent on creative individuals such as writers, journalists, copywriters, musicians or scriptwriters. It is frequently the case that such people are not directly employed by a cultural industries organization but work freelance, and their input needs to be managed. Most organizations have developed particular roles to do this (SEE: **producer**). Companies and organizations within the cultural industries are increasingly post-Fordist in structure, aiming to outsource many of their functions, and some, book publishing for example, have done so for a long time (SEE: **Fordism/ post-Fordism; outsourcing**). Although the cultural industries do produce physical products – books, records, etc. – their economic value resides primarily in COPYRIGHT and the rights that derive from it.

One last common characteristic of the cultural industries is the unpredictability of sales. A relatively small proportion of output, whether it is records, books or films, makes most of the money. The difficulty is that those who work in the industries frequently do not know what will sell well and what will not. Companies will adopt various strategies to manage this unpredictability, from hiring staff who appear to be able to pick winners to trying to repeat formulae that have been successful in the past. These strategies have only limited success.

SEE ALSO: **economics of the media**.

cultural materialism The theory, associated with RAYMOND WILLIAMS, that emphasizes the material significance of culture, in contrast to theories that focus on ideas, beauty and cultural ideals or see it a secondary product of economic and technological processes. Culture is, in this argument, neither simply reflective of economic forces and relationships nor an abstract, idealistic entity, but comprises texts that are produced and consumed through cultural and social processes and ways of life of particular groups. Culture is therefore material. Culture is also material in that it is made solid in a variety of forms, which are the products of industrial and social processes. Thus, television has an effect on society through the programmes that it shows. It addition, in related but slightly different senses, a television set is a material object that is located in private and public spaces. As an object it becomes part of the décor and the meaning of a living room and the rest of the décor may be structured around it.

cultural production The generation of cultural texts and practices. The idea of cultural production conveys the way in which culture is not simply created and delivered in an abstract manner which has no relation to other social practices. The production of culture is therefore in some ways akin to the production of any other material goods and services, but has the important distinctive quality that the products are envisaged as conveying meaning. The production of culture approach to the study of the media developed by RICHARD A. PETERSON identifies six different types of factor (technology, law and regulation, industry structure, organization, occupational career, and market) in the production of media products such as rock music. Approaches to the study of the media that concern themselves with patterns of ownership and control of media companies and those which look at the organizational processes at work in media companies emphasize production in similar ways. Other approaches may pay more attention to the analysis of the structure of texts (such as STRUCTURALISM and SEMIOLOGY), or to how audiences make meaning from texts (SEE: **audience**).

SEE ALSO: **cultural industries; political economy; producer; producer/ text/audience**.

cultural reproduction Idea derived from Marxist theory that conveys how culture is involved in the maintenance (reproduction) of a society which has unequal social relations at its core. Culture became increasingly important in the theories of a number of Marxist thinkers as a mode of explaining the continued acceptance of exploitation by many in capitalist societies.

SEE ALSO: **ideology; Marxism.**

cultural studies Approach to the study of culture that emphasizes the systematic study of all forms of culture, especially relative to power and inequality between groups. While the borders and boundaries of cultural studies are much disputed, as an academic activity it crucially developed at the Birmingham CENTRE FOR CONTEMPORARY CULTURAL STUDIES, where under the leadership of initially RICHARD HOGGART and then STUART HALL, there were developed a number of studies of culture that recognized textual complexity (from literary studies), social contextualization (from sociology and anthropology) and social change (from history). The key figures in the initial development of the approach were Hoggart, RAYMOND WILLIAMS and EDWARD THOMPSON. The development of a culturalized form of MARXISM was a key aspect of the initial phase of cultural studies, which led to an enduring interest in how culture and power are interconnected. Since its early days, cultural studies has grown into an area of academic life that continues to advance cultural theory, studies of different forms of culture and the critical analysis of how culture is implicated in the flow and distribution of power. While there are many contributors to cultural studies, the institutional location of the activity within universities has been relatively insecure. This is partly the effect of debates as to whether cultural studies should be, or is, a discipline with an established set of theories and practices or whether it is best seen as a space between disciplines that facilitates the interplay of different ideas and critical exploration (see further Baldwin et al., 1999; Couldry, 2000). Cultural studies today is closely related to media studies and continues to explore culture and power with respect most significantly to gender and racial difference and inequality.

culture 1 The arts and artistic practices. **2** The symbolic aspects of a way of life or ways of life. **3** A process of development. In the first sense culture is encapsulated in aesthetic and artistic practices and outputs, such as plays, the theatre, movies, books, poetry and so on. In some formulations this involves some kind of judgement of aesthetic worth that defines some things as culture (or proper or HIGH CULTURE – such as Beethoven) and others as worthless or trash (mass culture – such as Britney Spears). In the second sense attention is drawn to the range of practices that may characterize a social group (the working class), a section of a group (work-ing-class youth), a region (northern culture) or nation (England or Scot-land) and so on. The third sense developed from the idea of the cultivation of crops or animals. It now often refers to individual and social develop-ment as they become more cultivated. One of the problems of the concept of culture is the way in which these different meanings intertwine in sometimes-contradictory ways. Thus, the pop music of Bob Dylan might be studied as a form of aesthetic practice (sense 1, for example in terms of the imagery of his lyrics), in terms of its association with a form of culture in the 1960s or as part of the subculture of Bob Dylan fans (sense 2, the COUNTER CULTURE or the Bobcats), or as developing themes from earlier folk or blues music or in terms of its influence on subsequent writers and performers (sense 3).

SEE ALSO: **cultural studies**.

current affairs Type of television and radio programming that is con-cerned with the reporting and representation of contemporary events. The genre usually builds on events or narratives that are in the news and offers a more detailed view on particular aspects of them. Such represen-tation is often controversial because of the claims of bias from different points on the political spectrum and because of the way in which poli-ticians may be treated when up for scrutiny.

SEE ALSO: **documentary; news**.

cut Term used in related ways with respect to different media. It is common to hear the shout of 'Cut!' from the director of a film, to signify a point where filming is to stop. The term also refers to film editing, deriving from the literal cutting of the film that is part of film-making. This has led to the development of terms like 'rough cut' or 'first cut', to signal an initial edit of film that will not be the final and more polished version. The term is also used in the popular music industry with similar meanings and derivations. Here 'cut' came from the actual cutting of the groove into a master that would form the basis of the pressings of a recording in the days before digital recording techniques. Likewise, the term 'cut' refers also simply to a version of a tune or indeed to the tune itself. In radio and TV it is an excerpt from a longer recording.

cut-away In film-making a shot that is not a central part of the main narrative, but which may be used to add detail or develop a part of the dominant narrative or story.

cyberculture A term without precise definition that broadly refers to the attitudes, beliefs and bodies of knowledge of those heavily involved in computers and COMPUTER GAMES. It is also used even more generally to indicate the culture that might grow up in societies very heavily organized around computer systems.

cyberspace Used generally to describe any 'space' generated by computer networks, such as the INTERNET, VIRTUAL REALITY and the WORLD WIDE WEB. The term was used by William Gibson in his so-called 'cyberpunk' novels such as *Neuromancer* (1984), where he also introduces the idea of the 'matrix'.

SEE ALSO: **computer games; Haraway.**

cyborg See: HARAWAY.

cycles of concentration See: CONCENTRATION OF OWNERSHIP.

D

DAB (Digital Audio Broadcasting) See: DIGITAL BROADCASTING.

daguerreotype An early form of photograph introduced by Louis Daguerre in the early nineteenth century. The process used a metal plate that was covered with silver. The plate was sensitized by iodine fumes, exposed in a camera and then developed by being exposed to mercury vapour. The method required long exposure times in the camera together with a complex process of development. The resultant photographs were delicate, and prints could not be taken. Nevertheless, it was very popular for twenty years until it was superseded by photographs using paper, faster development and exposure times, and which could be copied many times.

SEE ALSO: **photograph**.

dailies 1 Newspapers that are published every day except Sunday. Most daily newspapers in the UK have a companion title published on a Sunday, e.g. *The Times* and the *Sunday Times* (SEE: **newspaper**).

2 The RUSHES of a film that are taken every day.

daily life Often used as another term for EVERYDAY LIFE. A more specialist use distinguishes everyday life as characterizing the consumer-based cultures and sections of cultures of the West from the daily life of other societies where the sheer task of getting through the day in physical terms is central (for example, in parts of Africa). The American writer Lawrence Grossberg (1992) suggests that the daily lives of those on the margins of American society, such as many Afro-Americans, often act as a resource for cultural and musical styles of the more affluent.

Dallas The title of one of the key television programmes of the late 1970s and early to mid-1980s. The best-known of the American prime-time soap operas, the programme was centred on the activities of the Ewing family in the American oil business. The settings and actions were primarily concerned with the interactions between various family members (especially J. R. Ewing, the anti-hero of the show) and others that they came into contact with. The immense popularity of the show led to its investigation by media scholars. Two main studies of the audience are of ongoing significance. First, the work of IEN ANG (1985) examined in a small-scale qualitative audience study the pleasures of *Dallas* for a female audience. This is one of the best-known of the wave of qualitative audience studies of the 1980s that were informed by developments in cultural and critical theory. Despite the relatively small size of the sample, the study has been very important to understandings of gender and TV. The second study was conducted by Liebes and Katz (1993) and sought to examine cross-cultural and cross-ethnic understandings and views of the programme. This is one of the most detailed and influential analyses of the audience for any one text. It made a number of points concerning the way in which the programme was understood from within the different cultural frames of various groups. Thus, some groups were concerned with the morality of the key characters, where others read it as a criticism of the American way of life. It also sought to examine the bases of the popularity of the programme.

SEE ALSO: **soap opera**.

dance The structured movement of the body in combination with music. There are as many different types of dance as there are societies and more. Like language, dance can almost be seen as a defining characteristic of human societies. This makes the relative lack of attention to the activity in academic circles all the more surprising. In recent years, this has begun to be rectified, though there is still a long way to go. Ground-breaking work was done on the importance of dance for young women in the context of studies of popular music and youth culture (see McRobbie, 1984). Previously, accounts of popular music had tended to neglect the significance of dance and concentrated instead on how music related to such activities as drug-taking and modes of dress. A renewed interest in dance also influenced the development of the many studies of rave and dance culture, especially noting the increased participation in dance by young men (McRobbie, 1993). Other specialist cultures based around dance, such as the phenomenon of Northern Soul in the North of England, have also received attention.

SEE ALSO: **youth culture**.

DAT Digital audio tape – tape used for digital, as opposed to analogue, sound recording.

Debord, Guy (1931–94) A radical French writer and film-maker who was active in the Lettrist and Situationist groups. His influence in media and cultural studies is most felt through his book *The Society of the Spectacle*

(1994, first published 1967), which anticipated a number of POSTMODERN-IST themes concerning the way in which social and cultural life was becoming both more spectacular and more commodified.

SEE ALSO: **spectacle**.

de Certeau, Michel (1925–86) A French social theorist who became influential in cultural and media studies in the 1980s and 1990s through his book *The Practice of Everyday Life* (1984), which emphasized the ways in which everyday cultural practices could be seen as oppositional or resistive to dominant power. For de Certeau, a mode of opposition does not need to be directly articulated as a strategy that would have explicit aims. Rather, he drew attention to the tactical evasions of everyday life through which people resist power. He used the term *la perruque* to capture the way in which employees do things in their bosses' time or use equipment provided by a company for their own purposes. Thus, an office worker may use internet access to book a holiday or the telephone to make personal calls. These ideas have influenced later theorizations of active and resistive audiences.

SEE ALSO: **active audience; everyday life; fan; Fiske**.

decoding See: ENCODING/DECODING.

deconstruction The practice of textual analysis associated with the French critic JACQUES DERRIDA. It pays particular attention to the identification of the multiple modes of writing in texts and undoes the strategies texts deploy to achieve the illusion of fixed meaning. This approach therefore undermines the idea that the text is unified as the creation of an AUTHOR, and has been seen as a form of POSTSTRUCTURALISM. Influence in media studies has been via more theoretical approaches to the study of DISCOURSE in texts.

SEE ALSO: **Bakhtin; dialogic**.

deep focus A film technique in which action and objects that are various distances away from the camera are all kept in focus.

delay system Technology used to hold back radio transmissions for a very short period, mainly so that potentially offensive material can be edited out.

democracy Originally, democracy meant government by the citizens as opposed to rule by a tyrant or an aristocracy. In modern societies, citizens cannot govern directly so they typically elect representatives to a parliament by means of a competitive party system. Democracy in this sense is often associated with the protection of individual freedoms, both from powerful groups and from the state. In turn, this is said to imply widespread educational opportunity, as much legal equality between citizens as possible and a free market based on private property. Another important constituent is a press, television, radio and book publishing free of interference by the state or by powerful groups. This is important because, in order to exercise their democratic rights, citizens have to be able to make choices based on good information and exposure to different points of view.

SEE ALSO: **elections; press freedom; public sphere; regulation**.

demographics The constitution of a population by such factors as social class, occupation, place of residence, education, gender, ethnicity. If you are going to sell or advertise a product or service, it is important to know as much as possible about the population to which the advertisements are to be directed. The demographics of a population are associated with CONSUMER BEHAVIOUR. For example, a person who has been to university is likely to have different tastes, buying preferences and income from someone who left school at the earliest opportunity. Thus, in planning a marketing campaign, an advertiser will want to know, for instance, the demographic make-up of the readership of a newspaper in order to ensure that the product is being advertised to people who are likely to buy it.

SEE ALSO: **geodemographics**.

denotation/connotation Within **semiology** or semiotic analysis, denotation refers to the most basic and specific level of meaning of a text or image. Thus, the denotative level of analysis of a photograph will concentrate on what is actually depicted in the frame. The contrast is with connotation, which refers to the much wider range of associations that the image or text might have. For example, while a picture of two clasped hands denotes a handshake, its connotation might be friendship or meeting for the first time. Or, the denotative meaning of the Cross of St George may be the English flag flown on ceremonial occasions but the connotative meaning of the image is of patriotism, nostalgia for empire or the England football team.

SEE ALSO: **Barthes; code; structuralism**.

deregulation There has been a long history of REGULATION of the media. Although many pressure groups have been concerned about the depiction of sex or violence in the media, especially television, and have asked for more regulation, business interests have pressed for less government intervention in the name of freedom of choice for the consumer. In the UK, this pressure for deregulation is not so much for greater freedom from censorship but for greater competition, particularly in television and radio broadcasting, and for an end to the monopoly enjoyed by the BBC. Within the last fifty years, governments have progressively dismantled the regulation of broadcasting by a variety of devices including the creation of Channel Four, the encouragement of cable and satellite and the relaxation of rules on the ownership of media companies.

SEE ALSO: **government and the media; self-regulation**.

Derrida, Jacques (1930–2004) An Algerian-born French philosopher best known as the main proponent of DECONSTRUCTION, which is a particular approach to the study of the text. His influential books include *Of Grammatology* (1976) and *Writing and Difference* (1978). His work is of most import in the humanities, cultural theory and the more literary versions of cultural studies in the 1980s and 1990s rather than in media studies. Derrida's demonstration of the manner in which texts contradict themselves and expose their confusions and hidden spaces was very influential in literary and cultural theory in the 1980s. While his approach still has adherents, its influence has waned.

desensitization The idea that the media have a negative effect on the ability of the audience to respond in a human or empathic way to social events. For example, the sensitivity of the audience to social and political crises, such as floods, earthquakes or wars, may be reduced by continued exposure to them on the TV and in other media.

SEE ALSO: **compassion fatigue**.

designer The role of designing the setting for a text or performance. The role of designer is often relatively neglected in academic analysis, although, for example, the look of a film or television programme has an important impact on how the audience responds to it.

SEE ALSO: **aestheticization of everyday life; costume design**.

Desmond, Richard (b. 1951) A MEDIA MOGUL with interests in magazine and newspaper publishing through his company Northern and Shell. He started a range of adult publications and launched *OK!* in 1993. However, he came to serious public notice in 2000, when his company acquired the *Daily Express* from United News and Media (SEE: **United Newspapers**). The purchase was controversial as Desmond was seen by some commentators as not a fit and proper person to own an important newspaper because of his association with pornographic magazines.

determinism Theories that assign causal priority to a single factor. MARSHALL MCLUHAN, for example, argues that major social changes are simply produced by the introduction of new technologies of communication, e.g. printing. Similarly, Marxist analyses of the media are often accused of using an economic determinism, in which all aspects of society, including the media, are determined by the economic structure of society or the relations of production.

SEE ALSO: **technological determinism**.

deviance The departure from social norms in a society or part of a society. This becomes criminal when laws are broken. The term has purchase in the study of the media in three main ways. First, media studies has been concerned with the depiction by the media of what have been defined as deviant groups. The classic study of this remains *Folk Devils and Moral Panics* (Cohen, 1973), which investigated the media reaction to the behaviour of young people at British seaside resorts in the mid-1960s. The book argues that the media reaction was a significant part of the generation of a MORAL PANIC (especially in the social control culture) around these folk devils. Significant attention continues to be paid to such issues of representation. Second, and in a similar vein, the way in which the media may play an important role in the generation of deviant behaviour is considered. There is a long tradition of work on the EFFECTS of the media that seeks to consider whether the media cause deviance. Third, the media contain many fictional representations of deviance. This can often be linked with the previous senses in that the way in which deviance is represented in fiction can be seen to have effects on how people react to factual deviance morally and in other ways. This means that fictional representations of deviance are often evaluated in moral terms. It would be very unusual for a criminal to be seen ultimately to be prospering in a TV series. The action may concern their attempts to gather wealth, but ultimately they are most likely not to 'get away with it'. CLOSURE tends to come on the terms of the authorities. While this may be seen as particularly important in those fictions that are centred on the police or detectives, the same points can be made about series where characters act in an 'immoral' way. Thus, for example, in SOAP OPERAS characters who act in ways that are anti-social to the community in which the series is set, and thus are deviant, are ultimately punished, expelled from the community in one way or another, or change their actions and character to fit in. Thus, while such action will often be a key aspect of the narrative in that it produces the aspects that interest and engage the audience, the characters that act in such ways cannot be a part of the community on a permanent basis.

SEE ALSO: **crime; police series**.

deviancy amplification See: AMPLIFICATION OF DEVIANCE.

diachronic Within SEMIOLOGY or semiotic analysis this refers to change in meaning over time. It is contrasted with SYNCHRONIC analysis, which takes a 'snapshot' of meaning at any one point. For example, a synchronic discussion of the Union flag would discuss the relationship between its different constituent parts, while a diachronic discussion would consider the way in which those parts came together at different times showing the change in the flag over a period of time. To take another example, a synchronic analysis of an advertisement would concentrate on the text of the advertisement itself, while a diachronic analysis might consider the way in which the advertisement was related to previous ones for the same product.

diagonal integration The diversification of activity by companies as they move into new areas. For example, when AOL and TIME WARNER merged in 2000, they hoped to take advantage of MEDIA CONVERGENCE. Time Warner, a major provider of content, was integrating with America Online, a major supplier of communication channels. The difference between HORIZONTAL INTEGRATION and diagonal integration is essentially one of degree. Within the last two decades there have been many mergers between media companies in different branches of the media, and it is difficult to say whether they represent horizontal or diagonal integration.

SEE ALSO: **concentration of ownership; vertical integration**.

dialogic A concept associated with the Russian writer M. M. BAKHTIN, which characterizes a text such as a novel as containing a range of discourses. Thus, rather than seeing a novel as representing a particular viewpoint, for example of the author, or of a social group, of which the author is a representative, the novel brings into dialogue a range of voices and ideas which may contradict each other. This idea can be generalized to other texts. Thus, media texts, such as television news, are often analysed in terms of the practices and ideas of those who produce them, journalists or studio producers for instance. In some Marxist analyses these practices and the dominant interests that control news are seen to produce a text that represents the interests of the dominant class. An approach influenced by dialogism, on the other hand, would argue that the news contains a number of discourses that exist in dialogue with one another. While this may be an unequal dialogue in that some discourses are more powerful than others, it is still there.

SEE ALSO: **deconstruction**.

diary method A method of media research that requires people to keep diaries of their media consumption. Some research into the media, especially television, demands a detailed knowledge of how people spend their time. Electronic surveillance methods, like the PEOPLEMETER, can give an idea of how viewers organize their television watching through the day. However, it cannot provide information about behaviour during programmes or attitudes towards them. For tasks such as these, a diary method is appropriate. The method can take a variety of forms. Viewers can keep a diary themselves and record what they are doing every fifteen minutes or so. Or an interviewer can ask them to recall what they did over the day, also in blocks of time. The drawback with the first is that it is demanding of the viewer. The defect of the second is clearly that it depends on potentially inaccurate recall by the viewer.

SEE ALSO: **audience research**.

diary story The sort of news story that is known about in advance so that journalists can plan to cover it. For example, the release date of an inquiry into an important public event will be known beforehand and the structure of the reporting of it anticipated.

diegesis The fictional world of a narrative. It is most often used to refer to the fictional world of a movie or to television programmes. Fictions construct a world that we are encouraged to believe in. For example, the soap opera *Coronation Street* shows a fictional world that makes sense to us. The world of *Coronation Street* would be disrupted if the characters walked out of the set. Thus, in REALIST texts of this kind, the diegesis is very important in constructing the sense that the fiction is real. This is despite the fact that *Coronation Street* is performed by actors and produced in Manchester by Granada TV. The use of voice over can further illustrate this idea. Some thrillers and action films use voice over to explain meaning. An example of this is *Merrill's Marauders* (dir. Sam Fuller, 1962), in which a narrator who is not a character in the film comments on the action, praising the bravery of the US soldiers. It therefore is part of the narration of the film, but not the diegesis. Music is similar in that it helps us understand the action, for example, by giving us a cue about whether the action is meant to be highly dramatic or romantic, but when it is on a soundtrack it is not part of the diegesis, as it is external to the world depicted. If it was being played by a band in the action it would be part of that diegetic world.

difference Some modes of cultural theory, especially POSTSTRUCTURALISM, emphasize the way in which cultures are constructed through the difference of one aspect of a culture from another. In some respects, built upon STRUCTURALISM'S emphasis on BINARY OPPOSITIONS, the idea of difference suggests that the relationship between different aspects is always in process and hence never settled. This has had some influence in the analysis of gender. A structuralist account would emphasize the definition of male and female as simple binary opposites. A poststructuralist, on the other hand, would argue that the difference between the genders is contingent and in play and one is always defined in relation to the other. For example, a structuralist analysis of a text would see masculine and feminine qualities as mutually exclusive and acting in opposition to each other. Such qualities would be reasonably easily defined and would often be clearly associated with a male hero and a female subordinate. An emphasis on difference involves consideration of how masculine and feminine qualities are produced by a text itself through a process. These aspects and qualities are not fixed or necessarily associated with one character rather than another. The idea of difference thus recognizes that there are clearly alternative forms of culture and discourse but the relations between them are complex.

diffusion Media messages and content are sometimes said to diffuse through the audience and society. For example, one person may see, hear or read a particular story and it will then rapidly be passed on to another person. This is significant as it shows how social processes are at work in the media AUDIENCE. Rather than an individual being directly affected by the content or message of a media text, they might hear about that text or a news report from another part of the world through a conversation with another person.

SEE ALSO: J Curve; two-step flow.

digital broadcasting Forms of broadcasting using digital rather than analogue technologies. Digital technology allows sound, images, text and data to be captured, stored and transmitted by the same method, giving much more extensive and faster integration between them (SEE: **media convergence**). Because digital signals take up much less space on the radio spectrum than do analogue ones, it is possible to have roughly ten times as many channels with digital technology.

digital community See: VIRTUAL COMMUNITY.

digital divide A great deal has been claimed for the INTERNET. It has been suggested that it will revolutionize the provision of information for all, improve the sense of community (SEE: **virtual community**), and even enable better democratic participation (SEE: **electronic democracy**). Unfortunately, all these features depend on easy and relatively equal access to the internet. All the evidence suggests that there is a digital divide, and many people do not have the access required. Elderly people, for example, find it difficult to keep up with technological change, and women make less use of computers, though this is changing fast. In 1999 in the UK, only 9 per cent of the over-65s, 3 per cent of the poorest 10 per cent, and 39 per cent of women were online. The situation is changing, though. For example, by 2003, some 9 per cent of the poorest 10 per cent of the population had access to the internet. The most important divide, however, is one of resources. Simply, those who do not have the money to buy the latest computer equipment or have broadband access or do not have the required skills will not be able to participate fully in the advantages conveyed by the internet. This divide exists within advanced Western societies. It is even wider between such societies and those that are less well developed. Only 3 per cent of the world's population are connected to the internet. Industrialized countries, with only 15 per cent of the world's population, contain 88 per cent of all internet users. Computer and internet access, in other words, reproduces the inequalities more generally found within and between societies.

digital editing Before the DIGITAL REVOLUTION, the editing of film or television material was a fairly clumsy process of physically manipulating the original film. Since sound, images and text can all now be recorded and processed using the same digital technology on computer, the editing process can be much faster and more effective. This is one of the technological changes that has facilitated the development of reality television programmes, as the vast amount of material shot can be edited very rapidly and economically.

SEE ALSO: **editing; offline editor**.

digital radio See: DIGITAL BROADCASTING; RADIO.

digital revolution A term loosely used in the press to describe the way in which different media are all using digital platforms. It is revolutionary in that it enables, say, sound, film, photographs and text to be originated, stored and edited all together more efficiently, accurately, effectively and quickly.

SEE: **media convergence; new information and communication technologies**.

digitization The process whereby material is converted into a form that can be processed by a computer using binary code of digits 0 and 1. In the media industries, the original form is still often ANALOGUE. So, for example, film for a television programme may have to be digitized before it can be edited on computer.

direct broadcast satellite See: SATELLITE.

direct entry Typesetting used to require a skilled operative who could turn an author's material into material out of which a printing plate could be made. Advances in word-processing software have now made it possible for journalists and others to prepare their text on computer and for it to go straight to the printer. This elimination of an extra stage in the printing process is one reason why costs in the newspaper industry fell during the 1980s and 1990s.

SEE ALSO: **print; Wapping.**

directness of address A way in which television addresses its audience. Television is essentially a domestic medium. One feature of this is that the style of television is everyday and conversational. Announcers, weathermen and -women, newsreaders, talk show hosts and many others face the camera directly and therefore give the illusion of having an intimate, direct, domestic conversation with the person watching. This sense of direct address is reinforced by the conversational and informal language used by television. Much of television actually is conversation or is simulated conversation. The language of television is the language of everyday life.

SEE ALSO: **household.**

director The person in charge of the making of a film or television programme. The director is usually seen as occupying the most important role in the making of a film, and it has become conventional to refer to film directors in terms that suggest they are the authors of the text. This approach developed under the influence of AUTEUR THEORY. While the director is crucial to the production of the film, the extent to which he or she is the sole creator can and should be disputed; the production process is generally far more complex.

The term is also used to refer to roles in the production of other media, but these are not normally seen as the most significant ones. For example, directors in TV are usually less important than PRODUCERS. The actual production of a television programme is very much a team effort, involving directors, writers, actors and technicians, and, as a result, the authorship of the programme is obscured.

SEE ALSO: **author.**

discourse A set of statements or body of language use on a particular topic or theme unified by common assumptions. For example, a television POLICE SERIES may contain a discourse of law and order, which suggests that the police are hard pressed in containing criminality, and a discourse of gender, where the issues of the relations between male and female police officers are examined. More specifically, discourse as an idea is most often associated with the work of the French author MICHEL FOUCAULT. For Foucault, discourses are important in defining the world. For example, discourses such as criminology have the effect of defining certain categories of people as criminal. Medical discourses define people as being ill or well in accord with concepts of disease. These concepts and discourses are historically, culturally and socially variable. Likewise, media studies as a discourse will define certain concepts in particular ways and exclude others. In these sorts of ways, discourses are connected to power, as being able to define certain categories of people in particular ways can reinforce and facilitate particular operations of power. Thus, the discourse of law and order in a police series may suggest that more funds need to be allocated to the police so that they can fight crime effectively. This might mean that resources are not directed to other purposes. Likewise, a discourse of gender may suggest that female police officers are better suited to some forms of police operation than others, or that high-ranking female police officers are subject to particular personal pressures and so on.

SEE ALSO: **ideology**.

discursive formation See: DISCOURSE.

disinformation 'Information' that is released by particular parties who are aware that the information is incorrect or partial with the aim of influencing others. Some of the best-known cases of this process have occurred in times of armed conflict or in the lead-up to it.

SEE ALSO: **spin**.

Disney The Walt Disney Company, founded by Walt Disney in 1923, has rapidly grown to be one of the most successful media CONGLOMERATES in the world, with sales in 2005 of some £14 billion per year. The company consists of four business areas: Disney Studio Entertainment, Disney Parks and Resorts, Disney Consumer Products and Disney Media Networks.

Disney Studio Entertainment has grown from the part of the company that became famous for the development of animated films. Disney produced some of the best-known examples of the genre (including Mickey Mouse) and led the way in the production of full-length feature cartoons (producing the first in *Snow White and the Seven Dwarves*). It also produces live-action films. The company distributes films under a variety of brands such as Walt Disney Pictures, Touchstone Pictures, Hollywood Pictures, Miramax Films and Dimension Films. Internationally, distribution takes place via Buena Vista International. The home-video and DVD market is serviced by Buena Vista Home Entertainment. This part of the company is also involved with live theatre production and music distribution.

Disney Parks and Resorts has responsibility for theme parks, where again Disney has been a prime mover and leading force. In 1952 Walt Disney Imagineering was founded by Walt Disney to develop Disneyland in Anaheim, California. The company now operates ten theme parks world-wide, as well as hotels and cruise ships.

Disney Consumer Products has responsibility for a range of products including clothing, toys, books, computer games, drinks and electronics. It also runs the Disney Stores network. Disney Media Networks controls television, cable and radio companies such as ABC Television, ABC News, Touchstone Television, ABC Radio, EPDN and the Disney Channel.

Disney has been at the leading edge of some of the key shifts in the nature of society and cultural life in the twentieth and twenty-first centuries. For example, along with McDonald's, the company is seen as a major contributor to the culture of the 'theme park experience'. More radical critics see this as part of a process of CULTURAL IMPERIALISM that spreads the hegemony of American life to the detriment of indigenous cultures. For others, Disney represents family values and family entertainment that has proved popular and enjoyable in a variety of countries and forms.

SEE ALSO: **ABC; animation; globalization**.

display advertising Advertising in newspapers and magazines which uses a variety of devices such as photographs or striking typefaces to catch the attention of readers. The contrast is with advertisements that are intended simply to convey information by pieces of text such as appear in the classified sections of newspapers.

dissolve In film-making where one shot fades in at the same time as another fades out.

SEE ALSO: **wipe**.

distanciation Process in film making that is intended to distance the viewer from the text. Mainly used in the context of radical film-making, where the intention is to disrupt the immersion of the audience in conventional realist texts.

SEE ALSO: **Brecht**.

distracted attention People watch the television set with varying degrees of attention (SEE: **regimes of watching**). Quite often, a household will simply be doing other things while the set is on and will only concentrate on it when something demands attention – a particular event in a soap opera, for example. This distracted attention is particularly characteristic of women, who typically are carrying out household tasks at the same time as watching.

distribution The supply of media products to audiences through consumption outlets, such as shops, theatres and cinemas. The process of distribution is central to a number of media, where, obviously, it can have significant effects on who receives a cultural product. For example, the control of distribution of films to cinemas can have important effects on popularity. Thus, in the heyday of the STUDIO SYSTEM in the USA, production companies were very keen to control the distribution of films to cinema chains that they owned. This is perhaps even more significant in the music industry, where being unable to purchase a popular record or track can mean very low sales. Making sure that a product is distributed properly can be as important as securing its adequate production in the first place. In the early days of the record industry, distribution was often very localized and in the USA records could be very significant hits locally (or in a particular sector such as the black market) and be unknown elsewhere. The pioneers of the independent sector would often go on long trips to distribute their product to radio stations personally to overcome such market constraints. In both the film and music industries smaller companies have joined together to sponsor independent distribution networks to make sure that their products reach the consumers who may desire them. One of the potential effects of computerized technology is to change the terrain of distribution. With access to the internet, a consumer can reach the website of a band and there find material that they can access directly. While, in itself, this is a form of distribution, the fact that in this case music does not need to be placed on a physical object (such as a vinyl record a tape or a CD) means that it can be distributed with far greater ease.

SEE ALSO: **independent company; magazine; music industry; newspaper.**

diversification A strategy pursued by companies to spread their range of activities and therefore to attempt to minimize risk to profitability. Media companies have diversified into a range of media, such as books, newspapers, magazines, film and television. In the past, such companies also diversified across industrial sectors so that they involved a large range of products that did not seem to relate to one another, though this process has now in large part been reversed as media companies have concentrated on media products. Where a company does operate across a diverse set of activities the brand of the company is important. For example, a company like Virgin can be involved in music retailing and train lines because of the familiarity of the Virgin brand.

SEE ALSO: **brand; conglomerate.**

division of labour The separation of a production process into its component parts each one of which is then carried out by a specialist worker. The division of labour allows for the more efficient production of goods, as in Adam Smith's classic discussion of pin manufacture. Rather than one worker producing the whole of the pin and thus needing knowledge about a diverse range of tasks, each task was separated off. This meant that tasks were simpler and could be performed more efficiently. This idea was most famously used in Henry Ford's development of production-line automobile manufacture. Here, the completed car is the product of the input of workers each performing a separate task as the car moves along the line. Media corporations exhibit a division of labour. Thus, a record company might consist of directors, a president or managing director, Artist and Repertoire, Marketing, Public Relations, Publicity and Press, Radio and Television Promotion, Sales, Business, Legal and Financial Affairs, Manufacture and Distribution, and Administration. The idea of a division of labour is that these different sections should work harmoniously together, though there are often conflicts between the different parts of any large organization. It also means that there is a need to integrate the different tasks that are performed. Another significant development has been the move of some of the different parts of an organization outside of the larger organization itself to other smaller companies. For example, much production of television programmes now takes place outside the larger organizations like the BBC in smaller, specialist independent production companies.

SEE ALSO: **Fordism/post-Fordism; music industry; outsourcing.**

DJ (disc jockey) The term disc jockey was developed to describe the then new role played by the announcer on radio programmes where rock and roll music was being played. Early disc jockeys became both famous (such as Wolfman Jack, as featured in the nostalgic film *American Graffiti*) and crucial as arbiters of taste. For example, many accounts have drawn attention to the role of Dewey Phillips' radio show in Memphis in promoting the early recordings of Elvis Presley on the Sun label. In the late 1950s in the USA, some DJs were found guilty of being paid by record companies to promote particular records, thus exploiting their potentially powerful position as arbiters of taste. The role of the DJ in bringing certain forms of music to the attention of the wider public and to specialist taste groups has been widely recognized and was much noted at the death of the British DJ John Peel in 2004. The term DJ also became associated with the rise of sound systems in reggae music in Jamaica and with hip-hop in African-American culture. In both cases the DJ was crucial in deciding which records were to be played at the live dance and then became seen as an important producer of new sounds in their own right. Thus, hip-hop culture developed from the way in which the DJ would move from one record or deck to another and thus cut sounds together. With the advent of rave or dance culture from the late 1980s onwards the DJ likewise moved to a pivotal role. Here, again, some key producers moved from a position where they were initially cutting together different records and sound in the live situation to making recordings that likewise bring together different sounds. In these senses the way in which much contemporary popular music uses samples and integrates different sounds can be seen as partly a product of initial innovations by DJs in the live situation.

SEE ALSO: **cut; radio**.

docudrama An example of the way that genres merge and cross, docudramas are documentary television programmes trying to make factual points but which consist wholly or partly of dramatic constructions. A noted example was a programme on UK television that was trying to show how the country's transport system is approaching gridlock. Instead of the traditional documentary format, the programme made its point largely by means of a dramatic construction of what would happen to a number of characters in an imaginary transport crisis in 2010.

SEE ALSO: **docusoap; genre; infotainment**.

documentary A GENRE of television, film, radio or photography which consists in a lengthier treatment of a factual topic than is possible in a news programme. In its filmic origins in the 1920s and 1930s, the genre of documentary was conceived partly as an important way of educating and informing and partly as a significant artistic form in its own right. This is what Corner (2002) refers to as the 'project of democratic civics'. A good example is the film documentary *Night Mail* (1936), about the mail trains which ran overnight, which had a spoken soundtrack written by the poet W. H. Auden and was presented in a dramatic style. The genre therefore merged into other forms at its boundaries – current affairs journalism, drama and advertising. This suggests two other important functions of documentary as 'journalistic inquiry and exposition' and 'radical interrogation and alternative perspective' (Corner, 2002: 259). With respect to the latter, film-makers would offer a radical and alternative critique of a social or cultural issue. Such approaches often came from those on the left politically or adopting a radical stance. The contemporary films of Michael Moore such as *Bowling for Columbine* (on US gun culture) or *Fahrenheit 911* (on the attack on the Twin Towers in New York in 2001) are good examples. While documentaries continue to exhibit the three functions and forms identified by Corner, there has also been a move to a different form, which has been termed 'documentary as diversion', where aspects of the documentary form have been fused with entertainment in forms like REALITY TV. Such programmes have proved to be very popular, leading to an idea that television has become dominated by a 'postdocumentary culture' (Corner, 2002), with many entertainment programmes being influenced by documentary approaches.

docusoap An example of a kind of television programme that blurs genre boundaries, docusoaps are documentaries in the sense that they record the experiences of real people living their real lives but are also soaps in that they follow those people in their everyday lives over time and choose to emphasize dramatic incident or feelings. A recent example in the UK is the series *Wife Swap*, in which two men exchanged wives for a short period.

SEE ALSO: **docudrama; genre; infotainment**.

dolly An apparatus, originally mounted on rails, which carries the camera and its crew and allows it to move and produce TRACKING shots. For much television and film work more recently, lighter and more flexible equipment is now available (See: STEADICAM).

SEE ALSO: **crane**.

domain name the name of a server on the internet. An example of a domain name is bbc.co.uk.

domesticity See: HOUSEHOLD.

dominant cinema Denotes those forms of cinema that follow HOLLYWOOD practices and realist NARRATIVE textual conventions (SEE: **realism**). Such practices and forms will often be opposed by radical film-makers or the AVANT-GARDE.

dominant ideology/culture The ideology or culture that receives the widest circulation in society. It is often claimed, especially by those influenced by MARXISM, that powerful groups in society are able to sustain their power by control over the way that ideas and knowledge circulate. This effectively excludes alternative ideas and moulds the beliefs and opinions of the population, providing an effective barrier to the formation of dissenting ideas. In the model, the media play an extensive role, for they are a major vehicle by which ideas and knowledge are made available, and the claim is that they provide only a partial view of the world shaped by the interests of the powerful.

This theory is much disputed. It is not at all clear that the media convey anything like a coherent set of messages, and it is uncertain what role they play in forming opinion and belief. Given these arguments, more complex versions of the theory have been advanced, such as that using the concept of HEGEMONY, which will recognize the complexity of media provision and audience response.

SEE ALSO: **bias; concentration of ownership; effects.**

dominant reading See: NATIONWIDE STUDY.

domination The power that one social group has over another, such as the domination held by one social class over another, by the old over the young or by men over women. The puzzle is to explain how that domination is secured given that it almost always will result in disadvantage to those who are dominated. There are two extreme kinds of explanation. At one extreme, it can be argued that one group coerces the other. For example, the old can effectively coerce the young by physical punishment or later in life by the withdrawal of financial or practical support. Lower social classes may be dominated by higher by the threat of loss of work or applications of the law. Although coercive measures of this kind may well work in particular circumstances, in contemporary societies they seem to be an implausible origin of domination. This suggests that another line of argument might be more effective. Perhaps subordinate groups accept their domination by others, not because they are forced to, but because of the beliefs, attitudes and values that they hold. Women, for example, may believe that it is the woman's role to make career sacrifices in order to care for children and acknowledge that men should have authority. The formation of views of the world of this kind lies primarily in the process of SOCIALIZATION – upbringing as a child, education and interaction with others. But it may also be the case that the media reinforce beliefs and therefore help to provide the means whereby domination is explained and justified.

Do the media work in this way? To some extent they do indeed provide one particular way of viewing the world (SEE: **cultural imperialism; gender; news; racism**). But does this amount to a provision of a distinctive worldview? There are two reasons for thinking that it does not. First, media organizations in all their variety do not provide a coherent set of messages for their audiences. For example, a glance at a TV schedule will show how diverse is the programming. Second, and more important, audiences do not simply accept the values, beliefs and opinions that the media may provide. Quite the contrary, they may actively resist them (SEE: **Nationwide study**).

dope sheet The catalogue of frames and sounds in an animated film before the final animations are produced.

SEE ALSO: **animation**.

dotcom An INTERNET-based company. The period in the late 1990s until 2001 is often known as the dotcom boom because the share price or market value of companies trading using the internet rose extremely rapidly and unsustainably. The subsequent collapse in values made investors very wary of new technologies, and the share price of companies of this kind only began to recover in 2004.

double exposure Two images placed on top of each other in a film or still photograph. For the amateur photographer, this may have been a common error in the past, but for some film-makers it has been part of a deliberate aesthetic strategy to show the complexity of meaning.

drama An acted fictional NARRATIVE, performed for an audience. Drama can be performed across a range of media, most commonly theatre, television, film and radio. It can be combined with the documentary form as in DOCUDRAMA. The main home for drama before the development of film and television was the theatre. The basic forms of drama as tragedy and comedy were set out by Aristotle. As drama progressed like many other forms it developed a number of realist conventions, such as using real names for characters, real places and so on. Drama attempted to be naturalistic, and the development of theatre in the nineteenth century increasingly centred the action in the enclosed spaces of the home rather than the public spaces of wider debate. RAYMOND WILLIAMS (1973) argues that in these forms of drama, such as the plays of Ibsen, the dramatic space of the room on the stage becomes a trap from which the characters cannot escape, showing them imprisoned by the rigidities of a hierarchical society. Authors such as BERTOLT BRECHT argued that this sense of social inevitability was underpinned by the naturalistic forms of the plays, which offered no alternative possibilities of action, and on the basis of MARXISM sought to develop a more radical dramatic form which aimed to place the audience at a critical distance from the events portrayed in the play. This has led to much debate about the extent to which drama can be politicized and be part of social change.

Radio drama was an important development and plays continue to be acted in the medium (SEE: **radio**). However, the most popular medium for drama is now television. In the early days of television, drama was performed and broadcast live but, as the medium developed, it was increasingly recorded. Drama now makes up a significant part of TV output, especially as drama series. The significance of this was recognized by Williams (1975), who pointed out that, because of television, never had so many people been able to watch so much drama. In the earlier days of television, single plays were of some significance, though they were often performed in series such as the *Wednesday Play* or *Play for Today* on the BBC or *Armchair Theatre* on commercial TV. These play sought to deal with controversial social issues such as homelessness (*Cathy Come Home* (1966), dir. Ken Loach) or vagrancy (*Edna the Inebriate Woman* (1971), dir. Ted Kotcheff). Other dramas were often controversial in that they were perceived to be breaking boundaries of representation of sex and violence and thus led to debates around morality and CENSORSHIP. They were also innovative in form and the representation of political events. Such drama was often significant in generating wider debate such as around Alan Bleasdale's *The Boys from the Blackstuff* (1982) and the issue of unemployment (Millington and Nelson, 1986). The representation of the British General Strike of 1926 in the drama *Days of Hope* (1975) led to consideration of the political impact and possibilities of REALISM in film studies.

While there is now much less debate about social issues in British society stemming from their representation in plays of this kind, it is important to recognize the ongoing popularity of TV drama, especially in the British continuous serial or SOAP OPERA. Programmes like *Coronation Street* and *EastEnders* regularly top the TV ratings and also address issues of social concern.

drive-time Period in late afternoon/early evening when commuters in their cars are expected to be listening to the radio on the way home from work. It is one of the focal points of radio scheduling, where prestigious current affairs and news programmes may be scheduled and where the mode of address to the listener on music stations will be as if they are driving home, even if they are actually listening in the home.

  SEE ALSO: **breakfast television; scheduling**.

dub See: DUB EDITING.

dub editing Where one image or sound is copied (dubbed) on to a storage medium or another image or sound. This process is now largely achieved by the use of digital technology. In the past, dub editing would be accomplished by one image or sound being physically cut (or spliced) into another. The practice is also known as dubbing.

dumbing down A criticism frequently made of the media, especially television, is that media content is intellectually undemanding and assumes that the audience is unintelligent and uninformed. Such accusations are often unaccompanied by any evidence of what the audience is actually doing with such content.

SEE ALSO: **effects**.

dummy A prototype or mock-up of a newspaper, magazine or book produced before final production runs are made. Dummies, often constructed in-house on computer, are used for a variety of purposes, e.g. to test reactions from consumers or to interest advertisers and retailers.

dumping The selling of a product at very low prices, even below the cost of production. Some countries, the United States and Brazil, for example, have large internal markets for television programmes. This means that television companies in the US can afford to produce programming which can be widely sold inside the country, thus covering costs. Those companies are then in a position to sell their product to other countries around the world at very low prices and still make a profit as a whole. This process of dumping programmes causes concern, especially in developing countries, because it is difficult for indigenous programming, which will be relatively expensive because the internal market is not large, to compete with the cheap imports. The risk, therefore, is that American television, and by implication American values, will crowd out all others.

SEE ALSO: **media imperialism**.

duopoly A situation in which only two companies are operating in a market.

duration Time that an item lasts in a radio or TV programme, which is usually given in seconds.

SEE ALSO: **concentration of ownership**.

DVD A digital video (or versatile) disc stores video information digitally allowing significant compression of material (hence more information can be stored on a small disc than a large tape) and enhanced picture and sound quality. The DVD has now superseded VHS video technology in advanced capitalist societies for the purchase of pre-recorded films and TV shows and is overtaking VHS as a home recording medium.

SEE ALSO: **digital broadcasting; digital divide; digital editing; digital revolution; digitization**.

e-book A book that is designed to be read, not as printed words on paper, but as a computer file on a device of some kind. A variety of devices can be used ranging from a personal computer to small handheld machines. There are currently experiments with devices with flexible, more book-like screens. E-books and e-book readers clearly have some advantages over traditional printed books. They can store a large number of books and an infinite number can be downloaded to them. The costs of distribution are very low. And they can even be read in the dark. However, with the current state of technology, e-book readers have more disadvantages. They are clumsy devices with a short battery life. Most customers find them difficult and tiring to read. And publishers have not yet worked out a satisfactory business model for them.

SEE ALSO: **e-zine**.

economics of the media Media products are not like baked beans, wardrobes or bicycles. They are largely intangible in that their value does not primarily lie in a physical attribute (a book or newspaper) but rather in their cultural meaning. This quality has two implications. First, the consumption of a media product by one person does not mean that another person cannot consume the same product. So, if I watch a television programme, then it does not prevent you from watching. If, on the other hand, I eat a tin of baked beans, you could not eat that tin (even if you wanted to). Media products are, in other words, public goods. More importantly, most media goods cost very little to produce and distribute to increasing numbers of consumers. Almost all of the cost of production is in the creation of the first copy. So a film like *Star Wars* costs a great deal to make but relatively little to show to each audience member. The costs to the producer and distributor hardly rise as audience numbers rise. This point has been emphasized by Anderson (2006) in his book *The Long Tail*, in which he argues that the internet further lowers the cost of distribution and digital technologies lower the costs of production. This helps to explain why ECONOMIES OF SCALE and ECONOMIES OF SCOPE are important in the media industries and why relatively few companies dominate the markets for media products (SEE: **concentration of owner-ship**). It also points up the critical importance of RIGHTS and INTELLEC-TUAL PROPERTY for media organizations. They sell intangible objects of cultural meaning – intellectual property – and their rights to intellectual property are by far their most valuable assets.

Of course, not all media organizations are profit-seeking. Almost all countries have bodies, television broadcasters, for example, that have other aims, most particularly to provide a public service (SEE: **public ser-vice broadcasting**). They are, however, constrained by much the same economic forces as commercial organizations. For example, the BBC has a need to maximize audiences in order to be in a strong position to negotiate with the government for increases in the LICENCE FEE. Not all branches of the media operate in the same economic environment either, and each will have particular features that affect their businesses (SEE: **advertisement; book publishing; magazine; new media; newspaper; radio; television industry**).

economies of scale The generation of economies in production coming from the enhanced efficiency stemming from specialization and the greater division of labour that is possible in larger firms. Media firms often seek to grow because they can achieve economies of scale which in turn mean greater profits. More importantly, most media firms incur the great bulk of their costs in producing the first copy of an item. Subsequent copies are very cheap to make, market and distribute. The larger the number of copies made, therefore, the greater the profit (SEE: **economics of the media**).

SEE ALSO: **economies of scope**.

economies of scope The generation of economies in production when a product can be altered only slightly, or perhaps not at all, and sold in a market different from the original one. This has become increasingly common in the media and underlies much of the merger activity between media firms (SEE: **concentration of ownership**). For example, a novel can be sold as a book and then made into a script for film or television. Or rock music can be sold in a CD but can also be used as film or television soundtracks or to accompany advertising. The very high initial costs of producing the book or record can be more than covered not only by selling lots of copies (SEE: **economies of scale**) but also by widening the scope of the product.

SEE ALSO: **economics of the media**.

editing Process of preparing raw material for publication or broadcasting. SEE ALSO: **cross-cutting; continuity; editor; montage**.

editor An occupational role in the media used loosely in two senses. **1** An editor is a person who prepares raw material for publication or distribution. In the print media, she or he receives text from a writer or a journalist and makes sure that it is fit for publication – ensuring that it follows the house style, is correctly punctuated, reasonably clear and properly integrated with illustration where necessary (SEE: **copy editor**). In film and television, editors take the raw rushes and cut them down into a form suitable for transmission, ensuring that the finished product meets transmission and quality standards and takes the form that the director intended (SEE: **offline editor**).

2 Confusingly, the term is also used, mostly within the print media, to describe people who coordinate the creation and production of texts. For example, editors in the book publishing industry are responsible for acquiring manuscripts suitable for publication and ensuring that they go through the publication process smoothly. They occupy a role not dissimilar to producers in the television industry (SEE: **book publishing; producer**). Similarly, editors in newspapers and magazines lead the team of journalists and set the tone, style and opinions of the publication.

editorial Material in a newspaper or magazine that gives the views of the EDITOR. In some publications it will be an opportunity to comment on current issues, while in others its scope is restricted to an introduction to the contents that follow. In some magazines editorials will also contain reference to advertisers and products, a practice which can make it difficult to establish where advertisement begins and editorial ends (SEE: **advertorial**).

SEE ALSO: **facing matter**.

effects It is a commonly held belief that the media have direct effects on the audience. For example, public discussion over the past century has been much occupied with beliefs that rock music causes adolescents to commit suicide, advertisements persuade people to buy things that they do not need, films induce violent behaviour in their audiences, television influences children's behaviour and attitudes, and newspapers mould the political views of their readers. In the earlier part of the twentieth century, academic work reflected this public opinion to a great extent. Researchers were impressed by the rise of radio and film and by their use in apparently moulding public opinion in fascist and communist regimes. From the mid-1930s to the mid-1960s, academic opinion was a good deal more cautious. Large-scale surveys or laboratory experiments did not find unequivocal evidence that exposure to the media has direct effects on the audience. There may be effects but they are mediated by other factors. Thus, the same social and cultural factors may influence behaviour and attitude but they also influence the response to the media.

Since the 1970s the pendulum has swung back somewhat. Much of the reason for this, in the UK at least, was that Marxist analysis became particularly influential in media studies. The proposition here was that the media have long-term effects in helping to create a dominant ideology that supports a capitalist society. Much of the attention, however, was lavished on the analysis of the content of the media rather than on the audience response. Little evidence was presented of actual media effects (SEE: **domination**).

Much of the difficulty in assessing claims about the significance of the media in moulding attitudes and behaviour lies in uncertainties about methodology. Many studies, particularly in the United States, derive their research methods from social psychology. There are three difficulties with this approach. First, it is largely based in the laboratory, using carefully controlled conditions, and it is unclear how representative of everyday life such conditions are. Second, it is not very good at measuring long-term changes. Third, it deals with very small-scale changes in attitude or behaviour and it does not contribute to large-scale theory of media effect. The response to these difficulties has been to use methods less based in the laboratory, although the validity and reliability of these methods is questionable (SEE: **audience research**).

The present state of research is, therefore, fragmented and much debated. The way forward is to concentrate on particular areas of media effect using a variety of methods rather than trying to formulate global theory. For example, the media may indeed have a decisive effect on strategically placed individuals who will be concerned about the image in the media. Politicians especially will alter their behaviour and even their policies in the light of media response. Again, the media may have an important role in focusing public anxieties, as in recent publicity in the UK concerning the MMR vaccine or genetically modified food (SEE: **moral panic**). More focused research in this area may additionally demonstrate how the media construct a framework within which public debate occurs (SEE: **agenda setting**).

SEE ALSO: **audience; children and television; cultivation theory; encoding/decoding; uses and gratifications; violence.**

elections Periodic events at which citizens in a democracy choose their representatives who will sit in a parliament or assembly. It has often been suggested that the media play a crucial role in the influencing of public opinion at election times. It was especially suggested in its early days in the 1950s that TV would have such effects directly. Like many processes that involve audiences, the actual evidence is rather mixed. Thus, on one hand, many recent commentators have argued that it is impossible to imagine the existence of an election outside the media events that in many respects constitute it. Thus, politicians are acutely aware of media deadlines and the need for soundbites and so on. The timing of statements and comments is made so that particular news programmes can cover them. However, somewhat paradoxically, the very prevalence and centrality of the media means that it is very difficult to evaluate any direct effect of the media on the voting preferences for one party or another. Thus, the concerns of those who thought that the media would directly influence voter behaviour in terms of preferences for one party rather than another, as was voiced during the period of rapid take-up of television during the 1950s, seem exaggerated now. However, the electoral process is completely media-drenched. Despite these ambiguities there is no doubting the fact that politicians are very concerned about the power of the media (including newspapers, television and radio and increasingly the internet) and have sought to make sure that any effect that they have is beneficial to their election strategies. For example, in the UK it has been argued that the policies of the Labour government led by Tony Blair towards Europe have been affected by the need to enrol the support of the MEDIA MOGUL RUPERT MURDOCH and consequently the endorsement of the *Sun* newspaper, which he owns.

electronic commons The idea that the **internet** should be open to all to express any opinion and should not be subject to private ownership or excessive regulation by the state or other agency. The term is taken from the principles of common ownership, particularly of land, which suggest that important resources should be held in common.

   SEE ALSO: **concentration of ownership; electronic democracy; new media**.

electronic democracy The use of the **internet** as an instrument of democratic participation. The internet is a powerful source of information and, potentially, of interaction between people across the world. These are also prerequisites of democracy. For this reason, those who have hoped to reinvigorate democracy have thought of the internet as a powerful tool. It not only provides a great deal of information, it also allows citizens to voice opinions, to debate with each other and to make complaints. It might even be a mechanism for voting. There have been a few develop-ments in this direction. The UK government, for example, does put a great deal of information from government departments on the web. Local authorities have experimented with online services such as the management of housing lists. Further development is hindered by reluc-tance on the part of citizens and by the fact that so many people do not have adequate access to the internet (SEE: **digital divide**). Critics fear that governments will simply use this as another means to control information – and may employ the internet as a means of sophisticated surveillance of citizens.

SEE ALSO: **government and the media**.

electronic newsgathering The use of electronic technologies in the production of news stories. Before the advent of the internet, journalists who were out of their office gathering news would convey their stories to a newspaper, radio or television station by letter or telephone. Now, however, journalists can do an interview, write a story and email it to their newspaper, where it can be edited on screen and then sent directly to print, thereby avoiding re-entry of the same text.

electronic publishing The production, distribution and sale of written material. Until very recently, PUBLISHING, whether of books, advertise-ments, magazines, newspapers or leaflets, took the form of PRINT. Com-puters and the INTERNET, however, make it possible to publish material which is not designed ever to be printed but to be read on screen.

This revolution in publishing occurred in two stages. In the first, material was entered into computer and transmitted by email to order or made available on the WORLD WIDE WEB. The reader was then expected to print it out for reading later. In effect this is simply a method of electronic production and distribution. In the second, the material is not only produced and distributed electronically, but is also read on screen and stored on computer for later reference if necessary.

Electronic publishing is cheaper in many ways. It integrates the whole publishing process, which is otherwise a set of separate steps. It does not require the production, storage and distribution of physically bulky objects. And it is, in effect, production on demand.

email A method of sending messages using computers or other electronic communication devices, either within an organization using an intranet, or across the INTERNET. The method is fundamentally asynchronous; the message is not read at the same time as it is sent. As such, as a method of communication, it is more like a letter than it is like a conversation. In this respect, it contrasts with INSTANT MESSAGING. The usefulness of email is being compromised by an increasing volume of junk mail and computer viruses.

embargo A ban on the publication of sensitive material until a particular date. In modern societies, all organizations of any size are very conscious of their public image and need good relations with the media. They therefore go out of their way to supply information to the press, radio and television. At the same time, they may wish to control the way that the media use any information. One way of doing this is to place an embargo on its publication – that is, to insist that publication is delayed until a certain time.

SEE ALSO: **public relations; spin.**

emergent culture A term coined by RAYMOND WILLIAMS to point out that, as cultures are always changing, at any one historical point there will be emergent cultures that are coming to prominence (or emerging). Thus, in popular music in the mid-1970s, punk rock was emergent in the sense that it was a new form of culture that was beginning to attract attention. In the late 1980s dance culture was emergent in the same way. If some cultural forms are emerging in this way others are declining. Williams used the term 'residual' for these forms. Thus, with respect to music in the 1970s, rock and roll could be seen as residual in the sense that it had been very popular at an earlier point in history but that it still had a following meant that it had not completely died out. Both of these types were contrasted with 'dominant culture' by Williams.

empowerment The capacity of individuals or groups to improve their life chances or situation. The media can be thought to do this for certain groups of individuals when confidence is imparted through some aspect of media involvement or consumption. For example, it has been suggested that involvement in rock music facilitated the communication of subversive messages for social and political change in the communist regime in the former East Germany (Wicke, 1992).

encoding/decoding A form of analysis of the creation and interpretation of media texts. The use of the term 'code' implies that the meaning and structure of a text is not always obvious but is buried or hidden. That meaning is put into the text by the encoder and interpreted by the decoder. Texts that permit a variety of interpretations by the decoder are often referred to as 'open texts' while those that limit the possibilities of interpretation are 'closed texts'. Most media texts are relatively open; street signs depend for their effectiveness on being closed.

The most influential version of the encoding/decoding model was developed by STUART HALL. It is tempting to think that media texts have a direct effect on their audiences; the meaning that is encoded in the text is the one decoded by the recipients. This is a view that gives priority to the encoder and the text. Hall argued, however, that the decoder has a significant role in being able to interpret the message in different ways. Hall further argued that the social position of the decoder influences the way in which the text is decoded. In particular, the decoder may take up a dominant, a negotiated or an oppositional reading of the text. If a dominant reading is adopted, the decoder accepts the PREFERRED READING. In a negotiated reading, the decoder may partly share the preferred reading but also modifies it. Oppositional readings bring an alternative frame of reference to the text which opposes the preferred reading.

SEE ALSO: **communication**; *Nationwide* **studies**; **open text**; **semiology**.

enculturation A term used most often in more anthropological forms of social research to denote the way in which people adapt to and take on new forms of culture.

end credits The credits at the end of a film or television programme. One of the significant points about contemporary end credits is the length and diversity of them. This signals the increased complexity of film and television production, but also the need to give recognition to even the most mundane role in the production process.

enigma Often the opening aspect of the narrative of a text, where questions or puzzles are posed for the audience. To take a relatively straightforward example, a detective story may operate with an opening enigma around who committed a crime, which an audience will expect the narrative to resolve at the end. However, the enigmas of texts may be more complex than this, often revolving around identity. Thus, in romantic fiction (SEE: **romance**), for example, a key aspect of the enigma may revolve around the characters of the hero and heroine, and how they are out of place or misrecognized socially. The narrative thus poses questions to the audience, but will resolve such questions of identity and place by having the hero and heroine becoming romantically involved at the end of the text. CLOSED TEXTS will tend to tie up the questions that are raised by texts, where OPEN ones will not. This is often a matter of degree, and some texts will do both. For example, early seasons of *The West Wing*, which was very popular prime-time TV, were sometimes criticized for the way in which narrative questions were left hanging.

enigma code Parts of the narrative of a text which pose questions that intrigue the reader or viewer. An example would be a murder story, such as *Inspector Morse*, where the text contains a prominent enigma code based around the question of who did the murder, how and why. However, the text will also contain other codes around visual display (for example, of Oxford and the surrounding countryside in *Morse*). It is also sometimes referred to as the hermeneutic code, deriving from the work of ROLAND BARTHES.

SEE ALSO: **code; enigma**.

entertainment All sorts of media perform the function of entertainment, often contrasted with the functions of information and education. Within media studies, entertainment has often been subject to a very critical eye for its allegedly political function – perhaps in the distraction of people from inequality and social injustice. More recently, entertainment, and especially light entertainment, has been valued more positively and the audiences for the form examined more substantially.

SEE ALSO: **Adorno; domination**.

enthusiasm A hobby or pastime in which people are very much involved. In the media, examples are the interest taken in cult films, such as *The Rocky Horror Picture Show*, pop music bands or television shows, such as *Star Trek*.

SEE ALSO: **fan**.

enunciation The act of speaking. The idea has been particularly significant in film theory, where it has been used to consider how films address the audience as spectators.

epic GENRE of film with a large budget, usually with an historical theme. Epics were significant from the early days of the cinema with an important example being *The Birth of a Nation* (dir. D. W. Griffith, 1915). These films were visually lush and opulent. The term is relatively little used now, and it can be argued that the form has been superseded by the success of the ACTION genre, which has taken over big budgets and visual spectacle, though not the historical or religious themes that often drove the epic.

escapism The way in which media provide a resource for the imaginative and physical removal of the self from the routines of EVERYDAY LIFE. This had tended to be neglected as an area of study until the advent of media and cultural studies. Popular music may be thought to play such a role in the activities of listening and attending live performance, and this has been considered in studies of FANS. However, the most extensive and important studies have considered popular romantic fiction (ROMANCE) and film. Thus, with respect to the former, the way in which the reading of successful romantic fiction provides a resource for the temporary escape from the confines of the everyday domestic activity for women has been researched and subjected to critique (Radway, 1987). With respect to film, writers have considered, *inter alia*, how the cinema as a physical space and imaginative resource provided an escape for women during the Second World War in Britain (Stacey, 1994). A similar sort of argument has been made concerning the pleasures of television soap opera for women, which have been seen as providing a space for relaxation and escape from domestic duties. The way in which films, novels and television offer escape still tends to be seen as a problem by some critics on the left and right. The former suggest that the escapism of, for example, fantasy genres, blocks proper consideration of the inequities of capitalist society; the latter will be more likely to see this as a symptom of cultural decline from the appreciation of more intellectual and sophisticated texts. It is significant how much attention has focused on the role of escapism for women with relatively little in detail on men.

SEE ALSO: **fantasy**.

establishing shot   The shot or sequence of shots in film or television that establishes a situation or location. It locates the initial meaning of the narrative. For example, the first shot of a soap opera will often be the buildings of the place itself, establishing that the narrative will take place in the locations of those streets and houses.

establishment   The interconnected group of people that occupies powerful positions in different organizations in the country. The proposition is that people in power, whether they are in the media, businesses, government, the judiciary, army or police or the large public services, are connected with each other by virtue of social background, attendance at the same schools and universities, overlapping memberships of organizations and continuing social contacts. From this it has been concluded that a fairly small group of people effectively run the country. The argument has a particular relevance to the media in that those who run large media organizations form part of the establishment and may be open to undue influence from other members. While it is true that there are indeed connections of this kind between powerful people, it is less clear that the establishment functions as a coherent group.

ethics   See: ADVERTISING ETHICS; JOURNALISTIC ETHICS.

ethnography   The direct observation of the activity of members of a particular social group, and the description and evaluation of such activity. The term has been used to describe the research techniques of anthropologists but has increasingly been applied in other social science and humanities disciplines. In media studies the idea and practice has been applied to studies of the AUDIENCE that sought to engage with how television was being consumed in the home. However, the earlier studies were based on relatively small amounts of observation which led to criticism of the depth of observation entailed. Subsequent studies have sought to counter this with greater involvement. Ethnography has also been used in the study of media production, as for example in the occupational cultures of journalists and news production. It has been particularly successful in the study of the occupational cultures of musicians and the way in which music is a key activity in everyday life. An example of the former is work on the practices and culture of American hip-hop producers (Schloss, 2004). The latter has manifested itself in more locality-based studies, such as ethnography of music practice in the English city of Milton Keynes (Finnegan, 1989) or the theoretically innovative investigations of popular music SCENES (Bennett and Peterson, 2004).

SEE ALSO: **participant observation**.

event One of the most significant developments as the media become more prevalent and influential in society is the media event, i.e. an event that is specially arranged to be shown on the media, or reported by it. It has been suggested that more and more events, such as an election, are being staged (the word is very suggestive in this context) for the media themselves.

everyday life Day-to-day activity and its study. In contemporary societies, the media are very much part of everyday life. Radio, recorded music and, especially, television are woven into the routines of domestic life. The conversational style of television and the scheduling and the content of programmes all reflect the domestic orientation of the medium (SEE: **directness of address; household**). Everyday life is given security and order by its own routine in which the media play such an important part. For example, one of the major ways in which everyday life is organized is by time. A sense of security is given by the routines that occur at more or less fixed times – going to bed, getting up, mealtimes – and the media, especially television, have a role to play in organizing those times. Theoretical approaches to everyday life in media studies take three main forms. First, there is a strain of Marxist-influenced critique of everyday life. Concentrating on the inauthenticity of everyday life in capitalist society, such approaches argue that the everyday is deficient and a pale shadow of what life could be like under a different system. The second offers a much more positive picture. Under the influence of POSTMODERNISM and the French theorist MICHEL DE CERTEAU it focuses on the resistances to power that are part of the everyday and the pleasures of the performance of everyday life. Both approaches have impacted on media and cultural studies, where they have often been caricatured. The former seeks to reveal the ideological role of the media in the concealment of power and inequality, the latter to show how media meanings are transformed into forms of resistance to power. This debate is limited by the over-attention to the dynamic between incorporation and resistance. In a third approach, which draws on the work of the sociologist A. Giddens, R. Silverstone (1994) has sought to retheorize the complexity of everyday life and the complex role of television in it.

exhibition The process by which cinema films are shown, a term derived from the idea of the art exhibition. Control over exhibition, like that over DISTRIBUTION, has been a very important production process. There is not much point in a film being made if it cannot reach an audience, however small or niche-like. Thus, powerful interests, especially the Hollywood studios, have sought, in the past, to gain control over exhibition.

eye-line matching The matching of shots in film so that the gaze of a character is seen to match to that of another character or to construct the consistent gaze of a character at a landscape or object. The shots are edited to create the sensation of continuity in the look. Thus, if one shot shows a character looking out, the next will often show what he or she is looking at from the angle and level that would suggest that the shot is from their eye-line.

e-zine A magazine published only online, available either on a website or by email. Because of its low costs of production, this method of publication has permitted the appearance of magazines that appeal to very small audiences. As a result, the majority of e-zines are run by enthusiasts and are free. Others finance themselves by charging a subscription.

F

facing matter Advertisements in a magazine or newspaper that are on the page facing the EDITORIAL, a position thought to be advantageous.

faction A type of narrative that follows the rules of fiction, but which is based on real events. This can be controversial in that the real is sometimes held to have been misrepresented in its conversion to the fictional form. An example of a faction film would be Oliver Stone's *JFK* (1991), which can be seen as arguing for a particular interpretation of the supposed conspiracy to kill President Kennedy. Those in favour of the form would tend to emphasize the significant impact that it can have compared with a more factual form.

    SEE ALSO: **actuality; documentary.**

fade The gradual appearance (fade in) or disappearance (fade out) in an image or shot in a visual narrative. Sound can also fade in or fade out.

family television Most television is received in a domestic setting – and almost all homes have a television. As a result, television is very much a domestic medium in its content, mode of address and scheduling (SEE: **household**). Although households in the UK and in many advanced industrial societies are becoming more diverse, including many single-person households and childless couples, for example, the prevailing form is still that of the family household. In addition, of course, many of those currently not living with children will have adult children living elsewhere and will tend to think of themselves as a family in that sense. Television producers therefore have to think of the family as a likely audience for their programmes. Media researchers have for some time also been interested in the way in which television is watched, not necessarily by individuals by themselves but by families.

    Television's content is oriented to families. Many of the most watched programmes, particularly soap operas and situation comedies, are about families and domestic life. Television scheduling has to take account of family routines. Children's programmes will be on at a time to suit them, programmes aimed at mothers again at a suitable time, and 'adult' programmes restricted to late evening (SEE: **watershed**). Less obviously, the family context of viewing is important. Television is frequently seen as destructive of family life. It may be wiser to see it as a question of families using television. This will take various forms at different times. Television may be used, for example, as a means of controlling children or of organizing mealtimes. More important still, television acts as a facilitator of communication. Several studies have shown how particular programmes will provide occasions for family debate and discussion about topics, such as drugs or sex, which are otherwise difficult to talk about in the abstract. Again, communal family watching of programmes provides opportunities for displays of family warmth and affection. Direct observation of families watching television has noted that parents and children touch each other and are more physically affectionate than they are at other times. It can also act as a source of domestic harmony as families laugh together or are harrowed together.

SEE ALSO: **television talk**.

fan An audience member who has some kind of intense and extensive admiration for an activity or a star. Commonsense and journalistic writing tends to be critical of such fans, as there is seen to be something wrong in admiration of this kind. Such individuals are thought of as 'sad', loners, hysterical, or, even, pathological. Media studies has developed an important strain of work that has contested such stereotypes, seeking to revalue and systematically investigate fans (Jenson, 1992; Sandvoss, 2005). There has been much attention paid to popular music fandom, often following aspects of the more journalistic and novelistic writing of authors like Nick Hornby (1992, 1994, 1995, 2003). While not often systematic, and remaining relatively underdeveloped theoretically, such studies do provide much evidence on contemporary fandom. The most extensive academic studies have been of television fandom, especially around cult TV (Hills, 2002) and *Star Trek* (Bacon-Smith, 1992; Jenkins, 1992; Penley, 1992). These studies have emphasized the creativity of fans in terms of their active interpretation of texts, the way in which they create new and often surprising new texts using the characters and situations from the original series, and the way in which the texts are embedded in different cultural forms such as song and dress. Through attention to these processes, these commentators have revalued Trekker culture. This has led to a great number of fan studies, which develop these key themes, with respect to other genres and cultural forms, such as work on *Buffy the Vampire Slayer* or on different forms of music. The danger has been that this attention neglects the relation between fans and other modes of audience activity (Abercrombie and Longhurst, 1998), which has been reinforced by the fact that the academic writers are often fans of what they are studying themselves (Bird, 2003). Fans are grouped into fandoms, and some of the literature considers the development of the fan as she or he becomes more integrated into the fandom, which is both a thing and a process. The term ENTHUSIASM is also sometimes used in this respect, though it may best refer to less media-driven forms of engagement, such as hobbies and sports activity (Bishop and Hoggett, 1986).

SEE ALSO: cult.

fantasy A GENRE of text that does not attempt to depict or capture the reality of everyday life, focusing instead on events and actions that are of an imagined and different other world – and a mode of audience experience that removes the consumer of a text from everyday reality. The genre of fantasy, like many others, covers a wide range of forms. However, it will usually not be set in a world that is ours (or it will alter that world in ways that make it less mundane), it will introduce events and activities that alter the rules of cause and effect in our world and will often involve some measure of playfulness on the part of the author. It is possible to see the *Harry Potter* series by J. K. Rowling as belonging to the genre of fantasy. Thus, while Harry's world connects to our world and experience, it is a world where magic is real and where concrete effects can be produced by it. Further, Harry's world is a parallel one to that in which we live and it can only be entered into by those who are in the know. For example, the train to Hogwarts departs from a platform that, despite being in a real station, only the enlightened can find. However, despite being fantastic in these senses, the world that Harry inhabits has much in common with ours, especially in the sense that events follow from each other. The narrative has to have plausibility within the world that has been set up by the author. So Harry cannot travel through time without this facility being explained in some way. As a genre, then, fantasy has some specific narrative features. It can also be explored in two other broad ways: as a mode of audience experience; and as articulating some deeply felt aspects of the human unconscious or human society. With respect to the former, and continuing the Harry Potter example, the reader of the books (or viewer of the films, or player of the games) will enter the fantastic world, he or she will be taken out of the everyday and escape to an alternative world; this may feel very relaxing in that the world is one where adults can relive a childhood, or where children can fantasize about using magic to get ahead of their boring parents (as Harry can if he wishes to deal with his 'muggle', substitute parents, the Dursleys). This mode of escapism has also been studied with respect to the way in which Hollywood movies provided the opportunity for female viewers to escape the reality of war-time experience (Stacey, 1994) and in connection with the way in which romantic literature also provides such opportunities for female readers (Radway, 1987). There has been a tendency within academic studies to neglect these modes of audience experience and pleasure, probably be-cause such removal from everyday life has been seen as serving dominant interests. For example, for the Marxist critic the audience member should attempt to engage with real life by trying to change it in some way or another, not escape from it. Likewise, those critics who tend to criticize forms of popular culture for lacking seriousness will also be critical of fantasy. Here, the genre and the experience does not lead to insight into the deeper values of society and its morality; again it would be suggested that it offers modes of superficial escape. Both of these sorts of approach not only tend to neglect the nature of the audience's experience and pleasure, but also do not sufficiently recognize the extent to which fan-tasy deals with the unconscious desires of the individual – wouldn't we all like to have magical powers that enable us to control situations? In addition, fantasy can also be seen as getting at deep-seated concerns of human life in the broadest sense – such as are there modes of experience in the world that are outside those that are defined by the rationalistic approach of natural science? In this way fantasy addresses aspects of our condition where we have some beliefs that might not be rational.

SEE ALSO: **escapism; realism; romance**.

fanzine A specialist publication that derives from the combination of fan and magazine. Fanzines developed around particular bands and types of music, especially punk (since the 1970s) and have been prevalent with respect to football in the UK (since the 1980s), where most clubs will have unofficial fanzines that discuss, often in a humorous and controversial way, their activities. In many respects internet discussion sites have now taken on many of the functions served by the fanzine.

SEE ALSO: **fan**.

fatwa A pronouncement or edict from an Islamic religious leader. The most famous fatwa, in effect a death sentence, was pronounced on the author Salman Rushdie by the Ayatollah Khomeini of Iran in 1989 after the publication of Rushdie's novel *The Satanic Verses* in 1988. The content and representations in the book offended many Muslims and others. Despite the fact that Rushdie had sought to open debate on how cultures interact and processes of faith in a globalizing (or postmodern) world, the fatwa forced him into hiding for a considerable period of time.

SEE ALSO: **globalization**.

fear of crime See: CRIME.

feature **1** In radio production a story that has been prepared beforehand.

2 Type of story in a magazine or in a magazine-type television programme. The feature may be one of the hooks of the publication or the programme, in the sense that, although feature stories are a regular aspect of the publication or programme, their content may be quite different from edition to edition.

Federal Communications Commission (FCC) Set up in the 1930s in the United States to protect the public interest in broadcasting, to regulate the content of radio and then television and to control competition in the industry, the FCC has more recently moved significantly towards deregulation. For example, from the 1980s onwards, the FCC has relaxed rules that previously made it difficult for one company to become dominant or that controlled cross-media ownership. Similarly, the rules regulating the amount and type of advertising have been progressively attenuated.

SEE ALSO: **regulation**.

femininity See: GENDER.

feminism Social, cultural and political ideas that seek to advance the place of women and the resulting social, cultural and political practices. Feminism has a long history, but feminist ideas have influenced the study of the media in several different ways since the 1960s (when so-called second-wave feminism was of particular influence). First, research has examined how women are represented in the media, in terms of the roles that they are seen to occupy and perform in particular texts. Second, there has been consideration of how particular texts appeal to women and connect to the nature of their everyday lives. Third, there has been influence from the different strains of feminist theory that have sought to show how sex and gender are socially and culturally constructed (SEE: **Butler**). There are a range of approaches in this respect, but they suggest that the media have a core role in the way in which gender is understood in contemporary societies.

SEE ALSO: **gender**.

fibre optics Technology that is based on the development of fibreoptic cable. This glass cable enables the transmission of digital information and can carry more information than previously dominant technologies.

SEE ALSO: **digitization**.

fiction Mode of NARRATIVE or story-telling that does not purport to be communicating factual information. While the distinctions between fact and fiction are actually very complex, as forms of fiction are very often based on real information and real feelings, and the communication of fact often involves the construction of narratives, the distinction between fact and fiction is commonsensically recognizable. Fiction occurs in various media and genres, but perhaps the most significant moment in its development was the creation of the realist novel in the eighteenth century. In this form many of the conventional features of familiar and popular fiction were created, such as real names for characters, setting in places that could be recognized as real, constructing the narrative to suggest the passage of real time and so on. There have been many different approaches to the study of the novel including STRUCTURALISM, POST-STRUCTURALISM, DECONSTRUCTION and the DIALOGIC which have also impacted upon media studies.

SEE ALSO: **realism**.

field 1 The space captured by a camera.

2 Within the cultural theory of PIERRE BOURDIEU, a space of operation of conventions or rules, such as the political and economic. One way to think of this is to refer to the field of play of a game – thus, hockey is played or a field of a certain size, within a set of rules that make some forms of behaviour acceptable (hitting a ball with a stick) and others not (hitting another person with the stick). Neither of these forms of behaviour would be acceptable within the field of the supermarket. This captures the idea that certain forms of behaviour are acceptable within certain fields, but not in others. Thus, skill with a hockey stick may be useful within the hockey field but pretty useless in that of the supermarket. However, in certain respects the fields overlap. Thus, skill with a hockey stick may generate sufficient income such that an individual never has to go shopping again and can avoid engaging with the supermarket field at all.

SEE ALSO: **convention; cultural capital; habitus**.

film Technically, the photographic substance on which images are recorded at several frames a second, which can then produce moving images when a light is projected through it on to a screen. More generally, the term for the texts created by this method, as well as by newer technologies such as video. In socio-cultural terms, film has since the end of the nineteenth century become one of the major art forms of contemporary culture. Film can cover almost any content with a wide range of forms but tends to exist as a NARRATIVE of more than one hour that in some sense or form tells a story. Film forms can range from the commercial to the AVANT-GARDE. Film is a part of many national cultures, where issues of particular concern are often considered.

SEE ALSO: **art cinema; Bollywood; cinema; Hollywood; photography**.

film noir A particular form of cinema that was developed in Hollywood during and after the Second World War. Often seen as a specific GENRE, film noir developed thriller conventions in a particular direction. A number of formal features of film noir have been much discussed. Four main aspects of film noir have usefully been identified. (1) A narrative based on investigation; (2) extensive use of devices such as flashbacks and voice over; (3) a complex representation of the female character, an emphasis on female sexuality; (4) a visual style that makes great use of shadow and contrast in black and white (Gledhill, 1980).

Of great interest to feminist film theorists, film noir is contextualized socially by analysis of the way in which women entered paid work during the Second World War, fulfilling the need for labour during a period when men were drafted into the armed forces. The argument is advanced that this both empowered women socially, but also meant that they had to be returned to domestic roles once the war was over. Thus, the film noir often centred on the exploits of a powerful yet dangerous woman, who would involve a male hero in her schemes (see, for example, *Double Indemnity*, dir. Billy Wilder, 1944). The narrative resolution of the film would involve the destruction of this female in one way or another. This dramatized the perils of independent women for men and society. The destructive and sexually free woman would sometimes be contrasted with a more nurturing and domestic woman. Film noir built on features of European art cinema (especially expressionism), using a characteristic style that used deep shadows which could be seen as visual metaphors of the themes of secrecy and moral ambiguity explored in the films.

SEE ALSO: **feminism; gender; police series**.

film studies The academic discipline that studies film in a systematic fashion. Film studies, while in some ways now a branch of media studies, has its own relatively distinctive history and approach. It is sometimes taught in relatively small specialist academic departments in universities, but also in larger formations that may combine film and media production, journalism and so on. Film studies has tended to concentrate on the textual analysis of film, showing its roots in approaches that were concerned with the analysis and interpretation of NARRATIVES. When taught in departments that engaged in film or media production this fed into the practice of making films. Where the study of film was carried out more in tandem with forms of literary analysis, there tended to be a relative neglect of the study of the production and institutional context of film, though this was not always the case and is now relatively rare. More often neglected was the actual consumption of texts (as opposed to the readings that critics or those producing films thought that audiences would make of texts). This continues to be a more serious gap – though there are studies that have made inroads to such research (e.g. Stacey, 1994; Kuhn, 2002; Staiger, 2005).

SEE ALSO: **cultural studies**.

film theory An aspect of film studies that concerns itself with the theorization of film, as opposed to the empirical investigation of it. Film theory has been particularly influenced by French-originated social and cultural theory (for example, AUTEUR THEORY, STRUCTURALISM and POSTSTRUCTURALISM), which has generated some of its key concepts and debates (such as around authorship, the MALE GAZE and the nature of NARRATIVE). Such theory itself was the product of different streams of analysis based in psychoanalysis and literary theory. It therefore concentrated on aspects of texts and their formal analysis. German social theory has also had impact through the take-up of the theories of writers like WALTER BENJAMIN and Siegfried Kracauer. Here, less emphasis is placed upon textual structure and more on how film connects to the unconscious, imagination and the flow of everyday life. Psychoanalytical work derived from Freud has impacted upon both these streams, leading to significant work in film theory on, for example, subjectivity and the dreamlike nature of film. This work has been of great significance in the production of a set of established ideas and concepts for the analysis of film. Less positively it has led attention away from more sociological analysis of institutions and audiences.

finance See: COMMODIFICATION; CONCENTRATION OF OWNERSHIP; ECONOMICS OF THE MEDIA; MEDIA IMPERIALISM.

fine cut Final edit of a film.

SEE ALSO: **rough cut**.

Fiske, John (b. 1939) Previously Professor of Communication and Cultural Studies at the University of Wisconsin-Madison. An influential exponent of media and cultural studies, who was subject to criticism for his perceived adoption of positions, in books such as *Reading the Popular* and *Understanding Popular Culture* (both 1989), that seemed to be suggesting that resistance to dominant cultures could be read into even the most commodified aspects of popular culture. This was criticized as a form of cultural populism (McGuigan, 1992). In many respects Fiske was a straw man for these sorts of position. He was co-author, with J. Hartley, of one of the first student-friendly books on the analysis of media texts, *Reading Television* (1978), and his most coherent overall statement can be found in *Television Culture* (1987). Both of these texts continue to offer much for the student of media studies.

fixed spot In radio, an item that appears at a regular place in a programme.
SEE ALSO: **diary story; off-diary story; spot news.**

flashback A part of a NARRATIVE that goes back to an earlier event or aspect of the story. This means that the narrative proceeds out of strict chronological sequence.

Fleet Street For a long period in the twentieth century, much of the national press had its headquarters, journalists' offices and printing presses in Fleet Street in London. The name came to stand for the newspaper industry in general, sometimes for dubious journalistic practices, and for traditional methods of organizing the production of newspapers. From the 1980s onwards, new technology forced changes in the printing of newspapers and in journalism, allowing various functions to be discharged more cheaply away from Fleet Street.
SEE ALSO: **newspaper; Wapping.**

flow Television as a continuous stream rather than a series of discrete programmes. Daily television consists of a number of different types of programme, and it may appear that viewers will choose to watch each programme having consulted a schedule in much the same way as they choose to read a book. Actually the experience of watching television is not of a set of discrete events – programmes – but is of a continuous flow, a term invented by RAYMOND WILLIAMS (1974), who noticed, when watching American TV, that it was difficult to separate programmes from each other and from advertisements. That is indicated in saying that we are watching television, not watching a specific programme. The flow is not random and chaotic, however, for there are two structuring principles at work. First, television producers put a great deal of effort into planning the sequence of programmes in order to keep viewers watching one channel (SEE: **scheduling**). Second, there is a certain unity given to the flow by the values of the culture (SEE: **structure of feeling**). Other authors argue that the word flow is misleading in that it implies a smooth and uninterrupted process. Actually, the flow is a procession of segments which are sometimes totally unrelated to one another. The way that advertisements punctuate an evening's viewing is one obvious example. The construction of news programmes as a set of unconnected items is another. The segmentation of the flow is emphasized by the characteristically fragmented camerawork of television.

SEE ALSO: **television**.

fly on the wall A term used to describe those television documentaries in which the participants seem to be relatively unaware of the camera and hence behave more naturally. On occasions, the camera may be literally hidden. In Britain, the 1970s series *The Family*, which followed the lives of a family group, was seen as a classic documentary of this type. Contemporary REALITY TV shares many of the features of the fly-on-the-wall approach.

FM (Frequency Modulation) See: AM.

focus group A technique made fashionable by the Labour Party in the UK, focus groups are used in qualitative research (SEE: **audience research**, in which a small group of people is asked to focus on an issue and discuss it in depth with an inteviewer, often on a number of separate occasions over time. It is used extensively in market research and political opinion polling as an alternative or supplement to traditional questionnaire surveys. While focus groups allow very detailed investigation over time, the very small sample size that they necessarily employ means that any conclusions drawn from the interviews are not generalizable to the population as a whole.

focus puller In film-making, the role that involves control of camera focus, usually the first assistant to the director of photography.

folio 1 A page in a book or magazine.
2 More rarely, a size of book at least forty centimetres in height.

folk culture A culture associated with a particular group, which is thought to be indigenous to the group and relatively unchanging, also often transmitted orally through song or recitation rather than written down. Most often now applied to music in the well-known idea of folk music. It is significant that many of the forms of music that were described as folk music, such as the blues, when it was recorded 'in the field' in the southern states of the USA by white middle-class men from the north, were played by performers who travelled round to perform in different locations and had in many cases heard recorded versions of the songs. Thus, these forms were not unchanging. While this is an important critique of simple understandings of folk culture, or folk music, it is important to suggest that folk can still be used to refer to forms of culture that are relatively located in place and social group, provided that it is recognized that such forms are subject to outside influence.

SEE ALSO: **globalization; mass culture.**

folk devil A social group stereotyped by the rest of society and treated punitively. Many societies scapegoat certain minority groups as being immoral or evil – that is, as folk devils – and deserving of control and punishment. In recent times in the UK, groups such as asylum-seekers, black youth, drug-users, travellers and football fans have been demonized in this way. In modern societies, this process is often promoted by the mass media, which may portray the groups in such simplistic terms that the police and the courts feel obliged to act against them. Such campaigns can become MORAL PANICS.

SEE ALSO: **amplification of deviance.**

follow focus In film-making, the process of moving focus so that a subject is kept clearly in focus during a shot.

font The style or design of the characters – the letters, numbers and symbols – used to print a book or newspaper. The term has come to have this meaning – the same as TYPEFACE – largely with the advent of computer typesetting and especially desktop publishing. Historically, it had other meanings.

footage The raw film shot for television or movies before it is edited. Can also be used simply for a section of film. The term probably derives from the way that film could be measured in feet.

footprint The particular area of the earth's surface within which television and radio signals from a SATELLITE in GEOSTATIONARY orbit can be received.

Fordism/post-Fordism Producing a book, a film or a record is not unlike other kinds of work, and organizing it poses similar problems. It is a complex process with a high degree of division of labour, that is, the production process is broken up into a number of stages. A considerable degree of standardization is involved – the repeated use of particular sets in film and television, for example. Each stage is carried out by skilled people who specialize in that activity and, especially in the media, these people may be freelance. Fordism is a method of organizing these production processes. It is named after Henry Ford, who pioneered production-line manufacturing of cars. The essence of this production system is mass production for mass consumption. Very large volumes of identical products are produced using machinery that can only make that one product. That standardization enables low prices, which, in turn, permit large numbers of people to buy the goods. Because each step in the production process is so specialized, only semi-skilled workers are required. On the other hand, a process that is so fragmented demands detailed management.

Within the last forty or fifty years, production systems have become more flexible. Markets are becoming more segmented (SEE: **market segmentation/differentiation**), consumer tastes are becoming more diverse, and greater choice is demanded. Mass-production systems which can produce only a narrow product range will no longer do. So, flexible systems using computer technology, and which can produce goods in small batches, are employed. Greater flexibility in production requires more skilled employees. Management techniques also change. Bureaucratic, centralized management is no longer appropriate, as it is inflexible and tends to stifle creativity, and is replaced with management that gives substantial powers to teams of workers. Companies aim to become leaner, subcontracting or OUTSOURCING parts of their production process.

Up until the late 1940s, films were produced in HOLLYWOOD by a factory-like process – the studio system. The studio was set up as an assembly line for large-scale production of a standardized film product. Film-production crews carried out separated, specialized tasks, and their skills were passed on through apprenticeships. Scenes were shot, not in chronological order, but in batches using the same actors and sets in order to maximize efficiency. Such a system needed fairly detailed management control, and this gave the producer, rather than the director or performers, the central place in film production. The studios stabilized their markets by vertically integrating production of films with their marketing, distribution and exhibition. In particular, the studios owned or controlled a substantial proportion of the cinemas and were thus able to guarantee an outlet for their production.

This was, then, a stable world. The studios' scale of output kept their costs down, their workers had secure employment, and markets were assured. All of this prevented serious competition, since it was difficult for any new company to become established. In the forty or so years since the late 1940s this system has gradually changed. The process was initiated by a court decision in which the studios were forced to divest themselves of their cinema chains. This deprived them of their guaranteed market and greatly increased the risks of making films. The second major force for change was the appearance of television, which slowly established itself as an important competitor for the consumers' time and money. As a result, the studio system slowly started to crumble. Throughout the 1950s the studios increasingly turned to independent producers to make films which would then be rented out to distributors by the studios. Initially this was an attempt to gain a greater variety of films (achieve product differentiation) but it also had cost advantages. Both the levels and security of employment of production and other staff declined. More production was also undertaken outside the United States, partly in an attempt to create films which could have an export market. These processes accelerated from 1970 onwards as the studios had their worst year ever. The major studios shrank in size to cut down their overheads. They sold off land and disposed of many of their production facilities. An increasing proportion of film-making was hived off to independent production companies, which in turn subcontracted to smaller specialized firms. These independent firms were effectively carrying much of the risk previously shouldered by the studios. The result is that the film production and distribution industry is now composed of a multitude of specialized units, which are no longer all within the same organization.

It is risky to exaggerate the differences between Fordist and post-Fordist production systems in the media. There is still, for example, a good deal of bureaucratic standardization. It can also be argued that the media industries have always been flexible in that they have always employed outsourcing for some aspects of production.

SEE ALSO: **individualization; market segmentation**.

foregrounding The process of bringing something or someone to the attention of an audience. The term is most often used in film-making to describe how action is brought to the front of the screen, suggesting particular significance.

form The shape or structure of a text. It is most straightforwardly distinguished from content. For example, a bottle of a particular shape or form may be used for a variety of contents – it might just as easily contain whisky or water. Form and content can be separated. However, they are often associated both by tradition and certain properties of the content. Thus, red wine bottles take a different form to those for sparkling white wine. The same is true of texts, where form and content are independent in many respects, but there are often clear associations between them. For example, punk, heavy metal or hip-hop music take a particular form and tend to be associated with a specific type of lyrical content. Punk music was fast and aggressive, and its lyrics were less concerned with romantic ideals than those of other forms of pop music. GENRES are also examples of form. WESTERNS, for example, have formal features in common, which are recognized by the producers and the audience. We know when we are watching a western because of the clothes that are worn, the guns that are carried, the landscape within which the action takes place and the characteristic antagonism between heroes and villains.

SEE ALSO: **formalism**.

formalism The approach to the study of texts that concentrates on the structural features of the text rather than its content. While in practice it can be quite difficult completely to separate form from content, the study of form is a very important aspect of media studies. The most important aspects of formal study in media studies tend to derive from STRUCTURALISM, SEMIOLOGY and POSTSTRUCTURALISM. In all cases, this involves attention to systems in the text that create meaning through formal features such as the conflict between hero and villain, rather than the specific features of the hero or villain in any one particular film. While these features may be an important part of the pleasure of the viewer, it is their formal features that are held to be most important to structural analysis. A danger here is that formal or structural features are emphasized to the detriment of other features of the text that may also be seen as important to audiences. In this respect, formalism has been criticized as being more interested in the mechanics of the texts rather than in how they are produced and received, and the meanings they contain, and the method needs to be treated as one approach amongst others.

SEE ALSO: **form**.

format Television programmes are produced in different genres – thrillers, soaps, situation comedies (SEE: **genre**). They also come in different formats. *Pop Idol* and *Big Brother*, for example, are programme formats, as distinct from specific programmes. Formats can be sold and exported and then varied to suit local tastes. The difference between genre and format is not entirely clear-cut, and a new format may be the beginning of a new genre.

Foucault, Michel (1926–84) A French philosopher and historian, whose work has been very influential across a range of social science and humanities disciplines since the 1960s. Foucault worked at a number of institutions of higher learning, before ending his career as Professor of History of Systems of Thought at France's premier academic institution, the Collège de France in Paris. Foucault's work traces how ideas are connected to power in complex and changing ways. He developed the idea of DIS-COURSE and showed how discourses structure the world in ways that construct certain categories of thought and understanding. He worked his ideas out over a number of specific studies, which have become classics. His first major book, *Madness and Civilisation* (1971, first published 1961), showed how conceptions of madness and reason are historically specific. Subsequent works such as *The Birth of the Clinic* (1973, first published 1963) developed these themes with respect to changing understandings of medical knowledge. He addressed the theoretical issues that underpinned his work in two key books that show the extent of influence of structuralist ideas on his work at this point, in *The Order of Things* (1974, first published 1966) and *The Archaeology of Knowledge* (1974, first published 1969). He carried on his investigations of power and knowledge in a series of texts, the best known of which are *Discipline and Punish* (1977, first published 1975) and *The History of Sexuality* (1979, 1987, 1990; first published 1976, 1984, 1984). Foucault's influence on media studies has been through the development of the concept of discourse and consequently on the analysis of media texts as consisting of discourses that construct and relate to power as well as the constitution and reconstitution of our identities.

SEE ALSO: **ideology**.

fourth estate The press and other forms of the media that provide information, opinion and comment. A common way of describing society in the eighteenth century and earlier was in terms of estates. There were thought to be three estates or groups of people – the aristocracy, the Church and the common people. In the late eighteenth or early nineteenth centuries, the term 'fourth estate' came into use to describe the press. Many reformers of that time saw the press as an important force in society able to act as a counterweight to the powers of the king, aristocracy and Church. The press acted as a source of information for a wider public but also, more importantly, as a forum of debate and disagreement with the activities of government.

The debate about the position of the press in society, and its power to influence opinion, has continued to this day and is complicated in contemporary society by the proliferation of media forms. For many, it has lost its capacity to promote rational debate and criticism as it is increasingly commercialized and trivial. For others, it has become over-mighty, capable of influencing governments in potentially undesirable ways or even of bringing down properly elected governments.

SEE ALSO: **concentration of ownership; public sphere**.

Fox Network A collection of American TV channels, the Fox Network is owned by NEWS CORPORATION and derives its name from the Twentieth Century Fox film studio also owned by News Corporation. The best-known of the channels is the Fox News Channel. This uses an approach to news modelled on talk radio and, perhaps as a result, has overtaken CNN in viewing figures. Fox News is often said to have a conservative bias, explicitly supporting the Republican Party.

frame **1** The smallest constituent part of a film, as the film is actually made up of a succession of still images.

2 To enclose a scene within a rectangle of the camera frame. The way in which an image is framed can create certain meanings.

3 A means by which people organize and interpret information and events (SEE: **framing**).

framing Means by which people organize and interpret information and events. The term is used in various ways in media studies. Journalists operate with a set of assumptions, or frames, which provide a way of organizing and filtering the information that they receive and which they subsequently transmit as news. For example, in the period 2002 to 2005 there was substantial media coverage in the UK of the combined MMR vaccine (for mumps, measles and rubella). The vaccine was alleged to have serious side-effects, including autism, which could be avoided by giving a vaccine against the three conditions one at a time. Journalists (though not all) framed this story as a conflict between parents, worried about the safety of their children, and the government anxious to save money by giving protection against three diseases in one inoculation. In this conflict the sympathies of the journalists appeared to lie with the parents, and the framing tended to focus on the alleged risk to children. (SEE: **news values**).

In a related sense, audiences will use frames to make sense of what they see on television or read in the newspapers. A study by Liebes and Katz of the very different ways in which viewers around the world approached the television series *Dallas* provides an example. These authors distinguish referential from critical framings. If an audience member uses a referential framing in talking about *Dallas*, it means that she relates the events of the programme to her own life. Critical framings, on the other hand, are used when audiences comment on the acting, sets and locations, narrative structure or themes of the programme (SEE: **television talk**).

franchise A time-limited licence to broadcast television and radio granted to commercial operators by government in exchange for a fee.

SEE ALSO: **Independent Television; television franchise.**

Frankfurt School The group of social and cultural theorists who were connected with Frankfurt Institute for Social Research, which was founded at the University of Frankfurt in 1923. Their work has been of wide influence, especially in media studies, in the ideas of the nature and effects of the culture industry and their critique of mass culture. The most influential members of the institute were Max Horkheimer, T. W. ADORNO and HERBERT MARCUSE. WALTER BENJAMIN had a significant association with the group. The most important contemporary exponent of the themes initially developed by the School is the German philosopher and social scientist, JÜRGEN HABERMAS. The group left Germany after the rise to power of the Nazis, due to their Marxist associations and the predominantly Jewish nature of the group. The rise of the Nazis (and totalitarianism) and the encounter with the nature of capitalism in the USA affected the thinking of the group in significant ways. Some members of the group returned to Germany after the war while others remained in the United States.

The Frankfurt School, in developing CRITICAL THEORY, was a key site of the reformulation of Marxism to accord greater weight to cultural themes. This meant looking to the effects of culture in the reproduction of forms of consciousness and culture that supported the rationalizing thrust of an increasingly bureaucratic and technocratic capitalism. The culture industry was thus a key site of such COMMODIFICATION and development of instrumental, standardized and limited thinking. The Frankfurt writers were thus very critical of the nature and effects of mass culture, which they saw as commodified and thus likely to lead to the incorporation of the masses into a restricted mode of capitalist thinking. The nature, and increasing prevalence, of the media in advanced capitalist countries were seen as important aspects of this process.

SEE ALSO: **cultural industries; Marxism.**

freedom of information The free flow of information is crucial for a properly functioning democracy. People need to have information in order to make judgements about current events, they need to know what information about them is held in order to check its validity, and information is required so that people can change their situation in life. It follows that the way that information is controlled is critical. Hence the phrase: 'knowledge is power'. Governments, corporations and powerful individuals may, however, wish to restrict access to information.

Governments will believe that some things that they do should remain secret, corporations will think that their commercial interests may be compromised if too much is known about them, and individuals may wish to protect their privacy. There is therefore a tension between revealing information in the interests of democracy and concealing it for reasons both good and bad. This tension is particularly acute in contemporary society because computer technology has simultaneously made it possible to store and access very large amounts of information and to distribute it widely via the internet.

SEE ALSO: **government and the media; public sphere**.

Freedom of Information Act 2000 This Act gives a general right of access (but with certain exemptions) to all types of recorded information held by public authorities and places a number of obligations on public authorities. Subject to the exemptions, any person who makes a request to a public authority for any information must be told whether that information is held. If it is, the information must be supplied, subject to certain conditions. In addition, all public authorities are required to produce a publication scheme, setting out how they intend to publish the different classes of information that they hold.

SEE ALSO: **freedom of information; Information Commissioner**.

free press 1 A press free of government control, censorship or too great an interference by owners who wish to promote their own views or commercial interests.

SEE ALSO: **censorship; concentration of ownership; government and the media**.

2 More recently newspapers and magazines that are distributed free to households, or in the street, and which depend on advertising for their revenue.

SEE ALSO: **freesheet; regional press**.

freesheet Free, usually local, newspaper. From the 1980s onwards, free newspapers and magazines became commonplace in towns and cities and have competed very successfully at the local level with newspapers that are paid for. In 1975, there were 185 freesheets published in the UK with 1,140 paid-for newspapers. By the mid-1980s, the numbers were about equal. Freesheets seek to make money, not from the cover price, but from the advertising that they carry, together with a small local news content. In this they are also very successful. Thus, in the early 1970s, the freesheets were taking a very small share of the total advertising revenue. Within twenty years, they were taking more than one-third. Since they are free, they do not use the traditional means of distribution, such as newsagents, but are delivered to households or handed out from stands in the street, and that has persuaded advertisers that more people will read them.

Freud, Sigmund (1856–1939) Austrian-born founder of psychoanalysis. His development of the basic concepts of psychoanalysis (*Five Lectures on Psychoanalysis* (1962, originally 1910)) has been very influential in the social sciences. His published work covered the application of psychoanalysis to a variety of areas relevant to the study of culture and the media; to jokes (*Jokes and their Relation to the Unconscious* (1976, originally 1905); art (*Leonardo da Vinci* (1984, originally 1910); dreams (*The Interpretation of Dreams* (1984, originally 1900); and the conflict between instinct and social order (*Civilization and its Discontents* (1930)).

Freud's work has been influential in the study of the media in several ways. First, his work has fed into film studies, initially through consideration of the dreamlike nature of the filmic experience and subsequently in discussions of the construction of sexuality through film, in discussions such as the construction of the MALE GAZE. Moreover, his work and that of subsequent psychoanalytic writers such as Lacan provided a framework and vocabulary for film theory especially in the consideration of ideology, subjectivity and spectator positioning. Second, more generally, Freud's work has been influential on a number of authors embracing CRITICAL THEORY who have sought to reformulate Marxism to take account of the increased role of culture and subjectivity in contemporary social relations.

SEE ALSO: **feminism; gender.**

Frith, Simon (b. 1946) Holds the Tovey Chair of Music at the University of Edinburgh. He is the best-known and most influential writer in the academic study of popular music and was the key figure in formulating the sociology of popular music. His book *The Sociology of Rock* (1978), which was rewritten as *Sound Effects* (1983), was, and remains, a key statement of the parameters of this mode of study, addressing how music is produced, the nature of aspects of its texts and how audiences relate to it. Frith contributed to the development of analyses of popular music, gender and sexuality (in work with Angela McRobbie: Frith and McRobbie, 1990) and co-edited a collection of articles that has further defined the field of popular music studies, *On Record* (Frith and Goodwin, 1990). His recent work has looked at popular music with respect to a range of issues concerning performance and value (Frith, 1996). He has argued, therefore, that the study of popular music has tended to neglect the different modes in which popular music is performed, and that much more attention needs to be devoted to how judgements are made about the worth of popular music by audience members. In this respect he has been critical of the ways in which cultural and media studies have neglected arguments about how the worth of popular culture and media can be discussed. He was also an active journalistic writer on pop music and has chaired the panel for the Mercury Music Prize for a number of years.

front projection Special effect in film-making which throws a projected image from the front of a performer on to a special screen behind him or her.

SEE ALSO: **back projection**.

full-out Printed text that is set to the full width of the page or column.

function The effect that a part of society has on the whole. Some approaches to the study of the media have drawn attention to the functions that the media have in social and cultural life. This can be at the level of the individual, in that the media serve the function, for example, of providing entertainment to the individual enabling him or her to relax and so on. This version of consideration of function was most systematically deployed in the approach to studies of the audience known as USES AND GRATIFICATIONS. In other respects, some writers emphasize how the media perform functions for society as a whole, such as acting as a kind of social glue that will bind people together in a common culture. This can be viewed positively, by functionalist theory advocates, as producing community, or, negatively, by Marxist writers who would suggest that such a mode of operation covers up social inequality and conflict. Developing this point, those who see benefits in this respect will argue that media are beneficial in that they can foster a common understanding or common cause. For example, the extensive media reporting of the death of Princess Diana in 1997 could be argued to have brought people together and provided a mode through which common feelings of grief could be articulated. The more critical or Marxist approach would argue that the feelings expressed were to some degree created by the overwhelming media coverage and that the binding of people together over this person deflected attention from much more significant modes of inequality and injustice, which are not commonly reported to a similar degree by the media.

SEE ALSO: **effects; Marxism**.

fusion The creation of new GENRES by the merger of two existing genres. For example, in the late 1960s and early 1970s, a new genre of music was developed labelled jazz/rock fusion, which quickly was simply called fusion. TV often innovates by fusing different forms and formats, creating new genres like DOCUDRAMA or INFOTAINMENT.

G

gaffer In film-making, the most senior lighting and electrical assistant to the director of photography.

Galtung, Johan (b. 1930) An influential Norwegian analyst of NEWS VALUES and leader of the development of peace studies, who founded the Transcend Institute in Norway in 1966. With Mari Ruge, he is the author of some influential work on the news, which considers how it is that an event is decided to be newsworthy and how processes (gatekeeping) and institutions/individuals (GATEKEEPER) are crucial to the process of deciding what is news.

SEE ALSO: **news**.

game show A GENRE of television and radio, organized, as the name implies, around a game of some kind, the most common of which is the quiz. Although formally about a game, the genre is also about a PERSONALITY (such as Cilla Black) and is a showcase for his or her talents. The attraction of the game show lies in the interaction – the chatting – between the celebrity presenters and those taking part. Game shows have a low status in the television and radio industries and outside them with the reputation as trivial and cheap entertainment. They attract large audiences, however, and represent a format used across the world.

gatefold See: CENTRE-SPREAD.

gatekeeper A person who is in a position to control access to the media. Examples would include JOURNALISTS, EDITORS in book publishing or television companies and A & R men in the music business. Positions such as these may carry considerable power. The political beliefs, opinions and tastes of gatekeepers may regulate who is published, what items are deemed newsworthy or who can bring their views to the public. The result is that particular values, beliefs or fictional works are excluded from exposure in the media.

SEE ALSO: **bias**.

gaze Rapt attention. People pay attention to the media to different degrees at different times. Television, for example, is, notably, a medium that demands attention – a gaze – at some times, but, at others, audiences will be less attentive and only glance. By comparison with television, other media, film or books, for instance, are more demanding, and audiences typically gaze rather than glance at them.

The term is also used to indicate that different people may have different ways of looking at the world, as in MALE GAZE.

SEE ALSO: **active audience; distracted attention; hot media; regimes of watching**.

gender The cultural and social construction of masculinity and femininity, where sex refers to the biological differences between men and women. Media studies has addressed gender in three key areas: texts, production and consumption.

Media texts have been considered with respect to gender in two broad ways. First, there has been consideration of how texts represent gender (or more often how they represent women). Thus, analyses of this type might focus on how the media represent women in particular stereotypical sorts of jobs or roles, or how women's magazines use advertisements that almost without exception deploy very slim women. This sort of approach was particularly prevalent in earlier stages of development of media studies, where writers sought to argue that such representations did not adequately represent the diversity of the experiences of women in the real world. Second, and related, there has been increased consideration of how texts construct images and ideas of gender, and how they may be said to contain gendered discourses or ideologies. Thus, a text in representing women (and men) in particular ways may be said to contain a DISCOURSE of gender. For example, contemporary magazines aimed at the young male market concentrate on images of young women who are scantily dressed (thus omitting images of, for example, women working in everyday occupations such as doctors, traffic wardens, school teachers and so on), and in so doing construct discourses of gender that suggest appropriate ways for women and men to behave. Women should attract men who are concerned with gadgets, female bodies and cars.

Further, it has been argued that texts can be seen as formally masculine or feminine. Thus, a masculine text might be characterized by action that focuses on the doings of a central male hero who through his action catches the villain (in TV police series) or saves the world from a criminal mastermind (in a James Bond movie). Such texts construct discourses that make some valued men active and individualistic (some men are of course boring and bureaucratic – usually M in the Bond series), while women are more passive, either helping the hero, falling under his romantic spell or waiting to be liberated from the clutches of the villain. A feminine text would be one where there are dominant female characters. A good example of this is British serial dramas (or soap operas) like *Coronation Street* or *East-Enders*. Here a community is 'led' by strong women, and the drama is centred on their efforts to maintain strength in the face of men who may be weak, devious or unreliable. This constructs a discourse of gender where women are strong, valued and collectively oriented, while men's individualistic activity leads to weakness and moral deficit (Abercrombie and Longhurst, 1991; Fiske, 1987). Texts can therefore be extensively analysed for the gendered representations and discourses that they contain and construct.

Attention to production can also illuminate a number of different dimensions of gender. Thus, analysis of the media industry, like many others, reveals that there is a gendered division of labour, in that women tend to be employed in certain jobs (such as make-up and costume) and less in others (such as film directors). It can then be argued that the nature of gender in texts is a result of the gendered nature of the production process. To take another example, women are very likely to be dominant in the varied production roles of a woman's magazine, but very much a minority in the similar roles of a popular music magazine or a magazine aimed at young men. Ways of behaving and acting as a producer are also gendered; thus, it is expected for (male) rock stars to be very masculine and seek to take drugs and sleep around, but if a female rock star sought to act in this way, she would likely be a figure of scorn (see, for example, discussions of the careers of the American rock stars Janis Joplin and Courtney Love). Thus, such male dominance of a part of the media production industry could result in the form called 'cock rock' (Frith and McRobbie, 1990), where male rock stars led bands that acted in aggressively masculine ways. This form was satirized in the movie *This Is Spinal Tap* (dir. Rob Reiner, 1983).

Audiences can also be considered with respect to gender. First, it is possible to examine how the audiences for certain texts divide along gendered lines. Thus, men form the larger part of the audience for texts such as television sport, but a minority of the audience for daytime soaps. Many television texts are more gender-balanced in their consumption, but there are clear patterns. This is also shown in those studies that have considered how texts are viewed and consumed as well as who consumes them. Thus, second, qualitatively researched audience studies show that women's television viewing is more likely to be inattentive than men's, that men tend to have control of the television remote control and so on, as well as the fact that they have different programme preferences (Morley 1986). In these ways television consumption can be said to be gendered. Third, there are analyses of how texts construct audiences that are gendered. The best such examinations have come in film studies, where the MALE GAZE has been considered. However, it can also be argued that other texts construct a male gaze. For example, it is not unusual for 'attractive' young women in a sporting crowd to draw the attention of the camera. In this sense the viewer is being constructed in a position of gazing at the woman in the crowd. In technical terms the audience member is being constructed as a male spectator, who derives pleasure from looking at the female form.

Lest it be thought that such gender patterns are unchanging, it is important to note that innovation has occurred. Thus, texts have been developed that have an active central female hero, for example, police series such as *Prime Suspect* in the UK and *Cagney and Lacey* in the US, or movies like the *Alien* series starring Sigourney Weaver. M in the Bond movies has been female, though we have yet to see a Jane Bond. Production processes have also been subject to change, as more women enter previously male-dominated occupations and roles, though the patterns are still clear – how many female guitar players are there in rock groups, compared to singers? Audiences are also in many ways more complex than simple division along gender lines would suggest. However, despite these changes, there are still clear ways in which media are gendered in textual form, production and consumption.

SEE ALSO: **feminism**.

General Electric Although primarily known as a producer of electrical equipment, General Electric is also a media company with interests in cable and broadcast television, e.g. NBC.

SEE ALSO: **media companies**.

genre A term that refers to a type of media product or work of art governed by implicit rules that are shared by the makers of the product and the audience for it. Examples are thrillers, soap operas, news programmes, documentaries, talk shows. Every genre has its own particular rules and conventions which distinguish it from others. To some extent these rules are about content. Particular types of character and event, for example, will routinely occur in particular genres and others will not. Domestic settings with everyday events will be the staple of soap opera but are unlikely to figure substantially in action movies. Narrative conventions also play a part in distinguishing one genre from another. Enigmas play an important part in thrillers and sometimes police series but are not usually so significant in situation comedy. Equally, visual or literary style can characterize a genre. It is almost immediately clear that we are watching a western from the opening or reading a book of fantasy from the first page. The credit sequences of soap opera and police series on television tell us instantly what genre is before us.

Media producers set out to exploit genre conventions. It is much easier and more economic to produce to a strict set of rules and to work to a formula. At the same time, it is possible to build up a loyal audience. Genres are a kind of complicity between producer and audience. The audience knows what it is getting and will come to a book, film or television programme with a set of expectations set by the genre. Part of the audience pleasure is in knowing what the genre rules are, knowing that the producer has to solve problems within the genre framework and wondering how it will be done.

The boundaries between genres, and the complicity between audience and producer in them, also make it possible to play with genre conventions. Some television programmes, *The Young Ones* or *The Kumars at No 42*, for example, deliberately parody, stretch or break the conventions. It is also important to realize that genres do change or even merge over time. A book may have genre conventions from both science-fiction and crime. Television, in particular, makes the boundaries between genres permeable, producing mergers between talk shows and situation comedy, costume drama and police series and even fictional and factual programming (SEE: **docusoap; infotainment**). Television's need for a constant stream of new programming means a perpetual tension between using genre conventions to retain audiences and keep costs down, on the one hand, and, on the other, breaking and crossing genre boundaries to attract new audiences and stay ahead of the competition.

SEE ALSO: **action; comedy; fantasy; film noir; horror; musical; police series; soap opera; western.**

geodemographics A method of classifying a population. Any population, including media audiences, can be seen as differentiated by demographic characteristics such as age, gender, occupation and social class. The geodemographics of an audience refer to a classification, not only by those characteristics, but also by where audiences members live. As it happens, people with similar characteristics of income, occupation, lifestyle and taste tend to live near one another and form relatively homogeneous neighbourhoods. That enables advertisers and others to target specific neighbourhoods if they wish to reach a particular group of the population, those with more than one car, for example.

SEE ALSO: **ACORN; demographics.**

geostationary Satellites in geostationary orbit are in a fixed position relative to the earth's surface.

Gerbner, George (b. 1919) Bell Atlantic Professor of Telecommunication at Temple University, Philadelphia. Gerbner has been a very important figure in the development of the study of media and especially of media violence. Today he is most influential through the ideas of cultivation – that is, that heavy media consumption (and in particular heavy consumption of TV) cultivates a set of beliefs in the audience (SEE: **cultivation theory**). A particular aspect of this is the process of mainstreaming (SEE: **mainstream**). These ideas have been extensively discussed in the study of audiences and in the debate around the fear of crime. Gerbner's work and that of his associates has been criticized for lacking an analysis of the meanings of media texts and also implying causal linkages between media and behaviour, which may not be sustainable.

SEE ALSO: **crime**.

ghost writer A person who writes for publication on behalf of someone else who is then credited with the authorship (or part of the authorship). People who are celebrities in some field of endeavour – sport, film or rock music perhaps – quite often publish books about their life. Many celebrities can't write, however, and, in these cases, the books are written by ghost writers, who write professionally.

Gilroy, Paul (b. 1956) Professor of Sociology at the London School of Economics. Gilroy's early work on race and culture appeared in *The Empire Strikes Back* (1982), a co-edited text from the CENTRE FOR CONTEMPORARY CULTURAL STUDIES, where he studied as a postgraduate. In *'There Ain't No Black in the Union Jack'* (1987) he carried out a multi-layered analysis that emphasized the complexity and centrality of interactions and struggles around race, class and nation in contemporary Britain. He has been critical of cultural studies' relative inattention to issues of race and has drawn attention to the significance of black expressive culture, especially in music. He has contributed to understandings and conceptualizations of black diaspora, globalization and identity and has also played a significant role in debates concerning the significance and function of black popular music (see Gilroy, 1993).

SEE ALSO: **race**.

Gitlin, Todd (b. 1941) Professor of Journalism and Sociology at Columbia University in New York City. Gitlin is both a radical critic of mainstream media and one of the foremost American writers on popular media fictions. He has contributed to the study of mainstream media in influential books like *Inside Prime Time* (1983) and *Watching Television* (1987).

glance See: GAZE.

Glasgow University Media Group (GUMG) This research group has been very influential in media research over a long time since its formation in the early 1970s. Often controversial, their work has frequently adopted a perspective critical of the media. The group is probably best known for pioneering and sustained work in the analysis of the content of the media, particularly in respect of news and current affairs. In a series of publications (SEE: **bad news studies**) they came to the conclusion that the news is biased, both in the selection of items and in the way that they were treated, and that the media are ideological. Hardly surprisingly, such a conclusion attracted hostility from media professionals. Academic criticism has focused on the methodology and conclusions of the content analysis and the tendency for the group to concentrate on media content rather than audience reaction. More recent work by the group has attempted to address this last point.

SEE ALSO: **ideology; news**.

globalization The process by which the world is being transformed into a single global system. The process has a number of dimensions. First, it is economic, which in turn has three aspects. The most important of these is the expansion of world financial markets. The globalization of financial flows, in which capital is moved around the world to finance international trade, accelerated rapidly in the last part of the twentieth century, helped by the development of information technology. At the same time there has been further growth of multinational companies, which operate in many different countries and are responsible for great increases in world trade. Further, large multinational companies are attempting to globalize their products and their production. They will, therefore, try to sell the same product in different countries and will distribute their production facilities around the world to obtain the lowest costs.

A second dimension of globalization is cultural. The media permit ideas, news and knowledge of other countries to flow round the world. The marketing efforts of multinational companies also help to bring different national cultures into closer proximity with one another. Lastly, mass tourism and increased migration increase cultural interaction.

Third, there are political dimensions of globalization. International organizations have become more powerful and, in certain cases, the World Trade Organization, the World Bank and the International Monetary

Fund, for example, can effectively regulate the behaviour of nation states. Many have argued that globalization is nothing more than an assertion of the economic and military power of developed Western countries, especially American. The result has been the development of political movements protesting against the social, political and cultural homogenization said to be produced by globalization.

SEE ALSO: **cultural imperialism; global media; glocalization; media imperialism**.

global media It has become a commonplace of contemporary debate that people's everyday lives are becoming more global, more affected by events taking place very great distances away (See: GLOBALIZATION). The media play a very important part in this process. First, media *content* is international. For example, for television it is not only news programmes that depict events in far-away places. Other programmes also use exotic locations and emphasize how any one country is affected by international events. Television is, in effect, constructing an international audience. Certain events, the second Iraq war in 2003 and 2004 or the taking over of a school in Russia by Chechen rebels in 2004, for example, are played out in front of an audience from every country. Second, the media *are traded and received* globally. The American film industry, for example, earns about £17 billion a year, much of which comes from selling films overseas. Nor is international trade in media entirely dominated by American media companies – though they clearly are easily the most important provider. Brazilian soap operas – telenovelas – are now also widely exported (SEE: **media imperialism**). Third, the media are internationally *owned* although overwhelmingly concentrated in the US and Europe. At the national level, the ownership of media organizations is becoming increasingly concentrated (SEE: **concentration of ownership**). The same is happening at the international level as relatively few large media companies operate across the world. This process of global ownership is much helped by the move to DEREGULATION by governments. Fourth, media products are made internationally. For example, satellite technology has accelerated the tendency to internationalize the production of television news. In the coverage of a news event, the engineer responsible for setting up the satellite link is usually the first on the scene, to be followed by the journalist who is to comment on the event. Similarly, television drama is increasingly globally produced. As the costs of production rise with improving production values, television companies have an incentive to cooperate in the production of drama. These CO-PRODUCTIONS take a variety of forms from the simple sharing of costs to full-scale cooperation in production, often using locations in the participating countries.

SEE ALSO: **media companies**.

global village A term invented and popularized by MARSHALL MCLUHAN. It implies both that information is available to very many people through the mass media and that it is available extremely quickly. In this view, the dispersed population of the world therefore increasingly resembles a village.

Globo A Brazilian media conglomerate with interests in Brazil in television, radio, newspapers and record production. The ownership of a television network is the most significant of these since it is now one of the largest in the world partly because of the size of the Brazilian population. The network is particularly known for its vast production of telenovelas (soap operas), which have been exported all over the world. Globo has expanded into cable and satellite.

SEE ALSO: **media companies**.

glocalization In recent years it has become fashionable to argue that there is a process of GLOBALIZATION, which is making local, regional and national cultures increasingly similar to each other. One of the agencies of this process is the media (SEE: **cultural imperialism; media imperialism**). In fact, local cultures are surprisingly resilient and maintain a considerable grip on the population. Sometimes what happens is a hybrid between globalization and localization whereby local cultures are blended with national and international ones, a process now known as 'glocalization' (Robertson, 1995). In addition, local populations may also easily maintain a separate involvement in both local *and* global issues. An obvious example is the way that the provision of news is organized in the UK. Local newspapers and freesheets are widely read in households that also take national newspapers.

Goffman, Erving (1922–82) Although he made major contributions to sociology, Goffman's impact on media studies lies in his view of EVERYDAY LIFE as performance. Here, his principal concern was with the constituents of fleeting, chance or momentary encounters. To grasp the orderliness of such meetings, Goffman employed drama as an analogy for the staging of social encounters in his *The Presentation of Self in Everyday Life* (1959). For Goffman, the social order is always precarious because it is disrupted by embarrassment, withdrawal and the breakdown of communication. He also contributed to the analysis of GENDER in *Gender Advertisements* (1979).

Google A company, started in 1998 in California, that manages the world's largest internet SEARCH ENGINE. Google escaped the DOTCOM bust of the late 1990s and early 2000s and has grown very rapidly to a stock-market valuation of over £50 billion in 2006. The company has ambitions to be the world's largest provider of information and, in pursuit of this aim, has formed partnerships with media companies.

government and the media Tyrannical and authoritarian regimes have long felt the need to control the flow of information and debate and to regulate the climate of public morals. Subversive views, opinions critical of the government and knowledge of what is going on in the inner workings of the state are all potentially dangerous to such regimes, which also feel that they need to control the expression of dissident religious or ethical views. And these, of course, are just what newspapers, radio, television and the internet do; they potentially put into the public arena all sorts of different opinions and bodies of information.

Many contemporary governments restrict the free operations of the media. For example, the Chinese government restricts access to the internet for its population and controls what can be seen on satellite television by agreement with News International (SEE: **Murdoch**). The government of Zimbabwe has closed down newspapers that have been critical of government actions. Western societies have a more remote history of similar behaviour. The free publication of books and newspapers was restricted until the nineteenth century by a mixture of direct censorship, taxation and the granting of monopoly privileges to favoured publishers (SEE: **book; print**). However, the pressures of democratization have brought greater freedom for the media in most Western societies (SEE: **public sphere**). At the same time, a growing COMMERCIALIZATION proved difficult to resist, and governments became used to encouraging the growth of business, including newspapers and eventually other forms of the media.

The result of the combination of democratic pressures and commercialization is a greater freedom from government control in the media, greater access by the public to a variety of views, a freer flow of information and an enhanced tendency for the media to investigate and challenge government. This is not to say that all is well in the relationship between governments and the media, and there is a continuing lively debate about just how much control governments should exercise. Some of this debate is about moral content. Many people feel that there is too much violence and sex, especially on television (SEE: **violence**). Governments have tried to exercise control in this area partly by forming bodies that deal with complaints and partly by making agreements with broadcasters. Again, governments try to regulate the flow of information about government activities. They actively conceal information, sometimes on the grounds of secrecy; this was an important point in the war in Iraq in 2003/4. Or they put a particular spin on news or try to work through or influence individual journalists. Most important of all, governments regulate the economic structure of the media. Through legislation they can encourage competition by, for example, controlling the degree to which media companies can acquire other companies or the degree to which there is CROSS-MEDIA OWNERSHIP between different branches of the media. On the whole, Western governments have tended in the last twenty years or so to deregulate and to permit, as a consequence, a concentration of ownership. Even if direct government control of the media in Western countries is less intrusive than it was even a century ago, many feel that it has been replaced by self-censorship and control by proprietors over content. The concentration of ownership of the media further threatens competition within the industry.

SEE ALSO: **censorship; freedom of information; lobby system.**

Gramsci, Antonio (1891–1937) An Italian political activist who was influential in the development of Marxist cultural theory. He is best known for his development of the idea of HEGEMONY, which has been utilized in radical and critical discussions of the place that media occupy in contemporary capitalist societies. From a Marxist point of view, hegemony is a concept that sought to explain how dominant groups held power, not only through their control over the economic means of production, but also by their ability to win consent from those economically dominated. Gramsci's influence in media and cultural studies came most importantly through the use of his work at the CENTRE FOR CONTEMPORARY CULTURAL STUDIES in the 1970s to inform cultural analyses of the role of the mass media in securing hegemony or ideological domination.

SEE ALSO: **ideology; Marxism.**

Granada A large UK-based media group but with significant interests in retail and football clubs and a long history of involvement in the hotel and catering industries. Granada's media interests include broadcast television, book publishing, film and television production and online products. It has also had a policy of diversifying its media presence by buying stakes in a variety of other media companies, including those involved in broadcast television overseas and in the UK and in newspaper and magazine publishing.

The origins of the company lie in the 1920s, when the brothers Bernstein started a chain of cinemas and became involved in the financing of film. In the 1950s, Granada was awarded the Independent Television franchise for the north-west region. Throughout the next decade, the company grew rapidly, but by diversifying into a range of industries including retail, motorway service stations and book publishing. In the 1990s, the group disposed of some of its hotel business and acquired more television broadcasting capacity. In the late 1990s and early 2000s Granada began to concentrate on the media and separated off its catering and hotel interests into a separate company. By 2002, Granada's TV broadcasting reached almost half of the UK population. In 2003, Granada merged with CARLTON to form ITV plc. Granada has produced some very well-known television including *Coronation Street*.

SEE ALSO: **Independent Television**.

graphical user interface (GUI) A piece of software that makes the operating system of a computer more intuitively usable by the use of pictures, e.g. icons for files. Designed in the early 1970s, but only emerging commercially with Apple computers some ten years later, GUIs were intended to make it possible for computers to be used by relatively untrained people rather than skilled technicians. They were therefore part of the move to make computers more interactive with their human users (SEE: **human–computer interaction**). GUIs, the best-known of which is Microsoft's Windows, now employ a standard set of conventions including windows, drop-down menus, icons and mouse pointing and clicking.

graphic novel Developed from comic books, the graphic novel uses themes and heroes from the comic books, especially in the USA and Japan, to reinvent and extend the more 'adult' themes that can be drawn from the comic-book tradition. One of the most influential graphic novels was Frank Millar's *Batman: The Dark Knight Returns* (2002, originally published 1986), which is credited with reinventing the Batman character and was then an input to the Batman cycle of films.

grazing In many countries, network broadcasting in television has been supplanted by cable and satellite broadcasting, greatly increasing the number of channels available. As a result, viewers have an ever-greater capacity to graze – to move restlessly between a large number of channels.

SEE ALSO: **audience; channel loyalty; gaze; zapping**.

grip In film-making the person responsible for movement of equipment that is related to the cameras, such as a DOLLY.

Grossberg, Lawrence (Larry) (b. 1947) Morris Davis Professor of

Communication Studies at the University of North Carolina, Chapel Hill. He has been one of the prime movers in the internationalization of CULTURAL STUDIES since the 1980s and has played a central role in the expansion of the discipline in the USA. Primarily a cultural theorist, he has used cultural studies positions to reinterrogate some key questions of philosophy. For example, he has sought to show how audiences become attached to particular texts through discussion of the idea of affect. Other most important writings for media studies have concerned the nature of rock music and how it has become part of a conservative culture, in books like *We Gotta Get Out of This Place* (1992). He has thus sought to show how rock music has been moved from a position where it could articulate critical responses to dominant powers to a place as part of the status quo.

SEE ALSO: **Centre for Contemporary Cultural Studies**.

gutter The space between columns of text on a printed page.

Habermas, Jürgen (b. 1929) Habermas is one of the principal exponents of CRITICAL THEORY and his main contribution to media studies lies in his analysis of the conditions of viable and rational COMMUNICATION and his formulation of the concept of the PUBLIC SPHERE. The main theme of Habermas' theory is that valid knowledge can only emerge from a situation of open, free and uninterrupted dialogue. The ideal society permits unconstrained communication and encourages free public debate. In *The Structural Transformation of the Public Sphere* (1989), he described the evolution of the public sphere in eighteenth-century Europe, in which public debate was possible, and charted its decline during the following centuries.

habitus An idea developed by the French sociologist PIERRE BOURDIEU (1930–2002) which refers to the way in which social groups classify the world. Rather than suggesting that particular groups have an IDEOLOGY, Bourdieu maintains that groups have habituated ways of classifying, seeing or engaging with the world. Groups inhabit particular cultures or ways of life. Thus, we will develop habitual ways of behaving that we often do not question because we have grown up with them. We may accept as normal some of the habits of everyday action and speech without realizing that others think of them in quite different ways. For example, the names given to mealtimes will vary by background and locality in different parts of Britain. The middle classes may refer to the midday meal as lunch whereas it will be referred to as dinner by the working classes, dinner being the evening meal for the middle classes, and so on. Likewise, eating habits vary across the world. For example, tourists from Northern Europe often comment that people in Spain eat much later than they do and this often catches out the unaware holiday-maker, especially at the start of the holiday. This idea can be used with respect to the study of media audiences, where the way in which particular sections of the audience respond, for example, to television can be seen to be related to their habitus. In this sense preference for types of programmes can be deep-seated and related to background, as can ways in which television is watched. The very location of televisions in rooms and the way that they fit into the décor of a house is related to background and thus to habitus.

SEE ALSO: **competence; cultural capital; field**.

hacker A person, often very skilled in computer programming, who gains, or attempts to gain, unauthorized access to a computer network. Motives for hacking may vary. Some, 'black hat' hackers, have a criminal or purely desctructive intent. Others, 'white hat' hackers, may be motivated by a cause of some kind.

Hall, Stuart (b. 1932) Jamaican-born intellectual and left-wing political activist who has been a crucial figure in the development of cultural and media studies. He spent a key period as director of the CENTRE FOR CONTEMPORARY CULTURAL STUDIES at the University of Birmingham before taking up the Chair of Sociology at the Open University in the UK. Hall had an early interest in popular culture and media and published on this topic in *The Popular Arts* (Hall and Whannel, 1964). He then wrote a number of papers on media topics. In particular he developed the influential idea of encoding and decoding. Through this idea, Hall criticizes models of media production and consumption that argue for too direct a causal linkage between what producers put into the media and what the audience derive from it. He suggests that the complex patterns of media production need to be understood in the context of capitalist production and exploitation. He argues that the resulting texts are complex phenomena that can be understood or decoded by audiences in different ways. Thus, while texts encode a range of DISCOURSES and have an IDEOLOGICAL function, they are not completely CLOSED. A text may have a preferred meaning, but other readings can be made of it. This idea that texts can be read within dominant, negotiated or oppositional modes became very influential in studies of the media audience. Thus, while Hall wrote from a Marxist point of view, which argued that the media would ultimately contribute to HEGEMONY, in that they are part of the ongoing reproduction of a society based on class domination and inequality, he also contributed to opening the way for further research on how the media so operated. He contributed significantly to a range of collectively authored books from the CCCS including *Resistance Through Rituals* (1976) and *Policing the Crisis* (1978), which explored these themes and many others. His work has therefore focused on the interrelations between ideology, culture, media, identity and politics and has been hugely influential.

Haraway, Donna (b. 1944) Professor of the History of Consciousness and

Women's Studies at the University of California, Santa Cruz. She has been one of the most important theorists of the idea of the cyborg (Haraway, 1991), which has been a key concept in literary and social debate about the intersection between human beings, animals and new technologies (e.g. Haraway, 1989). This has facilitated the posing of questions about the nature of what it is to be human and how human beings and technologies interconnect in complex ways. This has been particularly significant in the context of the development of computer technologies, and consideration of how access to the internet enables individuals to construct new identities. Thus, in William Gibson's classic cyberpunk novel *Neuromancer* (1984), the hero plugs himself into cyberspace, though which he can then travel. In important respects he is both human and machine. While this is science fiction, it has influenced the way in which the interface between identity, the body and technology can be rethought.

SEE ALSO: **feminism; gender; technology**.

hard news News which is thought to be reliable and accurate rather than speculative. The term is also used for news which involves topics of public interest rather than those concerned with human interest.

hard sell Advertising which is based on factual information about the product – how it works, what distinguishes it from other products, or its price, for instance. The contrast is with soft sell, which depends on an association of the product with feelings or lifestyle. Hard-sell techniques tend to be used for technical products such as cars or computers, while soft sell is deemed to be more appropriate for such products as cosmetics and drinks.

Hartley, John (b. 1948) Professor and Dean of Faculty of Creative Industries at the Queensland University of Technology, Brisbane, Australia. He has been an important figure in the growth of media and cultural studies, particularly in setting much of the ground for the cultural analysis of television texts and aspects of their contexts in books like *Reading Television* (Fiske and Hartley, 1978).

SEE ALSO: **Fiske**.

Hays Code The common name for the Motion Picture Production Code initially developed by William H. Hays to regulate the content of movies in the USA. Hays was Head of the Motion Pictures Producers and Distributors Association (which later became the Motion Picture Association of America). This organization had been set up by the movie industry in 1922 to self-regulate the content of movies, as the industry was concerned about the effect of several scandals on its business. The formal code was adopted in 1930, after the attempts to work by less formal means had floundered. Despite this formalization of the code, movies in the early 1930s did not seem much affected, so the code was revised in 1934. This led to the establishment of the Production Code Administration under the leadership of Joseph Breen. This then effectively classified and regulated the use of language and the representation of sex and violence in American movies until the 1950s. The code therefore operated across a range of representation to try to ensure that movies promoted moral conduct by controlling what words could be used and what acts could be depicted. Wrongdoing could not be condoned, sexual activity and violence only depicted in controlled ways and swearing and bad language not permitted. During the 1960s the code came increasingly under pressure and it was eventually abandoned in 1968, when it was replaced by a rating system for movies.

SEE ALSO: **British Board of Film Classification; censorship**.

HCI See: HUMAN-COMPUTER INTERACTION.

HDTV See: HIGH DEFINITION TELEVISION.

heads Shortened term for headlines in radio news. They contain summaries of the news stories that are deemed to be the most important of the day.

Hearst, Randolph (1863–1951) The American MEDIA MOGUL Randolph Hearst is usually credited with inventing tabloid journalism – sensational content, big headlines and lavish photography. He is often thought to be the model for the eponymous character of Orson Welles' *Citizen Kane* (1941). Hearst built up a large media empire including not only newspapers, but also radio stations, magazines and film studios.

hegemony Concept associated with the Italian Marxist political activist and theorist ANTONIO GRAMSCI which describes how domination of one group over another is produced politically and ideologically. Gramsci was concerned to explore the relationship between the coercive and cultural aspects of class domination and class rule in unequal capitalist societies. He thought that those in the working class gave their consent (and that they were not simply coerced by the dominant class) to class rule and wanted to explain why this was the case. He argued that culture is thus class-based and class-dominated and that a hegemony of shared values would operate in the favour of dominant groups. However, he also thought that hegemony was a process in the sense that it did not just happen but was produced through the relationships and struggles between different groups. There would be a role for certain institutions and groups in the production of hegemonic domination, but such groups, and the messages that they produced, would also be subject to contestation. For example, Marxists have argued that the media in capitalist societies act to produce hegemony for the dominant class. They do this by encouraging people in capitalist societies to think in similar ways and to offer narrow explanations for social and political phenomena. However, if hegemony has some degree of contingency, it must also be the case that there is some resistance or dissent from these messages. Hence, the audience for the media may, on the one hand, be seen as incorporated into a hegemony by the media or, on the other, resistant to it. Much research on the media audience has actually suggested that the reality lies between these two poles.

SEE ALSO: **Centre for Contemporary Cultural Studies; ideology.**

hermeneutic code See: ENIGMA CODE.

hermeneutics An approach to the interpretation of texts that has also been applied to the analysis of meaningful human action. It originated in debate about conflicting interpretations of the Bible among European scholars and was subsequently developed in Germany as a more general approach to the interpretation of texts and social life that emphasized the role of understanding and empathy, rather than the explanation of how social and cultural phenomena are caused by structural forces. A particular text is understood in the context of its times. For example, to understand a particular television police series of the 1970s such as *The Sweeney*, it would be necessary to consider it in the then current context of ideas about policing, how law and order was under threat, debates about corruption in the Metropolitan Police and so on. The text is understood in its context. This process of interpretation is called the hermeneutic circle. The process of interpretation also entails the interpreter seeking to put him- or herself in the position of the person whose actions they are trying to interpret. Thus, while it is possible to see *The Sweeney* as out of date and sexist, it should first be seen as meaningful in its context. Hermeneutics has been criticized as not being able finally to judge why one interpretation of a text is better than another.

SEE ALSO: **semiology.**

hero The plots of works of fiction usually have central characters around whom the plot is organized. Heroes are central characters of a particular kind for they are transformative – they are instrumental in changing things. Heroes are most common in popular genres – detective stories, science fiction or fantasy – and their activity is commonly contrasted with the inactivity of those around them. Science-fiction heroes therefore operate in rigid or repressive societies and detectives are often pitted against a bureaucratic police force. Heroes celebrate the virtues of the individual in societies of sullen conformists.

SEE ALSO: **individualization**.

hidden agenda People or organizations are said to have a hidden agenda when what they really want is hidden beneath what they actually say. Government briefings of the media are often accused of having a hidden agenda.

SEE ALSO: **bias; objectivity; spin**.

highbrow A term applied to people, judgements or cultural products. To call something highbrow is to imply that it is based on a restricted and elite taste, which depends on an advanced education and usually a particular social background.

SEE ALSO: **cultural capital; high culture**.

high culture Those works or artistic practices that are seen to have greatest worth or most sophistication. High culture is most often contrasted with mass or POPULAR CULTURE. It claims to be an authoritative statement of what is valuable and good in artistic, educational and cultural artefacts and experiences. Popular culture, on the other hand, is seen as vulgar, undemanding and commodified. High culture involves an analytical, disciplined and educated attitude to culture. Cultural appropriation is a serious matter requiring hard work. Furthermore, high culture is authorial. The text or artefact is produced by an individual artist by means of the exercise of his or her personal creative talents. Lastly, high culture stresses AUTHENTICITY – the representation of the real and meaningful experiences of human beings in culture or education as distinct from the mass-produced or commercial. So, on this view high culture is Beethoven; popular culture is represented by boy bands. High culture is James Joyce; popular culture is Jilly Cooper.

It is not at all clear that these contrasts are sustainable; popular culture has always had some of the characteristics of high culture. A good deal of the contrast is rather more an attempt to maintain distinction; high culture is an elite taste. Furthermore, in the late twentieth and early twenty-first centuries, the two categories have been even less distinct. High culture and popular culture borrow from each other, and audiences are more likely to sample from both (SEE: **omnivore**).

high definition television (HDTV) A method of transmitting television signals that gives higher resolution and a different ASPECT RATIO from those currently widely used. HDTV is digital and hence, in Europe at least, its introduction has been associated with DIGITAL BROADCASTING and the switching off of ANALOGUE signals.

Hoggart, Richard (b. 1918) Writer, teacher and administrator who has played an important role in the development of cultural studies. Hoggart's influence came in two major ways: first as author of the ground-breaking book *The Uses of Literacy* (1957); and second as the founder and first director of the CENTRE FOR CONTEMPORARY CULTURAL STUDIES at the University of Birmingham. *The Uses of Literacy* characterizes the component parts of the working-class culture of the type that Hoggart grew up in Leeds in Northern England. He shows a fine appreciation of the nuances of such a culture and analyses it with the tools of a sophisticated literary critic. His book is also a lament for the passing of this culture as it was replaced by a more glossy, commercialized culture of consumerism and celebrity. His work is therefore analytical, descriptive and critical. While the grounds of his critique have caused much debate, there is no doubt of the power of his analysis, which was a founding moment in the realization that popular culture and popular media were appropriate objects for detailed analysis. These were ideas that Hoggart fed into the initial direction of the Birmingham Centre, even if he would not have shared the turn that it later took towards Marxism.

SEE ALSO: **Raymond Williams**.

Hollywood The physical location of the US film industry (in Hollywood, Los Angeles, California) and a description of a type of film, film-making and studio system. Hollywood rose to dominance as the centre of the American film industry from the early twentieth century. For example, Universal City, the first true industrialized studio, was opened in Hollywood in 1915. It rapidly moved to global significance. This raised continuing fears of the way in which American products would marginalize and influence indigenous film (and subsequently television) in other parts of the world. Hollywood rapidly became the centre of a commercial and mass-market-oriented film-making system that created the STAR SYSTEM and the integrated studio system of production, DISTRIBUTION and EXHIBITION.

The key period of consolidation of the classic Hollywood era was in the 1930s and 1940s. During this period, the Hollywood (American) film industry was controlled and dominated by eight companies. There were five large companies that were vertically integrated (they produced films in studios, owned distribution companies and controlled the film theatres where the films were shown). The big five companies were MGM

(Metro-Goldwyn-Mayer), Paramount, RKO Radio Pictures, 20th Century Fox and Warner Bros. The so called 'Little Three' were Columbia, United Artists and Universal. The 'Little Three' companies were not vertically integrated and were therefore less powerful, but could show their films in the film theatres owned by the big five and therefore had access to audiences and prestige through this route. While the big five only owned a minority of the film theatres they were the most important as they were the so-called 'first run' theatres, where the new and therefore most profitable films would be first shown. This system of vertical integration was sustained through the 1930s and 1940s, but came under attack by the end of the 1940s, especially in 1948 by an anti-trust decision that led over a period of time to the studios having to divest themselves of theatre exhibition. While the companies fought this decision it was a key moment of change for Hollywood, which was also coming under pressure from the advent of television.

The studios had evolved a highly industrialized mode of film production. They produced large numbers of films as if from a conveyor belt. In such situations the companies are involved in satisfying demand from the audience, but also wish to make that audience demand predictable, so that products do not fail in the marketplace. There are two key aspects in this Hollywood process, which also apply to other sectors of the CREATIVE INDUSTRIES: the star system and the construction and reconstruction of GENRES. Stars were on contract to studios, which could thus promote films through their presence. It was hoped that the audience would want to see the latest film starring, for example, James Cagney, irrespective of genre. However, genre was also very important. This was a way of standardizing production. For example, similar sets and locations could be used for many western films, writers had a clear idea of what was needed in a western, and so on. It was also a way of standardizing audience expectations and of predicting where demand would be, if the audience attendance figures for various genres were relatively stable. While this can suggest that such companies were able to control the marketplace completely, they were in competition with each other, which led to the studios having their own strengths and styles and to their promoting innovation both technically (for example in sound and colour) and in terms of genre.

This system was dominant between the 1930s and the 1950s, when it began to decline in the face of the rising popularity of television (itself having a significant Hollywood presence). Despite this, Hollywood has remained as the centre of US global dominance of film-making. While the integrated studio system declined, the mode of film-making developed in Hollywood had set the parameters for the understanding of popular film-making. The significance of popular narratives with stars has become, if anything, more significant, and the Hollywood star remains at the top of the global star system. For example, an appearance at the Oscar ceremony is regarded as the pinnacle of achievement for film stars, and the award for best picture is still of great significance.

SEE ALSO: **celebrity; Disney; globalization**.

home cinema Technological developments have made it possible to create cinema-like effects in the home by the greater precision of image and surround-sound.

homology The manner in which apparently different phenomena are structurally similar (SEE: **structuralism**). The concept was much used in studies of YOUTH CULTURE from the Birmingham CENTRE FOR CONTEMPORARY CULTURAL STUDIES, where the different (and perhaps on the face of it contingent) aspects of a subculture were seen to be homologously related in that they had structural similarities. For example, in Willis' (1978) study of motor-bike boys, there is argued to be a homology between the exhilaration of riding a fast motor cycle and listening to aggressive rock and roll music. In punk subculture there would be a homology between the fast aggressive music and the effects of drugs that also 'speeded' up human action.

hooks, bell (b. 1952) A black American feminist author (born as Gloria Watkins), currently Distinguished Professor of English at City College in New York, who has contributed much to discussions of race, culture, gender and identity. She has demonstrated the complexity of identities in ways that show the power of cultural theory and cultural studies to address the dynamics of cultural change and processes of racism and gender exploitation. This can be significant, for example, in studying how the media represent such issues. Her many books include *Ain't I a Woman* (1983), *Black Looks* (1992) and *Reel to Real* (1996).

horizontal integration A method by which a company may enlarge its business by buying another company which is in the same field or at the same level in the SUPPLY CHAIN. In the media industries there is a powerful incentive to do this to capitalize on ECONOMIES OF SCALE (SEE: **economics of the media**) and to create a larger public and marketing presence.

SEE ALSO: **concentration of ownership; diagonal integration; vertical integration**.

horror One of the most popular GENRES of film and novels, though often subject to some critical disdain. As with other genres, there are variations in the types of horror, though the presence of some kind of 'monster' is crucial. The monster may be an alien or it may be a human serial killer, but in some sense it is outside 'normal' humanity. It may be that the monster has been created by human beings and then moves outside their control. This key theme was introduced most successfully and enduringly by Mary Shelley in her novel *Frankenstein* (1985, published 1818), which also addresses the issue, which has also run through the genre subsequently, of the problems that can be caused for human society by the development of technology. The popularity of the genre and its many subgenres has attracted academic attention, not least because it seems relevant to ask why it is that we enjoy being frightened. Answers often go in the same direction as the explanations for the popularity of other genres. Thus, some writers take a psychological or psychoanalytical stance, which may or may not place emphasis on the gendered nature of the victim and hero in the horror genre. In these accounts the pleasures of the horror film relate to the way in which it dramatizes the psychological processes of human development and gendered sexual relationships. Others adopt a more sociological view in which the fears addressed in the genre mirror the fears present in a society at any particular moment. For example, it has been suggested that the horror films of the 1950s in the USA were informed by the Cold War and the fear of the USSR and communism. Similarly, the later slasher movies, where women are under threat, have been seen as a response to the development of second-wave feminism from the 1960s onwards. As some writers have argued with respect to FILM NOIR, the 'problems' caused by the advance of women in society in the demands for equal economic and political treatment are dramatized in narratives that place women at risk. The films of Alfred Hitchcock have provided a fertile ground for critical analysis of how gender issues are addressed in the genre, especially in films like *Psycho* (1960) and *The Birds* (1963).

There have been textual analyses of the genre that are based on STRUCTURALIST principles. Thus, Tudor (1989) has examined horror in terms of BINARY OPPOSITIONS such as the secular and the supernatural, the known and the unknown and so on. He argues that there are three main narratives of the horror film based on how these oppositions work in different ways: knowledge, invasion and metamorphosis. In the earlier horror films, order is restored by the invention of humans and science, but in the films from the 1960s onwards, this becomes more problematic, and it is more difficult to return to the initial stability. Thus, in the *Aliens* series, Ripley is engaged in an ongoing struggle against the alien monsters.

SEE ALSO: **gender; western.**

hot media The distinction between hot and cold media was invented by MARSHALL MCLUHAN in his classic book (with Q. Fiore) *The Medium Is the Massage* (1967). Examples of hot media are radio, film, print and photographs; cold media include television, the telephone, speech and cartoons. The basis for the distinction is that hot media provide much more information and are, in that sense, much more intense uses of a single sense. McLuhan argued that cold media encourage participation, because the hearer or viewer has to fill in so much round the message itself. Hot media, on the other hand, give much less to do. He further suggested that the character of the medium as hot or cold has profound social effects. For example, the invention of print as a hot medium, in his view, led to the religious wars of the sixteenth century. McLuhan's TECHNO-LOGICAL DETERMINISM looks very odd now in that it represents a greatly over-simplified model of social change. So also does his hot and cold distinction. For example, current work would suggest that film is a high-involvement medium while television does not encourage participation (SEE: **regimes of watching**).

SEE ALSO: **The Medium is the Message**.

hot metal A method of printing using cast metal lines of type. Until the nineteenth century, printing depended essentially on the insertion of individual letters cast in metal which in a frame. With the invention of the LINOTYPE machine, it became possible to set entire lines of text in metal. This was done by creating a mould into which molten metal was injected. Because hot metal was present, printing was a fairly dangerous industry.

SEE ALSO: **print**.

household Many media of communication, film, for example, and even newspapers and magazines, are accessed in public contexts (SEE: **public sphere**). Television, however, is very much a private domestic medium; overwhelmingly it is watched at home by households and families. This domesticity is reflected in the content of television. Thus, viewers are treated, by newsreaders for example, as if they are participants in a domestic conversation (SEE: **directness of address**). A great deal of television is actually conversation. Many news, documentary and arts programmes, for example, consist of simulated conversations around a table. Other kinds of programmes like soap opera and situation comedy are about domestic situations, and their action largely consists in conversation. Further, the way that programmes are organized assumes the domesticity of television – and particular household arrangements. Television schedules (SEE: **scheduling**) are constructed around the constraints of the household

– mealtimes, bedtimes, the time when children come home from school and so on.

If households organize television, television also organizes households. Particular television programmes will act as fixed points and, despite the potential of the video-recorder, mealtimes, bedtimes and other appointments will be set around them. One study (Bryce, 1987) found differences between households in the way that they integrated television into daily life. One type plans television watching around other activities but, when the set is on, the family is expected to give its full attention to it. In the other type, all activities are organized around the television, which acts as a kind of clock, but members of the household do not give it much attention.

The television set plays a role in domestic relations of power. For example, there is often a process of negotiation over the use of the set. Most studies (e.g. Morley, 1986) show that, when families watch together, the men control what is watched and when and what will be recorded and played back. Children are the next most influential and women the least of all.

New technologies are widening the possibilities of leisure in the household. For example, the quality of film projection will be improved by home cinema equipment and popular music, television and the internet will be brought closer together (SEE: **media convergence**). An increasingly important question, therefore, concerns the ecology of the household – how members interact with each other in relation to different devices within the spaces provided.

SEE ALSO: **everyday life; privatization of leisure; public sphere; regimes of watching; television talk**.

HTML (Hypertext Markup Language) The programming language used to set up web pages. Web browsers, such as Safari, Firefox or Internet Explorer, interpret HTML so that web pages appear on screen as properly constructed pages of text and image.

human–computer interaction (HCI) A whole field of study has grown up which investigates the way that humans and computers interact. In the early stages, getting a computer to do what you wanted it to do was a clumsy, complex and technical matter, and specialized technicians had to do it. With the reduction in size of computers, better software and the production of input devices like keyboards and mice, the operation of a computer became a much less specialized matter. The development of GRAPHICAL USER INTERFACES further enhanced the ease of operation. These are all essentially measures which make it easier to control a computer. VIRTUAL REALITY systems represent an extension of these features in that there is a much closer and smoother relationship between computer and human. Further developments will embed computer devices more extensively in everyday life – from pieces of domestic equipment to the human body itself.

human interest A staple story of television magazine programmes, newspapers and magazines which seeks to capture some quasi-universal aspect of the human condition through an individual or group experience with which an audience may connect in a humorous fashion. The human interest story is often used to produce some 'light relief' at the end of television news programmes. There has been relatively little analysis of the human interest story, but its role in the ideological functioning of the British early-evening magazine show *Nationwide* was analysed by Charlotte Brunsdon and David Morley (1978). They argued that part of the significance of the human-interest story in a programme like *Nationwide* was to show how despite the diverse and fractured nature of British society, there is an essential human level on which we are all engaged and which thus represents our common humanity. In ideological terms, for such quasi-Marxist writers as these, this obscures the differences in wealth and status in a society such as Britain.

SEE ALSO: **news.**

Human Rights Act 1998 This piece of legislation arose out of giving legislative force to the European Convention on Human Rights. The Convention, and the Act which came into force in 2000, provide for a right to PRIVACY amongst other human rights. It is still very unclear how the courts will interpret the right to privacy. A number of celebrities have gone to court, without appealing to the PRESS COMPLAINTS COMMISSION first, claiming infringement of their rights to privacy when newspapers take intimate photographs of them or publish stories about their private life. The difficulty is that, however much people may disapprove of the actions of the newspapers from time to time, a full-blooded right to privacy could seriously damage investigative journalism.

hybridization The process by which different cultures, or aspects of different cultures, come together to form new combinations or hybrids. It is often argued that the process of GLOBALIZATION has led to the production of an increased number of hybrids. For example, it is noted how forms of indigenous music are affected by their contact with other forms, leading to new forms of music which combine different aspects of the two. Thus, the development of rock and roll music in the south of the

USA can be seen as a process of hybridization in which country music and the blues were brought together, especially in the work of Elvis Presley, to make a new and distinct type. Another example would be the way in which Bhangra music from India has developed in new ways through its contact with, for example, disco in the UK.

hyperreality A term developed independently by writers such as Umberto Eco and JEAN BAUDRILLARD to capture the way in which representations in contemporary cultures are becoming more real than the reality they depict. These hyperreal representations may be SIMULACRA in the sense that what they depict may never have existed. For example, our notion of the reality of small-town USA may be derived more from the idealized versions represented in DISNEY theme parks than the actual towns themselves. For writers such as Baudrillard, hyperreality has effectively usurped reality entirely, so there is in a sense no reality beyond that created in media images and simulations.

SEE ALSO: **simulational culture**.

hypodermic needle model In popular discussion, the media are often said to have direct EFFECTS on people, causing them to act in certain ways. Violent films, for example, are claimed to cause viewers to act violently, almost as if the media message of violence was injected directly (by hypodermic needle) into the minds of the audience. The idea has also been used by some commentators in discussion of the way in which some people may be affected by the lyrics of rock music to commit crimes of violence and self-harm. Such a view is now much contested by more sophisticated understandings of the interconnections between texts and audiences.

SEE ALSO: **audience**.

hypothesis A proposition or propositions put forward for empirical testing. The term is also used more loosely to mean suggestion, explanation or theory. A common view of theory construction and explanation in the natural sciences runs as follows. Scientists think up a theory which might explain certain phenomena. They then deduce logically from that theory certain more specific propositions – hypotheses – which take the form of predictions about what will actually be found in nature. These hypotheses are then subjected to empirical tests in the laboratory. The predictions will either be true or false. If false, the theory is said to be disconfirmed. If true, it is confirmed, although always liable to be disproved in further laboratory tests. In practice, such a rigorous method is not often adhered to in the natural sciences. It is difficult to employ in media studies, and other social sciences, because laboratory conditions are not commonly attainable and the social world is too complex. As a result hypothesis testing in these subjects typically takes a different and less rigorous form.

SEE ALSO: **qualitative research; quantitative research**.

iconography An icon is a SIGN that works through a mechanism of resemblance to its REFERENT. Iconography is concerned with the sets of signs that have a familiar set of resemblances within a particular type of media. Thus, the iconography of the WESTERN might involve large hats, spurs, pistols and rifles. These are the familiar signs of the GENRE, which do actually appear in the films. It is important to recognize that iconography can change. Thus, for instance, long 'duster' coats became part of the iconography of the western from the 1960s onwards, but had not been there previously.

SEE ALSO: **semiology; structuralism.**

ICT (information and communication technology) The computer-based technology that has enabled the rapid, efficient and accurate processing of information and the communication of text, audio, graphics and video material.

SEE ALSO: **new media.**

identification The process through which audience members identify with media texts or STARS. The idea has been most used in the study of cinema and film, where it was derived from psychoanalysis and Marxist theories of IDEOLOGY. In the former, identification tends to refer to the way in which the individual is constituted as a knowing being, who has a sense of themselves as a distinct person. In the latter, the emphasis is placed on the way in which subjectivity is partly constructed through media identification to produce subjects who are constrained by the operation of ideology and power. Thus, who we are is affected by what we watch and listen to, and we are made in this way to suit dominant interests. This process has been more often theorized than investigated empirically. There are exceptions. Stacey (1994), for example, shows that identification occurs both when a film is being watched in the cinema and outside it. Thus, when we are watching a film we may identify with the actions of the hero and feel that we are engaged in the action from the point of view of, for example, Ripley in the *Aliens* series. We may also identify outside the film by copying the hairstyle Ripley has or mimicking her mode of dress. This shows that films (and other media texts) contribute both to who we are, but also to how we fit into a system of gendered power, in this case through the position of an active woman.

SEE ALSO: **male gaze.**

identity The sense of self and the process of definition of that sense. Numerous disciplines and thinkers have sought to explain how our identities are constituted through a range of psychological, cultural and social processes. It is often argued that identity is something that is subject to historical change. For example, the idea that we each have our own individual identity is a product of the development of modern societies, which have been centrally based around the idea of the individual. Such societies, as they develop, then produce relatively stable identities based around, for example, the experience of the family or work. Some writers have suggested that contemporary identities are now much more fluid and subject to a range of influences in their construction (Hall, 1992). It has become much more common to argue that media play some (and perhaps an increasing) role in such processes. This process has been explored with particular respect to young people and a range of media and cultural activities in the work of Willis et al. (1990), who concentrate on the role of popular music and television in the lives of young people. In addition, some writers on popular music suggest that music plays an important part in the constitution of identity as it both engages imagination and affects how we move our bodies (Frith, 1996). Such ideas have also been explored with respect to visual media such as film and television, where texts may provide resources for how we think about ourselves. For example, an individual may define him/herself as a *Doctor Who* fan.

idents Mechanism for identifying a radio station so that the listener is aware what station he or she is listening to. Presenters state the name of the station for this reason.

ideological state apparatuses A mechanism by which states ensure the compliance of their populations. According to the Marxist writer LOUIS ALTHUSSER the state operates through repression, or the repressive state apparatus, and IDEOLOGY, or the ideological state apparatuses. For Althusser, the media are one of the ideological state apparatuses as they perform a key way in constructing forms of subjectivity that reinforce social (and especially class) domination.

SEE ALSO: **Marxism.**

ideology While it has earlier beginnings, the concept of ideology has been most developed in the work of Marx and subsequent MARXISM. It is possible to distinguish two broad strands in the conceptualization of ideology. First, ideology understood as the ideas that are linked to one particular social group; and second, ideology as referring in some sense to ideas that are false or illusory. With respect to the first account, ideology may be linked directly to a particular social group, such as the dominant class or the working class. Alternatively, the ideas of the dominant group overpower those of others due to the control by the dominant group of the means of communication of ideas. This is one of the ways in which ideology has been considered in media studies. For some Marxist commentators, the media, due to the fact that they are in some sense controlled by the dominant class, put out messages that are broadly in the interests of that class. There are some influential analyses of television news that argue along such lines (e.g. GLASGOW UNIVERSITY MEDIA GROUP, 1976, 1980). With respect to the second sort of account, which holds that ideologies contain illusory ideas or induce false ideas or false consciousness in those who are the target of the ideas, there is also a role for the media. Some Marxist analysts have argued that people are in thrall to false ideas pumped out by the media or, perhaps, the very way that they think is structured by the particular content of television programmes. Some of the work of the Marxist critic T. W. ADORNO on popular music adopts such a position. For him, the standardized products of the popular music industry divert the masses from the real pleasures of non-commodified music that might inspire critical reflection on society.

SEE ALSO: **critical theory; dominant ideology; Frankfurt School; rhetoric.**

idiographic Methods of study of individual, unique persons, events or phenomena. These methods do not attempt to find or describe general laws.

image 1 What appears in the photograph or on the screen in front of us. Much of the work of media studies is concerned with the analysis of images. Semiotics and SEMIOLOGY are probably the most popular.

2 Term used to refer to the representation constructed of the STAR. An issue here is the extent to which the image (which may be an important way in which the BRAND of the star is constituted) is separated from the real personality of the star. Within the STAR SYSTEM part of the desire of the fan is to explore this relationship to come to better knowledge of the real personality and the real person. It has been suggested that this is an important part of the appeal of reality TV programmes and perhaps especially those that are based on the activities of a group of celebrities.

SEE ALSO: **cinema; photography.**

image system When a number of images are connected to produce a coherent grouping or network. This may be true of textual images or the images of stardom. Thus, in a STAR TEXT, a range of different images of the star that are related (and thus systemic) are brought together to construct a NARRATIVE of development over a period of time. For example, Madonna's star text has developed over the years to include her flirtation with pornographic forms of representation and her 'maturity' into a middle-aged mother, resident in England.

imaginary In psychoanalysis, a phase or aspect of the process of development of human personality. In general theoretical terms, this idea has been much used in film studies in ways derived from psychoanalysis and Marxist theory to examine how spectators are constituted by film texts. It has also been used to examine how individual subjects are constructed through imaginary relationships to their real existence. Crudely, I may imagine that I am a free individual actor, but in reality my life is subject to massive constraints put on me by others in society. It is sometimes thought that media play a key role in such processes, as they provide the resources for such imagined connections.

SEE ALSO: **Althusser; identity; ideology**.

imagined community In the social sciences, community is a rather loosely used term which indicates a group of people who have something in common with each other which in turn distinguishes them from other groups. There is a shared experience giving a sense of belonging. Imagined community is a term coined by BENEDICT ANDERSON (1991) to refer to a community whose members cannot know each other but who nevertheless have a collective sense of belonging largely created in the imaginations of the participants. An important example is the nation. The media (newspapers in Anderson's historical analysis) play a critical role in the formation of the imagined community of the nation by promoting and assuming the idea of nationhood. It has also been suggested that music can play a role in producing an imagined community of people who feel close to each other on the basis of their shared appreciation for an artist or genre of music. These ideas were prevalent with respect to the role of rock music in the constitution of imagined links between members of the counter culture of the 1960s. It is thought by some that artists such as Bruce Springsteen still possess aspects of such power. It is also used with respect to genres such as hip-hop.

SEE ALSO: **audience; habitus; virtual community**.

IMAX A system of WIDESCREEN screen projection, which has been installed in specially built cinemas. It produces a three-dimensional experience and, like previous innovations in widescreen technology, directs attention to visual effects rather than to NARRATIVE.

immediacy The way in which a text works on the audience in a direct fashion. It has been suggested that much contemporary cinema is concerned with immediacy in that the ACTION genre, utilizing spectacular effects, has become very popular, and the audience does not have to work hard to gain the meaning of the text. This can be contrasted with those texts that need more work on the part of the audience to uncover meaning. The implicit, and sometimes explicit, point is then often made that immediacy is something to be scorned.

SEE ALSO: **spectacle**.

impartiality A judgement or piece of reporting that is free of bias and does not take one side or another.

SEE ALSO: **bias; objectivity**.

improvisation The creative departure from a pre-existing script or pattern/score of music. With respect to the former, it is most often found in comedy, in the idea of the 'ad-lib', and with respect to the latter, in jazz. Jazz is often defined in terms of the importance of improvisation, and the talent of the jazz musician will be crucially evaluated through their ability to improvise. Some film-makers and theatre directors use improvisation in the development of their texts. An example of this is the body of work associated with Mike Leigh.

incorporation For Marxist and Marxist-influenced writers the process by which the media perform a role in the bringing of the population to believe in the DOMINANT IDEOLOGY or dominant culture of a society. Once these are incorporated, the population will not question the fundamental assumptions and nature of the culture and society.

SEE ALSO: **hegemony; ideology; Marxism**.

Independent Broadcasting Authority (IBA) The agency that replaced the Independent Television Authority. The IBA had the responsibility for providing television and radio services additional to those of the BBC and it acted as both regulator and broadcaster. The IBA had wide powers to preview programmes while also entering into contractual arrangements with independent television companies for the supply of programmes. It was replaced by the INDEPENDENT TELEVISION COMMISSION in 1991.

independent company A small commercial enterprise, privately owned, not listed on the stock exchange and independent of the dominant or major companies. In the music industry it is often thought that such companies have the capacity to produce especially innovative forms of music. There are many examples of this in popular music, such as the role of Sun Records in early rock and roll, Atlantic Records and Chess in soul and rhythm and blues, Stax in soul and Stiff in punk. However, other commentators suggest that such companies are not actually independent in any real sense as they still act as commercial enterprises. Other processes are also at work here. First, the 'independent' company can act as a talent scout for larger or major companies, who then subsequently sign an artist on a longer contract. For example, Elvis Presley initially recorded for the independent company Sun, based in Memphis, but his contract was sold after two years to the major company RCA in 1956. Second, the independent company can be taken over by a larger one, once it has proved its success in the market. Stax was taken over in this way. Third, the larger companies have now often adopted a strategy whereby they set up labels that look as if they are independent, as these are seen to be more authentic by consumers, whereas they are simply the major operating in a different way.

SEE ALSO: **conglomerate; cultural industries; music industry**.

independent production company During the late 1970s and early 1980s, a series of economic, political and legislative changes produced important changes in the media industries. Previously media organizations had been vertically integrated (SEE: **Fordism/post-Fordism**). Television organizations, the BBC for instance, kept all functions – technical, production, editing, transmission – in house. Under pressure to reduce costs, however, they started to put some of these functions out to independent companies that could do the same work more cheaply because they were specialized and did not carry the same administrative overheads. In the UK and USA these tendencies were reinforced by governments anxious to encourage competition and enterprise. Thus, CHANNEL FOUR was set up deliberately to make use of independent production companies. Subsequent legislation in the UK specified that a given proportion of programming had to be carried out by independent production companies. The result was that independent production companies (examples are Hat Trick and Lion Productions) sprang up to produce complete television programmes or series, leaving the existing large companies free to concentrate on commissioning, distribution, marketing and broadcasting. An additional advantage claimed for this OUTSOURCING is that independent production companies are able to bring a creativity and freshness lacking in large organizations, especially the BBC. Inevitably, some of these companies have grown large, and there have been mergers between them. In addition, the existing large television companies have bought into the independents. These tendencies will undermine the original intentions.

SEE ALSO: **producer choice**.

Independent Television (ITV) A term introduced in the 1950s in the UK to describe television broadcasters that were independent of the BBC and financed largely by advertising rather than by a licence fee. Such broadcasters were heavily regulated in their early days via the mechanism of the TELEVISION FRANCHISE by the INDEPENDENT BROADCASTING AUTHORITY in the content of their programming and in their ownership. This regulation has been progressively relaxed over succeeding decades. Public standards of media content have changed considerably since the 1960s, and all forms of media are freer. Since the independent commercial television sector was set up in part to offer competition for the BBC, it was felt that the sector itself needed to be competitive. Consequently, the rules on ownership of licences inhibited any one operator from owning more than one. However, these rules have been relaxed over time, and it became possible for one broadcaster to operate more than one franchise. By 2002, two companies, CARLTON and GRANADA, between them controlled television broadcasting to almost the whole of the UK population. In 2003, these two companies merged to create ITV plc.

SEE ALSO: **BBC**.

Independent Television Commission (ITC) Set up in 1991 to succeed the Independent Broadcasting Authority, the ITC acted as a regulatory body for the independent television sector in the UK. Its powers and responsibilities were transferred to OFCOM in 2003. The ITC's aim was to promote and safeguard the interests of all viewers of commercial television while fostering a competitive marketplace. It had a particular interest in regulating ownership of television companies holding licences and in setting engineering standards. The ITC Codes of Practice set out rules on taste and decency, impartiality in news and factual programming and offence and harm in advertising.

Independent Television News (ITN) Founded in 1955, ITN supplies news to INDEPENDENT TELEVISION companies, cable companies and most commercial radio stations in the UK. It also makes documentaries and operates a large archive of news footage. Originally owned by fifteen regional independent television companies, ITN is now owned by ITV PLC (with 40 per cent), Daily Mail and General Trust, United Business Media and Reuters, each with a 20 per cent shareholding.

index A SIGN that is directly related to its REFERENT, or a SIGNIFIER that is directly related to a SIGNIFIED. For example, a bell on a bicycle is an index of the bicycle. The headlights of a car are an index of the fact that a car is there at night-time.

individualization An idea common in social science is a contrast between mass society and an individualized society. In the former, society is seen as composed of people who are largely similar to each other in their conditions of life, their paths through life and their tastes and attitudes. While such societies may in fact be composed of large blocks, social classes for instance, whose members are different from one another, within each block people are similar. The contrast is with a society in which people are much more individually different. Even within a social class, individuals will have differing aspirations, tastes and attitudes and different courses through life. It is unwise to take this sort of contrast too literally. There never has been a mass society of the kind described, and a society of individuals without any degree of social aggregation is an impossibility. However, the contrast is useful in drawing attention to a change in many Western societies, including Britain, towards a more individualized composition. The growth of a consumer society has produced a greater range of tastes. Changing occupational structures have fragmented (though not obliterated) traditional social groupings including social class. Most important of all, the pattern of people's lives is more individualized. This point can be illustrated by looking at the way in which age is a less good predictor of social situation than it was. For example, those in their forties or fifties have become a more diverse group than their parents were at that age. Some will have taken early retirement, some will be retraining, some will be progressing through careers, some will be temporarily unemployed. Domestic situations will be similarly various. The traditional nuclear family is no longer the norm, and households have become increasingly diverse: single people living on their own, or as single parents; couples – both heterosexual and homosexual – cohabiting; couples who have postponed parenthood or elected not to have children; divorcees living with new partners and with second families. Similar arguments can be applied to young people.

What has this got to do with the media? Individualization of the kind described will segment or fragment the audience for the media (SEE: **market segmentation/differentiation**). No longer, for example, can television producers assume that their audiences have roughly similar tastes or, indeed, watch in similar circumstances surrounded by a family of a particular kind. Comprehensive broadcasting of the kind practised by the

BBC in the 1950s, 1960s and 1970s assumed a kind of audience which is in decline. Such tendencies also undermine the idea of public service broadcasting. Faced with such social changes, broadcasters have every incentive to avail themselves of the technical possibilities of multi-channel broadcasting. An individualized society is therefore faced by a more individualized set of channels of media communication which reflect differences in taste.

SEE ALSO: **Fordism/post-Fordism**

influence The capacity to persuade. There are those who have influence over others. Such people may be in public life or they may be members of the local community. They may be celebrities, politicians, vicars or academics or simply those who are regarded as having a knowledge of the world. Influential people of this kind are generally users of the media and they therefore act as translators or interpreters of media content for a wider audience.

SEE ALSO: **amplification of deviance; two-step flow**.

information and communication technology See: ICT.

Information Commissioner The supervisory authority which enforces the FREEDOM OF INFORMATION ACT 2000 and the Data Protection Act 1998.

information rich Contemporary advanced societies are sometimes described as being information rich in that they have increasing amounts of information available in a more accessible form for larger numbers of people than had hitherto been the case. One key cause of this situation is the effect of the world wide web and the internet, which have led to huge amounts of information being available at the press of a button. However, it must be remembered that possession of the internet is itself socially patterned – crudely richer people and those in particular occupations are more likely to have access to it – and information may be of variable quality. The richness of the information available has led some commentators to suggest that some societies have reached information overload. The problem here then becomes how one distinguishes useful information from mere 'noise'.

SEE ALSO: **digital divide**.

information society Societies whose productive capacity is based on the use of knowledge. Before the industrial revolution in Europe in the late eighteenth and early nineteenth centuries, economies were based on agri-culture and extractive industries like coal-mining. For much of the nineteenth and twentieth centuries, the economies of advanced industrial societies were based on manufacturing and, latterly, on the provision of services. These societies now, however, are increasingly dependent for their economic prosperity on the discovery of knowledge and the provision and dissemination of information. Agriculture, extraction, manufacturing and, to a lesser extent, services are increasingly carried out by less-developed economies.

infotainment Media products, especially television, that mix information and entertainment. Various methods are used from dramatic reconstructions of historical events using actors to employing a great deal of visual illustration (SEE: **docudrama**). The term is often used slightly by people who believe that the mixture of fact and fiction risks confusing viewers, misrepresenting matters of fact and lowering standards of factual journalism. The opposite point of view is that an entertaining method of presenting factual material helps the audience to grasp what is being said.

SEE ALSO: **genre**.

Innis, Harold (1894–1952) A Canadian political economist who argued that the technological nature of communication was an important determinant of the form of a society. For example, the shift from a technology of print to that of screen would be seen to have a fundamental effect on society. While Innis' own ideas have had some continued influence on the study of the media, especially from the view of political economy, he is often seen as an important influence on the far better-known MARSHALL MCLUHAN, who was also employed at the University of Toronto.

SEE ALSO: **Toronto School**.

instant messaging A method of exchanging messages over the internet in REAL TIME. The technology means that messages are more like conversations – parties almost see the words being typed – than they are like letters, which are effectively the format for emails. Instant messaging is possible over both computers and mobile devices. A large number of sites and technologies are used for instant messaging and, at present, there are no common standards. Most of these sites will allow parties to know whether particular people are online, and available, and offer facilities equivalent to a telephone messaging service. Particularly for young people, instant messaging is associated with creating and maintaining social networks, which will use a particular site (SEE: **LiveJournal**; **MySpace**).

integration The process by which people become part of a society, culture or group. It can be suggested that media sometimes perform such a function in the sense that they can bond people together, perhaps especially during points of social stress, such as wartime or during processes of relocation to new societies and cultures.

SEE ALSO: **imagined community**.

intellectual property The constitution of ideas as a form of ownable and tradeable property. Modern economies are increasingly dependent on knowledge and ideas. Value is created not so much by extraction of raw materials or agriculture, or even by the manufacture of physical objects, but by the ideas that lie behind the goods and services of modern society. This has come to include not only scientific ideas, but also such intellectual products as music, artworks, books, designs, brands or logos. Those ideas become very valuable; they become a form of property. The question then is: who owns this property and who is allowed to use it and under what conditions?

The use of intellectual property is legally regulated, usually in the form of patents, TRADEMARKS or COPYRIGHT. Inventors or others can register a novel design, device or manufacturing process and receive a patent which protects their ideas against infringement. Trademarks which cover such items as logos or brand names can similarly be registered. Copyright is more complicated. Any original work, whether it is a picture, a book or a piece of music, belongs to the originator, who only has to claim copyright to warn others not to copy it without permission. That copyright can be voluntarily given away (usually in exchange for money) or the copyright holder can license someone else to use her creation.

The whole area of intellectual property is an area of urgent and increasingly angry debate. On the one side are those who want to widen the scope of intellectual property to protect the financial investment in the production of ideas. On the other side are those who argue that knowledge should be freely available for the benefit of all humankind. This debate has been particularly fierce in such areas as pharmaceuticals. The insistence on the restricted ownership of the intellectual property in modern drugs has often meant that sufferers, particularly in the developing world, are deprived of drug treatment because they are too expensive. In the media, the copying of films on DVDs or the downloading of music from the internet have sparked similar controversy.

SEE ALSO: **brand**.

interactive media Media which permit audiences to respond directly to what they see or hear. In their origins and for quite some time, media organizations provided one-way communication. Media audiences were *addressed*, whether by film, book, radio, television or record. Although producers of the media were naturally interested in the views of audiences, for marketing purposes, if nothing else, there was a limited degree of interactivity between producer and audience. Audience members might be encouraged to fill out questionnaires or to telephone or write in, but these methods clearly do not provide genuine interaction. The DIGITAL REVOLUTION does give greater opportunities, however. INTERACTIVE TELEVISION, for example, allows much greater audience participation. Audiences can, to a greater degree, determine which parts of a record or film they watch and can manipulate images and sounds using computer technology.

SEE ALSO: **active audience**.

interactive television Television used to be thought of as a medium that made for passive viewers who simply watched what was on. Technological innovations, especially CABLE TELEVISION, have made it possible for viewers to relate interactively with television content. With a handset, viewers can answer questions posed in a programme, participate in an educational programme or choose a camera angle. As yet, the interactivity of television is not well developed but it will be possible to greatly extend its scope.

SEE ALSO: **electronic democracy; TIVO**.

International Telecommunications Union (ITU) An organization with about 190 member states, the ITU promotes the efficient operation of telecommunications globally. In particular, it is concerned to make sure that international standards are created which make possible effective communications between countries. In addition, it assists in the development of telecommunications in developing countries.

internet A method of connecting together computer networks; a network of networks. Given that the internet is now a part of the everyday life of many people in Europe and the United States (though still only around 3 per cent of the world's population), it is sometimes difficult to remember how recent a phenomenon it is. The first graphically based internet browser, Mosaic, only became available in 1994. Since then, usage has grown rapidly. In 1995, there were perhaps about 100,000 users of the internet worldwide. By 2001, there were almost 500 million.

The internet permits EMAIL, CHAT ROOMS, BULLETIN BOARDS and the WORLD WIDE WEB. On the face of it, it encourages limitless possibilities of communication with friends and strangers and gathering of information and opinion of all kinds. At the same time, it is feared, because people will become addicted or because it allows governments to monitor the activities of their citizens. This contrast between optimistic and pessimistic views is actually characteristic of the introduction of any new technology. Television, for example, is still in the grip of a similar debate, some fifty years after its introduction (SEE: **moral panic**). Unfortunately, although there is a mountain of speculation about the internet, there is little serious research which might help us to arrive at sound conclusions.

There are a number of questions which may be posed. First, what is the relationship between the internet and power (SEE: **domination**)? Proponents of the internet have argued that it allows critics of government to debate freely and to organize more effectively. Certainly, it is true that some governments have sought to control internet usage precisely because they feared that dissidents would be better informed and organized. However, it is less clear that the internet does pose threats to any government, at least partly because of the capacity of many intelligence services to intercept internet communications. Second, can the internet create an environment in which citizens can debate and thereby create a more healthy democracy (SEE: **public sphere**)? There may well be serious possibilities here. Certainly, the web can enable citizens to be better informed, and local organization can be facilitated by the internet (SEE: **electronic democracy**). However, as yet, this is not what the majority of people use the internet for. Furthermore, the great majority of the world's population do not have access to the internet (SEE: **digital divide**). Third, can the internet enhance contact between people and enable new communities to grow up (SEE: **virtual communities**)? Again, there are possibilities. Chat rooms and email do allow people to make contact with strangers, and the internet has helped those with similar interests to interact. However, the evidence is that, so far, the internet has actually reinforced existing social contacts of family and friends rather than created new ones. Fourth, does the internet encourage solitariness and addiction? There is some early evidence that some people, especially middle-aged women, are addicted to internet use, but, since much the same claim has been, and is made, about both television and computer games, more systematic and long-term research is needed. Fifth, does the internet encourage a more ACTIVE AUDIENCE than other media? Claims have been made that internet users are able to be more creative and the medium permits greater INTERACTIV-ITY. However, it seems that the bulk of internet activity consists in surfing the web, which is not, in itself, a particularly interactive form. Sixth, how does business relate to the internet? Commercial enterprises were fairly slow to make use of the internet, but now the bulk of traffic is commercial. Business websites are commonplace, and a rising proportion of them have ordering and other facilities. The internet is now responsible for about 5 per cent of total worldwide advertising spend, and commercial junk email is now notorious. Early predictions that the internet would herald totally new ways of conducting business have, however, proved false – or at least premature.

SEE ALSO: **cyberspace**.

interpellation Term devised and popularized by the French Marxist LOUIS ALTHUSSER to characterize how IDEOLOGY works to construct social subjects. In Althusser's view, interpellation works through a process of 'hailing'. For example, if we turn when someone shouts at us in the street (when we are hailed) we are being positioned as a subject which is defined by how that person addresses us. Our identities, our sense of who we are, are produced through such processes. Thus, for Althusser, the media hail us and interpellate us as subjects of ideology. For example, the cover of a magazine like *Loaded* addresses or hails us as young men who are interested in viewing the bodies of young women. It thus contributes to the identities of young men as having this as one of their core interests.

SEE ALSO: **Centre for Contemporary Cultural Studies; discourse; dominant ideology; identity; imaginary**.

interpretive community A community is based upon the shared interpretation (or debate over interpretation) of a text. One of the earliest uses of the concept was in the work of the literary analyst Stanley Fish in his studies of the readers of literary texts (Fish, 1980). More recently, in her classic study of romantic fiction, Radway (1987) showed how a group of women shared interests in the reading of particular types of romances. In addition, many of the studies of FANS have shown how they form groups to discuss texts (in addition to engaging in other activities) and can thus be seen as interpretive communities.

SEE ALSO: **imagined community**.

intersubjectivity The process whereby the sense of the self of individuals is shared or communicated to produce some degree of commonality or understanding. Can be used especially with respect to audience processes, where meanings are shared. Thus, FAN groups would show a degree of intersubjectivity in their common understandings of the appeal of texts to them and how they are significant to their identities.

SEE ALSO: **audience; habitus; imagined community**.

intertextuality The process by which meanings from one text become part of, or refer to, another. This process can be deliberate, for example in the way that a comedy may parody other texts, or in the way that post-modern texts are thought to operate by the incorporation of other texts or fragments of texts (SEE: **postmodernism**). For example, the film *Wayne's World* makes numerous references to other texts. However, those writers such as ROLAND BARTHES and MICHEL FOUCAULT (e.g. Barthes, 1977; Foucault, 1977b), who have heralded the end or the death of the AUTHOR, would hold that, in effect, all texts are produced through a process of mobilization of other texts and DISCOURSES, such that the text is actually made up of many other texts, and is written through the author. In this sense, intertextuality is not a deliberate tactic of an author, but the way in which all texts are produced.

SEE ALSO: **auteur theory; dialogic; poststructuralism**.

interview A method of obtaining information from individuals. Interviews may either be formal, using a structured interview schedule, or informal, the interviewer being able to follow up points made by the interviewee. Interviews may also provide either quantitative or qualitative data. Doubts have been expressed concerning the reliability of the interview, as its social nature can lead to various sorts of unreliability. Interviewers may introduce bias, by the sort of questions that they ask or the way that they ask them. Interviewees may choose not to answer truthfully. A third element of bias may occur as the result of the social interaction between the interviewer and interviewee.

SEE ALSO: **open-ended question**.

introductory cue The command or message given to an announcer on radio or TV so that he or she knows to begin or to go to a new item.

invasion of privacy See: PRIVACY.

ISDN (Integrated Services Digital Network) A way of transmitting digital signals through a telephone line.

SEE ALSO: **digital broadcasting; digital revolution; digitization**.

italic See: TYPEFACE.

ITC Code See: INDEPENDENT TELEVISION COMMISSION.

ITV plc See: INDEPENDENT TELEVISION.

J

James, C. L. R. (1901–89) An historian, political activist, literary critic and cricket fan, James was an influence on the development of the study of race. He made contributions to the study of revolt and resistance, for example in *The Black Jacobins* (1980, originally published 1938), to literary analysis and to the investigation of cricket in its cultural and political context. His study of culture in the context of politics and the development of a cultural MARXISM drew important lessons for cultural studies. He has also been an important influence on the development of studies of POSTCOLONIALISM and postcolonial theory.

SEE ALSO: **globalization**.

J Curve A graphical representation of the percentage of a population who have heard of a news event, plotted against the percentage that have heard of it from non-media sources. The method can illuminate the different ways in which people hear about such an event and the relative power of the media. It can therefore be used to classify how different types of news event are spread. It was produced through the study of DIFFUSION of awareness in the USA by Bradley S. Greenberg's (1965) work on the assassination of President Kennedy in 1963.

JICRAR (Joint Industry Committee for Radio Audience Research) The body formerly responsible for commercial radio audience measurement in the UK, now superseded by RAJAR.

SEE ALSO: **audience**.

JICTAR (Joint Industry Committee for Television Advertising Research) The body formerly responsible for audience measurement for commercial television stations in the UK, now superseded by BARB.

SEE ALSO: **audience**.

jingle A short piece of music that identifies a radio station, a show, a presenter or a part of a show.

jouissance French word used in cultural and media theory to describe forms of pleasure from texts that are non-rational, concerned with emotion and physical sensation and which are therefore often difficult to put into words. The contrast is with *plaisir*, which is used for more cognitive and rational pleasures. In POSTSTRUCTURALIST thought, in particular the work of ROLAND BARTHES, *jouissance* is the pleasure derived from those sorts of AVANT-GARDE texts that open up the play of meanings and frustrate any attempts at closure, whereas *plaisir* is the pleasure of those texts that seem to close off the play of meanings in order to attempt to achieve intelligibility.

journalism The demand for journalism and journalists has increased radically within the last few decades. Although the traditional home for journalism – NEWSPAPERS – has been in decline, the burgeoning of television and radio channels and the proliferation of both free and paid-for magazines has meant a greater demand for those who provide information professionally (SEE: **information society**). Journalists now cover a wider variety of fields, particularly in entertainment topics such as sport, cookery and celebrity, than in the past, but most of the issues arising in analysis of journalistic practices come from news journalism.

Some 20 per cent of BBC television and 30 per cent of BBC radio output consists of news journalism. Journalists working in this area are therefore important in simple volume terms but they are also significant in that they may influence the way that the audience constructs the world (SEE: **agenda setting; public sphere**). In writing a story, a journalist, of necessity, has to select what to include and what to leave out. The issue then is: what factors influence that selection (SEE: **news values**). There are many different answers to that question. Some analysts argue that the social background of journalists influences the manner in which they work. Others suggest that the way in which media organizations are owned constitutes an important source of pressure. Thus, owners or advertisers may directly interfere with what journalists write. Still others note that the professional culture of journalists determines what is to count as news. The most probable account is some combination of all these. What that conclusion suggests, in turn, is that there is unlikely to be a systematic and long-term bias in the media but rather a set of shifting and sometimes contradictory emphases around a rough consensus (but SEE: **manufacture of consent**).

The solution to the possibility of bias in the news is the need for journalists to be objective in their work – and they are trained to be scrupulous in the use of sources, to check facts and to look for different views on a news item (SEE: **objectivity**). Actually, this pursuit of objectivity is a phenomenon dating only from the second half of the twentieth century. Before that, journalism was a more straightforwardly partisan occupation, and journalists were more preoccupied with putting forward a viewpoint than they were with maintaining a strict objectivity. The ideal here is a kind of marketplace of ideas in which partisan views compete for the attention of the reader. One might argue that the pursuit of objectivity is a consequence of public service broadcasting in which there is an obligation to be impartial (SEE: **journalistic ethics**).

SEE ALSO: **news**.

journalistic ethics Clearly, journalists occupy a responsible position in that they inform the public and play a significant part in public debate, whether they work for newspapers, radio or television. In presenting their material, they have an obligation to be objective and accurate (SEE: **bias; objectivity**). Of course, these values are open to interpretation, and, particularly in the press, objectivity does not always seem highly valued. There are, furthermore, many cases where journalists actually invent stories or photographs.

Ethical issues do not, however, only arise in the presentation of material but also in its acquisition. For example, it is difficult to assess how far journalists should go in invading the privacy of public figures let alone private ones (SEE: **privacy**). To what extent should journalists be allowed to use confidential material? Should informants, often closely connected with crime, be paid for information? Should newspapers be allowed to print the names of people they believe to be involved in anti-social or criminal behaviour with sometimes drastic, and unmerited, consequences for those individuals?

For many members of the public, journalists go too far in their search for the newsworthy and sometimes, indeed, effectively create the news rather than report it. The response from newspapers that they are only acting in the public interest rings somewhat hollow at times (SEE: **regulation**). Surveys of opinion suggest that the public has very low levels of trust in journalists generally. Many European countries have codes of behaviour for journalists, but they are voluntary, and it is not clear that they are effective in preventing abuse.

SEE ALSO: **government and the media; journalism; Press Complaints Commission**.

jump cut In film, a cut which removes some frames from the middle of a shot, causing the action to 'jump' forward in a discontinuous manner. Such a cut can be used by radical or alternative film-makers to disrupt the conventional flow of narrative and thus to force the audience to contemplate the nature of the text before it.

justification Alignment of the margins of a body of text on a page. Text may be justified to the right, in which case its margin on the right-hand side forms a straight line down the page. Similarly, it may be justified on the left or may have both margins justified. In printing, justification of these kinds is achieved by altering the spacing between words in each line. Alternatively, lines of text may be left ragged, which means, usually, that the left hand margin is fully justified but the right hand margin is not. Spacing between words is kept regular with the result that lines on a page end at different points.

The term is also used only for even margins on both right and left. If only one side is left even, then, in this usage, the term 'range' is used, as in 'ranged right or left'.

K

karaoke The practice which originated in Japan in the early 1970s, where it is immensely popular, of singing along to a backing track in public. The term karaoke is also used to refer to the technology that makes up karaoke equipment. This consists of five parts: a sound source, a visual source, a microphone, sound and visual distribution and accessories (Mitsui and Hosokawa, 1998: 8). As the technology has developed, these different components have increased in sophistication.

The success and popularity of karaoke in Japan is shown by the fact that in the early 1990s the turnover of the karaoke industry was around one-third of that of the record industry in that country (Mitsui and Hosokawa, 1998: 21). There are divisions within the practice of karaoke in Japan, where different markets have been developed for the daytime participants such as women and school students and the night-time users. Karaoke also takes place in different places such as bars, clubs and homes.

While the basic idea of karaoke and its technology is common, the practices associated with it have evolved in particular ways in different societies. This has much to do with previous traditions that have existed in the society for singing in public (Lum, 1998). Thus, the antecedents of karaoke in the UK include pub sing-a-longs and audience participation in music hall. In Japan karaoke bars are more communal places, where there is more of an expectation that all will sing than in other societies. This phenomenon was captured memorably for Western audiences in the hit movie *Lost in Translation* (dir. Sofia Coppola, 2003).

Katz, Elihu (b. 1926) Distinguished Trustee Professor of Communication at the Annenberg School for Communication at the University of Pennsylvania. He was one of the key movers in the development of the study of the media in the USA, especially of the audience. Katz's long working life has involved the study of personal communication in media audiences, and he was an important contributor to the development of the USES AND GRATIFICATIONS approach to the study of media audiences. He has also been concerned with the conceptualization of the public sphere and media ritual. He has worked in the USA and Israel and conducted a seminal cross-cultural study of the television programme *Dallas* (see Liebes and Katz, 1993).

SEE ALSO: **audience;** *Dallas.*

Kellner, Douglas (b. 1943) George F. Kneller Professor of Philosophy and Education, Chair in Social Science and Comparative Education, University of California at Los Angeles (UCLA). Kellner has worked at the intersection of media studies and cultural theory. He has studied media spectacle and postmodernism and is a prominent commentator on the work of JEAN BAUDRILLARD.

kerning The process by which the spacing between letters in a proportional FONT is adjusted to improve the aesthetic appearance or to enhance legibility.

key drawings Term used in animation for drawings that capture the end and beginning of a movement. These can be used to provide a key that can then be filled in by other animators.

SEE ALSO: **animation; cartoon.**

knowledge society A society in which knowledge, or information, has become central. Key aspects of this idea are: that the production and consumption of knowledge have become as, if not more, important than the production and consumption of things; that knowledge and things are inherently related and connected anyway (thus, for example, unless people possess certain knowledge, they are unable to operate a computer); and that knowledge itself has become increasingly commodified – i.e. something that can be bought and sold in a marketplace like any other good. This last point implies the development of a knowledge economy with an increasingly large network of commercial organizations which effectively buy and sell knowledge.

SEE ALSO: **information rich.**

Kristeva, Julia (b. 1941) Bulgarian-born literary critic and philosopher who has lived and worked in France since 1966. Her work has been influential on feminist, literary and film theory, especially in the working out of STRUCTURALIST and POSTSTRUCTURALIST themes. Her work on transgression has formed an aspect of the development of those forms of politics concerned with the nature and transformation of identity, and her ideas have been used in work on film that has been influenced by psychoanalysis. Examples of this can be found in work on the HORROR film and on IDENTIFICATION.

SEE ALSO: **film theory.**

L

labelling process Sociological theory which proposes that, once some-one has committed a criminal or deviant act, others will treat him or her as a criminal or deviant. Once labelled, the person will be more likely to reoffend as they come to believe that they are indeed criminal or deviant; it becomes part of their identity. The media have an important role to play in this process in that they contribute to the designation of an act as deviant or criminal. For example, over many years, the newspapers and television have defined drug-taking of all kinds as deviant, and this has, in turn, persuaded governments to introduce legislation and enforce it.

SEE ALSO: **amplification of deviance; moral panic**.

language Language in many respects defines what it is to be human, and all human societies have some kind of language. Human languages consist of combinations of sounds called phonemes. These phonemes are arranged in different ways in particular languages to produce words. These words are further ordered into sentences and phrases, which are governed by conventions of syntax. A key part of being socialized into a culture comes from the learning of the conventions of the language of the group. This may be very localized as, for example, certain words and accents are specific to regions or areas of a country. This illustrates that language has a degree of cultural specificity. The relationship between words, thought and things has been puzzled over by many philosophers. Some writers, as in the Sapir–Whorf hypothesis formulated by Edward Sapir and Benjamin Lee Whorf, have argued that there are culturally specific thought worlds that are created by language. The regular use of specific language produces particular and habitual thought worlds. If language is specific in this way, one possible step is to suggest that in some sense language is constructing the world, rather than representing it. However, this immediately introduces other issues. How, if language is so culturally specific, do different cultures communicate with each other? Or how can one culture know another? There is much debate about this issue, especially within the study and the practice of translation from one language to another. However, despite the existence of different words for similar things in different languages, it is clearly possible to translate between them.

The most influential approach to the study of the meaning of language, which has become a crucial aspect of how texts are studied in media studies, is SEMIOLOGY (or semiotics). Based in structuralist ideas, this method has examined the structure of the SIGN, which refers to a REFERENT, dividing it between the SIGNIFIER and the SIGNIFIED. Meaning is generated at denotation and connotation levels (SEE: **denotation/connotation**). The work of ROLAND BARTHES argues that representation is intimately linked to IDEOLOGY and the unequal distribution of power in society. Thus, some representations will work to produce ideas that are in the interests of dominant and powerful groups. For example, the Glasgow University Media Group (1976, 1980) showed the significance of the use of language in television NEWS. Such ideas have been explored by many other writers who have drawn attention to the significance of language in, for example, inequalities in class, gender and race.

The sociologist Basil Bernstein (1971, 1973, 1975) drew a distinction between what he termed restricted (spoken by the working classes) and elaborated (used by the middle classes) codes of language. The latter conveyed educational advantage on the better-off members of society. In Bernstein's analysis, this difference both represents the class structure and disadvantage and reinforces and constitutes it as an ongoing set of inequalities. Similar arguments have been made for how gender and race are represented in language and the way that this reinforces systematic inequality and disadvantage. Those who suggest that confronting inequality entails changing the language of everyday life (for example, by using the word 'person' to represent a human being, rather than the word 'man') have often been ridiculed in some parts of society, but it can be suggested that, if the weight of academic research on the role of language in inequality is recognized, then cultural change in at least partly dependent on language change.

SEE ALSO: **structuralism**.

langue Within STRUCTURALISM, SEMIOLOGY or semiotic analysis, *langue* refers to the structure of a language that underlies or underpins everyday speech, which is referred to as PAROLE. For example, the rules of a sport like football are like *langue*, and they permit a range of different events and outcomes at the level of *parole*.

SEE ALSO: **sign**.

Lazarsfeld, Paul F. (1901–76) An Austrian sociologist who emigrated to the

USA in 1933, Lazarsfeld was an important influence in the development of quantitative methods in the study of mass communications. He is perhaps best known for his studies of the impact of the media on political attitudes and of the role of opinion leaders in influencing voting (SEE: **two-step flow**). He also did work on radio, noting, for example, that the less well-educated tend to be relatively more dependent on radio (and now television) for their information.

lead The most important piece in a news programme, which will be narrated first.

leading The space between lines on the printed page. The term derives from the days when printing was by HOT METAL and the spaces between lines was created by the insertion of a strip of metal.

leak Most journalists dealing with issues of public interest have sources inside government or business which will give (leak) them information or documents unofficially. Governments are very touchy about such leaks. Since leaks of this kind gain substantial publicity, those who do the leaking may be working to an agenda of their own. For example, politicians may leak deliberately to undermine policies with which they disagree. Or the government may use unofficial channels to leak its own policy proposals in order to test public reaction in advance of any formal announcement.

legitimation Process by which an action, policy or person becomes viewed as legitimate, i.e. accepted as right or proper. Marxists and those on the political left have drawn attention to the role of the media in the legitimation of capitalist societies. In this view, the media focus on selected issues and neglect others in ways that serve the interests of those in power. Thus, from this perspective, television in liberal democratic capitalist societies, while seeking not to favour one political party over another, will continue to emphasize the legitimacy of parliamentary democracy.

SEE ALSO: **Glasgow University Media Group; hegemony; ideology; news.**

leisure Rather obviously, leisure is conventionally defined as the time left over after paid work. This definition is misleading for those who do not have paid work in the conventional sense – the retired, the unemployed, the young.

The amount of time that people spend at work in the UK has been declining steadily since the beginning of the century, from about fifty-three hours per week to forty hours for industrial manual workers. There are signs that, for some categories of worker, this decline is being halted or even reversed. Clearly, there are many different ways of spending leisure time, but most of it is taken in the home (70 per cent for men and 80 per cent for women), chiefly watching television. There are, however, gender, class and life-cycle differences in leisure patterns. In particular, men are more involved in leisure pursuits outside the home, and women, whether in paid employment or not, have less free time. Professional and managerial classes do more in all fields of leisure than other social classes, partly as a reflection of their greater financial resources. The young and the elderly have more free time than other age-groups, and their lives typically are organized around leisure pursuits.

With rising incomes in the West, many households have more money available for their leisure pursuits. This is related to the growth of a leisure industry, which clearly affects the media. These developments have led some commentators to argue that a leisure society or a CONSUMER SOCIETY has been created in which a person's identity is given less by their paid employment or by their social class or family background than by their leisure pursuits.

letterer This is a person who draws by hand (rather than use a standard FONT) the letters used in advertisements, magazine covers and, above all, comics and comic books. The craft can be used to create a distinctive visual style.

letterpress A printing process consisting in using a block or plate which has the letters raised above the surface. Ink is then spread on the raised portions of the plate and applied, using a press, to paper. For centuries, printing has effectively taken the form of letterpress printing.

SEE ALSO: **print**.

licence fee The fee paid by every user of a television set in the UK to the government which, in turn, provides the bulk of the funding for the BBC. This system was adopted because the BBC was providing a public service open to all. The licence fee method of funding, however, has attracted increasing controversy since the 1980s. Commercial radio and television providers continue to object to the system because they claim that it constitutes unfair competition, especially when the BBC turns to commercial activities to enhance its income. More seriously still, as digital broadcasting produces a very large number of channels, much of the audience for radio and television may not be using the BBC at all. Thus, it is asked why people should pay for a service that they do not use.

The term is also used more generally for the money paid to the government by commercial organizations for licences to broadcast.

SEE ALSO: **economics of the media; public service broadcasting**.

lifestyle The patterned way in which individuals organize their everyday lives. In both society and academic study the increased use of the term is related to the development of CONSUMER SOCIETIES and consumerism. It is often argued that, as a consequence of the development of consumer societies in the West, individuals are free to construct their own lifestyles and that, furthermore, the consumption of goods and services is a key part of such constructions. Thus, in this view, consumption cannot be linked to class, gender or occupation in direct and straightforward ways, but, rather, lifestyles are constructed on the basis of a complex interaction of influences such as occupation, place of residence, age, stage of life-cycle (being married, retired and so on). Media consumption can then be studied as an aspect of lifestyle. In this sense, it can be suggested that lifestyles are at least partly constructed by individuals as they interact with media in different ways.

SEE ALSO: **daily life; everyday life; identity**.

lighting The processes of the illumination of sets or scenes in film-making can be explored in two main ways, either technically or ideologically, though there are important connections between the two. The conventional way to categorize lighting of a shot or scene is in terms of the key light, the fill light and the back light. The key light is the main source of light, and is the most directed of the three modes of light. The fill light is not directional and fills in some of the shadows created by the key light. A light placed behind the main subject provides greater depth to it. The positioning of these lights and all other aspects of lighting is under the control of the cinematographer (SEE: **cinematography**) in the example of film-making. Overall, the lighting can be high-key or low-key. High-key lighting is bright and is used, for example, in musicals. Low-key lighting offers a greater contrast and produces more shadows and was used to important effect in FILM NOIR. Thus, there are important connections between technical decisions about lighting and the meanings of GENRE in texts. An influential account of the ideological (SEE: **ideology**) aspects of lighting has been provided by Dyer (1997), who argues that the mode of lighting deployed under the influence of Hollywood has been based around the production of whiteness. This favours whiteness as a dominant cultural form and also means that black features end up illuminated in ways that suggest their subservience to whiteness.

lighting cameraman See: CINEMATOGRAPHY.

linear editing See: NON-LINEAR EDITING.

link Narration that joins one section of a programme to another in TV and radio.

linotype A typesetting machine invented in the nineteenth century. It replaced an earlier technology, which involved placing individual metal letters in a frame. The linotype operator sat at a keyboard and typed out what needed printing. The machine then created, by a HOT METAL process, whole lines of type set in one block of metal (called a slug). Linotype machines dominated printing, especially in the newspaper industry, until late in the twentieth century but have been superseded by phototypesetting technology.
  SEE ALSO: **print; slug.**

lip-sync The synchronization of sound to the visual representation of a performer so that speech corresponds to the movement of the lips.

literary agent A person who acts for authors in dealing with book publishers. Agents scout for authors for books that they know publishers are looking for or look for publishers for books or ideas that they have received from authors. Many literary agents will also deal in film or television scripts or other work destined for print. In return for their work they receive a percentage of the money the author eventually receives from the publisher. Literary agents are gradually taking over the role of dealing with authors previously discharged by COMMISSIONING EDITORS. In this respect they are like other kinds of agent in the media.
  SEE ALSO: **agent; book publishing.**

LiveJournal The brand name of a website that allows its users to create, sustain and enlarge their social networks, primarily by posting material about themselves and communicating with each other via the site.
  SEE ALSO: **MySpace; virtual community.**

Livingstone, Sonia Professor of Social Psychology at the London School of Economics, she has played an important role in the development of AUDIENCE and reception studies in the UK. She has studied the audience for various genres of TV programmes, especially soap opera, and explored the role of TV in contemporary democracy. Recent work has focused on young people and new media.
  SEE ALSO: **soap opera; youth culture.**

lobby system The lobby, founded in 1882, was the name given to a small group of journalists from the press, radio and television who had privileged access to politicians. They were entitled to interview MPs in the members' lobby of Parliament as long as they did not attribute any information to those who had released it. Lobby correspondents were also invited to 10 Downing Street for daily briefings by ministers and press officials. Again, these briefings could not be used directly by journalists and were intended as background to the day's events. Journalists were recommended by their employers for membership of the lobby and would then be given permission to join by the Serjeant at Arms; membership could be withdrawn if it was felt that a journalist had transgressed a lobby rule by, for instance, quoting a source from a lobby briefing.

The lobby system was extensively criticized. It was felt that it was too secretive, in that remarks could not be attributed, and too small for the increasingly large number of media outlets and journalists, and the method of appointment meant that the government could pick and choose which journalists should have access to information. The government, in other words, used the lobby system to control the media. Partly in response to these criticisms, the Labour government has introduced some changes. For example, against the wishes of most members of the lobby, foreign journalists are now allowed to attend the daily briefings given by ministers and official spokesmen.

SEE ALSO: **government and the media**.

localization Process by which culture or cultural processes become more locally based. It is often assumed that in the contemporary world social, political, economic and cultural processes are becoming more global such that what happens in one place may be much the same as in any other (SEE: **globalization**). While this is undoubtedly true in many respects, it can be argued that it should not be assumed that the same culture or processes are occurring everywhere. The opposite tendency would be for processes to become more locally based, where there is, for example, a resurgence of attempts to use local shops rather than out-of-town shopping centres. Another example would be where local radio stations or local programmes on TV remain very popular. The fact that local processes are still important has been recognized in the development of the term GLOCALIZATION (Robertson, 1995). Thus, while there may be local forms of culture and they develop in particular locales, they do so in interaction with processes which are also happening on a global scale. Music is therefore often made by people who live close to each other and shows the influence of place (as captured in the idea of SCENE) but those people will also be affected by the circulation of music that comes from a variety of places.

SEE ALSO: **cultural imperialism.**

local newspaper or local press See: REGIONAL PRESS.

local radio Radio in many countries has tended to have a local, rather than a national or even regional, focus. In the USA, for example, much radio was broadcast to particular cities and regions, even if in earlier times network programmes were also broadcast and stations were affiliated so that particular programmes (such as the *The Grand Old Opry*) could be spread around a region. In Britain, radio was national (though with variations across England, Scotland and Wales) until the advent of local commercial radio and BBC local radio stations in the 1970s. Today, local radio is of importance like the local press in addressing community issues and local news. In a context where there is increasingly proliferation of radio stations, radio can serve niches in a variety of ways; in addition to broadcasting specialist music, it can be directly related to localities and communities that may be concentrated by residence in particular areas of cities and so on.

SEE ALSO: **radio.**

local television There have been a number of attempts to develop a truly local television service that would appeal to the same audience as is currently served by the local press. There clearly is a demand for local, as distinct from regional, news, and there is scope for using a local service for such activities as electronic democracy. As yet, a successful and replicable business model for local television has not been developed, but the potential is there with digital technology, especially cable.

long shot In film a shot taken from a distance that is used to convey a sense of space or to locate action in a specific place.

Long Tail, The See: ECONOMICS OF THE MEDIA; NEW MEDIA.

Lull, James (b. 1950) Emeritus Professor of Communication Studies at San Jose State University, USA. His earlier work on AUDIENCES for television around the world was an important part of the move towards a more sophisticated understanding of audiences, based on ethnographic and qualitative research, rather than questionnaires and surveys (Lull, 1988 and 1990). He has also written on a range of other topics in media studies including media communication, media scandals and global media culture.

Lyotard, Jean-François (1924–98) French philosopher and literary theorist, who held a number of academic positions in France and other countries. He is best known and most influential for his contribution to the development of the analysis of POSTMODERNISM and POSTMODERNITY in his book *The Postmodern Condition* (1984, originally published 1979), which argued that knowledge was locally contingent and that therefore grand or master narratives of identity and knowledge were in decline.

lyrics Words of a piece of music or song. There has been a debate in studies of popular music as to how important lyrics are to the creation of meaning (SEE: **Frith**, 1988), by comparison, for example, with the melody or with the nature the voice. For some people, lyrics are very important in how they understand the piece and its resonance for them. Those analysing popular music will also often focus on lyrical content. This is especially the case when the work of particular artists such as Bob Dylan is analysed as poetry by those who have a literary training. Other people are less concerned with the lyrics and focus more on the overall sound of the music or the quality of the singer's voice. Roland Barthes (1990) captured the latter in his idea of the 'grain' of the voice. There are also various methods for the study of lyrics, including CONTENT ANALYSIS or DISCOURSE analysis. One way of thinking about this whole issue is to consider the number of ways in which lyrics are misheard in contemporary music. Listeners often get the lyrics wrong and then may build their own interpretation of the song on the basis of their mistake.

SEE ALSO: **language; microphone; voice.**

M

McDonaldization Invented by George Ritzer in *The McDonaldization of Society* (1993) to describe the way in which commercial products and human experiences are all being reduced to a standardized, bland uniformity – rather like McDonald's hamburgers. According to this view, there is little diversity or originality in media products, whether these be rock music, television programmes or Hollywood films. In addition, as the United States continues to dominate the world's media, localized diversity is squeezed out by standardized American media products (SEE: **media imperialism**). A countervailing view is that media industries, like any other, require constant innovation in order to stay competitive; media markets are becoming increasingly fragmented, leading to increasing diversity (SEE: **audience differentiation**); and, in the world generally local media forms are flourishing.

McLuhan, Marshall (1911–80) A Canadian academic, who was an influential theorist of the media. He is chiefly known as a proponent of the idea that the intrinsic character of a medium is important in itself, irrespective of the content of the message that medium is conveying (SEE: **hot media**). He also invented several phrases which have entered everyday language. The best known are 'THE MEDIUM IS THE MESSAGE' and 'GLOBAL VILLAGE'. Most influential in the 1960s, he was subject to a revival of interest in the 1990s under the influence of POSTMODERNIST ideas and interest in the effects of technological innovation.

SEE ALSO: **technological determinism; Toronto School**.

McQuail, Denis (b. 1935) Emeritus Professor of Mass Communication at the University of Amsterdam. McQuail has been a key figure in the codification and development of the systematic academic study of the media. He has conducted a number of studies of different aspects of the media, including the democratic roles and responsibilities of the media (e.g. McQuail, 2003) and media audiences (e.g. McQuail, 1997), where he was an important proponent of the USES AND GRATIFICATIONS approach. He has produced a number of well-known textbooks on the media, which have proved to be very popular with successive generations of students (see, for example, especially McQuail, 2005).

McRobbie, Angela (b. 1951) Professor of Communications at Goldsmith's College, University of London. She has combined the study of different dimensions of YOUTH CULTURE with analysis of developments in cultural theory, texts and politics. Her best-known and most influential work centres on the discussion of GENDER in YOUTH CULTURE and youth subcultures. She was critical of the malestream (which signals the male domination of mainstream thinking) approach of the writing on youth culture at the Birmingham CENTRE FOR CONTEMPORARY CULTURAL STUDIES. She has produced a range of writings to correct this perceived imbalance, which have drawn attention to the nature of media in youth culture. In particular she has considered magazines for young women and the changing nature and significance of popular music. Her most important works in these respects are McRobbie (1991 and 1994).

SEE ALSO: **feminism**.

magazine With their origins in the eighteenth century, magazines or periodicals, published weekly, monthly, quarterly or even annually, were originally sold to the relatively well-off. When they started to take advertising, however, their cover price could be reduced and readership expanded as a result. They now constitute a successful and growing sector.

There are some 10,000 magazines published in the UK. That figure includes the well-known consumer magazines (ones sold in newsagents or by subscription), such as *Hello!* or *Loaded*, but the majority of titles are given away to customers (by supermarkets, for instance) or as a benefit of membership of an organization. Thus, the magazine with the largest circulation in 2005 was the *Asda Magazine*, which is distributed to about 5.5 million customers. The ten magazines with the greatest circulation include supermarket magazines and TV listings publications. In 2004, the list of the top-ten weekly consumer magazines was dominated by women's and TV magazines. At the head of the list was *What's on TV*, selling over 4 million copies, with *OK!* at 3.6 million. Monthly women's magazines also sell well.

Sales of magazines are increasing. During the 1990s, for example, the number of copies sold increased by about 30 per cent. As with the media more generally, there has been a CONCENTRATION OF OWNERSHIP in the consumer magazine sector, which is now dominated by EMAP and IPC, with the BBC a third important player. National Magazines and Condé Nast publish well-known magazines (for example, *Good Housekeeping* and *Vogue* respectively).

For consumer magazines about 40 per cent of the revenue comes from advertising and about 60 per cent from the cover price. One way in which to look at the economics of magazines is to see them as devices for the delivery of audiences to advertisers. The success of the industry has come, not on the whole from publishing titles that appeal generally – to all women, for example – but rather from aiming at market niches – vintage car enthusiasts or young men, for example. Advertising can then be targeted at that readership. The publishers' main difficulty, besides ensuring the loyalty of its specialized audience, is keeping the cover price low enough to ensure a large enough readership for its advertisers.

SEE ALSO: **newspaper; women's magazines**.

mainstream 1 Core or conventional culture in a society. Despite the everyday use of the term, often by those who seek to separate their activities from what they think of as the mainstream, or the conventional, it is often quite difficult to describe what the mainstream is! This is rather like ideas of DOMINANT IDEOLOGY/CULTURE, where it is assumed that everyone knows what is meant, but where there are as many different versions of the concept as there are commentators. In one sense, mainstream television may be thought to be that which is broadcast in the prime-time hours, say between 7 and 10 p.m. However, when the content of such television is considered, it is actually quite varied and differentiated, even taking into account terrestrial channels only. The consideration of satellite channels would introduce further complications. Thus, the mainstream may have greatly fragmented through the rise of cultural diversity and the increase in media providers.

Studies of popular music sometimes make play of the difference between specialist musics and the mainstream. Fans of specialist musics are even more likely to make this distinction as a way of separating themselves from what they see as the mainstream or commercial culture. One of the difficulties with this process is that the idea of what the mainstream is shifts and is contested. It is also often stereotyped.

The process by which people in a society become inducted into the mainstream values and beliefs of a culture has been called 'mainstreaming'. The idea is chiefly associated with the work of GEORGE GERBNER and his colleagues (especially Larry Gross: see, for example, Gross, 1989) in the cultural values project, who have studied the effect that heavy TV viewing tends to make people more believing of the mainstream values of a society.

SEE ALSO: **cultivation**.

2 Movement in jazz in the 1950s.

majors Large companies that dominate the market for popular music globally. There are currently four such companies – Sony/BMG, EMI, Universal and Warner – based in different countries of origin. The majors seek to control markets through CONCENTRATION OF OWNERSHIP and diversify by the processes of conglomeration.

SEE ALSO: **independent company; music industry**.

male gaze According to the film analyst and film-maker LAURA MULVEY (1981), cinema constructs a male gaze, by positioning women on the screen as objects to be looked at by men. Through this process, the spectator for cinema is placed in a powerful male position. Based in a psychoanalytic perspective, Mulvey's argument is that narrative cinema of the classic HOLLYWOOD type provides two particular forms of pleasure for the audience. First, there is scopophilic pleasure – sexual pleasure derived from looking. Here, we are separated from the action on the screen and feel that we are looking in on it. Hence we derive pleasure from looking at another person as a sexual object in a voyeuristic fashion. Second, we derive pleasure from IDENTIFICATION with what is happening on the screen in front of us. This process tends to break down the gap between the spectator and the screen that is a key part of the first form of pleasure as we feel ourselves become part of the action that is going on in front of us. The form of identification is most often with the male hero as he controls the action of the film. In the course of the action of the film, women are displayed on the screen for the male hero to look at. Having the female characters in roles that offer them up to be looked at does this. For example, they may be showgirls or prostitutes. The hero looks at them, but the audience is also placed in a position where they are looking too. Thus, rather than the gaze at the woman operating to disrupt the narrative flow of the film, this is integrated within the narrative, and the two forms of pleasure are connected. The spectator for dominant Hollywood narrative cinema is therefore constructed in a male position, which disempowers women. Mulvey thus offers a very strong critique of the male pleasures of dominant cinema, which acts against the interests of women, and through her critique and her own cinematic practice she seeks to offer alternatives. This work has been highly influential though often criticized. First, it has been suggested that Mulvey ignores actual audience responses to the text, which may vary significantly; second, that she oversimplifies the complex ways in which women are represented, especially as women have been placed in the central hero role; third, that she ignores the way in which males are offered up for the gaze. Despite this broad point, the construction of the gendered gaze remains an important area for the investigation of film texts.

SEE ALSO: **film noir; gender**.

manufacture of consent A term originated by Ed Herman and NOAM CHOMSKY in *Manufacturing Consent* (1994) to describe the way in which the news media in the United States and other countries put across one particular view of news and current affairs. Deprived of alternative views, people give their consent to policies of their government that they would resist were they to be properly informed. The hypothesis works best in times of international conflict. The media in the US, for example, did clearly adopt a view partisan to the interests of the United States during the Cold War and to some extent during the Vietnam war, both wars with Iraq and, more generally, with countries defined as enemies or potential enemies.

SEE ALSO: **bias; domination**.

Marcuse, Herbert (1898–1979) Trained at the Universities of Berlin and Freiburg, Marcuse went to the United States in 1934. The central issue in his work is the possibility of an authentic existence in modern capitalist society. He argued that the mass media promote inauthenticity and REPRESSIVE TOLERANCE, chiefly in the way that they help to maintain a consumer society and to encourage obedience in the people.

SEE ALSO: **critical theory; effects; Frankfurt School**.

market Where goods and services are exchanged. Media markets may be relatively open and easy to enter. For example, people may trade tapes of the recording of a band with each other, perhaps in return for a small amount of money as well. However, in many other areas, the market is dominated by a small number of very powerful companies. Media texts are, therefore, commercial products that are related to markets and commercial activities. This leads to a number of different ways of studying and conceptualizing how media texts are produced for sale on a market and how they are consumed.

SEE ALSO: **commodification; economics of the media; market segmentation/differentiation; media companies; monopoly**.

marketing The process of preparing a media product for sale in a market by such means as advertising (SEE: **advertisement**) and promotion. As the culture industries have become more commercially oriented and consumerist, marketing departments have taken on a more prominent role in media organizations. This tendency has caused controversy. In the music industry, for example, some of those working in A & R have thought that marketing departments have gained too central a role in the development of an artist and the shaping of careers – processes historically seen to be the province of the A & R department. Equally, in book publishing, editorial staff have resented the increasing importance of the marketing function, arguing that it produces an aversion to risk which is both commercially and artistically damaging.

market research Any commercial enterprise will want to know as much as possible about its customers and the reasons they have for buying goods and services. Market research will also be useful for finding out about the competition, evaluating the effectiveness of advertising campaigns or testing different versions of a potential product to find out which suits the market best. Commercial investigation of media audiences is clearly a form of market research.

SEE ALSO: **audience measurement; audience research**.

market segmentation/differentiation Over time, a market that was fairly uniform in the wants and aspirations of consumers and in the kind of products provided may become more segmented as consumers start to differ in their tastes. For example, cars used to be provided in a relatively small range of colours, with one or two engine sizes and a restricted range of optional equipment. Now, there is a much greater range provided to suit different tastes. Similarly with the media, there is a greater range of choice available because the market is more segmented. For example, readers are not simply confronted by a few women's magazines that are much the same as each other as they were in the 1960s, say. Women's magazines differ more from one another and appeal to distinct market segments. Market segmentation is likely to be underpinned by social changes (SEE: **individualization**).

SEE ALSO: **Fordism/post-Fordism**.

Marxism The approach to the study of society and culture derived from the work of the German scholar and political activist Karl Marx (1818–83). Marxism has been influential on media studies in a range of ways. First, there are approaches that consider the nature of the political economy of the media to show how the form and content of texts are determined by political and economic processes in society in the widest sense. Second, organizational processes can be examined through the lens of Marxism, considering, for example, processes of exploitation in media workplaces. Third, the approach can be used in the study of texts and in the nature of media output. Work on television news that suggests that it is constructed in accord with particular dominant social interests would fall into this category (see, for example, GLASGOW UNIVERSITY MEDIA GROUP, 1976, 1980). Fourth, the perspective has been influential in theories of the media audience – tending to suggest that the audience is in some way affected ideologically by the media. Many contemporary qualitative media audience studies offer a version of this view in seeking to show the relationship between ideological incorporation and resistance in the audience. Fifth, the approach has been influential in general theoretical terms through its impact on many social and cultural theorists, who have in turn influenced the development of media studies.

SEE ALSO: **Centre for Contemporary Cultural Studies; critical theory; domination; Frankfurt School; ideology.**

masculinity Characteristics culturally ascribed to men. Many societies have ascribed different and distinctive qualities to men and women. In modern Western societies, it is considered 'masculine' to be aggressive, independent and active. It has been argued that, in contemporary societies, there is a 'crisis of masculinity' because women are entering the workforce in increasing numbers, and many traditional male occupations in heavy industry have disappeared with modernization, leaving men to compete with women in the service sector. These concerns inform the presentation of masculinity in television and film, and, although the differences are less clear-cut than they were, certain GENRES, e.g. POLICE SERIES or WESTERNS, are masculine, while others, e.g. SOAP OPERA and ROMANCE, are more distinctively feminine.

SEE ALSO: **gender.**

mass audience Especially in the early days of the development of the mass media, the audience tended to be thought of as an undifferentiated mass of people who have similar characteristics. This usage was derived from mass society or mass culture theory. In such theories a mass society was produced by the processes of industrial development, which led to the grouping of people together in new industrial towns and by the way in which the extension of the franchise brought increased proportions of the population into the political process (to its detriment in some elitist views). Developed by cultural critics on the political left and the right, such theories often held that mass culture was a symptom of cultural decline brought about by commercialism. The mass audience were then either dupes of the capitalist system or lacking in true cultural discrimination, or both. The mass audience could be manipulated by advertisers or politicians as it would be made up of individuals without powers of discrimination. These individuals had been separated from their traditional groups and thus were more open to persuasion by the new mass media. Though elements of the theory still surface, especially in public discussions of the media, it has largely been discredited in academic circles.

SEE ALSO: **audience; mass communication; mass media.**

mass communication Idea that communication involves the mass production of media texts or messages that are then distributed to a MASS AUDIENCE. The idea is thus contrasted, on one level, with communication that takes place between individuals on a face-to-face basis, or through immediate human contact between people who are in the same place. On another level, the idea is also contrasted with theories of communication that emphasize how culture is produced in small groups and understood or decoded in a large variety of different ways according to social group membership. The roots of mass communication theory can be found in a set of theories and approaches that are often termed mass culture or mass society theories.

SEE ALSO: semiology.

mass culture See: MASS AUDIENCE.

massification See: MASS AUDIENCE.

mass media The term is now usually used synonymously with media, in that we tend to think of all media as being distributed to a large mass of people. However, despite this relatively commonsensical understanding, which has fed into the ways in which media studies has been defined as a field of academic activity, the idea of mass media carries a certain degree of intellectual baggage or currency with it. Thus, the term comes from the same intellectual stable as MASS COMMUNICATION, mass culture and mass society. It tends to suggest a particular understanding of how media production works, what the media are like themselves and how they are consumed.

SEE ALSO: mass audience.

mass production Production of goods, services and texts that involves the generation of large numbers of the same good in an industrialized way. The key moment in the development of mass production came with the innovations of Henry Ford in the manufacture of cars in the early part of the twentieth century. Mass production was then rapidly applied to a range of goods, including those that have been defined as cultural and involving the media. Thus, radios and gramophones were rapidly mass produced, moving on from the way in which they were initially built by enthusiasts from kit form, as were gramophone records, leading to the potential for sounds to become much more widely circulated, more quickly than had hitherto been the case. While the rapidity of these developments was affected by economic depression in the 1930s, the main aspects of mass production of media and culture were in place by the Second World War. While mass production is still a core aspect of the

CULTURAL INDUSTRIES, there has been a move to the more niche production of goods, in that wider ranges of texts are produced in shorter runs, suggesting that consumers now have greater choice and are not subject to constraint to the choice of that which has been mass produced.

SEE ALSO: **Fordism/post-Fordism; mass audience; music industry.**

mass society See: MASS AUDIENCE.

masthead The title of a newspaper at the head of the first page.

Maxwell, Robert (1923–91) Starting his career as a publisher of scientific books and journals, Maxwell went on to run MIRROR GROUP NEWSPAPERS, which published, amongst other titles, the *Mirror*, the *Sunday Mirror* and the New York *Daily News*. Notorious in his day as a ruthless entrepreneur and proprietor, his newspaper empire collapsed amid allegations of financial irregularities, including stealing from the firm's pension funds. Maxwell's death by drowning was widely thought to be suicide.

mechanical reproduction The process by which an original work is reproduced, so that a large number of copies are made. It is particularly associated with the Marxist writer WALTER BENJAMIN, who, in a very famous and influential work (Benjamin, 1970), considered the effects of the mechanical reproduction of works of art. In particular, he argued that the removal of the singular work of art from its context would lead to a loss of aura, while also being part of a process of the democratization of culture.

SEE ALSO: **critical theory; cultural industries; Frankfurt School; Marxism.**

media amplification See: AMPLIFICATION OF DEVIANCE; MORAL PANIC.

media buying Most advertising agencies will have departments dedicated to buying advertising space in newspapers, magazines, television and radio. Those who work in this area will have to be well acquainted with the DEMOGRAPHICS of the media, their cost and their effectiveness in generating sales.

SEE ALSO: **media planning.**

media companies The media landscape of the world contains thousands of different individual organizations. Many of these are so well known that they, in effect, function as BRANDS. *The Times*, Sky and Twentieth Century Fox, for example, are all recognizable brands within their media fields of newspaper publishing, television and film production respectively. However, what is less well recognized is that many of these individual organizations or brands are, in fact, owned by a few large media

CONGLOMERATES. Those three examples, for instance, are all owned by NEWS CORPORATION.

Within the last two decades, there has been a greater and greater CONCENTRATION OF OWNERSHIP of the media. The world's media is now dominated by five companies – TIME WARNER, DISNEY, News Corporation, BERTELSMANN and VIACOM. These companies – four based in the US and one in Germany – have grown by acquisition and merger and have all pursued much the same strategy. They all have a global reach, not only selling their products internationally, helped by the English language, but also acquiring companies in many countries so that products can be local in language and culture. Importantly, they have also diversified within the media field by HORIZONTAL INTEGRATION and DIAGONAL INTEGRATION. They may have strengths in particular sectors. Bertelsmann, for example, has a powerful presence in music and book publishing, while Disney is especially strong in film and television. However, they all have tried to acquire stakes in several sectors of the media to take advantage of MEDIA CONVERGENCE. All of them have also invested heavily in the possibilities of digital technology (SEE: **digital revolution**). The most notable example of this was the merger of America Online – an internet service provider – with Time Warner – the largest media company – although the success of this venture has yet to be proved. At the same time, there has also been a move into leisure fields related to the media. The big five have, for example, become owners of sports teams and constructors of theme parks. This diversification has also meant that very big media companies have developed by concentrating on the media. They have tended to shed other non-media interests in order to provide the capital for further growth in the media. While twenty or thirty years ago, well-known media organizations may have been owned by large conglomerates with extensive non-media interests, that is no longer the case. Only SONY (in music and film) and GENERAL ELECTRIC (in television) remain important global players in the media while being primarily invested in other fields.

SEE ALSO: **digital revolution; global media; media imperialism.**

media convergence In their origins, the various branches of the media utilized different technologies. Until fairly recently, for example, newspapers and books were typeset in hot metal, films were shot and edited on celluloid film, and songs were recorded by analogue means on to vinyl discs or magnetic tape. With the advent of computer technology, however, the production systems of media organizations are being brought together. Books, newspapers and magazines can all be originated on computer and sent directly to be typeset. Photographs and illustrations can be inserted directly at the origination stage. Film can be shot on a digital camera and edited on computer. The use of computers and appropriate software not only makes the production of media products faster and cheaper, it also enables print, visual images and sound to be integrated very much more easily and to be stored economically. In turn, this makes it possible for media organizations to take content from one form to another and to experiment with cross-media forms.

SEE ALSO: **digital revolution**.

media drenching See: MEDIA SATURATION.

media imperialism A means by which powerful countries dominate others through their control of the media. For centuries, some countries have sought to dominate others economically and politically. When successful this is usually accompanied by cultural domination (SEE: **cultural imperialism**). The media may be an important means by which cultural domination may be secured.

The starting point for an exploration of this topic is the international trade in media products. The issue is that American and, to a lesser extent, British products dominate the market. American films, television and popular music can be found more or less everywhere on the planet. In 2002, for example, of the twenty top box-office films worldwide, nineteen were American. Similarly, the majority of films shown on European television are American. Indeed, the American film industry is one of the very few American industries to have a positive net balance of trade with the rest of the world. Britain is very much a junior partner but still exports internationally.

People across the world are watching or listening to a great deal of American film, television and music. The point is significant because of the assumption that, as a result of this dominance, people in every country will be taught what to think by American media products. At this point, the argument about media imperialism becomes less clear, because it sees the audience as essentially passive. The first point to make is that American culture does not seem to overwhelm audiences. Quite the contrary, audiences will use their own cultural assumptions to interpret, and even criticize, the American material that they see. For example, the American soap opera *Dallas* was sold in over ninety countries and became a craze in many. In the Netherlands, for example, over half of the population watched the series at the height of its success. The reaction to this popularity on the part of politicians and opinion-formers was almost uniformly hostile. They saw *Dallas* as merely the latest symbol of the domination of American popular culture. However, the fact that the programme appealed so very widely to viewers across the world does not mean to say that it appeals in the same way, that audience reactions and interpretations are all identical. Indeed, it may be its very openness to different interpretations from different cultures that explains its global success, as one particular study argues. At its extremes, this variability of response is shown in countries in which *Dallas* was not a success. In Japan, for example, the programme was a dismal failure (Liebes and Katz, 1993).

A second issue with the media imperialism thesis is that what may happen as a result of the intrusiveness of Western, and especially American, media is a mixing of cultures rather than the simple domination of one over others. Popular music is a good example of this. New musical forms are generated out of the mixture of Western and non-Western indigenous traditions.

Most significantly, local cultures may be much more resilient than a pessimistic view would have us believe. Less-developed, and even some more-developed, countries will have difficulty in creating media industries with access to the equipment needed to serve the demands of their populations. Print-based industries – newspapers, magazines and books – are relatively simple to develop and will serve local cultures. Recorded popular music demands a recording industry as well as a method of distribution. Broadcasting and film require even more capital to start up. In these circumstances, it is not surprising that American products will arrive to fill a vacuum. Alternatively, multinational media companies may adopt the strategy of operating in developing countries *within* the language and culture of the society. Then, as indigenous media companies start up, they will have the capacity to respond to local cultures. Some of these have become important providers and now *they* export to other countries. Good examples are Indian cinema (SEE: **Bollywood**) and Brazilian and Mexican soap opera (SEE: **globo; televisa**).

SEE ALSO: **concentration of ownership; globalization; global media; media companies.**

media mogul or **media baron** An entrepreneur with a significant public presence who runs (and partly owns) media companies and who, thereby, wields considerable power and influence. Past examples include Lords BEAVERBROOK and NORTHCLIFFE, who were newspaper proprietors. Contemporary examples are SILVIO BERLUSCONI and RUPERT MURDOCH, both of whom have interests in television and newspapers.

media planning The organization of advertising campaigns which use the media. Advertising agencies will employ, either directly or indirectly, people whose job it is to advise clients on the most cost-effective media in which to advertise. Judgements about this cost-effectiveness will depend on a knowledge of the likely effectiveness of media in the generation of sales of the particular product together with an understanding of how the product is designed to appeal. Media planners will work within certain constraints. For example, they will be given a budget, the client will have decided what the target market is to be, and the length of the advertising will be set. Planners then have to balance a whole series of decisions. Media have to be chosen which will be seen, heard or read by the target audience. Will it be bus shelter posters, cinema, television or newspapers or some combination of all of these? Coverage – the number of people in the target market reached by the media – has to be balanced within the budget against the frequency with which advertisements are projected at the market. Should advertisements appear in a large burst, perhaps in several media, to make an impact or come out slowly over time to maintain exposure? Different media will be able to satisfy different objectives. Clearly radio is only suitable for sound. Television is better for creating an image. Telephone or direct mail marketing is used when the consumer is expected to do something quickly in response.

SEE ALSO: **advertising agency; advertising campaign.**

media policy The regulation of media by government or approach to media by organization or group. This is now often a central aspect of the aims of governments and states. All media are regulated in some form, and the prime way in which this is done is in national frameworks. In addition to this essentially political and legal mode, there is normally recognition of the importance of the media in economic and cultural terms. Thus, media are important in the generation of national wealth and prosperity, through sales both within a society and externally. Media are also important through cultural aspects of policy, where there is often a desire to protect national identities, normally from the perceived threat of the influence of American media. These different dimensions are increasingly important at the local and regional levels as well. Thus, most cities now have some form of cultural and media policy that will involve the role of these aspects of life in the regeneration and continued prosperity of the locale. Many organizations will also feel that they require a policy towards the media, in order to encourage good publicity for their aims. In some respects these different aspects of the importance of the media in policy are an impetus for the development of media studies and its expansion within academic life.

SEE ALSO: **censorship; globalization; government and the media.**

media saturation Some events attract so much media attention that it makes sense to refer to them as media saturated. Media organizations put great resources into covering them, and their reporting occupies many hours of broadcasting or pages of print. The funeral of Princess Diana or the Iraq war of 2003/4 are examples. Like the related idea of media drenching, it also is used to point to the way that media have become a core aspect of society and culture in general.

mediascape A term coined by the cultural theorist Arjun Appadurai (1993, 1996), to denote one of the scapes that he sees as of increasing importance in the contemporary world. The concept has become important as a way of conceptualizing how we live in a world where media are all around us and a part of our everyday lives. Thus, it is argued that, as we live in a landscape or a cityscape, so we also live in a mediascape of some complexity. The strength of the idea also comes from the fact that, while we can in many ways steer our own course through a landscape, in that we can keep to a path or cut across a field, we are also constrained by our habits and the legislation and practice that puts some areas out of bounds to us. Thus, with the mediascape – in some ways we create our own paths in that we prefer some television programmes to others, or listen to some types of music but not others, but we are also to some degree constrained by what we can watch or listen to by, for example, the law and our financial resources.

SEE ALSO: **audience**.

media streaming Media in which delivery and consumption occur simultaneously. A book is a non-streamed medium while television is streamed. The term is most commonly employed in discussions of video streaming over computer networks. Because video computer files are relatively large, successful large-scale transmission of video over networks has had to wait for powerful computers with large storage capacity and a means of transmission with extensive BANDWIDTH.

SEE ALSO: **video-on-demand**.

media technology See: TECHNOLOGY.

mediated communication Communication that passes through a third party. A simple and direct act of COMMUNICATION is a conversation between two people. Still fairly simple is a performance of a rock band in a stadium or of a stand-up comedian in a pub. These are direct communications between performer and audience. Communication is mediated when such direct communication passes through a third party. In this sense, all activity by media organizations is an example of mediated communication. If an audience listens to a record of a rock band, the communication is mediated by the techniques of recording and the whole apparatus of the music company, which produce an entirely different sound from the live performance. Confusingly, communications involving the media may themselves be mediated. Thus, a person may hear about the news of the day, not directly from a newspaper, but from someone else who has read it.

SEE ALSO: J Curve; two-step flow.

mediation The process by which an institution or individual impacts upon another institution or individual elsewhere, often involving some degree of change in the original and that which is being impacted upon. Negus (1996) identifies three main senses of mediation: (1) the 'idea of coming in between', (2) 'a means of transmission' and (3) 'the idea that all objects, particularly works of art, are mediated by social relationships'. He argues that these ideas can be applied to the media in ways that illustrate some important institutional processes. Thus, in the first sense people can act as GATEKEEPERS in the way that studies of news have identified. Thus, journalists and editors will treat some of the events that happen in the world as news and others as not. Or they decide that some events are more important than others. With respect to the second sense, media technologies themselves act as mediators. Media technologies such as television mediate between events that happen in the world or the drama recorded in a studio and the audience. The third sense of mediation identified by Negus emphasizes that all media are involved in social relationships – they are not simply technological processes at work – and these social relationships are infused with power and power inequalities. Thus, the relationships involved in media production and consumption are mediated at a variety of levels, which involve power in different ways. This might be the power of the MEDIA BARON or the power of men in the household to determine what other members of a family watch on TV through their monopolization of the remote control.

mediatization A process whereby media become more important in society and culture. For example, it has been argued that sporting events in contemporary society have become mediatized in a number of ways. Sports personalities are increasingly promoted through the media, the nature and timing of the events themselves are affected by TV schedules, and the actual events are increasingly being judged through the use of media technology. Similar arguments can be made about a number of other areas of life, such as the political process. Many critics see mediatization as pernicious and as detracting from the authentic nature of the original event. However, while there is certainly an argument to be made along these lines, one also has to consider the possibility of the positive effects of mediatization in that, in sport for example, more people are able to see events and the quality of refereeing.

SEE ALSO: **audience.**

media violence See: VIOLENCE.

Medium is the Message, The A phrase invented by MARSHALL MCLUHAN in his *Understanding Media* to describe the importance, in his view, of the medium of communication rather than the content of the message. Some media, radio, for example, convey much more information more intensely by requiring only one of the senses than others, say television, and this intensity has important social effects. The introduction of print as an intense, information-rich medium was an important cause of the religious wars of the sixteenth century, independent of the content of the printed publications.

SEE ALSO: **hot media.**

melodrama A GENRE of cinema and theatre that centres on women's experience, interpersonal conflict and heightened emotion, and which usually places a strong emphasis on visual richness of scene and costume.

SEE ALSO: **romance.**

merchandising The process by which goods are produced in association with a media product, which can then be sold to consumers. Many successful films, such as *Star Wars* or *Spiderman*, have greatly increased their revenues by licensing the ideas, script, images or soundtrack from the film to companies which will release products associated with the film. Associated with *Star Wars*, for instance, are toys, clothes, books and games. While merchandising in not in any sense new and has been connected to a range of artists in the past – witness the explosion of goods associated with popularity of The Beatles in the 1960s including Beatle hats and plastic Beatle wigs – the process is now seen by many commentators as core to the promotion of media products.

Merchandising is in essence an exploitation of a BRAND. Although at its clearest in film, other forms of the media seek to maximize revenues from their successes in much the same way. Television series, *Teletubbies* for instance, will also have everything from sweets to books as associated merchandise. Computer games will have toys and books associated with them. Rock bands will sell T-shirts.

SEE ALSO: **advertisement; cross over; sponsorship.**

message A unit of communication between a sender and a receiver. This apparently simple definition conceals difficulties of interpretation. It would be possible, for example, to concentrate on the sender of the message and ask how effective the message has been in conveying the sender's intentions. Alternatively, one can focus on the receiver and ask how the message is interpreted. These two foci effectively assume different notions of what kind of thing a message is. The first suggests that the meaning of a message is fairly unequivocal. If the sender's intentions are misread by the receiver, that is because the message was carelessly phrased or because the receiver was distracted. In other words, poor communication can be remedied. The second approach is more radical in that it suggests that the meaning of messages is more plastic and variable and much more open to different readings by the receivers. In particular, one cannot assume that sender and receiver occupy the same *cultural* universe. What the first approach may characterize as miscommunication, the second may see as a fact of life.

SEE ALSO: **communication science; semiology**.

metaphor The figure of language where something stands for something else. For example, if we say a performer was on fire, we do not literally mean that he or she was in flames, but that the quality of the performance was such that it had fiery, inspirational or dramatic qualities that can be understood by this substitution. Metaphor is a fundamental part of LANGUAGE, but is also much used in communication in advertising.

SEE ALSO: **semiology**.

method acting Type of acting developed by Constantin Stanislavsky in the Soviet Union (therefore sometimes called Stanislavsky's method) that emphasizes how the actor should 'become' the character that he or she is playing. The method was developed by the Actors Studio in postwar USA and deployed by a number of actors and screen stars in the 1950s, most notably by Marlon Brando. The idea has also influenced the style and approach of more recent performers such as Robert de Niro.

metonymy The figure of language where a part of something stands as a representation of the whole. Thus the political process of a country may be referred to by the name of its capital city, as in the phrase 'Washington says . . .'

SEE ALSO: **semiology**.

microphone A device that converts sound into electrical energy, which can be amplified and reconverted into sound. The microphone is seen as one of the technologies that had an effect on the development of popular singing styles, especially with the advent of the so-called crooners such as Bing Crosby in the 1920s and 1930s. The use of the microphone permitted a different and more intimate singing style and conveyed relaxation. It also contributed to the promotion of the individual singer as a key focus on stage, rather than the singer being part of the band. Subsequently microphone technology and styles have developed enormously, and microphone technique is an important part of learning how to sing.

SEE ALSO: **lyrics; technology; voice.**

mimesis The process of copying, reproducing or imitating something. Thus a REALIST or NATURALIST text may seek to copy or imitate the real world. A related idea is that of mimicry.

SEE ALSO: **language.**

minorities For much of the twentieth century, the media were aimed at mass or large audiences. The result was – and to a large extent still is – that many minority groups within the population felt that their cultures or tastes were not being served or were being represented unfairly within mainstream media. Homosexuals, for example, argued that there was little television programming that directly addressed their interests, and the portrayal of homosexuals in television drama was stereotyped and unfavourable. Ethnic and religious minorities felt similarly treated. Two changes in the way that the media are provided has begun to change this situation. First, government has insisted that minorities be catered for in those media over which they can have influence (SEE: **Channel Four**). Second, it has become economically and technologically possible to cater for minorities. As minorities gain in wealth and status, it becomes worthwhile starting up newspapers, magazines or radio stations for them. DIGITAL BROADCASTING has reinforced that tendency in that it permits a multitude of channels appealing to very different markets and lowers the cost of producing radio and television programmes.

SEE ALSO: **gender; race.**

Mirror Group Newspapers (MGN) Owners of the *Daily Mirror*, the *Daily Record*, the *People*, *Sunday People* and a share in the *Independent*, MGN has taken some time to recover from its association with ROBERT MAXWELL and has lost market share to the *Sun*. In 1999, the group merged with Trinity, which published regional newspapers and the merged group – Trinity Mirror – claims to be the largest newspaper publisher in the UK.

SEE ALSO: **newspaper.**

mise-en-scène Combination of the elements seen on the screen, or in a shot in CINEMA, which might include the setting, landscape, costume and lighting. The term is often used in analysis to draw attention to particular modes of composition of images and elements and thus to the skills of particular film DIRECTORS. This can then be contrasted in analytical terms with, for example, the script, attention to the NARRATIVE of the film (how the story is told) or the role of the STARS and celebrity. For example, Monument Valley in the USA has become a key aspect of the mise-en-scène of the westerns of the director John Ford, which often starred John Wayne.

SEE ALSO: **auteur theory**.

mixing The process whereby different instruments or sounds recorded on separate channels or tracks are brought together to produce the final product that can be released for sale on the market or broadcast on radio and TV. As recording technology has increased in sophistication with the development of increasing numbers of tracks for recording and computerization, the scope for the mixing of music in different ways has increased significantly. In the early days of recording, music was recorded 'live' in the studio. The musicians would be located in different places in the same room and would play together. If a mistake was made then the whole 'take' would have to start again. As technology developed, it became possible to record the drums on one track, the bass guitar on another and the piano on another and so on. This then meant, for example, that the keyboard player could add his or her 'part' to the complete tune at a different time (or even from a different continent) from the bass player or the drummer. It also opens up the possibility that music can be mixed in different ways to produce different sounds – the voice might be mixed up or down or strings might be added to the basic tracks (as by Phil Spector in the famous case of The Beatles' *Let it Be* (1970) album). This gives the person in charge of the mixing (most often the PRODUCER) significant power over the final sound. The process of mixing is also a part of the 'live' performance of music. The sound of the live band will be controlled from the mixing desk. Also, live dance music will involve mixing as a creative act. Here the DJ will mix different sounds together to produce one overall effect. The salience of this practice in dance culture was signalled by the title of the UK magazine of this type of music – *Mixmag*.

SEE ALSO: **music industry**.

MMS See: MULTIMEDIA MESSAGING SERVICE.

mobile communications Many forms of the media are used in fixed locations television, film and radio, for example. Technological changes have meant greater mobility with the advent of portable radios, CD and

DVD players and even televisions. However, the use of newer technologies, especially digital rather than analogue signalling, radio and miniaturization of computer devices has enabled further opportunities for mobility. This is illustrated by the mobile phone. It has now developed so that it can not only be used for voice conversations, but also for texting, email, and downloading music and pictures. Further development will allow greater integration of media and better performance, meaning that one single device will play films and music and be used for communication between people.

SEE ALSO: **media convergence; new information and communication technologies.**

mobilization The process by which people become involved in an activity. Most often used with respect to political movements, with the idea that individuals or groups can be drawn into an activity, a protest movement, for example, through a variety of factors. One of these factors could be the media. Thus, images of starvation in Africa on television and newspapers concentrated attention on the problem and mobilized sectors of the population to contribute financially to events such as Live Aid in 1985 (Garafalo, 1992). Mobilization has also been considered in a more negative fashion through, for example, the role that newspapers and radio have played in the mobilization of people to engage in extreme political campaigns and parties, such as the Nazis in Germany in the 1920s and 1930s.

model sheet Set of drawings used in the animation process to provide examples of feature characters.

SEE ALSO: **animation.**

mode of address When one party is communicating with another they will use different modes of address in different circumstances and with different purposes in mind. For example, when giving a speech to a large audience, the speaker will use relatively formal language appropriate to a public event. Similarly, television in its early days used a mode of address that suited a public event. In a private conversation between two people, however, a public mode of address would be inappropriate, and an altogether more intimate tone will be adopted. It is argued that the mode of address of television has changed. Although it is a public medium, it is received in homes, which are private spaces. As a result, it has adopted a mode of address more like a conversation that is suited to a domestic environment.

SEE ALSO: **directness of address.**

modernism Term used to characterize a broad movement in the arts in the late nineteenth and early twentieth centuries. The movement contested previous REALIST forms and led to a new emphasis on experimentation with form. Examples of modernism would include James Joyce and Marcel Proust in the novel, T. S. Eliot and Ezra Pound in poetry, Pablo Picasso and Georges Braque in painting and Igor Stravinsky and Arnold Schoenberg in music. Modernism in literature and art made the familiar world as depicted in realism strange or opaque, used narratives that were fragmented, rather than having a clear beginning, middle and end, and foregrounded its own production, through the often strong intervention of the artistic strategy of the author. Modernism, then, often appears 'difficult' by comparison with some realist forms. Modernism was also very influential in new movements in architecture from the 1920s onward through the Bauhaus and the work of Le Corbusier. This led to an architecture that emphasized the use of modern materials such as concrete and the removal of ornamentation from buildings to allow the foregrounding of function.

monopoly A situation in which one company or organization is the only one operating in a market, so reducing competition. Although in other fields this term is applied to commercial situations, in the media (and other public services) it has also been used to describe the situation in which a public broadcaster dominates broadcasting. For example, the BBC was set up in the 1920s quite deliberately as a monopoly. In the 1950s, it was believed that this monopoly was a poor idea and viewers and listeners deserved greater choice. Commercial or public service monopolies are a particularly sensitive issue in the media since such monopoly providers may be biased in their provision of news, comment and debate while impartially provided information is critical for a healthy democracy. Worries of this kind have surfaced in connection with NEWS INTERNATIONAL in the US, the UK and globally and Fininvest in Italy.

SEE ALSO: **concentration of ownership; economics of the media.**

montage The process of film editing that combines shots that may seem to be narratively disconnected in order to produce a complex overall meaning. One of the most discussed examples of this process is the use made of it by the Russian film director Sergei Eisenstein in his film *Battleship Potemkin* (1925), where, in the famous 'Odessa Steps sequence', he edits together a range of images that are narratively 'impossible' to create a range of new meanings which connect events and ideas together.

SEE ALSO: **auteur theory; language; semiology.**

MOO See: MUD.

moral entrepreneur See: MORAL PANIC.

moral panic The populations of contemporary societies appear to be faced with successive crises or panics of different kinds – AIDS, global warming, asylum-seekers, mugging, flooding, excessive drinking by women, pensions, GM crops, to name but a few. These social anxieties have a number of features in common. They are panics or explosions which appear suddenly, perhaps triggered by an event of some kind, only to subside fairly rapidly to be replaced by a new one. They tend to encourage a sense of the apocalypse while, at the same time, they exaggerate the degree of risk. For example, numerous surveys show that the elderly are worried about being assaulted in the street, although the chances of this happening are comparatively low and much lower than the chances of a young man being attacked. The media play a critical role in organizing and disseminating these anxieties, and this is enhanced by the tendency for elements of the media to take up stories from each other. Anxieties of this kind are not without historical precedent. Medieval societies, for instance, were plagued by mass movements of people who believed that the world was coming to an end. But their intensity and frequency are particularly modern, not least because of the much greater efficiency of contemporary systems of mass communication.

Despite the common features of mass anxieties, there are also differences between them. Some, for example, have identifiable perpetrators who can be blamed, and anxieties of this kind are known as moral panics. These, as the name implies, involve a moral judgement about the behaviour of a particular group of people – paedophiles, asylum-seekers, young people. Because of a newsworthy event, an issue is identified that appears to pose a threat to the basic values and way of life of society. A group of people is named as responsible. The media take up the story and extend it by implying that there is a general danger of which this story is but an example. Influential people ('moral entrepreneurs') organize a campaign, forming associations with like-minded others. The media report their activities, giving a further turn of the screw. Government agencies feel that they have to respond. Politicians make speeches, the police may be more vigilant, governments threaten new legislation. There is a cycle whereby the original event is amplified, tapping into people's anxieties and sometimes having very real social effects. The press, television and radio provide the oil whereby this cycle is kept going.

SEE ALSO: **amplification of deviance; Cohen; folk devil.**

Morley, David (b. 1949) Professor of Communications at Goldsmiths College, University of London. He has made contributions to the study of audiences, especially in the ground-breaking *Nationwide* studies (Brunsdon and Morley, 1978; Morley, 1980), and on the place of television and other home technologies in everyday life (Morley, 1986). More recently he has written extensively on the nature of global cultural change and its effects on media consumption, especially in the influential book *Home Territories* (Morley, 2000).

SEE ALSO: **audience; Centre for Contemporary Cultural Studies**.

motivation 1 The reasons that people have for consuming different media or different aspects of the media according to what it is that motivates them. This is an aspect of those analyses of the AUDIENCE and consumption that place greater emphasis on the psychological aspects of human action. An issue here is that, especially with respect to a medium like television, which is mainly watched in the home, there may be a range of motivations for watching a particular programme that are not simply to do with individual preference. For example, programmes may be watched because another person in the household has a preference for them.

2 Used in acting to refer to the ability to capture what it is that impels the character that they are playing. This is an important aspect of trying to convey the reality of a character or situation. Actors have often gone to great lengths to empathize with their character, changing their body shape, for example.

SEE ALSO: **method acting**.

movie mogul Term developed to characterize those with the greatest power within the film industry. With respect to the early Hollywood system (1920s–1940s), the term is applied to the heads of studio, who carried huge power in decisions about all aspects of the film-making process. Examples of these powerful men include: Jack Warner (Warner Bros), David O. Selznick (RKO), Darryl Zanuck (Twentieth Century Fox), Adolph Zukor and Barney Balaban (Paramount), Louis B. Mayer and Irving Thalberg (Metro-Goldwyn-Mayer), Carl Laemmle Jr (Universal) and Harry Cohn (Columbia).

SEE ALSO: **Hollywood; media mogul**.

MP3 Format for the storing of music on computers and digital music players such as the Apple iPod. MP3 stands for Moving Pictures Experts Group – ½ Audio Layer 3. It is a format that allows for the condensing of large amounts of information into small files. Such compression allows for the storing of a whole collection of albums on a digital music player, which is then portable. It also facilitates the rapid downloading of music from the internet.

SEE ALSO: **digitization**.

MTV (Music Television) A television channel that began transmitting in the USA in 1981, but which has gone on to become a global player. In its early period of development it was intimately connected with the rise of the MUSIC VIDEO, leading to much debate about whether the video was eclipsing live performance and recorded sound as the main way in which popular music would be conveyed and understood. This debate has now died down, but the importance of MTV as a key specialist channel (even though it carries a greater variety of programming beyond videos) and its effects on the music and media industries, in terms of sales and generation of audience interest, remains significant.

SEE ALSO: **music industry**.

MUD (multi-user dungeon) Originally a text-based computer game which could be played by several people via a dial-up or broadband connection. It consisted of a series of rooms and involved the solving of puzzles, searching for treasure and fighting. More recent versions, called MOOs, use images and more closely resemble games run on a personal computer.

SEE ALSO: **computer games**.

mug shot a photograph in a newspaper of a person's head only.

multimedia Describes the combination of media into one form that shows the integrated effects of this new combination. The term is used in art to refer to the way in which an art text may combine a range of media, such as video, music and sculpture, breaking away from, for example, the use of paint and canvas alone. The idea connects to that of CONVERGENCE in that technologies are coming together to integrate previously separate experiences. For example, contemporary digital TVs and DVD players can receive radio and play CDs as well as receiving TV and being used to play DVDs.

SEE ALSO: **digitization**.

multimedia messaging service (MMS) A means of sending messages containing multimedia material, e.g. video, music, images, rather than simply text, to mobile phones and other handheld devices.

SEE ALSO: **short messaging service**.

multiplex Type of cinema, consisting of a number of screens, that is increasingly located outside of city centres along with shops and gyms.

This process of suburbanization of leisure can have significant effects on the centres of cities and towns as they 'empty out', producing 'edge cities'.

SEE ALSO: **cinema**.

multi-tracking In the early days of recording, music was recorded live in the field or live in the studio. This meant that it was impossible to mix the music in any other way than that in which it had been recorded. The advent of multi-tracking, which means that each instrument or sound can be recorded on a different track, created the possibility that sound could be manipulated to produce many different versions of the 'original' sound. This technology created new jobs, such as that of the mixer, and new forms of creativity, which have fed into the creation of new forms of music such as electronic music.

SEE ALSO: **mixing; music industry**.

Mulvey, Laura (b. 1941) Professor of Film and Media Studies at Birkbeck College, University of London. A British film theorist and AVANT-GARDE film-maker, she is most influential for her analysis and critique of the gendered nature of visual pleasure in dominant Hollywood cinema and the way in which this constructs a MALE GAZE. These controversial ideas have led to extensive further research and debate.

SEE ALSO: **feminism; gender**.

Murdoch, Rupert (b. 1931) The son of an Australian newspaper proprietor, Rupert Murdoch has built up a global media group embracing newspapers, magazines, film production, television, book publishing and radio. One of the strengths of his company, NEWS CORPORATION, is that the family continues to own a substantial stake in it, and Murdoch has appointed members of his family to key roles within it. One of the most powerful figures in global media, if not the most powerful, Murdoch attracts substantial criticism. He is commercially very aggressive and has used his influence to lobby governments sensitive to potential criticism in his newspapers in order to further his interests. Ex-employees of News Corporation have said that Murdoch's own right-wing politics influences the content of television and newspapers that he owns. He has even attracted criticism from neo-conservatives in the United States for the low moral standards of the Fox television network.

SEE ALSO: **media mogul**.

music Systematic arrangement of sound. It would appear that almost all cultures and societies will have generated some form of music. In that sense, it is almost as basic to human society as LANGUAGE. The systematic study of music is musicology. The study of popular music has considered a number of different aspects of music. On one level, there has been attention to the texts of music and especially to those of popular music. A key debate here has been over the extent to which the tools of conventional musicology, such as attention to the score and the notes, can be applied to popular music, which may not exist in such a form. While this debate is ongoing, popular musicology has developed its own approaches using ideas from SEMIOLOGY as well as concepts such as DISCOURSE and MEDIATION. Other branches of popular music studies have considered the political economic context of the MUSIC INDUSTRY, the social production of music in bands and localities, the nature of the popular music audience and how music is part of subcultures and everyday life (Longhurst, 2007; Shuker, 2001).

SEE ALSO: **beat; lyrics; mixing; voice.**

musical A GENRE of cinema film that has music at the core of its narrative. As with all genres, there are a range of different types of musical or subgenres. These will involve different combinations of song, dance, performance and narrative (Cook and Bernink, 1999). It is significant that the film that is used to date the beginning of the 'talkie' era was a musical (*The Jazz Singer* (dir. Alan Crosland, 1927)). Many musicals include dance routines that have involved some of the most famous stars in cinema history, such as Fred Astaire and Ginger Rogers, who starred in a number of musicals in the 1930s. Also well known and much discussed are the 1930s films of the choreographer Busby Berkeley, which use spectacular dance routines to produce geometric effects. Musicals, especially the musical drama form, often had a group of musicians, singers or dancers as central characters, thus providing a narrative explanation for the prominence of music. For example, in *Gentlemen Prefer Blondes* (dir. Howard Hawks, 1953) Marilyn Monroe and Jane Russell played singer/dancers on a ship carrying the Olympic team from the USA to France. Musicals have continued to be important, though they are much less significant than they were. The genre accommodated the advent of ROCK AND ROLL in the 1950s, and Elvis Presley spent much of the period from 1956 to 1968 starring in a succession of Hollywood musicals. This practice carried on into the 1960s, when many popular groups, most notably The Beatles, starred in British films like *A Hard Day's Night* (dir. Richard Lester, 1964) and *Help!* (dir. Richard Lester, 1965). While these sorts of musical are less common today, the Spice Girls made a successful foray into the form with *Spice World* (dir. Bob Spiers, 1997). Other musicals such as *Saturday Night Fever* (dir. John Badham, 1977) have proved to be very popular. Explanations for the success of the genre have often been found in the possibilities that it provides for ESCAPISM. One more recent twist to the tale of the interconnections between the visual, sound and narrative has been the more recent sales success of film soundtracks showing the influence of the MUSIC VIDEO form.

SEE ALSO: **cinema**.

musician A player of music. The development of a distinct profession of musician is a relatively recent phenomenon. Musicians are normally categorized as amateur, semi-professional or professional, though the boundaries between these categories are inevitably blurred. There have been a small number of influential academic studies of musicians. The work of H. Becker (1963) on jazz musicians of the 1940s illuminated the occupational culture of this group, with its contempt for the non-musicians, labelled as 'squares'. It also demonstrated the ways in which the demands of the commercial marketplace and authenticity produced dilemmas for the musicians. H. Stith Bennett (1980) developed aspects of Becker's interactionist approach in his influential study of rock music copy bands in 1960s USA. More recently, to take some important examples, Ruth Finnegan (1989) has explored the role of everyday music-making in the English town of Milton Keynes. S. Cohen (1991) has examined the 'indie' scene in Liverpool with particular reference to gender and commercialization, J. Schloss (2004) has considered the practices of hip-hop producers, and J. Toynbee (2000) has offered an overview of musical creativity.

SEE ALSO: **music industry; scene**.

music industry The music industry is concerned with the production of musical forms for sale on the market. The industry globally is dominated by the power of a small number of very large firms, which have risen to dominance by controlling markets and by processes of merger and acquisition. Currently four such companies dominate: Sony/BMG, EMI, Universal and Warner which, between them, produce approximately 75 per cent of recorded music globally. Two of these companies (Sony/BMG and Universal) are parts of other larger companies, whereas two (EMI and Warner) operate outside a wider CONGLOMERATE structure. The music industry has been concentrated (SEE: **concentration of ownership**) in this way for a significant time, though there are cycles of concentration. There are also smaller producers, often called independents (SEE: **independent company**).

The industry has products (such as CDs, vinyl records and tapes) which act as repositories of musical texts. In 2002 the value of such sales was $31 billion, showing a significant decrease from the near $40 billion reached in 1996 (Laing, 2004), with the USA being by far the largest market followed by Japan and the countries of Western Europe. The industry is also increasingly concerned with the protection and exploitation of various rights (SEE: **copyright; intellectual property**).

The industry is structured by a division of labour within companies, which produces a variety of tasks and occupations such as A & R, PRO-DUCERS (who guide the creative process in the studio), engineers (who ensure that the right sound is produced in the studio technically) and MARKETING (who publicize the products). As with other media industries the music industry is increasing globalized as it acts across the world with little respect for national boundaries. Moreover, the industry in increasingly integrated with other industries, television and film, for example, that have historically been concerned with different products. It is likely that this process of CONVERGENCE will continue to break down the barriers between the different aspects of media industries. This will be reinforced by computer technologies and digital downloading, which will increasingly affect the purchase of the formats (e.g. CDs, tapes and records) that have successively sustained the industry throughout its history.

SEE ALSO: **majors.**

music press Newspapers and magazines devoted to music. The music press plays a significant role in the promotion of particular music, tastes and ways of understanding music (Shuker, 2001). There are newspapers and magazines for all specialist modes of music. While a music press has existed since the early days of the music industry, notably in the UK with the *Melody Maker* (1929–2000), a key development beyond the trade papers such as *Cashbox* (USA) and *Music Week* (UK) came with the advent of the rock magazines like *Creem* and especially *Rolling Stone* in the US in the late 1960s. This rapidly led to the development of the 'inkie' rock press in the UK, in such publications as *Melody Maker*, *New Musical Express* and *Sounds*. These were seen as engaged in a more sophisticated sort of criticism than the previously existing teen/fan publications, such as has continued in the UK in *Smash Hits*, and have been seen as very important in the development of rock culture and criticism. In the 1990s a new wave of glossy monthly magazines, such as *Q*, *Mojo* and *Uncut*, were developed to cater for different segments of the ageing rock audience.

SEE ALSO: **music industry.**

music video Music video developed as a distinct type of text in the 1980s. There were precursors that combined music, visual image and NARRATIVE image, such as the musical film and short films made for cinema or television. However, taking a cue from the film produced for Queen's very successful 'Bohemian Rhapsody', music video came of age with the development of the dedicated television stations for their programming such as MTV. In their early days such films were called promos, as they had the key function of promoting a particular band, singer or, most likely, particular track or song. In this sense, music videos can be seen as a form of advertising. Some commentators have classified music videos into different types, most notably the film writer E. A. Kaplan (1987). Her analysis sought to show the connections between music videos and the development of postmodern textual forms. This approach, while influential, has been criticized for its focus on the visual aspect of the video and neglecting the music. This argument was most clearly advanced by A. Goodwin (1993) in the most comprehensive analysis of the earlier period of music video and MTV. In the 1980s there was some degree of concern that music video would have a detrimental effect on the quality and variety of popular music. Such criticism often came from musicians who had been schooled in rock traditions and was most clearly represented in Dire Straits' hit single 'Money for Nothing' – itself a big MTV hit. Such criticism is now rare, and music video has spread across the range of genres of music.

SEE ALSO: **cinema**.

MySpace The brand name of a website, now owned by NEWS CORPOR-ATION, which offers a range of features that help social networking. Of particular note are the capacity to post personal profiles, which can include video, photographic material or music, combined with an INSTANT MESSAGING service. Although reliable evidence is scarce, it is said that the site is mostly used intensively by groups of young people who use it to sustain and enlarge their social networks. It is also used by people who are trying to make a career and find it an effective form of self-marketing. Worries have surfaced in the press that MySpace, and sites like it (SEE: **LiveJournal**), are used by sexual predators.

mystification The way in which an activity or process is made obscure. It is held by Marxist critics that the media are centrally involved in mystification in advanced capitalist societies in the sense that they deflect attention from inequalities of power and status and conceal the exploitation of one class by another that lies at the heart of capitalist society. The engagement of the population with popular media and personalities is held to lead them away from the 'real' issues confronting society.

SEE ALSO: **critical theory; hegemony; ideology; Marxism**.

myth The narratives of society that, when analysed, reveal core aspects, understandings or assumptions of that society or culture. These are often part of commonsense ideas that people have about their society and culture and are mobilized in new narratives that may inflect them in particular directions. For example, the WESTERN may be thought of as condensing myths about American society and culture concerning the call of the wild and individual achievement, and specific westerns will occupy themselves with different aspects of individualism or the relationship between the individual and society. More specifically ROLAND BARTHES (1973) used the idea of myth to capture how the connotation (See: DENOTATION/CONNOTATION) process involved in SIGNIFICATION is myth-like. Here, in Barthes' view, myths operate more specifically in a society like France in favour of the dominant class in a capitalist society. Thus, in one of Barthes' most famous examples, a black soldier saluting the French flag is part of a myth of the inclusiveness of the French imperial 'family', which transcends and obscures ethnic differences and effectively suppresses conflict based on ethnic difference.

SEE ALSO: **hegemony; ideology; language; semiology.**

Napster Website that facilitated free access to music on a file-sharing basis. It was shut down in 2000 as the result of a court case, but it has now reopened on a subscription basis (in 2004 in Britain). Napster is one of the largest of such services, but there are a number of others.

narcotic Many of those who are critical of the media suggest that the effect of the media is much like that of a drug and, similarly, induces a dulling of the critical faculties.

SEE ALSO: **Frankfurt School**.

narrative The way in which a tale or story is told. Narratives tell a story through a sequence of actions and events. They may be very simple or more complex. An example of a very simple narrative is 'The cat sat on the mat.' Here, the story is told through one sequence of events and involves only one active participant. Most narratives are much more complex than this, involving many sequences of action and many characters. For example, the narrative to the British continuous serial *Coronation Street* has been developing without a break since 1960, involving thousands of characters and stories. Despite such complexity, STRUCTURALIST analyses have suggested that many narratives involve a relatively limited number of key characters (or character functions), the HERO or the villain for example, and a fairly consistent set of actions and sequences of events. Influential examples of this approach can be found in Wright's (1975) analysis of the narrative structure of the WESTERN film or Radway's (1987) consideration of the romantic novel (SEE: **romance**). Narrative analysis has been applied to many media that involve fiction. However, the techniques used can also be applied to factual television or documentary. Here narratives are used to report or comment on real events.

Another important distinction in narrative is between OPEN and CLOSED TEXTS. The former leaves more scope for interpretation by the reader and the latter less so. The texts of MODERNISM or POSTMODERNISM are often more open in that the links between different aspects of the narrative require more work on the part of the viewer or reader. Closed texts may be more simple and often have much less scope for interpretation. Thus, 'The cat sat on the mat' is both simple and relatively closed. However, there is still scope for the reader to imagine different sorts of cats and mats, as well as perhaps a coal fire burning in the background, or sunlight streaming through an open door.

SEE ALSO: **genre.**

narrowcasting See: BROADCASTING.

nation See: NATIONALISM.

nationalism A set of beliefs in the unity of the population of a nation-state founded in some common characteristics, such as language, religion or ethnicity. It is often argued that the media, and especially the news-papers, are nationalistic, promoting the idea of Britishness by contrasting what they take to be the British way of life with that of other countries. It is useful to distinguish hot from cool nationalism. The former is manifested in the kind of fervour, often violent, that has characterized such countries as Iran or Serbia in recent times. Cool nationalism, on the other hand, is the routine, everyday acceptance of nationality. Part of this everydayness lies in the way that media organizations assume that their audience members are part of one nation. The very language is of us and them. Newspaper reporting of immigration throughout the second half of the twentieth century has contributed to this, by contrasting the culture of immigrants with the assumed way of life of the British. Cool nationalism is not just restricted to the presentation of news or current affairs. Soap opera and situation comedy on television, for instance, similarly invoke stereotypical images of other nations, with the French and Germans coming in for particular notice. In the reporting of sport, particularly football, cool nationalism becomes a bit hotter. In sum, the media are contributing to the construction of the nation as an 'imagined community'. The nation is a bit like the local community in which we live in that we feel secure and we know its ways. But it is imagined in that we cannot possibly know everybody concerned, and that act of imagination is greatly helped by the language of the media and the portrayals of Britain and other countries. In practice, of course, nationalism does not work in the media quite as smoothly as that. Although the media may portray the United Kingdom as one nation, actually there are nationalisms within it. The Welsh and the Scottish, for instance, frequently wish to see their nations represented in the media as nations and to have their own language used. There are Welsh-language television soap operas, for example, and audiences identify strongly with the Welshness that is portrayed.

SEE ALSO: **gender; imagined community; race; stereotype**.

National Readership Survey (NRS) A non-profit-making limited company, formerly called JICNARS, which provides an estimate of the number of readers of newspapers and magazines and of the demographic characteristics of those readers in terms of sex, age, nationality and occupation. These data are used by advertisers to plan advertising campaigns. NRS interviews about 35,000 individuals per year, a large sample which gives the ability to offer detailed analyses.

SEE ALSO: **Audit Bureau of Circulations; circulation**.

***Nationwide* study** An important study of the way that audiences interpret – or read – television (SEE: **encoding/decoding**). The emphasis here is not on the effect of television on audiences or the use that they make of it but rather on the *meaning* of television. In the *Nationwide* study, Morley (1980), much influenced by STUART HALL'S work on ENCODING/DECODING, argues that social background and context determine the way in which television is interpreted. His method was to show an example of a current affairs magazine programme, *Nationwide*, to different groups of people each of which represented a different social position – apprentices or black further education students, for instance. There was then a discussion of the programme in the group which showed the interpretations that the groups gave. Morley classified these interpretations into three types. Some groups, bank managers, for instance, gave *dominant* readings, which embodied the values, beliefs and attitudes that are dominant in society. *Oppositional* or *critical* readings were given by groups, shop stewards, for example, which contradicted the dominant beliefs and values. Thirdly, some groups produced *negotiated* readings, which involved a meaning system that could live with dominant values without necessarily fully believing or accepting them. Morley points out that this classification into three types of reading is itself crude in that there are differences within each type. Thus, shop stewards and black further education students both adopted oppositional readings but the former were actively radical, seeing the programme as biased against working-class interests, while the latter effectively withdrew, seeing *Nationwide* simply as not relevant to them.

SEE ALSO: **aberrant decoding; effect; ideology; preferred reading; uses and gratifications**.

naturalism 1 With respect to methods of investigation, this refers to approaches to the study of the media in society that rely upon methods that are commonly associated with the natural sciences, such as seeking to prove an HYPOTHESIS or engaging in the use of testing of models. For example, an investigation of the television AUDIENCE that relied upon the use of questionnaires to count the number of hours watched by different households or groups would be naturalistic.

2 A type of text. Naturalistic texts are those that in some way seek to show the detail of the EVERYDAY LIFE of people. There is much confusion between REALISM and naturalism. However, key exponents of naturalism within the nineteenth-century novel such as Emile Zola sought to show both how everyday life could be depicted in detail in the novel and also the effects of heredity on the actions of those depicted. This usage has some commonality with sense 1, as naturalism as a textual strategy has many affinities with the desire to study human life in a scientific way.

SEE ALSO: **genre; narrative**.

NBC (National Broadcasting Company) Founded in the mid-1920s as a radio network, NBC started television broadcasting in the late 1930s. It was originally owned by RCA but is now part of General Electric. In the 1930s, the FEDERAL COMMUNICATIONS COMMISSION found that NBC controlled the majority of radio audiences and forced the company to divest itself of part of the business, which became ABC.

SEE ALSO: **CBS; Fox Network**.

needle-time Time that a radio station is allowed to broadcast commercially recorded music. The term is derived from the dropping of the stylus or 'needle' on to a disc. The restrictions on needle-time impacted upon the development of popular music in Britain in the 1960s. The pirate stations could play recorded popular music without restriction (as they operated outside the law), but the BBC, once reorganized in 1967, was under restriction. One consequence of this was 'live' formats were developed, and 'sessions' were included in programmes that otherwise played records. The most famous of these were the 'Peel Sessions' on John Peel's programme, which often gave new bands the chance to be heard by a wider audience.

negotiated reading See: NATIONWIDE STUDY.

Net Book Agreement (NBA) Towards the end of the nineteenth century, booksellers and, to a lesser extent, publishers became worried that the practice of selling books at a discount was undermining booksellers' profits and making it difficult to sell books with a small readership but which were, nevertheless, of considerable artistic or intellectual merit. Eventually, an agreement, the Net Book Agreement, was signed between the

Publishers' Association, the Society of Authors and the Booksellers' Association. The NBA stipulated that publishers would supply books to booksellers on condition that they sold them to the public at the price specified by the publisher (the net price). The publisher would give a discount on the published price, which gave the bookseller his income.

The NBA was a form of price-fixing. As such it came under attack from the very beginning from those who argued that it restricted competition and was in restraint of trade. It proved, however, extraordinarily resilient until the late 1980s and early 1990s. Publishers and booksellers, probably with increasing uneasiness in the case of the former, supported the agreement because it ensured the continuation of independent bookshops in many towns and allowed shops to stock a wide variety of books, not just best-sellers. Governments were similarly unwilling to act against what was a restrictive practice and for the same reasons: reading and books were privileged. However, the agreement collapsed in the 1990s. Large bookshop chains appeared that carried considerable clout with publishers. In order to stay competitive they preferred to have the opportunity to discount the publisher's recommended price, especially for best-sellers. Smaller independent bookshops were indeed squeezed out of business, and, as a result, there are fewer bookshops and there are some towns without one. A similar process occurred with small independent record shops. These tendencies have been exacerbated by the growth of internet bookselling. However, there is as yet no evidence that fewer books are being published.

SEE ALSO: **book publishing**.

network See: TELEVISION NETWORK.

network society The idea that society, or smaller forms of social organization, can be described as a network, a set of elements loosely and flexibly connected. In the social sciences there are several approaches to the study of society that use differing forms of network analysis. A very influential and fairly recent one has been developed by Manuel Castells (1996), who argues that networks have become the dominant form of social organization in an INFORMATION or KNOWLEDGE SOCIETY. For him, the crucial point is that the elements in the network are related to one another by flows of communication or information. The media, and even more the NEW MEDIA, form a critical and growing means of providing this flow.

SEE ALSO: **digitization; globalization**.

new information and communication technologies (NICT) Within the last thirty or forty years, the development of new technologies has begun to change the way in which the media industries produce and distribute content and the manner in which audiences relate to that content. The main driver for these changes is the greatly increased use of digital technologies (SEE: **digital revolution**). In assessing these changes, it is wise, not only to be cautious about claimed revolutions, but also not to overstate the importance of technological changes by themselves.

All the media – print, sound, film, television, photography – use digital platforms for much of their production processes. This makes production easier, cheaper and faster. Visual and sound material can be integrated smoothly and efficiently with text, making it much easier for producers to pull different media forms together. CROSS-MEDIA OWNERSHIP therefore makes more financial sense. These changes have had major impacts on the working lives of employees in the media industries. For example, production in most print media involved several stages each of which was carried out by a specialized and skilled person – author, editor, typesetter, printer – and involved entering the text more than once. The process is now much less fragmented, text is entered by the author, and fewer specialized and relatively expensive staff are employed. Digital platforms do allow audiences to interact with the media to an extent. They also permit audience involvement in production – downloading music, editing film, integrating photographs with text, for example. Much more significant for the audience, however, is the reduced cost of media provision and the increase in choice. Digital television, for example, provides for an enormous increase in the number of channels, allowing those channels to be more specialized. Broadcasting is being replaced by narrowcasting, and the media market is less of a mass market and more of a differentiated one (SEE: **market segmentation/differentiation**).

The ideal of PUBLIC SERVICE BROADCASTING is based on the idea that the public as a whole will be served by the same broadcaster. If the public takes to a multi-channel offering, then the ideal is undermined. In the UK, technological changes have therefore forced reconsideration of the position of the BBC as a provider of *mass* media and a public service broadcaster, and the Corporation has started up number of specialist digital TV channels. Similarly, older patterns of REGULATION of the media are threatened by new technologies. Clearly, regulation is much less easy if there is a multitude of channels and providers. This is a particularly obvious difficulty in the case of the internet. New technologies pose a similar threat to attempts to control the market by producers. For example, it is so much easier for people to copy digitally produced film, music and text. That threatens traditional notions of the rights that authors have in their work (SEE: **copyright**). Such trends also make it necessary for companies to work out new ways of charging for their products, thus altering the business models of media industries.

New information and communication technologies have therefore significantly affected audiences and producers of traditional media. They also have the capacity to generate new forms. In this the communication aspect is particularly important. For example, the INTERNET is potentially a new form even if it has been over-hyped in recent years. Then again, the development of MOBILE COMMUNICATIONS allied with smaller computers may give audiences different ways of accessing and using media. It is far too early to tell if any of the claimed potential of new technologies will actually come to pass.

SEE ALSO: **active audience; interactive media; new media; technological determinism.**

new media Media of communication based upon digital technology and access to the internet. Within the last two or three decades, the production, distribution and consumption of media of all kinds have been substantially transformed by NEW INFORMATION AND COMMUNICATION TECHNOLOGIES. These changes have also been assisted by alterations and relaxations in the regime of REGULATION.

As far as *production* is concerned, the use of digital technologies has made the production process in all branches of the media more streamlined and efficient. For example, film editing is now done on computer, shortening the time involved radically. The production of printed material now requires only one input of text, instead of two or even three. The use of digital technologies has also led to MEDIA CONVERGENCE. Because images, film, text and music are all stored and transmitted digitally, it is much easier to mix material from different media.

The *consumption* of media has also been transformed by new technology. For example, with television, people are now able to watch their favourite programmes at a time and place of their choosing rather than being subject to the scheduling of the broadcasters. In addition, the PERSONALIZATION of media is becoming common. Instead of simply being members of a mass audience, all of which listens to or watches the same material, consumers can choose what interests them. MP3 players can assemble favourite tracks from different sources and TIVOS can record favourite television programmes. The *distribution* of media, in other words, is changing. People do not have to gather round an object of some kind at a pre-determined time. Instead, they can choose what to have transmitted to a portable device – mobile phone, MP3 or portable computer.

Technological and regulatory changes are beginning to have an effect on the *business models* employed by media companies. Traditional mass media companies are constructed on the basis of building large audiences and holding them relatively passive, while they make their money from sales of the product or advertising. Media organized around digital production, distribution and consumption can go for smaller and more specialized audiences. Anderson (2006) argues that the internet makes possible the development of NICHE MEDIA and NICHE MARKETING: it is now possible to sell economically very small numbers of any product and to keep them for sale indefinitely. The impact of the internet and digital production technologies on most branches of the media is becoming obvious. A long-term decline in NEWSPAPER sales is being accentuated by the growth of online media, focusing on journalism or advertising. The industry has reacted by creating ONLINE NEWSPAPERS, but it is unclear whether these will be profitable. Similarly, PODCASTING, which enables consumers to be selective in their listening and to cut out advertising, has been making inroads into traditional commercial RADIO. Music is increasingly being distributed by downloading rather than by physical media such as CDs.

Claims are also made for the potential participative, interactive and democratic possibilities of new media, sometimes comparing their impact to the appearance of the printed BOOK. The traditional media essentially *address* their audiences, while the new media *interact* with them. Even with new technology, the traditional media model is of *downloading* material to the audience, while the new technology makes it possible for audiences to *upload* material. For example, there are numerous websites where people can contribute journalism, photographs, music or novels. A good deal of this material is finding its way into traditional outlets such as newspapers. But many argue that the possibilities of new media go beyond the participative or interactive in which ordinary people can make their own media product and get it to an audience however small. In this view, the new media can create an ELECTRONIC COMMONS, in which anyone can express a view on anything, can contribute to any debate and become heard by others. In this sense, the new media will recreate that PUBLIC SPHERE that the traditional media helped to establish in the eighteenth and nineteenth centuries but which has subsequently become lost. Arguments of this kind are associated with others that stress the manner in which new media, far from encouraging individualism, actually promote social bonds between people by creating VIRTUAL COMMUNITIES.

It is important not to be carried away by arguments about the new media. The alternative position is that it is still unclear how radically new the effects will be in respect of content, audience reaction and the structure of the industries. For example, much of the material available on the internet is actually taken from more traditional media. Newspapers are put online, music otherwise available on CD can be downloaded as can trailers for films which will be exhibited in the usual way. The internet, in other words, is simply being used as a means of distribution rather than the means of enabling a new media form. Again, whatever the potential for greater interactivity and participation, the significance of present levels of participation is not clear. They may simply be a reaction to a new form and may decline as media producers of a more traditional kind respond. And for the majority of the population, the use of new technology is still fairly passive; the use of the world wide web, for example, can be much like reading a book or a newspaper.

Lastly, it can be argued that the new media have not forced many changes in the media industries, particularly in their ownership. While there are new media start-up companies that have become very large (e.g. GOOGLE), the provision of new media is still likely to be in the hands of the very large old media companies, which have bought into the new technology.

In sum, it is too early to determine what the impact of the new media will be.

SEE ALSO: **blog; concentration of ownership**.

news Every day, news comes at us from many different sources – regular radio and television bulletins, newspapers and magazines, the internet. All these sources claim to be providing an accurate description of what is going on in the world around us. Often, this is clearly not true. There are many countries in which the government controls the media and what purports to be news is actually a censored account. But, even in countries with a free press, news stories involve *selection* of what appears. It is the journalist's job to select what news stories to present to the public and what aspects of news to include. Necessarily, this involves leaving something out. The point here is not that journalists conspire to mislead the public. They clearly do not. It is simply that they, and the organizations that they work for, could not operate unless they made some decisions about what to include and what to leave out in a news report.

That raises two interconnected questions. First, how is the selection made? Second, does the construction of news reports amount to bias?

The flow of presented news is a product of a variety of overlapping factors. Although it is not at all clear that the media have direct effects on individuals (SEE: **effects**), organizations tend to be very sensitive to what is said about them in the media. As a result, governments, public bodies and commercial organizations will go to great lengths to manage news that concerns them (SEE: **public relations; spin**). They will have entire departments dedicated to briefing journalists, trying to counter unfavourable publicity or creating stories which put them in a good light. Governments, and to a lesser extent other organizations, will also control access to their inner workings. Government action of one kind or another will often *be* the story and officials can choose which journalist to brief officially or unofficially and what information to provide (SEE: **gatekeeper; lobby**). As a result of these processes, journalists may well start with partial information on which to base their news stories. Media organizations themselves will also be a factor in the way in which news is produced. In the second half of the nineteenth century and the first half of the twentieth, owners of powerful newspapers like BEAVERBROOK, HEARST, NORTH-CLIFFE and Rothermere expected that their publications reflected their social and political views and would interfere if necessary with editorial decisions. Although more recently such partiality from owners has been less obvious as newspapers have become absorbed into large corporations, there are cases of interference. For example, both ROBERT MAXWELL and RUPERT MURDOCH have been accused of using their newspapers to press a particular point of view or of censoring material that might harm their business interests. Nor does this stop with print media. For example, NEWS CORPORATION operates an important news channel in the United States, Fox News, which has a significant right-wing bias.

The factors mentioned so far are deliberate attempts to structure the news in particular directions. They are not, however, as important in this respect as the entirely unconscious processes built into journalists' practices themselves. The best way of exploring these is via the concept of NEWS VALUES. If some event fits in with these values it is likely to be reported. If it does not, it is likely to be missed. It is important to stress again that the presence of news values is a necessary part of any news-gathering process; journalists have to have some way of organizing what they report. Analysts of the media have identified a number of news values (Galtung and Ruge, 1973). First, newsworthy events tend to be recent and of a frequency that fits in with the production cycles of media organizations. Journalists tend to pick up events that occur in a 24-hour cycle, and one of the consequences of this is that the history of those events is missed. Secondly, there has to be a measure of cultural proximity in news items. What appears on British television, for example, has to be meaningful in terms of British culture and experience. Similarly, the American media are notoriously parochial and will only deal with events that affect the United States. Third, news items have to be surprising.

What is newsworthy is what disrupts the normal course of life. Routine events are not of interest, but the sudden, unpredictable or deviant are. Fourth, the more the event concerns elite nations or elite individuals, the more probable it is that it will become a news item. The concentration is on people and events in the public eye, not on the everyday, private sphere. Fifth, the more the event can be seen in personal terms, the more likely it is to serve as a news item. It is more newsworthy to treat an event as produced by a named (and photographed) individual than it is to see it as caused by social, economic or political forces. Sixth, the more negative an event is in its consequences, the more likely it will be to become a news item. The news, as many often say, is frequently bad news. This leads to a stress on such topics as social conflict, crime or natural disasters.

News values therefore provide a filter through which some items pass to become news stories and others do not. What determines the manner in which the items that do pass through are treated? Again, the treatment is not some automatic process; it requires the active intervention of a journalist who has to make a story out of bits of information. Journalists do not go out into the world unequipped. On the contrary, they go with a set of assumptions, or FRAMES, which provide a way of organizing the information that they receive and which they then transmit in news stories. For example, reporting of events in Iraq since the removal of Saddam has tended to be dominated by the frame of insurgency. Events that could be fitted into this frame – suicide bombings, attacks on police stations, deaths of British or American soldiers – were reported, but much else was ignored.

Do the processes of the selection and subsequent treatment of news items amount to systematic bias in the news (SEE: **bias**) in the sense that the news presents a coherent view of the world which is biased? At a very general level, and for certain issues, that is more than likely. During times of international conflict, for example, the media adopt a very nationalistic stance (SEE: **manufacture of consent**). At other times, for terrorism or other serious crimes perhaps, where there is a widespread consensus, the media are similarly biased. But generally there will be so much disagreement in the media as a whole that systematic bias across all forms of media is unlikely, and the requirement for balance in television news, particularly, is a further safeguard.

SEE ALSO: *Bad News* studies; framing; journalism; news values; strategies of containment.

news agency Not to be confused with shops that sell newspapers, news agencies are organizations that gather raw news from across the world and then supply it to the press, radio and television. The best-known, AGENCE FRANCE-PRESSE, ASSOCIATED PRESS and REUTERS, were all founded in the nineteenth century and were global players from the start. Before their appearance, and for some time afterwards, newspapers relied on rumour and gossip, on foreign correspondents who might write for several publications or their own overseas staff for foreign news and on their own journalists for domestic news. The result was often inaccurate – and much delayed – reporting, particularly concerning overseas events. The news agencies transformed this situation by being able to supply accurate and timely raw material to newspapers throughout the world, thus creating a large pool of customers, which made a profitable business possible. This was greatly helped by the invention of the telegraph in the mid-nineteenth century, which permitted much faster communication. The agencies prided themselves on a strictly factual presentation without comment. It was left to the individual newspapers to write up the stories in whatever way they wished.

As well as the international agencies, nationally based ones began to appear in several countries in the nineteenth century and have continued to do so. Indeed, the bulk of the business of both Associated Press and Agence France-Presse derives from their domestic markets. Many of these national agencies are cooperatives started by newspapers clubbing together. The best-known UK agency is the PRESS ASSOCIATION.

As there has been a proliferation of media forms, particularly with the development of radio and television, agencies have started up dealing with these new forms or the old agencies have adapted to take on the new technologies. As the internet has become significant, the agencies have further adapted to become internet-based. This, in turn, is related to a change in their customer base. While they started as suppliers of news to newspapers and then to radio and television organizations, they now provide, via the internet, regular news updates directly to individuals. At the same time, some media organizations are looking more like news agencies in that they also are using the internet to supply raw news for others. An example is CNN.

News Corporation A large, globally significant media company (with sales of about £10 billion), News Corporation has RUPERT MURDOCH as its major shareholder and managing director. The company controls, amongst others, newspapers (e.g. the *Sun* and *The Times* in the UK, the *New York Post* in the US), cable, satellite and broadcast television (e.g. BSKYB in the UK, FOX NETWORK in the US, Star TV in Asia), film (e.g. Twentieth Century Fox) and book publishing (e.g. HarperCollins). As with other global media companies, News Corporation has attracted substantial criticism for its dominance in the market, especially for news and particularly as Murdoch has strong political views which do colour the company's output.

SEE ALSO: **concentration of ownership; media companies**.

news cut A short extract from a recording of a person speaking. It is most usually used with respect to radio news. Many of those involved in public life now make pronouncements that they know will be cut to a sound bite by the media.

news-gathering See: NEWS.

newsgroup A discussion space organized in computer networks. The use of the term is restricted to a technology – usenet – that preceded the INTERNET. Access to usenet is controlled but fairly easy and, despite the availability of alternatives on the internet, newsgroups continue to flourish. Usenet classifies newsgroups by type, e.g recreational, scientific. One of these types, known as alt, short for alternative, has attracted wide attention, since it permits discussion of topics that are regarded by some as deviant, subversive, dangerous or simply eccentric.

newspaper Printed newssheets began to appear in Europe in the sixteenth century, and daily newspapers were established from the early seventeenth century onwards. The first newspaper in the English language was actually published in Amsterdam in 1620 but it was rapidly followed by a London publication. Daily newspaper publication had to wait until the early eighteenth century. Throughout the seventeenth and eighteenth centuries, newspapers were extensively controlled. Initially, they were effectively restricted to the reporting of events overseas and were readily closed down if they showed any inclination to comment on national politics. Later, restriction on publication was achieved by the imposition of a tax (stamp duty) which severely limited the readership (SEE: **government and the media**). This tax was gradually phased out and, in the nineteenth century, newspapers became relatively cheap; with greater literacy in the population, readership expanded rapidly. The nineteenth century also saw a number of technical and marketing innovations. Printing presses were greatly improved, illustrations appeared, and photography was used towards the end of the century, advertisements were introduced, and the invention of the telegraph made news-gathering so much easier. Journalism also became much more professionalized. Towards the end of the nineteenth century and on into the first half of the twentieth century a new type of owner appeared – the so-called press baron (SEE: **Beaverbrook; Northcliffe**).

Newspapers began to receive significant competition from other media, especially radio and television, after the Second World War, and from the internet more recently. The CIRCULATION of all national daily newspapers has declined over time. For example, in the mid-1990s some 17 million daily newspapers were sold in the UK. By the end of the 1990s this had dropped to just under 14 million. This pattern of decline is by no means repeated worldwide. In Asia, for example, including Japan, newspaper sales have increased over the same period, as they have in parts of Europe, Germany, for example. In terms of sales per 1,000 of the population, the UK is at the mid-point globally.

For much of the early history of newspapers in the UK, publication and readership was centred on particular cities. From the mid-nineteenth century on, however, newspaper publication became much more national, and regional newspaper sales went into decline. The UK press is unusual globally in that it is dominated by newspapers that are produced in London and have national coverage, though often with regional editions. It is true that in recent years there has been something of a revival in the fortunes of the more local press (and the Scottish press is particularly different), but this is due almost entirely to the introduction of free local papers solely dependent on advertising (SEE: **regional press**).

The ownership of newspapers has also become more concentrated over time (SEE: **concentration of ownership**). In the late 1990s, four newspaper groups (Associated Newspapers, MGN, News International, United Newspapers) between them commanded almost 90 per cent of daily national newspaper sales in the UK.

One response to the presence of other competitive media has been for newspaper companies to diversify into other media. News International, for example, not only owns *The Times* and the *Sun*, but also has interests in television, film, book publishing and radio. It has simultaneously become more expensive to start up a new national paper with the result that any new newspaper has to achieve higher circulation figures to break even. The effect of these trends is that there is less competition between newspapers, readers have a more limited choice, and minority opinions are squeezed out. Because the costs of setting up INTERNET publications are so much lower, this has become a way of representing a variety of opinion, some of which is downright eccentric, in something of the same manner as early nineteenth-century newspapers did. Newspapers are having to come to terms with the internet as readers desert them. Some have invested heavily and successfully in their own internet publications. The online version of the *Guardian*, for example, has as many readers as does the newspaper itself. In one month its site receives 10 million visitors, only one-third of whom are based in the UK. It is not yet clear, however, how newspapers will make money from their internet activities.

The concentration of ownership and the power of the large media groups raise anxieties about the OBJECTIVITY of newspaper reporting and opinion. These anxieties derive from a number of sources. Newspapers, like any other form of media, have to construct the news out of the torrent of everyday events. To do so they will have to use frameworks of assumptions to make sensible stories. The result, inevitably, is that news stories will adopt a particular perspective (See: BIAS; NEWS; NEWS VALUES). In a competitive market that perspective is likely to be closely matched to that of the readership. In addition, the reporting and opinions of newspapers may be pushed in very definite directions by the commercial and political interests of owners. This was famously the case with the newspaper barons of the first half of the twentieth century, who sometimes saw the newspapers that they owned as mouthpieces for their own opinions. But it remains true for the barons of today. BERLUSCONI, MURDOCH and MAXWELL, when he was alive, all interfered in editorial content. More seriously, corporations, as well as individuals, will have interests that will colour the content of their publications.

Newspaper Publishers Association (NPA) Founded in 1906, the NPA is the trade association for national newspapers and it represents and promotes the national newspaper industry. Its current members comprise ASSOCIATED NEWSPAPERS, Express Newspapers, Financial Times, Guardian Newspapers, Independent Newspapers, Trinity Mirror, NEWS CORPORATION and the Telegraph Group.

Newspaper Society Founded in 1836, this organization promotes and represents the UK's regional and local press, currently made up of some 1,300 daily and weekly, paid-for and free, newspaper titles.

newsreel A film of news items that was shown in the cinema. Newsreels were shown from the earliest days of the cinema and, prior to the advent of television, were the main way by which people could see moving images of news events. Newsreels were sustained into the 1960s after the introduction of TV by, for example, using colour in advance of its widespread use in TV, but rapidly died out afterwards.

news release Story prepared for the media to communicate a group's or individual's point of view. This is one way in which organizations seek to influence media content.

SEE ALSO: **embargo; public relations**.

news values The starting point for any analysis of the presentation of news in the media is the relationship between the flow of events in the world and the news story. The media – television, newspapers, radio – have to make sense of the multiplicity of events that occur. To do that journalists have to decide what is news and what is not, and how to present a news item so that it can be understood by a very diverse audience. A number of news values contribute to this sense of newsworthiness. For example, newsworthy events tend to be recent; the closing of a hospital is news, but its construction is not. The more an event concerns elite or celebrity individuals, the more likely it is to count as news. Typically, news items have to be surprising; what is newsworthy is that which disrupts the normal course of life. In turn, that news value is related to another, in that the more negative an event is in its consequences, the more likely it is to be reported. More obviously still, newsworthy events have to fit into the national culture; in the United States, events that concern that country are much more likely to figure in the news than ones affecting other nations. Lastly, journalists, as a rule, are not comfortable with abstract questions and they prefer to report items that can be seen in personal terms. It is important to emphasize again that news values are a necessity in constructing news out of the welter of daily events. Whether or not they are the right values, or whether they distort reporting, is a separate question.

SEE ALSO: **agenda setting; bias; framing; journalism; news**.

newsworthy SEE: **news values**.

new wave A significant new group of producers in the media. There have been two particular movements that the term has been most prominently applied to. First, there was the group of film producers (initially critics) who led the development of a new cinema in France from the 1950s onwards. Combining new modes of film-making and in various degrees forms of radical politics, film-makers like François Truffaut and Jean-Luc Godard were to become very influential. Second, in popular music, the term was applied (often interchangeably with PUNK) to the generation of rock bands that became influential in the mid-to-late 1970s initially in the USA and UK (see Heylin, 1993).

SEE ALSO: **auteur theory; director**.

niche audience See: AUDIENCE DIFFERENTIATION.

niche marketing The practice of marketing to groups of people with specialized interests. As markets differentiate (SEE: **market segmentation/ differentiation**), small specialized markets develop which companies can appeal to. The large range of magazines now aimed at particular interests and hobbies is an example. The advertising and marketing techniques therefore need to be adjusted to appeal to niches of this kind. The internet, offering an inexpensive form of marketing, is ideally suited to targeted niche marketing.

SEE ALSO: **Fordism/post-Fordism**.

niche media Media directed at niche audiences. The media have traditionally been directed at a mass audience. For example, BBC television, until the 1990s, took the form of comprehensive broadcasting which was intended to serve all social groups and all tastes and values, even if particular programmes appealed only to a section of the audience. However, changes in the audience (SEE: **individualization; market segmentation/ differentiation**), in the regulatory regime (SEE: **government and the media; regulation**) and in technology (SEE: **digital broadcasting**) have made it possible to reach more specialized audiences. For example, there are now many television channels available, and there will be more, and these can be dedicated to particular types of programming. Print media have always reached niche markets but have been limited by the costs of production and, above all, of distribution. The internet, with relatively low costs of distribution, is well suited to reaching niche markets.

non-linear editing The editing of film by taking frames from any point in the sequence without physically cutting the source material. Before the widespread use of computer technology in film and video editing, any editing had to be done by processing strips of film or tape. In its crudest form, this consisted of cutting the film and splicing in frames taken from elsewhere in the film. This is a form of linear editing, so called because it can only treat images in a single straight sequence. DIGITAL EDITING has fundamentally changed the process of editing. It is now possible for a non-linear approach to be used whereby images can be selected quickly from any point in the film or tape and moved to any other point.

non-verbal communication Communication that takes place without the use of sound or speech. This can involve facial expressions, hand movement or positioning of the body.

SEE ALSO: **language**.

Northcliffe, Lord (1865–1922) Born Alfred Harmsworth, Northcliffe with his brother, Harold Harmsworth (1868–1940), subsequently Viscount

Rothermere, founded a newspaper empire, and, together with BEAVER-BROOK, came to typify the PRESS BARON in the UK in the first part of the twentieth century. The Harmsworths' empire came to include, amongst other titles, *The Times*, the *Daily Mirror* and the *Daily Mail*. They were particularly successful in winning a working-class and female readership.

Northern and Shell See: DESMOND.

OB (Outside Broadcast) Radio and television material that comes from recording outside the studio.

objectivity A view of the world that is free of bias and self-interest and represents the truth. For most journalists objectivity is a key value. Similarly, the public in most developed countries expects that the reporting of news that they get is free of bias, is impartial and represents a political balance, not favouring any particular interest. That public conviction is reflected in attitudes to news organizations. Thus, surveys in the UK show that the public trusts television news far more than that in newspapers because they believe that the latter tend to favour a particular political stance.

Clearly, objectivity is a slippery idea and it continues to be fiercely debated. Governments and politicians, for example, frequently accuse the BBC of bias. The Corporation's coverage of the second Iraq war in 2003/4, for example, resulted in a serious breach with the Labour government of the time and the subsequent resignations of both the Chairman and the Director-General of the BBC.

The problem is that total objectivity, at least in the sense of a complete and transparent description of events in the world, is an impossibility for anyone and is inconsistent with the way in which the media work. Thus, any news presentation is a relationship between the flow of events and the representation of those events. News programmes or stories have to make sense of the flow of events and that sense-making is a *construction*. It involves, for instance, deciding what is news and what is not or how to present a news item so that it can be understood by a very diverse audience. That construction is produced by a variety of devices (SEE: **framing; news values; strategies of containment**). Those devices will of necessity produce a particular view of the world, and thus it will always be possible to argue that that view is biased.

So, given that most people would wish to avoid bias, what role can be given to objectivity in the media? Objectivity should not be seen as content – as a more or less truthful account at any one time. Instead, it should be seen as a *process* whereby, over time, media organizations are able to challenge and revise past accounts offered by others and, indeed, themselves.

SEE ALSO: *Bad News* studies; bias; news; truth.

obscenity That which a society considers indecent. Concern with the meaning and (control) of the representation of the obscene has run through the whole history of art and media. Ultimately, the definition and the extent of control of the obscene are both controversial and socially contextual. However, this does not prevent REGULATION through legislation like the Obscene Publications Act.

SEE ALSO: censorship; children and television; gender; pornography.

Ofcom (Office of Communications) Formed in 2003, Ofcom is the regulator for the UK communications industries, with responsibilities across television, radio, telecommunications and wireless communications services. It took over the roles of the Broadcasting Standards Commission, the Independent Television Commission, Oftel, and the Radio Authority. As a result, Ofcom has very broad powers and handles complaints, regulates competition, monitors standards and deals with licences.

SEE ALSO: regulation.

off-diary story News stories that occur as unexpected events. The contrast is with a DIARY STORY.

SEE ALSO: news.

offline editor Person who processes the raw film straight from the camera to a finished edited programme or movie, using a copy of the original in a different medium. The distinction between offline and online editing in television and film POST-PRODUCTION is becoming eroded as technology improves. Working with the director, theirs is a creative job to do with the content of a programme, with communicating information or telling a story. Online editors have a much more technical role. They may add visual effects, sounds or captions, but their most important task is to ensure that the final product is of the right technical quality for broadcasting. Offline editors tend to be freelance, online are more usually employed in-house in broadcasting organizations. As the computer technology employed by offline editors improves and lowers costs of production, they are able to take over more of the work traditionally done by online editors.

offmike Sound that is included in a broadcast in radio that is not directed at the microphone.

Oftel Set up under the Telecommunications Act 1984, Oftel had responsibilities for promoting competition in the telecommunications industry and for making sure that telecommunications services were provided, especially emergency services, public call boxes, directory information and in rural areas. Its powers and responsibilities were transferred to OFCOM in 2003.

oligopoly A situation in which only a few companies are operating in a market. Some media commentators fear that this is the situation developing worldwide as media companies merge to create very large enterprises which dominate the market.

SEE ALSO: **concentration of ownership**.

omnivore A person who engages with a wide range of cultural texts or practices of diverse kinds. It has been argued that in the United States there has been a shift from a division between the elite and the mass in culture. In particular, it is maintained that middle-class groups have become more omnivorous in taste (Peterson and Kern, 1996). So, for example, in the past, a highly educated person might have been interested in the classics of literature and classical music; now they are likely to read detective novels, watch soap operas on TV and listen to popular music from around the world as well. They are thus omnivores in that they consume both high and popular culture. According to this account, those at the bottom of the social scale are univores in that their cultural consumption is more restricted and constrained by material factors (Bryson, 1997). Evidence for the omnivore thesis was initially produced with respect to the consumption of music in the US. The thesis is now subject to empirical investigation and theoretical refinement in a number of other countries (see Peterson and Anand, 2004).

SEE ALSO: **high culture**.

180 degree rule In cinema and television the audience is presented with a point of view from one side of the action. For example, a football match is shown from one side of the pitch. This prevents confusion on the part of the viewer, who might otherwise be misled by teams seeming to kick in different directions in rapid succession. 'Violations' of this convention are explained to the viewer, to make the point that action is being shown from a different point of view. Such violations of the rule are becoming more common, as in the rapid cutting between different camera angles in some TV interviews.

SEE ALSO: **camera angle; narrative**.

online community See: VIRTUAL COMMUNITY.

online editor See: OFFLINE EDITOR.

online game A COMPUTER GAME played in REAL TIME on a large remote computer connected by a network, usually the INTERNET, to many players often distributed around the world.
    SEE ALSO: **MUD**.

online newspapers As use of the INTERNET began to spread, the alternative press (SEE: **radical press**) found that publication of their material on the internet was cheaper than using the traditional print medium and they were still able to reach their target audience. Many of the more orthodox newspapers have followed suit and have online editions in addition to their standard print format, and there are now several news services online that offer continuously updated news.
    SEE ALSO: **newspaper**.

open-ended question In INTERVIEW research, a kind of question that allows respondents to say what they want, rather than require them to choose among answers that the interviewer has fixed in advance. Interviewers write down or tape-record the answers. The replies of all respondents are considered together later and are either coded for statistical analysis or used as they are for the purposes of interpretation or quotation.

open source The way in which software is distributed free to users of computers and computer networks, often as part of a concern about the monopoly control of much software by large companies. Also referred to as shareware.

open text The sort of text that is open to a range of different interpretations. The contrast is with a CLOSED TEXT. Examples of open texts are often given from the more AVANT-GARDE forms of cultural production, where forms of writing and depiction are seen as difficult and innovative and where the reader is required to exercise skill in understanding the different and complex aspects of the text. However, these ideas have also been applied to more popular texts in media studies. For example, television SOAP OPERAS have been seen by some analysts as open and complex texts as they deploy a range of different storylines within the overall narrative and rely on the deployment of skill by the reader to make sense of the complexity. It has also been suggested that the meanings of such texts are relatively open in that a range of issues are opened up for consideration, especially concerning gendered social interaction, which are closed down by other, and perhaps more ideological, texts. However, an alternative view would suggest that soap operas are actually relatively closed texts, as only a restricted number of narrative outcomes are possible. Thus, those who break the law will ultimately be punished in one way or another, even though it may take years for the punishment to come. Therefore, soap operas would not leave a moral ambiguity about whether a crime will pay, even if the audience's sympathies have been engaged in different ways during the course of the progress of such a narrative.

SEE ALSO: **avant-garde; ideology; narrative; semiology.**

opinion-leader or -former Those people who are particularly influential in forming the opinions of others. While such people clearly exist in all communities, workplaces or families, the term is more usually restricted to those who have a platform of some kind in a newspaper, magazine, or radio or television programme.

SEE ALSO: **influence; persuasion; primary definer.**

opinion poll The testing of the views and intentions about an event or action through the use of survey methods. Often used now in the context of run-ups to general or major elections and having been developed with increased sophistication since the middle of the twentieth century. There are linkages between opinion polling and consumer research, where companies seek knowledge about the purchasing intentions of consumers, and audience research, where commercial broadcasting agencies also require information about who is consuming a programme, so as to be able to deliver a predictable audience to an advertiser.

SEE ALSO: **elections.**

oppositional reading See: NATIONWIDE STUDY.

oral culture That form of CULTURE that is transmitted to successive generations through word of mouth, rather than being written down. While this is often seen as a feature of more 'traditional' societies that do not have a written culture, it is important to recognize that forms of oral culture are very much part of contemporary and recent cultural life and change. A good example is American blues music, which was developed by a number of black artists who each gave an oral culture resource a particular inflection in their own performances and subsequently in recorded performances. These traditions and performances were subsequently copyrighted, in some famous cases by white performers, leading to disputes over the nature of authorship.

SEE ALSO: **author; black music; folk culture.**

other The idea that cultures construct outsiders (or those who are other) who are radically different, strange and perhaps threatening. These 'others' are contrasted with those believed to be legitimate members of society or insiders. The category of person that fits into the category of the other can vary between societies and even between parts of them and across time. Thus, EDWARD SAID'S (1978) study of *Orientalism* shows how the orient was constructed in Western DISCOURSE as the exotic other to the West. Likewise 'immigrants' to advanced Western societies are constructed as other, or radically different to the established population. The study of how categories of people are constructed as 'other', or what may be termed the process of 'othering', is an important trend of development in cultural and media studies.

SEE ALSO: **difference; globalization; identity; ideology**.

out See: OUT CUE.

out cue The cue at the end of a news item or story that indicates the turn of the next speaker.

outsourcing The placing of activities important to an organization's business with another, separate organization. Many companies have found that it is more efficient to outsource some of their activities so that they concentrate on the core of their business. For example, a large firm may get a specialist company to run their catering for their employees or a small firm may give their bookkeeping to a company that specializes in that service. The point is that the specialist firm is more efficient in gaining ECONOMIES OF SCALE. Media organizations have always used this practice. Book publishers have, as a rule, outsourced their printing and typesetting since the nineteenth century. Similarly, authorship has been an out-of-house function for a long time and, more recently, independent free-lancers have acted as COPY EDITORS and even COMMISSIONING EDITORS. There is now, however, an increasing tendency for a variety of media organizations to outsource in pursuit of lower costs. Most post-production television is outsourced, and INDEPENDENT PRODUCTION COMPANIES are generating much of television's content. Many people have expressed concerns that outsourcing will lower quality and will degrade the conditions of work of those who are employed by the outsourcing companies or are freelancers.

SEE ALSO: **casualization; Fordism/post-Fordism**.

out-take A portion of film that is not used in the final complete version.

OVS (over-the-shoulder shot) A point of view in film or television that appears to be from over the shoulder of a participant or actor.

ownership and control The idea that the ownership of goods, property or rights is a process that can be distinguished from the control of them. In the nineteenth century and before ownership and the effective control and management of commercial enterprises were unified, owners tended also to be the managers. With the widespread adoption of the joint-stock company, however, ownership and control were prised apart. Professional managers control large media companies, while shareholders own them. At the same time, one should remember that large media companies like NEWS CORPORATION are identified with individuals (MURDOCH) who will also own substantial numbers of shares.

SEE ALSO: **concentration of ownership; media mogul; movie mogul.**

P

page traffic The number of readers reading a page of a newspaper or magazine.

panning The movement of a camera fixed to a stand from right to left or vice-versa.
SEE ALSO: **static shot; tilting; tracking.**

panopticism A form of detailed, rational and bureaucratic surveillance operating in society (SEE: **surveillance society**). The term derives from Jeremy Bentham's design for a prison where a large number of prisoners are kept under surveillance by a small number of guards located in a central viewing tower. This idea was developed as an analysis of power and regulation by MICHEL FOUCAULT. CCTV can be seen as a form of panopticism, where a camera controller can keep different locations (and hence large numbers of people) under surveillance.

paparazzi Named after a character in Federico Fellini's film *La Dolce Vita* (1960), these are journalists who specialize in obtaining news or photographs of the rich and famous. They tend to follow their quarry around and use any methods to obtain their material and are therefore frequently accused of invasion of PRIVACY. The paparazzi have been blamed for the death of Diana, Princess of Wales, in that they harassed her by following, on motorcycles, the car in which she was killed.

paradigmatic Within STRUCTURALIST analysis, a set of words that have some common features and which can be substituted in a sentence or string of words that create meaning. For example, the sentence or syntagm 'the cat sat on the mat' could be changed if a paradigmatic term for floor covering was inserted, for example, carpet. Thus, a set of words in a paradigm of floor covering could begin with mat, carpet, rug, vinyl and so on.
SEE ALSO: **semiology.**

parallel action A specific narrative of action that is developed in combination with another without (at least initially) being linked. Thus, we may be shown one person arriving at a place in one set of actions and then arriving at a quite different place in a parallel action. We expect these to be linked at some point in the overall NARRATIVE, but this may only become clear as the text develops fully.

parasocial interaction A form of social relationship at a distance alleg-edly encouraged by the media. Theatre audiences tend to be intensely involved in the performance while the play lasts but, at the moment it ends, they re-enter the ordinary world. Television, radio and cinema, on the other hand, produce a continuous interplay between the world of mundane reality and that of the performance. Some writers claim that the appearance of the mass media generated a new kind of social relation-ship, the parasocial, in which a bond of intimacy is struck up between medium and performer on the one hand and audience members on the other.

SEE ALSO: **regimes of watching**.

parole Within STRUCTURALISM, SEMIOLOGY or semiotic analysis, *parole* refers to the surface level of language such as everyday speech. The con-trast is with LANGUE, which is the deeper level of structure that underpins the surface level of everyday speech acts. Thus, for example, *langue* is like the set of rules of football that permit a range of different games which exist at the *parole* level.

SEE ALSO: **myth**.

participant observation A research technique in which the researcher observes a social collectivity of which he or she is also a member. An example is the study of fan communities by Bacon-Smith (1992). Partici-pant observation can take two forms. Covert observation takes place when the collectivity is not aware that it is being studied. Overt observation, on the other hand, describes a form of observation in which the observer is known to be an outside investigator by those being studied.

The advantage of the covert approach is that the setting remains natural and the presence of the observer creates no artificial changes, which is a major risk of open observation. But it raises an ethical dilemma, whether one should observe people as objects of study without their consent. Both forms are confronted by the same problem, that the observer may gain only a restricted and partial understanding of the situation, because the observer's role may not provide access to the total population under investigation. For this reason, participant observation is sometimes supplemented by other forms of data collection.

passive audience See: ACTIVE AUDIENCE.

patriarchy The dominance of men over women. While male dominance is often explained biologically, most social scientists argue that patriarchy refers to social, not natural relations. There is considerable debate about the sociological explanation of patriarchy. Many explanations have been offered, including men's dominance of the workplace and a widespread socialization process that insists that women's primary role is to be a wife and mother. One important element in this socialization process that is often cited is the media industry. Television and women's magazines, especially, are accused of promoting stereotypes of femininity which reinforce patriarchy.

SEE ALSO: **gender; masculinity.**

payola Payments made to disc jockeys to play or 'plug' particular records. This caused a major scandal in late 1950s USA.

SEE ALSO: **DJ; music industry.**

pay-per-view Most television is effectively funded either by advertising, by the state, by subscription or by a licence fee. However, some services delivered by satellite or cable, largely in the United States, are funded by viewers paying directly every time they watch a programme or group of programmes. In the UK, some SKY services, chiefly sport, are delivered in this way.

PDA (Personal Digital Assistant) A handheld device which can carry out many of the functions of a desktop computer, e.g. calculator, address book and diary. PDAs are now commonly combined with mobile phone technology to give access to the INTERNET and therefore permit not only voice calls, but also EMAIL and web browsing.

Peacock Committee Set up in 1985 by a government hostile to the BBC, the remit of the Peacock committee was to review the licence fee method of funding. Although expected to propose serious changes which would have significantly altered the nature of the BBC, Peacock actually endorsed the licence fee as a method of funding the BBC because it ensured quality. Although the committee favoured opening up broadcasting more to private broadcasters, it also endorsed a mixture of private and public broadcasters. Some of Peacock's recommendations found their way into the BROADCASTING ACT 1990.

peak time That time in the day when large numbers of adults will be watching television. Although now important to all television producers who will want to produce competitive programming and maximize their audience, peak time was originally significant to COMMERCIAL TELEVISION because that was the time that advertisements would be seen by the buying public.

SEE ALSO: **drive-time**.

Peoplemeter The television industry needs to measure audiences to establish the level and nature of audiences for programme monitoring and for the selling of advertising airtime. Since 1981, BARB has been in charge of audience research for the industry, and since the early 1990s, measurement of audiences has been done electronically by means of the Peoplemeter. This is a device placed inside the television set which can record when the television is on and what channel is being watched. It can also record who is watching, since each member of the household (and visitor) presses a button on a handset to indicate that he or she is watching. In addition, the meter will report data on video-recorder usage, including its use in recording programmes off the television for viewing later on. A great deal of care goes into the construction of the sample of households that will have a meter installed. The sample reflects different household structures, made up of the interaction of three variables – stage in the life-course (for example, whether the household has children), occupational and educational status of the head of the household and household size.

SEE ALSO: **audience measurement**.

perfect binding See: BINDING.

performing rights Anyone who wishes to perform a song or a piece of music in which they do not hold the COPYRIGHT must apply for performing rights from the copyright holder and in most cases pay a fee. Such payments are often collected by the PERFORMING RIGHTS SOCIETY.

SEE ALSO: **author**.

Performing Rights Society The principal agency for the collection of PERFORMING RIGHTS revenue in the UK. The society was founded in 1914. Its membership is made up of writers, publishers and copyright owners and successors. There are four main sources for the income that derives to this membership on the basis of their possession of performing rights: public performance royalties, radio and television royalties, overseas royalties and investment. In 2005, there were 36,748 writer members, 2,261 publisher members and 1,813 successor members. The distributable income of the society in 2004 was £256 million (www.mcps-prs-alliance.co.uk).

SEE ALSO: **copyright**.

periodical A booklet or book that comes out periodically, typically weekly, monthly or quarterly. The term is often used synonymously with magazine, but sometimes means something more serious or weighty, such as an academic journal or political, economic or current affairs publication (SEE: **magazine**).

Periodical Publishers Association (PPA) The trade association for UK magazine publishers. It currently represents some 300 firms which between them publish 3,000 magazine titles of different kinds.

personal influence The manner in which one person affects the views or behaviour of another. The way in which the media have effects on the audience is rarely direct but is mediated by a variety of factors. For example, particularly influential individuals or opinion-formers may well have an important role in interpreting reported events and ideas in the media to others in their community. This view was originally advanced in a study of an election campaign in the United States and has been used to counter propositions that the media are all-powerful. Subsequent evidence appears to indicate that the role of personal influence actually varies considerably from situation to situation and may, indeed, simply reinforce the effects of the media rather than resist them.

SEE ALSO: **two-step flow**.

personality Television does not seem to have the STAR SYSTEM of film, in which audiences identify with the star. On the other hand, television does have performers who, while not being stars, are *personalities*. These personalities are central to a particular programme, viewers will know them by name and programmes almost become vehicles for them. Such personalities are particularly found in chat shows (e.g. Paul O'Grady) and in game shows (e.g. Graham Norton), but the phenomenon is gradually creeping into news, documentaries and current affairs (e.g. Jeremy Paxman). So developed is television's personality system that some chat and talk shows have turned to parody; the personality performer parodies the fact of personality on television (e.g. Dame Edna Everidge).

SEE ALSO: **celebrity**.

personalization The tailoring of media products to the particular wants and needs of individuals. Until the advent and widespread adoption of electronic communication, the media were *mass* media. That is, media producers treated their audiences as composed of people who were more or less the same as each other and who would all therefore receive the same media content. For example, all those who read *The Times* newspaper received the same newspaper every day, whether they were young or old, living in Bournemouth or Bolsover or were men or women. Similarly, those who turned on their television would have available the same set of programmes as their next-door neighbour. Of course, the media exploit market niches (SEE: **niche media**). But, within each of those niches, everybody receives the same product despite the fact that they will have different wants and tastes. With print and broadcast media it is very difficult to personalize media products so that individuals receive the kind of material that they want. Electronic media move closer to this possibility, however. Individuals can assemble together tracks from different rock bands, edit film or photographs or have television programmes recorded according to their known tastes (SEE: **TIVO**). Of course, one could readily argue that extreme personalization has very definite drawbacks since exposure to the same media products gives people something to talk about.

SEE ALSO: **individualization**.

personal media Media content that is chosen personally by an individual and delivered to them at a time and a place also of their choosing. The term is also used to describe those devices, e.g. MP3 players, personal computers and TIVO, that allow the consumer to filter out unwanted material and decide when to watch or listen.

SEE ALSO: **new media**.

persuasion Some acts of communication are attempts to persuade others to do or to think something. For example, advertisers are attempting to persuade us to buy something, politicians to agree with their policies, moral reformers to change our beliefs. Such attempts at persuasion can be overt or covert. In wartime, for instance, propaganda about the enemy is overtly an attempt to encourage a population to greater efforts. Persuasion can be less obvious. Thus, advertisements differ in the extent to which they overtly attempt to persuade; in some cases it is obvious what they are attempting to do while in others it is not even clear what product is being recommended.

Persuasion is essentially a question of changing attitudes, and most research into persuasion consists in measuring attitude change. Typically, two groups will have a questionnaire designed to elicit their attitudes towards something. One of them will then be exposed to some material, a film or a text perhaps, that is designed to change their attitudes, while the other group (the control group) is left alone or is exposed to neutral material. Both groups then have their attitudes remeasured to see what, if anything, has changed. Experiments of this kind show that persuasion – of anything serious and long-lasting – is not an easy matter, and any change in attitudes requires a campaign of persuasion not a single event. The research – chiefly of interest to the advertising industry – does show certain factors which can affect attitudes, at least in the short term. These include the order in which material is presented, the credibility of the source and the impact of fearful messages. Some research has detected a sleeper effect in which some change in attitudes is detected long after exposure to the persuasive message.

Classical persuasion research tends to allocate a subordinate role to the receiver of the persuasive message, who is treated as essentially passive, an improbable assumption. Furthermore, there are other reasons for being sceptical about the capacity for successful persuasion. Even if people are persuaded to change their attitudes, that does not mean that the change is stable, nor does it have obvious implications for their actual behaviour.

SEE ALSO: **brainwashing; rhetoric**.

Peterson, Richard A. (Pete) (b. 1932) Emeritus Professor of Sociology at Vanderbilt University, Nashville, USA. Peterson has been a prime mover in the study of culture and media from a sociological perspective in the USA. His most well-known contribution is in the development of the production of culture approach, which, as the name implies, argues for the importance of a range of economic, political, legal, organizational and social factors that influence the production of culture (Peterson and Anand, 2004). He has conducted a number of empirical studies that have developed this framework. He has also turned his attention to how culture is consumed, especially via the development of the OMNIVORE thesis. An excellent representation of the different strands of this overall approach can be found in his book on the construction of authenticity in American country music (Peterson, 1997).

SEE ALSO: **music industry**.

photography It is generally recognized that the first photograph was produced by Joseph Niépce in France in 1826. Early photographs were uniquely produced by the action of light on a chemically treated plate. Subsequent innovations include the DAGUERREOTYPE, named after Louis Daguerre, which was supplanted by the calotype invented by William Henry Fox Talbot in 1841. This had the advantage that a picture could be taken quickly and that multiple copies could be produced from a negative. These processes generally remained in the hands of the professional or dedicated enthusiast. However, from the late nineteenth century onwards photography became a popular form through such inventions as the Kodak box camera, marketed by the American Max Eastman in 1888, and especially the Brownie box camera. Through the twentieth century technical innovation fuelled the development of photography as an art form, as an aid to reporting and the documenting of events and as a popular everyday practice. Important innovations include the 35 mm camera (the Leica, 1925), the Polaroid instant camera (1947), the Instamatic (1963). From the 1960s onwards colour became more widely available (Baldwin et al., 1999: 377–8). Since the 1990s digital cameras and associated technologies have become increasingly commonplace.

While photography is an art form in its own right, with a history of innovation, which has also involved MULTIMEDIA activities and practices, it has also functioned as a technique to document events, and some well-known photographs provide a crucial representation of key events. This is especially the case with war photography, despite the fact that some supposedly documentary photographs were actually staged after the events (e.g. the US marines raising the flag on the island of Iwo Jima in the Second World War). Photography is also a key part of everyday life. It is unthinkable that key ceremonial events such as a marriage could pass off without being photographed. Photo albums are also used to record the important parts of family lives and operate as a key device through which the NARRATIVE of life is assembled.

SEE ALSO: **camcorder; cinema**.

photo-journalism Although journalism is often thought of as exclusively to do with the written word, some journalists specialize in photography to be used in newspapers and magazines. As a form, photo-journalism became particularly popular in the years after the Second World War with publications such as *Picture Post*.

photomontage An image created by putting together elements from several different photographs.

photo-story A piece in a newspaper or magazine that is very largely composed of photographs.

Pierce, Charles Sanders (1839–1914) One of the founders of the science of signs, which he termed semiotics. This is the term which is still most often used in the USA for this academic activity. In Europe the term SEMIOLOGY is more common, deriving from the work of Ferdinand de Saussure.

SEE ALSO: **Barthes; structuralism**.

Pilkington Committee Reporting in 1962, the Pilkington Committee was asked to review the services then provided by the BBC and the independent companies and to recommend whether there should be new services provided by other organizations. In the event, the committee was critical of the programming and advertising standards of independent television.

piracy Most often used to refer to the illegal copying of music, film or video. Marshall (2005) distinguishes between six types of piracy in the music industry (which can also be applied to other media industries): counterfeiting (where the intention is to copy the whole of a product including the cover); pirating (where only the sounds are copied and it is not intended that the copy should look like the original); bootlegging (where unreleased material is produced for commercial gain); tape trading (where tapes or CDs of the same type of material as contained in bootlegs is swapped); CDR burning or home taping (which is non-commercial copying of officially available material on a small scale); and file-sharing (where material is shared via the internet). It is suggested by video and music industries that the scale of piracy is huge – though it is actually very difficult to arrive at true figures and the estimates often elide the categories identified above. There is also debate over the extent to which music companies lose from these practices. Thus, while counterfeiting might involve significant profits for those engaged in it, home taping may simply mean that a single copy is passed to another person who would not have bought the original.

SEE ALSO: **author; copyright**.

pitch An event at which the writer or originator of a film idea presents the idea to the executive or executive team who have the responsibility for commissioning film. This process was satirized in the movie *The Player* (dir. Robert Altman, 1992).

SEE ALSO: **cinema**.

place See: SPACE.

plaisir See: JOUISSANCE; PLEASURE.

play-list Most radio stations will operate with a play-list, which is the internally approved list of music that will be played most often during a set period of time. It is clearly important for music companies to ensure that their releases are on radio station play-lists and they employ people known as pluggers (SEE: **plugs**) for this task. It is clear that there is significant scope for corruption here as those in control of a play-list might be influenced to favour particular releases. This is one aspect of the process known as PAYOLA.

SEE ALSO: **DJ**.

pleasure As the study of the media developed it became clear that one of most neglected areas of research concerned the way in which audiences derive pleasure from engagement with media. In the early days of work with the concept, it tended to be used in ways that derived from psycho-analytic attention to the role of sexual desire, especially in visual texts like film. In addition, in French STRUCTURALIST thought a distinction was made between *plaisir* (or pleasure) and JOUISSANCE. The former implied more rational and cognitive pleasure, the latter a more bodily and sexual response. Subsequently, pleasure became used in a more general way to indicate the enjoyment of the media and the manner in which this mode of engagement could itself produce an oppositional, active or resistant outcome.

SEE ALSO: **Barthes; male gaze; voice**.

plugs The process by which a particular piece of music is promoted to radio stations by employees of the music industry known as pluggers, who will travel to radio stations to encourage the station to agree to play their product.

SEE ALSO: **DJ; payola; play-list**.

podcast A method of transmitting multimedia files (audio, video or music) over the internet to personal computers or, more fashionably, to handheld devices such as mobile phones or MP3 players such as iPods. The word, indeed, comes from 'broadcast' and 'iPod'. The advantage of podcasting is that the material can be seen or heard at any time and any place – and can be replayed as many times as one wishes. It also allows consumers to construct the mix of material that they prefer, rather than to take what they are given, and to avoid advertisements. Some podcast provision will come free, and others will come via a subscription. It is unclear as yet what the impact of podcasting will be, particularly on the radio and music industries. It will surely be a source of competition for commercial radio. It will also attack the method of distribution used by the music industry.

SEE ALSO: **new media; personalization; radio**.

point of view Where the action in film or television is shown from the perspective of a participant in the action. As an audience, we may know more than the point of view of any particular character or than the participants in the action. In addition, the process of identification of the point of view with a particular character can encourage sympathy with the character, even if he or she might have engaged in criminal or immoral actions.

SEE ALSO: **180 degree rule**.

point size The size of characters on the printed page, measured in points. SEE ALSO: **typeface**.

police series There are a number of variations of this GENRE, but all have the police as the most significant characters. They are a series in the sense that each episode has the same central characters and has similar settings. There is also a tendency for the setting to be urban, though this is not always the case. While some of the conventions of the police series are based on those of the detective story, they developed with television itself during the 1950s and have continued as one of the most popular of TV genres. In broad terms, there are two key variants of the genre. The first centres on the activity of a male policeman. He is often individualistic and seeks to act to defeat the criminal using his own methods. This may involve him in breaking the procedural rules of the police force, which can often bring him into conflict with his more rule-bound superiors. The international success *Inspector Morse* would be a good example. Morse essentially acts as an individual supported by his more procedural helper (Lewis) and operates at the edge of the rules, consistently annoying his superiors. This marks Morse off as an individual, as do his own patterns of taste in music and cars. The second variation is more like a SOAP OPERA. Here, the focus is on the activities of a group or community of police officers, based in one location. The relationships between the officers are of central narrative importance, as they go about attempting to maintain law and order on their 'patch'. The most popular series of this type in Britain currently is *The Bill*, and *Heartbeat* is another example.

In the earlier days of police series the central characters were male, but as the genre has developed, gender and the place of women in the police have become more significant. There have been series with a central female hero, who also acts individualistically, such as *Prime Suspect*, and women feature more heavily as part of the community of officers in series like *The Bill*.

It has been suggested that all police series have an ideological function in securing the message that the police are in broad terms a key agent of keeping law and order to the benefit of all. Thus, while Morse may bend the rules, we can see that he does it to capture the real murderer. It is almost never the case that the police corruption is depicted as systematic. While there may be seen to be 'bad' officers or issues of race and gender prejudice, these are often explained as part of the problem of a particular individual rather than being the fault of the system. More radical critics see the police series as part of HEGEMONY in securing the consent of the population to inequalities in society.

SEE ALSO: **gender; ideology; western**.

political economy In broad terms, the political economy approach has been concerned to stress the way in which the economy is the most important factor in social life, including the media. In recent years there has been debate in media studies about the relative merits of a 'political economy' approach compared with 'cultural studies'. CULTURAL STUDIES approaches are more concerned with the nature of texts and how they are consumed and tend to neglect the economic and political dimensions. In many ways this is a very sterile debate as any full analysis will pay attention to all dimensions, recognizing the importance of the production of texts, the nature of texts and the ways in which they are consumed by audiences.

SEE ALSO: **Marxism**.

politics The part of human life concerned with power and its exercise and distribution. Various areas of media have been seen to be political in different senses. A good example is the nature of the debate around the politics of popular music. There are two main dimensions to the discussion of this issue. First, there is the way in which popular music is thought to be oppositional to power holders, authority, or established values in the most general sense. Second, there is more detailed and specific discussion of the way in which particular types of music and musicians have opposed (or supported) dominant or oppositional parties and groups (see Longhurst, 2007; Shuker, 2001).

SEE ALSO: **critical theory; Frankfurt School; hegemony; ideology; Marxism**.

polysemic The way in which texts can contain multiple sign systems, which give rise to a range of possible meanings and consequently interpretations on the part of the audience. The contrast would be with very simple or CLOSED TEXTS, where meaning is much less complicated.

SEE ALSO: **semiology; sign**.

popping Distortion in radio sound produced by a speaker being too close to a microphone.

popular culture Popular culture is most often contrasted with HIGH CULTURE and mass culture. There are two broad senses of the term. First, it can be used to refer to the culture that is most widespread in a society. In this respect, it will be differentiated from high or elite culture, which will be a minority taste. High culture is usually defined through particular types of text – 'classical' music pieces or 'difficult' novels – and is seen as appealing to particular sections of the upper classes. Second, popular culture is distinguished from mass culture. The latter term is associated with mass-society theories and tends to be considered in a negative way as a form of culture that is in some respect inauthentic. Popular culture as a term has fewer negative connotations and is sometimes used to refer to culture that is organically linked with the lower or working classes. In this sense, popular has less to do with the way that the culture is widespread and more to do with how it is linked to a particular class.

As media and cultural studies developed from the 1960s onwards they tended to use the term popular rather than mass culture to refer to forms of culture that were widely appreciated in society. This signalled a shift from the approaches of mass culture and mass-society theory towards a more sophisticated understanding of the complexity of popular culture in both textual and social aspects.

SEE ALSO: **omnivore**.

popular music In the most general sense music that is popular in having an appeal to a large number of people. More specific uses entail the connection to the working class as understood as the 'popular' classes; or the distinction from serious music as in the influential work of the Marxist critic T. W. ADORNO. Adorno was very critical of popular music as he saw it as the commodified output of a culture industry. However, some draw a distinction between pop and popular music. Pop music is often criticized in ways that reflect Adorno's approach. It is seen as manufactured, designed only for commercial appeal and to be liked by those who lack true discrimination. An example of such criticism of pop music would be the way that boy bands are often written about by the music press. By contrast some forms of popular music are held to be more serious, less designed for the market and to be produced by authentic musicians. A classic example of this is the idea of 'rock' music. Rock is then able to be popular (in that some artists will sell large numbers of records) but is distinguished from pop music. Other forms of popular music are also 'rescued' from the taint of the culture industry in similar ways – a good example would be 'folk' music. This can be popular among particular groups, but authentic as well.

SEE ALSO: **critical theory; Frankfurt School; rock and pop**.

populism A political movement that seeks to mobilize the general population or sections of it to a cause which established political parties are perceived to have neglected or ignored. They may often be based on a single issue or be locally based in one area of a country. The term is then also often used negatively to capture the ways in which political parties and movements seek to gather popular support through direct and often over-simplified appeals to the voters. The idea has some resonance in media studies in the debates around cultural populism. Thus, the work of some writers, especially JOHN FISKE (1989a and 1989b), was held, by authors such as McGuigan (1992), to be exaggerating the potential of popular fictions to be used by audiences creatively to resist the ideological messages of capitalism. This was argued to neglect the real constraints on the interpretation of texts that result from the capitalist production process and the organization of production, giving too much weight to the importance of popular texts and the popular audience.

SEE ALSO: **hegemony; ideology.**

pornography While there are many debates on the definition of pornography, the key idea is that pornography is a form of representation that depicts sexual activity with the aim of sexually stimulating the (usually male) consumer. There has also been wide debate on the effects of pornography (like the debate on the representation of sexual activity more widely). It has been held by a number of critics that pornography is harmful. It can be thought of as detrimental in different respects, from the way in which consumption of pornography could have led a person to commit a violent sexual crime to the way that the types of representation of women in pornography leads to particular views about how women should behave and be thought of by men in society. The evidence for the harmful effects of pornography has been heavily disputed. In broad terms there are two camps – the more liberal camp, which suggests that there should be a degree of personal freedom in what individuals consume and that harm is not straightforward to detect; and the writers who suggest that pornography can be shown to be directly harmful and that it should be censored and controlled. These positions do not map simply on to the left and right in politics, say between liberal on the one hand and conservatives on the other. For example, there has been much debate on pornography within FEMINISM, between those who assert that pornography is harmful to women and should be banned or controlled and those who adopt anti-censorship positions (while often being anti-porn). These are only the broad streams in a debate that has involved much discussion about the possibility of a feminist erotica and the pros and cons of any forms of censorship.

SEE ALSO: **censorship; gender; male gaze.**

positional goods These are those goods or services whose desirability lies in the fact that they are difficult to obtain or expensive or both, such as Porsche cars, Armani suits or Rolex watches. Objects such as these gain cult status, but the paradox is that, if more people acquire them, they start to become less desirable.

SEE ALSO: **consumer society**.

positioning Refers to the ways in which texts locate members of the audience. Thus, texts place the reader into particular ways of viewing and thinking, which may have effects upon him or her. For example, the depiction of a woman on screen may position the male viewer in certain ways that he may find comfortable or uncomfortable. The viewer of an adventure film may be positioned to identify with a male hero, who is active and powerful and in that sense sympathetic, but whose politics and views may have more or less appeal. For example, the character Harry Callaghan, played by Clint Eastwood in the *Dirty Harry* series of films, could position the male liberal viewer as in sympathy with his ability, skill and 'cool' but also induce anxiety about his breaking of the rules of procedure and evidence. In this respects positioning does not necessarily determine views or behaviour but it may exert a strong force.

SEE ALSO: **male gaze; ideology; interpellation**.

postcolonialism Like the related term imperialism, colonialism refers to the way in which one society or power takes over another society or region and dominates it economically, politically and culturally. For example, Britain colonized India in the eighteenth and nineteenth centuries. Post-colonial societies are those that are formally independent but are still involved in a relationship with the former colonizers. A key work on postcolonialism is EDWARD SAID'S *Orientalism* (1978). The term is also used to characterize the literature produced in a country that was previously colonized.

SEE ALSO: **difference; globalization; hegemony; media imperialism**.

post-dubbing the process of adding actors' speech to a film in the studio after it has been shot.

post-Fordism See: FORDISM/POST-FORDISM.

postmodernism A movement in painting, literature, television, film and the arts generally. There is disagreement as to what its main features are but they include the following. (1) Pastiche: a putting together of elements of style from radically different contexts and historical epochs.(2) Reflexivity: the capacity to be self-aware, often accompanied by a sense of irony or playfulness. (3) Relativism: the absence of objective standards of truth. (4) An opposition to certain classical artistic techniques such as NARRATIVE – telling a story in an ordered sequence closed off at the end – and representation – attempting to depict reality. (5) A disrespect for, and a wish to cross, traditional artistic boundaries such as those between popular and high culture and between different artistic forms. (6) A lessened belief in the importance of the author as the creator of the text.

Rap music or the 1970s/1980s group Talking Heads are given as examples of postmodernist, popular music, while *Twin Peaks* is theorized as a post-modernist television show (see Connor, 1989). The latter had a narrative that was based around cause but it also made direct reference to other genres of television and popular culture – such as the police series, the horror film and the teen flick. Moreover, in being constructed in this way, the text was often playful, in that it was asking the audience to spot these references and connections. The world depicted in *Twin Peaks* was both familiar and strange and partly structured around these references to other texts. It might be argued that these features have become increasingly salient in much popular television, especially that produced from sections of the television industry in the USA. Thus, shows like *Buffy the Vampire Slayer*, *The Sopranos*, *Six Feet Under* and *Desperate Housewives* can be all be seen as postmodernist.

Sociologically, the interesting question is the relationship of post-modernism to POSTMODERNITY – whether the former is the culture of the latter. The issue for both is whether they represent genuinely new cultural and social forms or whether they are merely transitional phenomena produced by rapid social change.

SEE ALSO: **poststructuralism; realism.**

postmodernity Social scientists often use the term modernity to describe the state of industrial, capitalist societies of the West in the period from the industrial revolution in the early nineteenth century to the middle of the twentieth century. Some analysts have argued that these societies are entering (or have entered) a period of postmodernity characterized by the fragmentation of the system of social classes, the emergence of CONSUMER SOCIETY, post-Fordist (SEE: **Fordism/post-Fordism**) systems of production and marketing and a declining role for the state in economic and social life. Many theories of postmodernity also give cultural factors a central role. The media are seen as central to everyday life in a manner impossible in previous societies and POSTMODERNISM is seen as a cultural form typical of postmodernity.

post-production The whole process of producing a film or video can be divided into a number of phases. The PRE-PRODUCTION phase consists of detailed planning, setting up locations where necessary and hiring a production crew. The production phase involving actual filming needs to be kept as short as is possible since it is very expensive. Much television is, of course, live or produced relatively cheaply and, in these cases, the pre-production phase may be relatively short. However, all film and television will require a post-production phase in which the results of production are prepared for broadcasting or distribution. Most important of all there has to be a process of editing of the raw RUSHES into a coherent film or television programme (SEE: **editing**). For many recent films (e.g. *Lord of the Rings*) which involve complex visual effects this can be a long and expensive process (SEE: **computer-generated image**).

poststructuralism A movement in the social sciences and humanities that developed from a critique of STRUCTURALISM. Rather than being concerned with the correct identification of the deeper meanings or the underlying structure of a text, poststructuralism sought to elucidate the play of different meanings within the text itself and to show how the text often undermined its own claims. Interpretation is therefore always in dispute and can never ultimately be resolved. This introduced a measure of critique of the scientific pretensions of structuralism into textual criticism. The work of French writers such as JACQUES DERRIDA (e.g. 1976 and 1978) and JEAN BAUDRILLARD (e.g. 1988) exhibits many of these poststructuralist traits. Derrida shows how texts subvert themselves, and Baudrillard offers a critique of the attempt to analyse culture through the identification of mutually exclusive BINARY OPPOSITIONS. Poststructuralist ideas were also influential in some forms of FEMINISM, as the approach could be used to overcome simple oppositions between categories of man and woman and to explore how concepts like man and woman, masculine and feminine were discursively constructed in different ways in different times and societies. Such writers saw how poststructuralism could be politically progressive through the destabilization of such established and perhaps conservative meanings. Others were more critical, seeing the abandonment of claims to the identification of truth as opening the doors to forms of relativism and disorder, where anything would go.

SEE ALSO: **postmodernism**.

power The capacity to impose one's will on others. It is often argued that the media have too much power. Parents will be worried that their children are exposed to undesirable influences by television, film or rock music. Politicians are dismayed that their policies are not presented in the way that they think is necessary. Minorities of all kinds feel that their views and way of life do not get an airing or are treated by the media in a positively hostile way. Celebrities and others feel that some elements in the media are too intrusive into private lives. Ordinary people believe that the media present a distorted picture of the world around them. Some of these concerns are to do with the ethics of the media. Others stem from a belief that media organizations are insufficiently regulated (SEE: **govern-ment and the media; regulation**). Still others are convinced that the media really do have the power to mould beliefs and attitudes and have effects on the way that people act (SEE: **domination; effects**). Much of the research indicates that the power of the media is exaggerated both by politicians and by the public. Thus, it is unlikely that media exposure is an important factor in the formation of fundamental values and beliefs. Neither is it probable that, for example, violent films cause people to be violent. On the other hand, politicians, and other public figures, are very sensitive to the way that the media report their activities and may alter policies to fit in with what they perceive that the media are saying. It is also likely that newspaper or television reports will affect the ATTITUDES that members of the public will take towards particular issues at particular times. For example, it is often held that the media are partly responsible, through their reporting of crime, for attitudes and beliefs that the public hold about the prevalence of crime, tending to exaggerate the frequency of street crime, for instance.

SEE ALSO: **moral panic**.

preferred reading There is potentially a large number of ways of inter-preting a particular media text whether it is television, radio, rock song or newspaper. In many cases, however, one set of meanings is given prominence in a media message and other possibilities are subordinate or absent altogether. This may be the deliberate intention of the producer or it may be an unconscious preference. The media, in other words, help to define the world in particular ways. It is a further and more doubtful claim that this dominant meaning – or preferred reading – reflects the dominant values of society (SEE: **dominant ideology**) *and* effectively con-strains the audience into making one interpretation that fits with those dominant values. It is unsafe to overstate this argument since many tele-vision texts contain more than one set of meanings, and audiences are likely to produce a mixture of readings.

SEE ALSO: **active audience; agenda setting; encoding/decoding; ideology**.

pre-production The processes that are involved in film and television production in the period leading up to the shooting of the film itself. The period after shooting is known as POST-PRODUCTION. For example, before a film or TV show can be shot, actors need to be cast, costumes designed, a script written, props and possible locations found and so on.

press See: NEWSPAPER.

Press Association (PA) Founded in 1868, the PA is the national NEWS AGENCY for the United Kingdom and Ireland. It supplies a variety of services including latest news, video footage and access to a photograph archive. It operates as a private company, and most of its shareholders are national and regional newspaper publishers.

press baron The powerful newspaper proprietors of the period from the end of the nineteenth century to the Second World War. Men such as BEAVERBROOK, NORTHCLIFFE and Rothermere built up substantial newspaper companies but also saw their newspapers as providing a platform for their own political, social and moral views. Since the Second World War newspapers by themselves have become less important, particularly as their circulations decline. Newspapers now often form part of large media groups which will also have interests in other media such as radio and television. Proprietors have continued to have a substantial public presence, however, and continue to exercise influence over the content of the media that they control (SEE: **Maxwell; Murdoch**).

SEE ALSO: **concentration of ownership; media mogul.**

Press Complaints Commission (PCC) An independent body which deals with complaints from members of the public about the editorial content of newspapers and magazines. In 2002 it dealt with 2,630 complaints of which about 60 per cent were to do with accuracy and about 40 per cent were to do with the invasion of PRIVACY. Almost all of these complaints were dealt with by the PCC informally. It made a formal adjudication in only thirty-six cases, and any that were critical of the newspapers concerned were published in those newspapers.

The PCC is an example of self-regulation and it has been extensively criticized as weak and ineffective. The commission operates according to a code drawn up by newspaper editors, and almost half of the membership of the commission is composed of senior staff in newspapers. Above all, critics make the point that newspapers apparently continue to publish inaccuracies and invade privacy.

SEE ALSO: **regulation.**

press freedom A free press prints what it believes in and is free of governmental controls over what it can print and of interference from large corporations. This ideal is unlikely to be attained; the question is how close one may get to it.

SEE ALSO: **concentration of ownership; government and the media; public sphere.**

pressure group A formally constituted organization which is designed, at least partly, to bring pressure to bear on government, civil service and other political institutions to achieve ends that it favours. In Britain in the 1960s and 1970s the National Viewers and Listeners Association formed and led by Mary Whitehouse campaigned vigorously against what it saw as falling moral standards and indecency on British television. Another good example of pressure group politics can be found in the activities of the Parents' Music Resource Center (PMRC) founded by Tipper Gore (the wife of Al Gore, Vice-President to Bill Clinton in the late 1990s) and other 'political wives' in the 1980s to campaign against eroticism, sadism and violence in the lyrics of popular music. One result of this activity was the parental advisory stickers that appear on CDs that may 'offend' in these terms.

SEE ALSO: **censorship; pornography.**

primary definer Those persons or institutions that have the capacity to define, judge or describe events with the likelihood that their definitions are taken by the public as authoritative. Examples are experts of various kinds, the police, judges, some religious figures and even some politicians. These primary definitions only come to public attention because they are taken up by the media, which are therefore acting as secondary definers.

SEE ALSO: **amplification of deviance; moral panic.**

primary media Media that are consumed in an attentive manner, such as a newspaper or a book. Of course, any particular medium may be consumed in this way, or in a secondary fashion – where it is part of the background. TV is a good example of this. It may be a primary medium when we give it our full attention, or secondary if it is switched on when we are reading a newspaper, for example. Media can also be in a tertiary position, in which they form part of a background to which we pay no attention at all. Background music in a supermarket may be like this.

SEE ALSO: **active audience; mediascape.**

print The invention of printing in the fifteenth century was crucial in the development of modern media, much of which is print-based. Modern printing began with the invention of the first printing press by Johannes Guttenberg in 1436, although there is evidence that the Chinese had made a similar invention in the eleventh century. The printing press was introduced into England by William Caxton in 1476. Guttenberg's innovation was the use of movable type made of iron, which could be inked and then pressed on paper in a wooden machine worked by hand. Previously, the type was carved into blocks of wood on which the paper was pressed, giving an inflexible process. The basic principles of Guttenberg's press remained unaltered for more than 300 years. During that time, there were improvements in inks and paper and a great deal of experimentation with typefaces, but the process, although faster than in Guttenberg's time, remained slow and laborious. Books were, as a result, restricted to a small group of people who could read and therefore relatively expensive. The industry was also hampered by the restrictions placed by a government worried about the subversive possibilities of books and pamphlets.

The late eighteenth and early nineteenth centuries, however, saw the introduction of a series of technological innovations which transformed the printing industry. Taken together with the spread of literacy and the growth of a READING PUBLIC, these innovations enabled the production of large numbers of copies of relatively cheap books, as well as pamphlets, periodicals and newspapers, throughout the nineteenth century. Two of these changes were of particular importance – the use of iron in the manufacture of the entire printing press and the introduction of steam-powered presses. Throughout the nineteenth and twentieth centuries, further changes were made. Machines were invented to set up the type on the printing plate via a keyboard. Previously letters were inserted in a frame by hand. Printing presses became much faster and capable of printing in colour and incorporating illustration with ease. Latterly, the computer revolution has radically changed the typesetting function, allowing pages to be set up on a computer.

With computers becoming more important in everyday life, there has been much speculation about the disappearance of print. There has as yet been no sign of this. Indeed, a media-saturated society seems to generate more printed material not less.

SEE ALSO: **book; letterpress; newspaper**.

privacy There is an active debate in most Western societies about the degree to which people have a right to privacy. While there is much dismay about the extent to which the media intrude into people's private lives, ordinary people as well as celebrities, there are also anxieties that any attempt to control the media may end up with an unjustified curtailment of PRESS FREEDOM. The recent behaviour of the media has prompted calls for legislation to strengthen the right to privacy, and there have been some high-profile legal cases. Michael Douglas and Catherine Zeta-Jones, for example, sued *Hello!* magazine for infringement of their privacy and had partial success. Media organizations usually respond that self-regulation is the best way and that organizations such as the PRESS COMPLAINTS COMMISSION are successful in controlling the worst excesses of invasion of privacy. It is not at all clear that this is true, although it is usually celebrities and politicians who complain most, and some people maintain that those who often court publicity shouldn't complain when they get the wrong sort.

SEE ALSO: **Human Rights Act 1998; private sphere.**

private sphere Often contrasted with other terms (SEE: **public sphere**), the private sphere is usually taken to mean the sets of relationships and activities within the family and the home. The boundary between the private and the public is becoming increasingly blurred by the media. For example, television brings the world directly into the home in ways that make it difficult for parents to prevent exposure to events that they may wish their children to avoid. The internet can act in a similar way.

SEE ALSO: **privatization of leisure.**

privatization of leisure The argument is often made that, since the mid-twentieth century in Western societies, there has been an increasing diversion of time, energy and loyalty towards the immediate family and the home (SEE: **private sphere**) and away from other relationships in, for example, the local community. One aspect of this concentration on the private sphere is that leisure is taken in the home rather than outside. In households in the UK, for example, some two-thirds of leisure time is spent at home, and a great deal of that is centred around the media, especially television (SEE: **leisure**).

It is not absolutely certain that there is a long-term privatization of leisure. The data do not exist to make accurate comparisons over time, and it may be that any changes that have occurred are short-term. However, it is clear that whole industries have grown up to cater for home-based leisure.

SEE ALSO: **everyday life; household.**

process model A model of the chain of communication from sender to receiver where the direction of meaning from the sender to the receiver is primarily determined by the messages sent by the sender. The receiver is therefore subservient to the sender.

SEE ALSO: **communication.**

producer All media organizations have to manage the relationship between the commercial and creative sides of the enterprise. Particularly in the larger organizations, these two aspects are separated out into different roles which then have to relate to each other. In the print media, for example, EDITORS organize the creative input whether that be from book writers or journalists. There is then another role, often called publisher, that deals with strategic, financial and organizational aspects. Similarly, in visual media, film and television, for example, there is a distinction between producers and DIRECTORS, the former more like a publisher and the latter more like an editor.

The balance between the two kinds of role varies between different media and different organizations, and they should not be separated too rigidly. Television generally, for example, is a producer's medium, and the role straddles the creative and organizational functions. The producer organizes and manages, making sure that the various elements of the production system are there at the right time and that the whole process is carried out within the budget. For some producers, that may be a detailed, day-to-day matter, while for others it may involve more remote control. At the same time, producers are actively involved in the creation of programmes, are often responsible for the original idea and work closely with writers. In the MUSIC INDUSTRY, the record producer has the job of coordinating the production of a record.

There are several different ways of being a producer. Perhaps most significantly, producers can function at different levels. For example, within the British television networks, there is a distinction between the series producer, who will be in daily detailed contact with programme-making, and the executive producer, who will have overall responsibility for several programmes or series and hence will not have any detailed involvement.

Film producers are not unlike television producers in being a bridge between financial and management constraints and the creative process of making the film. However, cinema tends to give more power to the directly creative people, especially the director of the film. Television, as an industry, works to much more demanding timetables and has to produce more material within restricted budgets. These exigencies tend to demand tighter management in general and hence favour the role of producer.

The term is also used simply for those who produce media texts of whatever kind.

producer choice In the 1980s and 1990s, media organizations in the UK and the USA became much more competitive, a tendency encouraged by governments (SEE: **Fordism/post-Fordism; independent production company**). Thus, in the late 1990s, the then Director-General of the BBC, JOHN BIRT, introduced a system of producer choice whereby programme makers could go outside the BBC for people to work on programmes. It was believed that such a system would reduce costs while also enabling creativity to be brought into the organization from outside.

producer/text/audience A model for the analysis of the media introduced by STUART HALL. It is based upon the assumption that any full analysis has to pay attention to three closely related aspects – the media producer, the media text and the audience. The starting point is usually the text, the media product, whether it is an individual television programme or a set of programmes, a book, women's magazines or tabloid newspapers. The analyst will be interested in the form and content of the text, in what is left out, what language is used or what view of the world is presented. There is a temptation to stop at that point. For example, claims that television programmes are violent are frequently made, and it is often simply assumed that there will be an effect of some kind on the audience, perhaps making particularly susceptible individuals commit violent acts. However, such a claim cannot be made without an investigation of the audience – and in this example it is by no means clear that there will be any such effect. So, direct study of the audience and its interpretations and reactions is required. Similarly, in order to explain how a media text takes the form that it does a study will be needed of how that text comes to be generated by looking at the people and organizations that produce it. For example, if an investigation of newspapers comes to the conclusion that the news is biased, an explanation of that bias will need to come from a study of journalists, of the organization of newspapers and of the large media companies that ultimately own and control newspapers.

SEE ALSO: **encoding/decoding; news; violence**.

product placement The display, use or mention of a commercial product or service in a film or television programme that is not intended to carry advertising material. Advertisers look for ever more ingenious opportunities for promoting products. One relatively recent one is product placement, in which particular products are obviously used in a film, television programme or book, and care is taken to place company logos and names in clear view. Product placement helps the film company to finance the film. The company concerned not only receives the publicity directly but is also able to exploit it in a subsequent advertising campaign. Product placement has been much criticized for contributing to a blurring between what is advertisement and what is not.

SEE ALSO: **advertising ethics; merchandising; sponsorship**.

promotional culture The way in which a society's culture has become drenched or saturated with the activities and values that were once the narrower province of ADVERTISING. The term suggests that contemporary culture has become more concerned with the selling of things and the values associated with this, but also that people's identities and presentation of self have become more promotional and therefore more performed and less authentic.

proof A fully typeset, but not yet printed, copy of a book, newspaper or magazine. Proof copies will be used for final checking of the text before printing (hence the verb 'to proof') and may also be used for promotional purposes, especially in the book publishing industry.

SEE ALSO: **dummy**.

propaganda Messages or texts that are produced to deliver a set of ideas that are distorted or untrue, in the service of a political interest.

SEE ALSO: **censorship: ideology**.

Propp, Vladimir (1895–1970) Russian theorist of NARRATIVE structure. Best known for his authorship of *The Morphology of the Folk Tale* (1968), which is a structural analysis of Russian folk tales or fairy stories. Propp argues that the folk tales are constructed from a limited number of generic character types or functions. Narratives move through a sequence of actions or segments that can be identified in general terms. This idea has been very influential on STRUCTURALIST analyses of media and culture. For example, the idea that the basic functions or types in the WESTERN are the hero, the villain and society, and that these general functions move through a set of actions that are common to all examples of the western form (Wright, 1975), is derived from the approach initiated by Propp.

SEE ALSO: **binary opposition**.

prospects The schedule of stories in radio news to be covered in any particular day.

psychoanalysis See: FREUD.

public broadcasting service To be distinguished from PUBLIC SERVICE BROADCASTING, which refers to a set of values that may underpin all broadcasting, public broadcasting services are those that have non-profit aims and attempt to provide broadcasting in the public interest in areas that commercial organizations will not enter. The Public Broadcasting Service in the United States, for example, is a private, non-profit enterprise delivering programming and education services via more than 300 TV stations and the internet. It is owned and operated by licensees which include educational institutions, community organizations and municipal authorities. Much of this activity is funded by the Corporation for Public Broadcasting, which in turn is funded by the American government.

public opinion The opinions that the population of a country are thought to have. However, although politicians frequently refer to the 'public' or the 'people', it is unclear that there is a unified public or a coherent public opinion. Most contemporary societies actually have within them a diversity of opinion at any one time. Moreover, the attitudes and opinions that people have can also be quite volatile over time. There are, of course, occasions when a large majority of a population have the same opinion about some issue or set of issues, at least as measured by OPINION POLLS. Obvious examples are in wartime or at other moments of national crisis.

SEE ALSO: **public sphere**.

public relations The cultivation by an organization of a positive image of its activities in the public mind. Commercial enterprises actively promote their goods and services to their markets. Public relations forms part of this promotional work together with such activities as advertising and SPONSORSHIP. The idea is that all these elements will fit together in an organized whole. For example, at the same time as a company concludes a major sponsorship deal, it will conduct a public relations exercise and an advertising campaign. As BRANDS have become more important in marketing, so also has public relations, which aims to give more prominence to a brand by whatever means possible at the same time as protecting the brand name from unfavourable publicity. Richard Branson's adventures in hot-air balloons, for example, give prominence to the Virgin brand.

Public relations activities can take more or less any form and will be addressed to different audiences. Issuing press releases, talking to journalists, putting out leaflets, lobbying government agencies, involving celebrities in promotional activities, arranging social events for influential people are all examples of public relations work. Government ministers, civil servants, journalists, customers, employees, shareholders and the general public are all audiences which have to be managed in a coherent fashion.

Public relations essentially consists in giving out messages about the company, about the brand or about its products. In this respect, therefore, the relationship to the media is critical. Companies need beneficial exposure but journalists also need copy.

While public relations is of great and increasing importance to organizations operating in a commercial environment, public bodies of all kinds are increasingly interested in communicating effectively with those who use their services. Government departments, universities and NHS bodies, for example, are all actively involved in public relations.

public service broadcasting Broadcasting in the UK since its origins in the 1920s has been influenced by the ideals of public service. In earlier formulations, particularly as advanced by JOHN REITH, public service in broadcasting had several features. First, it meant that every household in the UK had equal access to broadcasting, which therefore had a democratic function. Second, content should not be driven by market considerations, but should be the best available, reflecting the highest cultural standards. Broadcasting, in other words, should not only be used for entertainment, but should also educate and inform. Third, it was felt that the achievement of the first two objectives would only be possible if there was a single provider of broadcasting which could ensure that programming of the required quality was delivered to every citizen. Fourth, a system of funding was required which enabled these objectives and was independent of commercial considerations. The solution in the UK was a licence fee payable by everybody who had a radio receiver (and, later, a television).

The ideal of public service in broadcasting has been progressively attenuated throughout the twentieth century under commercial pressures. This accelerated after the Second World War with the advent of television, which has much greater commercial possibilities than radio and is visible in the reports of committees and the subsequent legislation (SEE: **Annan Report: Broadcasting Act 1990; Broadcasting Act 1996; Peacock Committee; Pilkington Committee**). In the UK, the major breach in notions of public service was effectively to end the monopoly enjoyed by the BBC and introduce commercial competition (INDEPENDENT TELEVISION), funded firstly by advertising but then as well by subscription and pay-per-view. Besides that, there has been a gradual relaxation in control over content, although the principle of mass access to broadcasting survives.

The result of this attenuation of the original public service ideals is an uneasy tension in the broadcasting system in the UK (and in other countries). Many elements of the ideal persist. The BBC and the licence fee are still with us, but there are many arguing that the first should be broken up and the second abolished. Government still keeps control over the system as a whole by an insistence on licensing broadcasters, although there are progressive relaxations of the regulatory regime. And the ambiguous position of the state – and successive governments – continues to be a further source of tension. The state has effectively acted as guarantor of the public service ideal. However, it has also frequently fallen out with the BBC because the latter's programming does not accord with the views of the government of the day. At the same time, governments have allowed the intrusion of commercial interests which are not beholden to government at all.

The future of public service broadcasting is not clear. Commercial pressures will continue to mount as terrestrial, satellite and cable broadcasters challenge the BBC. These pressures will be accentuated by technological changes. Digital television, in particular, allows for a very large number of channels. That has two effects. Firstly, it is likely to encourage specialization. The idea of comprehensive programming on a few channels will begin to look increasingly anachronistic. Indeed, the BBC has itself developed a range of specialist digital TV channels. Second, with such a wide choice, many viewers will stop watching the BBC altogether and they may well resent paying the licence fee to fund the BBC when they make no use of the service. Over the next few years there will be a major public debate about the reconstruction of public service broadcasting.

SEE ALSO: **BBC**.

public sphere An area of public life within which a free debate about issues of widespread concern can be developed, leading to the formation of an informed public opinion and the development of rational public policy. Some social theorists (most particularly HABERMAS, 1989) have argued that the public sphere was most highly developed in eighteenth-century Europe, promoted by the appearance of an urban culture, places where people could meet to argue and debate, the widespread use of newspapers and the growing importance of a social class of entrepreneurs who had an interest in challenging a state dominated by king and aristocracy. This public sphere of well-informed, rational debate became corroded, so the argument runs, throughout the nineteenth and twentieth centuries. A major part of the reason for this is that the media have trivialized and commercialized what they produce, no longer giving people the opportunity for informed debate.

There is continuing disagreement about the role of the media, especially television, in the formation of a public sphere in contemporary societies.

Some would argue that the media have cheapened public debate and will point to the obsession with celebrity as an instance. Others reply that the question is not only what the content of the media might be but also what it is that audiences do with that content. For example, TALK SHOWS are often cited as an example of trivialization, yet research shows (Livingstone and Lunt, 1995) that people will use the topics aired in such shows as a basis for discussion at home and at work.

Publishers Association (PA) The trade association for book, journal and electronic publishers in the UK, the PA promotes the interests of its members and provides a range of services to them including training.

publishing industry To publish something is to bring material, usually written material, to the attention of the public. The activity becomes commercially viable when members of the public in large enough numbers are prepared to pay for the material. In turn, that depends on a spread of the ability to read (SEE: **reading public**) and the invention of a printing technology which allows written material to be produced relatively cheaply.

In contemporary society, the publishing industry is usually taken to comprise the production and sale of BOOKS, NEWSPAPERS and MAGAZINES. These are, of course, all PRINT media, but a growing segment of the publishing market is online publishing or ELECTRONIC PUBLISHING.

puff A promotion of a product or service. The term is most usually used for a covert promotion in which a journalist or author promotes a product while writing about something else.

SEE ALSO: **advertorial**.

punk A form of rock music that developed in the UK and USA from the early 1970s onwards, reaching a height of popularity and influence in the period 1976–9. The form was characterized by short, loud songs and a return to 'basics' in instrumentation. The term itself was derived from US prison slang for a homosexual man and filtered through 1960s American 'garage' bands. This taking on of 'outsider' terms has become a very common activity in contemporary culture. Punk music was associated with bands like The Sex Pistols (Savage, 1991) The Clash (Gilbert, 2005), The Damned and The Buzzcocks in the UK and groups like The Ramones, Richard Hell and the Voidoids and Blondie in the US (Heylin, 1993). After its initial popularity punk still influenced a range of political bands (of the left and the right) around the world, which continued to be attracted to the simplicity of the music and the opportunity for declamatory lyrics (Laing, 1985). The other key development was into what was termed post-punk (Reynolds, 2005), where musical experiment and AVANT-GARDE claims were the order of the day. The influence of punk styles on music continues.

SEE ALSO: **new wave; rock and pop**.

Q

qualitative research See: AUDIENCE RESEARCH.

quality television High-status, valued television with expensive pro-duction values. While everybody seems to have views about quality tele-vision, it is actually more difficult to define than one might think. If the term is used, it is often assumed that no real definition is needed or that the listing of some programmes that are held to be of the cateogry will do. In Britain, this will often be a high-cultural ADAPTATION, such as *Brideshead Revisited* or *Jewel in the Crown*, with lavish production values. The problem with the term is that it comes with some baggage. Thus, certain forms of television, soap opera for instance, which are often popu-lar with large audiences, will not fit into the category, especially if they are television originals, rather than adaptations. In addition, it is sometimes thought, especially in the UK, that quality television is non-commercial television, even though the commercial sector produced *Brideshead Revisited*. Despite the difficulties of definition, those bidding for indepen-dent television franchises in the UK have to satisfy a quality threshold as well as succeed financially. This is to make sure that they will be able to meet established norms of what counts as acceptable quality standards.

SEE ALSO: **high culture; mass audience; popular culture.**

quantitative research See: AUDIENCE RESEARCH.

queer Historically this denoted strangeness but became a slang and degrading term for a male homosexual. In the context of gay sexual politics it has been reappropriated in a similar way to that in which some black people have adopted the term 'nigger' or 'nigga' as a form of positive identification, seeking to turn around a previously abusive term. This has led to modes of analysis (e.g. queering, queer theory) that approach texts and cultural practices from the 'queer' viewpoint and seek to reanalyse and reinterpret them to produce new meanings.

questionnaire Used in survey research, this is a set of questions given to respondents and designed to provide information relevant to the research area. Questionnaires may be completed by the respondents themselves or be completed by an interviewer. The questions may be CLOSED-ENDED, in which case the respondent simply selects from predetermined answers such as yes/no in the simplest form, or from a list of predetermined answers in more complicated forms. Or the questions may be OPEN-ENDED, in which case respondents answer as they wish. When questionnaires are completed by the respondents, for example when the research is conducted by mail, or when the level of literacy among respondents is not high, it is common to use the closed-ended format as much as possible.

quota A limit placed on something to restrict availability. Governments have sometimes tried to establish a quota on the amount of 'foreign' material broadcast on radio and television or exhibited in cinemas. This may be done to protect the indigenous media industries or to prevent the national culture from being 'infected' by ideas from outside.

SEE ALSO: **globalization**.

R

race There has been much debate about the concept of race. Historically, the term has been used to group people with (supposed) physical similarities, whether observable or not, and has become a subject of political and social controversy. Despite this, the term has been used as part of everyday speech and adapted in numerous ways to inform political and social discourse in such ideas as racial discrimination and institutional racism. Rather than talking of racial groups, the term ethnic group is now more common. Both race and ethnic identifications have tended to be used positively and negatively within media and cultural studies. Taking music as an example, that produced for the 'black' community in the USA was originally termed 'race' music, which was then replaced in the later 1950s by identifiers such as 'rhythm and blues'. In this context, race would have been seen as having negative connotations. In other contexts, the appellation of black would be seen as positive in, say, much BLACK MUSIC of the late 1960s and early 1970s. While race as a 'scientific' or analytical concept is highly disputable, its resonance and use more widely is clear and ongoing.

racism This term is usually used to describe actions, policies or attitudes that are determined by beliefs in racial characteristics such as that white men are naturally superior to black men. The media have sometimes been accused of fostering racism in their audiences or readers or even of being directly racist themselves, by using STEREOTYPES of ethnic and racial groups. For example, television drama, especially in the 1970s and 1980s when it had black characters, frequently depicted them in subordinate roles. More seriously, same newspapers have a tendency to exaggerate the importance of certain types of crime, e.g. mugging, which are claimed to be carried out by black youth. Again, in 2003 and 2004, the British press was obsessed by the issue of asylum-seekers, who were presented as causing serious social problems. In turn, those people were largely described in terms of their racial or ethnic origin – gypsy or black African for example. There is thereby conveyed an association of social problem with race.

radical media/radical press Media that espouse views alternative to, or critical of, MAINSTREAM or conventional opinion. Some people think that the media in the UK, and in all developed societies, tend to represent the middle ground of political and moral views, or, especially in the case of the press, a more right-wing approach, perhaps reflecting the views of owners (SEE: **bias; concentration of ownership**). One response to this is to set up a newspaper, magazine or radio station which expresses a more radical viewpoint, from either the left or the right. One difficulty is that the costs of doing this can be very high, or, in the case of television, prohibitive, especially given that the audience is likely to be relatively small. The term 'radical media' is usually used for those publications expressing a political view opposed to the mainstream while 'alternative media' is used for those advocating moral views at variance with those prevailing in society.

radio A hugely significant part of everyday life. While much attention in media studies has focused on television, leading to a relative neglect of radio, this situation is now changing. In 1998 each British household had on average between five and seven radio sets and in 2000 it was reported that 'Nine out of ten people in the UK listen to radio every week for an average of three hours a day, representing over one billion listening hours a week' (Fleming, 2002: 1). There are 'almost 70 separate owners of independent radio licences' (ibid.), and in '1999 there were 257 radio stations – local, regional and national – operating within Britain, and the list grows by the month' (Barnard, 2000: 2). One of the particular characteristics of radio is that it is very easy to listen to it while doing other things that require some attention. Thus, while this also happens with television to some extent, there are situations such as driving where screens are not appropriate and indeed illegal (SEE: **drive-time**). Radio has sometimes been termed a secondary medium (SEE: **primary media**) because of this characteristic.

While the technology of radio is a late nineteenth-century invention, like many media technologies, it was not initially seen as a consumer technology in the sense that it would be used to broadcast programmes to a large and diverse audience. The significant development of radio in this sense came after the First World War. It is possible to divide the history of radio in institutional and technological terms since then into three broad phases (Barnard, 2000), with the distinct possibility that we are entering a new and fourth phase. The first phase lasted from the late nineteenth century until the end of the Second World War in 1945. During this period, radio moved from the first transmission of electromagnetic waves by Rudolf Hertz in 1887 in Germany, Marconi's experiments in Italy in 1894 and his patenting of wireless telegraphy in the UK in 1897 to being a mass medium. In this period two relatively distinct institutional forms for radio emerged, which continue to this day. The UK adopted a public service model (SEE: **public service broadcasting**) while the USA developed a commercial model (SEE: **commercial television**). The British Broadcasting Company was formed in 1922 and became the British Broadcasting Corporation in 1927. Radio broadcasting had begun in the UK in 1920, but rapidly developed via the BBC during the 1920s. In the USA, radio developed as a commercial activity via networks like the National Broadcasting Company (NBC) and the Columbia Broadcasting System (CBS), which were to become familiar and powerful networks. Radio stations were financed through advertising and sponsorship, and local stations were affiliated to one of the networks. Local stations (identified by sets of letters) would combine networked programmes with local broadcasting and would cover a particular area (SEE: **transmission area**).

By the end of the Second World War, radio had established itself as a mass medium that was extremely popular in the UK and USA. By 1946 the BBC was broadcasting three national stations – the Home Service, the Light Programme and the Third Programme, which are the ancestors of the current Radio 4, Radio 2 and Radio 3. The USA networked local stations in a commercial model. This had been a twenty-year success story. A key development that was to affect this situation was the advent of television (which also affected the film industry). As television rapidly developed as a mass medium during the 1950s, radio changed. It is important to note that features of television both institutionally and in programming (see further below) came from transfers from radio. Thus, during the 1950s successful radio programmes featuring variety and comedy were transferred to television. This meant that in some respects radio carried on with its successful mass broadcasting (as there was still an audience for it), but also developed its own niches. Thus, between 1945 and 1978 we can identify a second period of 'contraction and repositioning' (Barnard, 2000). In the UK, this is marked by the development of commercial pirate radio stations broadcasting pop music to regional areas in the 1960s and the government action against them which led to the introduction of Radio 1 in 1967. The passage of the Sound Broadcasting Act in 1972 led to the introduction of commercial or independent radio in Britain. LBC was the first independent station and began broadcasting in London in 1973. BBC local radio had been launched in 1967. Technologically this period saw the introduction of FM radio in the USA (SEE: **AM/FM**), which had become more popular than AM by 1978. This period therefore sees a mixture of public service and commercial radio, new technological developments and new programming for specific tastes and localities in the UK.

From the late 1970s, radio entered a period which Barnard labels 'Deregulation and Convergence' (SEE: **deregulation**). With the election of the Conservative government in the UK (1979) and that of Ronald Reagan as President in the USA (1980) and further technological shifts, radio continued to change. National commercial stations started in the UK, and the 1990s saw the development of digital technologies which promoted MEDIA CONVERGENCE. This, it can be argued, is leading to a fourth era in radio. There has in recent times been a proliferation of radio stations in both the BBC and independent sectors. These serve particular tastes. Digital radio has been introduced to the UK, and numerous radio stations are available on digital boxes that play through TVs. Radio is also available through the internet, and broadcasters are providing programmes and selections as PODCASTS that are available for downloading from computers to MP3 players. While many of these developments can be seen as continuing innovations from the third phase, they are opening up new possibilities leading to further digitization and convergence. There are also further developments in specialized forms of radio that are outside the mainstream. These include contemporary pirate stations that serve specialist audiences in urban areas and forms of alternative radio.

Radio programming falls into four broad types: fictive, music, news and talk or speech. Music and speech are dominant. Some stations cover all four with a variety of programming, while others focus more narrowly. There are various forms of fictive programming including situation comedy, variety shows, the radio play and the daily serial or soap opera. Radio soaps became very important in the USA in the 1930s. Indeed the name stems from the sponsorship of the programmes by soap-powder companies, and a number of these programmes, such as *The Guiding Light*, were subsequently transferred to TV. In Britain the best-known example is the still-continuing *The Archers*. Radio drama of various types has been very popular in the past. One of the best-known episodes in radio history is the panic generated by the transmission of Orson Welles' dramatization of H. G. Wells' novel *The War of the Worlds* in the USA in 1938, which people found so convincing that they believed that the Martians had landed. Radio adventure series were also very popular in the heyday of mass radio. However, most radio programming now combines music, news and talk. Even programmes based around music include large amounts of talk. Disc jockeys have become important arbiters of musical taste in a range of fields (SEE: **DJ**). There have been important developments in these sorts of formats, such as the rise of the shock jock, who takes an aggressive and provocative stance towards the audience, and the zoo format, where the DJ interacts with a group of 'friends' in the studio. The fact that so much radio involves talk has led to the development of interactive forms in which members of the public phone in. On the back of such developments it can be seen that radio can often act as a kind of political forum for the airing of views and advice, especially in local areas.

The radio audience, like other media audiences, is researched commercially and academically, using qualitative and quantitative measures (SEE: **audience measurement; audience rating; audience research; audience share**). Audience figures are produced in the UK by the Radio Joint Audience Research (RAJAR), which also records what people think of what they are listening to. Academic research on radio audiences has a long history; indeed, some of the pioneering media audience research was done on radio audiences in the 1930s and 1940s. While such research has tended subsequently to be overshadowed by that on television audiences, there are studies which show how important radio is in accompanying domestic tasks, at work and in the car. Radio is also used to punctuate the day. Further, radio can for some people become an important part of their identity, in that how they think of themselves is bound up with their radio listening.

There is little evidence that radio will decline in importance in the future. However, together with television, it will be likely to adapt to a new media environment characterized by digitization, technological convergence, proliferation of stations, downloading and increased personal choice.

SEE ALSO: **local radio**.

Radio Authority See: OFCOM.

Radiocommunications Agency See: OFCOM.

radio spectrum The range of possible frequencies on which broadcasts of radio and television can be made. The government controls what frequencies a broadcaster can use in order to make sure that one broadcaster does not interfere with another. Successive governments have argued further that, since the radio spectrum is a finite resource, it has to be regulated by licence.

ragged See: JUSTIFICATION.

random sample A selection from a population that is studied instead of the whole population. A random sample is taken where any member of the population has an equal chance of being sampled.

range right or left See: JUSTIFICATION.

ratings See: AUDIENCE RATING.

rationalization Process whereby different modes of production of goods or services are brought together within larger units and aspects of the process are made more efficient. One common way to describe the process of rationalization is the concept of 'McDonaldization' coined by the American author George Ritzer. Ritzer (1993) argues that many contemporary processes are being rationalized along the lines of a McDonald's fast food restaurant. This is done with the aim of making the delivery of goods and services more efficient, calculable, predictable and controllable. It has been suggested that this process is affecting, for example, music in a number of ways. The production of music can be rationalized by bringing together music actually recorded in different parts of the world. The texts are rationalized by reducing the actual variation in sound, through the use of computer-generated sounds for instance. Consumption is rationalized through the dominance of retailing through large music supermarkets.

SEE ALSO: **concentration of ownership**.

reach See: AUDIENCE REACH.

reader As media studies developed the idea of TEXTS, so it also energized the ideas of the reader and reading. In this sense all sorts of texts, including film and television, are said to be read. This has now tended to be subsumed in broader processes of understanding of the AUDIENCE.

readership See: BOOK; CIRCULATION; NEWSPAPER; READING PUBLIC.

reading public Generally used for those who read books, reading public also has a more specialized and meaningful sense. The extension of the audience or market for books, newspapers and magazines was clearly only possible because of the development of an education system which taught large numbers of people to read. This process is usually said to have started in the eighteenth century with the middle classes, and especially women, receiving an education which gave them the ability to read. However, even by the end of the century, only about half of the population could read, and books were relatively expensive still. The reading public expanded greatly in the nineteenth century with the development of public libraries, the extension of educational opportunities and the appearance of cheaper books, newspapers and periodicals.

SEE ALSO: **book; newspaper**.

realism Not so much a particular form as the claim, implicit or explicit, of a text that its representations are a direct, unmediated reflection of real life, and hence that its meanings have a value of truth. Critics of realism would argue that such texts merely disguise their nature as DISCOURSE and that their meanings do not spring naturally from empirical observation, but are constructed by IDEOLOGY. Thus, although the novels of Emile Zola appear to consist of directly observed details of French society at the end of the nineteenth century, they also propose a model of human behaviour based on discourses of heredity and biological determinism that seem to preclude the possibility that political action could ameliorate or change the social conditions described. Another problem is that any text must necessarily be selective in what it portrays. Thus, although some forms of BLACK MUSIC are thought to offer a realistic portrayal of the everyday life of black people, there is a whole range of black experiences that they do not represent, so any claim to comprehensive realism must be questionable.

Despite these difficulties and confusions, it is possible to argue that there is a basic textual structure to realism. Realist fictions have three broad characteristics. First, they offer a window on a world that is defined through human actions; second, they use narratives of cause and effect and often have a clear beginning, middle and end; third, they conceal the fact of their own construction as texts. Thus, in a realist television fiction such as *The Bill*, the world that is depicted is a plausible one of inner-city policing and it concerns the actions of police officers as they go about their professional and personal lives. The narrative links those actions together and the connections between events is shown to us. The fiction is presented as if we are watching the events unfold; if a camera appeared in shot it would be seen as a disaster, even if we as the audience know that we are actually watching something that has been shot in this way. This model of realism distinguishes the form from MODERNISM and POST-MODERNISM (Abercrombie, Lash and Longhurst, 1992).

SEE ALSO: **naturalism**.

reality TV A type of television programming in which real people (who are not acting a part as in scripted drama), previously strangers, come together in a contrived setting – a house or a desert island, for example. The programme purports to explore the relationships of the people concerned. The best-known example is *Big Brother*. Reality TV has attracted a good deal of unfavourable comment, being criticized for being boring and, worse, for lowering standards of programming. Audience studies have explored viewers' motivations for watching, showing that there is a desire to explore the extent to which the participants are behaving authentically.

SEE ALSO: **surveillance society**.

real time 1 In computer games, television programmes or films in which events occur in time at the same rate as they would do in real life.

2 Communications that occur between parties at the same time (synchronously) rather than being delayed and responded to at some later time.

real-time viewing Broadcasting that is received by audiences at the same time as it is produced by filming events as they happen. Most television is recorded for later transmission, but programme-makers are experimenting with real-time broadcasting. News is the obvious example, but REALITY TV offers the same possibilities.

reception See: AUDIENCE; READER.

red top A TABLOID newspaper, so called because its MASTHEAD is in red.

referent In semiotics or SEMIOLOGY, the object or event in the real world to which a SIGN refers. For example, within the English language, the referent of the sign 'dog' is a four-legged animal while the sign for the same referent in French is 'chien'. Thus, while referents remain common across languages, signs usually differ.

referential code Those parts of a text that come together to form a CODE that refers to cultural information, a set of cultural understandings or to a body of knowledge. An example would be the religious knowledge in the best-selling novel *The Da Vinci Code* by Dan Brown (2004), or the use of scientific knowledge in science fiction. The term comes from the work of ROLAND BARTHES.

SEE ALSO: **discourse**.

referential framing See: FRAMING; TELEVISION TALK.

reflexivity 1 Theories that refer to themselves. This is often supposed to be a characteristic of POSTMODERNISM.

2 The way in which, particularly in modern societies, people constantly examine their own practices and, in the light of that examination, alter them.

regimes of watching People watch television with varying degrees of attention. Even when the television is switched on, some members of the household are not watching at all. Others may be doing something else at the same time as half-watching – homework or a crossword puzzle, for instance. Women are particularly notable for this kind of 'distracted viewing' while doing domestic tasks such as cooking or ironing. Still others may be concentrating hard on the programme. In any period of viewing any one person may go in and out of rapt attention. The capacity to engage in distracted viewing or to move in and out of attentive viewing is an acquired skill. In the early days of television, audiences tended to give the set all their attention all the time, rather as if they were at a cinema.

There is, therefore, a continuum of attentiveness. Different media are also associated with different degrees of attentiveness. Typically books, plays and films appear to demand and receive attention while television, popular music, radio, magazines and newspapers do not or do not much of the time. It is difficult to know how far to press this distinction, however, since high-attention regimes of watching are more highly valued in society than low-attention ones.

SEE ALSO: **distracted attention; hot media**.

regional media See: LOCAL RADIO; REGIONAL PRESS.

regional press Although national newspapers have suffered a decline in circulation, regional newspapers, on the whole, seem to be doing rather better (SEE: **circulation; newspaper**), although this is mostly to do with the popularity of FREESHEETS rather than paid-for papers. For example, in 2004, the circulation of all regional daily titles was over 8 million by comparison with 8.9 million for the *Sun* in the same period. In 2002, nearly 41 million paid-for regional papers were sold and 29 million free papers were delivered every week.

Just as national newspapers have, over time, been aggregated together in groups under the same ownership, so also have the regional press. Important groups include Reed Regional Newspapers, East Midlands Allied Press and Westminster Press. These groups have responded to the competition for advertising posed by the freesheets by acquiring or starting freesheets of their own. National newspaper groups have also been for some time owners of local papers. Associated Newspapers, United Newspapers, the Trinity Mirror Group and the Guardian Group are particularly prominent.

SEE ALSO: **Newspaper Society**.

register A form of speech that operates under its own set of CONVEN-TIONS and in specific contexts. For example, the register of speech and vocabulary at a football match may be very different from that appropriate in a professional meeting or a court room.

SEE ALSO: **field**.

regulation Media organizations, whether they are in public or private ownership, are heavily regulated in almost all societies. There are several reasons why societies should seek to regulate. First, non-democratic governments will fear criticism from newspapers, books, radio and tele-vision and will seek to control them. The government of Zimbabwe, for example, closed opposition newspapers in 2003. The media in China are only now slowly emerging from strict control. Indeed, so sensitive was the Chinese government to media criticism that it sought to control access by its population to foreign television and newspapers. Second, almost all societies seek to regulate the content of the media in the interests of public decency, taste or sensibility. For example, pornographic content is generally controlled, films are given certificates that relate to the depiction of sexuality or violence, and expressions of race hatred are forbidden by law. Third, since it is widely accepted that the media should play a major part in informing citizens about current events in the interests of democ-racy, there are some attempts to encourage objectivity in reporting and to discourage BIAS. In most Western societies, and particularly in Britain, such a notion is very much bound up with the ideal of PUBLIC SERVICE BROADCASTING. One aspect of this ideal is that the public should be offered impartial broadcasting, which is guaranteed by the state. Nobody expects newspapers to be impartial, but television and radio are expected to be, and this affects commercial broadcasting as well as the BBC. There are, as a result, occasional conflicts between the BBC and successive governments about the objectivity of particular items. Fourth, there are sometimes technical reasons for regulating the behaviour of the media. For example, until fairly recently, the RADIO SPECTRUM was treated as a scarce resource, and governments had to regulate broadcasters to make sure that they do not interfere with each other's transmissions. Lastly, for several centuries, the media have been a source of revenue for govern-ments. Quite often, taxation has simply been a means of control rather than a pure revenue-raising device, as in the eighteenth-century taxes on paper. However, in recent years, governments have made substantial amounts of money by selling licences to television companies and to mobile telephone companies.

The most obvious source of regulation is government. However, media organizations are controlled in effect by other agencies as well. The most significant are those agencies of self-regulation set up by the industry itself, of which the ADVERTISING STANDARDS AUTHORITY and the PRESS COMPLAINTS COMMISSION are examples. This form of regulation is often thought to be ineffective but, equally, government regulation carries its own dangers (SEE: **self-regulation**). Other forms of regulation are rather more covert. Owners of commercial media companies have put pressure on their employees to promote particular social or political views. That is most obvious, and explicit, in the case of newspapers but is beginning to creep into television as well (SEE: **Beaverbrook; Fox Network; Murdoch**). This is, perhaps, at its most dangerous when a media group dominates provision in a particular country and its owner is also politically involved (SEE: **Berlusconi**). Given an increasing CONCENTRATION OF OWNERSHIP in the media industries, there is a growing danger of a conflict between commercial freedoms and the freedom of expression. Lastly, there is the possibility that journalists censor themselves. News stories will be cast in a particular way, or even never see the light of day, because journalists are worried about the effect that they may have or because they operate with certain assumptions derived from the culture around them (SEE: **news**).

SEE ALSO: **government and the media**.

reinforcement Process by which messages and the meanings they contain are made stronger by media coverage or by other forms of communication. It has been suggested that one function or effect of the media is to reinforce, i.e. make stronger, the beliefs and opinions that people already have rather than change views or introduce new ones.

SEE ALSO: **effects; hegemony; ideology; propaganda**.

Reith, John One of the most famous figures in the history of broadcasting, John Reith was responsible for making the BBC into a major force as a public service broadcaster. Born in 1889, Reith became an engineer specializing in radio communications. In 1922, he was appointed as general manager of the British Broadcasting Company, an organization set up by a group of radio manufacturers. In 1927, he became the first Director-General of the newly established British Broadcasting Corporation and stayed in that post until 1938. On the outbreak of war in 1939, he was invited to join the government, and he occupied various ministerial positions until the end of the war. He died in 1971.

Reith had very strong views about the role of the BBC although, as broadcasting developed, these views became increasingly out of date. He was, for example, not keen on the introduction of television because it might lower broadcasting standards. He early argued that the BBC should educate, bring the nation together as a moral community, promote the highest standards of taste and, by the provision of information and argument, help to create a rational democracy. In order to fulfil this mission, broadcasting should be a monopoly as a corporation in the public sector, able to ensure that standards were met. Such a mission clearly brought the BBC into a very close relationship with the state and this was, and has continued to be, an awkward one, as arguments over the corporation's reporting of the Iraq war in 2003/4 shows.

SEE ALSO: **public service broadcasting**.

repertoire The menu of actions that a performer or speaker can engage in. For example, a singer will know a number of songs that he or she is able to perform. The idea is used in forms of communication theory to refer, in a similar way, to the vocabulary or to the basic stock of knowledge or form of communication available to a group or an individual.

SEE ALSO: **code; discourse; language;** *langue*.

representation One thing standing for something else in the sense of *re*-presenting it. Most simply then, texts are often thought to represent some form of external reality, more or less accurately. For example, black people may be represented in particular jobs in television programmes. Asian people are nearly always shopkeepers in British soap operas, despite the fact that, statistically, this is a minority occupation for such groups. In part, this is due to the SOAP OPERA form, which over-represents the prevalence of small businesses in general. On a more philosophical level, there is debate about whether art can represent anything outside of itself. Much contemporary painting since modernism, for example, is a comment on the nature of art itself and form, rather than an attempt to represent reality in any accurate or even particular way. There may be a range of different representations of groups or individuals in texts or cultures. Thus, rather than speaking simply of the representation of a group it is important to pay attention to diversity. This sort of move is reflected in the increasingly common tendency in the English language to create new plural forms of words that were hitherto singular. For example, the term 'musics' signifies the diversity of musical forms around the world.

SEE ALSO: **language; realism; semiology**.

repressive tolerance Generally speaking, the toleration of rival beliefs is understood to be a feature of democracies to be welcomed. The media play a major role in sustaining such tolerance in that, taken as a whole, they represent a variety of viewpoints and encourage debate even if they do so within particular limits. There are those, however, who believe that such tolerance actually neutralizes true dissent. It acts as a kind of sponge, allowing disagreement but confining it within limits. Destructive dissent is simply defined out of existence. Hence repressive tolerance, a phrase attributed to HERBERT MARCUSE.

SEE ALSO: **domination**.

residual culture See: DOMINANT CULTURE; EMERGENT CULTURE.

resistance Audiences are said to be resistant when they do not accept, or they actively oppose, the dominant meaning of a media text (SEE: **preferred reading**).

SEE ALSO: **active audience; encoding/decoding; *Nationwide* study**.

responsibility It is frequently argued that the media have great power in society (SEE: **domination; effects; moral panic**) particularly in their capacity to influence those who hold political power. This is perhaps most obvious in law and order matters. For example, in running stories about illegal immigrants or violence in the street, the media contribute to a climate of opinion in which the risk of harm is exaggerated. Those institutions that have considerable power over others should, the argument runs, be accountable for their actions. That is, there should be some means by which they are judged and, if they have behaved irresponsibly, they should make some reparation, which, in the case of a newspaper, for example, could vary from a written apology to the payment of a large sum of money. At present, the means of holding newspapers to account are relatively weak. Recourse to the law is expensive and uncertain of outcome. The PRESS COMPLAINTS COMMISSION is widely thought to be toothless. Arguments of this kind have become more convincing as the press in particular has become more aggressive. However, if the press is over-controlled, there is a risk that free speech is compromised. There are in any case doubts as to whether the media do have long-term effects on attitudes and beliefs.

SEE ALSO: **censorship; freedom of information; government and the media; regulation**.

returns Those copies of books, magazines, newspapers or CDs that are returned unsold to the publisher by the retailer. Whether or not returns can be made depends on the contract between publisher and retailer. Thus, in return for a lower price of supply, retailers can take the risk of not being able to sell all copies ordered from the publisher.

Reuters Founded in 1851 as a company owned by the newspaper press of the UK and Ireland, Reuters is now a large commercial company with a Stock Exchange quotation headquartered in London. It owes its financial success to a diversification of its business in the 1970s and 1980s into financial information and transactions, which now provides some 90 per cent of its turnover. As a result, Reuters had a turnover of more than £3.2 billion in 2003, although, in its news agency business strictly considered, it is about the same size as the American ASSOCIATED PRESS.

SEE ALSO: **news agency**.

rhetoric Traditionally, rhetoric is the art of formulating arguments, or of using language to persuade others. In classical civilizations it was taught as a body of rules. In contemporary social science, the term has been employed to point to the importance of argument and persuasion in the spoken word or written text (SEE: **persuasion**). Some analysts of the media are interested in investigating how rhetorical devices in the language of media texts effectively persuade an audience to a particular point of view. For example, newspapers in the UK adopt a NATIONALIST rhetoric in their contrasts between Britain and other nations (Billig, 1995).

SEE ALSO: **ideology**.

riff An often relatively simple musical phrase that is repeated. Most commonly associated with guitar-based, blues-derived and Anglo-American rock music.

right of reply There have long been concerns that the media, newspapers and magazines especially, can present the views or behaviour of members of the public in an unfavourable and untrue light and invade their PRIVACY. One remedy is for anyone who feels that they have been treated in this way to complain to the PRESS COMPLAINTS COMMISSION. However, this rarely proves satisfactory. An alternative would be to have a right of reply in the newspaper or magazine concerned. There have been proposals to formalize this right but, so far, without success.

rights See: COPYRIGHT; INTELLECTUAL PROPERTY.

road movie A GENRE of film centred on the characters' movement across a landscape and the adventures that they have on the way. The manner of transport is usually the car or the motor-cycle. The fact that the characters are on the move often allows the narrative of the film to address issues of personal and social freedom. For example, a movie like *Easy Rider* (dir. Dennis Hopper, 1969) portrays the adventures of two male motor-cyclists from the counter culture of the 1960s (who are joined by another character who has 'dropped out' of conventional life), and the extent to which their new lives are sustainable. Given that they are murdered, the film can be read pessimistically. While such films are usually based around male heroes, the genre was used to explore the limits of female freedom in *Thelma and Louise* (dir. Ridley Scott, 1991). Again this can be read pessimistically with the main characters' suicide as CLOSURE in the movie. However, this has also been interpreted as a positive act on their parts.

rock and pop There has been much debate about the differences between rock and pop music. Despite the difficulty of making a clear musical distinction, the terms are still prevalent in everyday discourse. While both may be seen as forms of popular music, rock is often held to signal a greater musical complexity and authenticity than pop, which is held to be simplistic, 'manufactured' and commercial or market-driven. Deeper investigation problematizes the distinction. For example, rock music is often relatively simple and commercial. The pejorative use of the term 'pop' is at some times seen to derive from some measure of contempt for its supposed audience, as young and female. The perceived tendency of the rock audience to be older and male provides a legitimation for a particular set of male tastes, enabling identities to be constructed around ideas of AUTHENTICITY and REALISM. Critics have at times rejected these ideas, with female writers valorizing pop and critics of the rock tradition and its constraints seeking to draw on pop values of superficiality and danceability.

SEE ALSO: **gender; popular music.**

rock and roll The standard description, derived from black slang for sexual intercourse, of the form of music that came together in the USA in the mid-1950s from influences in rhythm and blues, country and folk. There are many variations of rock and roll. More specifically there is sometimes a distinction made between the original rock 'n' roll (which is held to be more authentic) and the later rock and roll, which was more commercial and sanitized (see Gillett, 1983). Gillett argues that the description rock 'n' roll should be applied to the music between 1954 and 1958, with that existing between 1958 and 1964 being referred to as rock and roll. This difference is most commonly represented by the difference between Elvis Presley's pre- and post-army work. Elvis went into the US army in 1958 and did not record new material until 1960. His work prior to 1958 is seen as ground-breaking and innovative but after that time as weak and commercialized. This representation is actually very simplistic, ignoring the actual diversity of his work. Rock music developed from 1964 onwards with the unprecedented success of The Beatles in the US in that year, which involved taking American forms back to their country of origin, inflected by British experience.

Gillett (1983: 23) identifies five forms of rock 'n' roll: 'northern band rock 'n' roll' (e.g. Bill Haley), the 'New Orleans dance blues', 'Memphis country rock (also known as rockabilly)', 'Chicago rhythm and blues' and 'vocal group rock 'n' roll'. This is significant as it shows the diversity of rock and roll from its very beginnings. However, despite the important roles of performers like Chuck Berry, Little Richard, Jerry Lee Lewis and Carl Perkins in the innovation and popularization of the form, the key figure was Elvis Presley both for his own innovation and the way in which he represents how the different sources of rock and roll came together in particular places (in this case Memphis) to produce a new form that has continued to influence popular music ever since.

SEE ALSO: **punk; rock and pop**.

romance A GENRE of popular culture involving love and physical and emotional bonding. Media studies has developed a literature on the representation of romance. There have been three broad trends in the analysis of romance, which have influenced each other in some respects but have also had to operate in relative isolation, probably because the approaches have been applied to different media.

First, romance has been analysed with respect to the novel and especially in the context of how romantic fiction is read by a predominantly female audience. The best-known example of this comes in Janice Radway's influential book *Reading the Romance* (1987). Radway carried out a STRUCTURALIST analysis of the type of romance that she found to be popular with a group of women in a town in the mid-west of the USA. She contrasted this ideal romance with those romances that were not popular with this group, which she termed 'failed'. The key reason for the success of these novels was that they provided an escape route from some of the domestic trials and mundane aspects of the everyday lives of the women. Thus, on the one hand the novels were valued, for Radway and the women she studied, in that they provided a mechanism of escape and, in this, resistance to day-to-day life. However, in Radway's view, in the end, through their NARRATIVE conclusions and the women's pleasures in such solutions, they did not offer a more radical alternative. In this respect they operate ideologically. Thus, while Radway's text is one of the most influential audience studies it is constrained by the incorporation/ resistance paradigm in audience studies (Abercrombie and Longhurst, 1998).

Second, analysis of romance has taken place through work on

MELODRAMA in film. With particular reference to the melodramatic films of the 1950s, a number of features of such films have been isolated (Gledhill, 1987). (1) The plot or narrative of such films revolves around the misrecognition of the characters. Characters may therefore be out of place, for example, in that they are in the wrong social group. (2) The narrative has an emotional or personal life focus. (3) The films appeal to the sensations rather than directly to the intellect. (4) The films tend be spectacular and to have a strong visual pull. (5) The performances by the actors in the film are deliberately exaggerated. (6) The music soundtrack to the film is emphasized. Feminist writers argued that such films should be reevaluated and in many respects revalued as they articulated modes of experience often derided as female and were also innovatory in form, in moving away from the constraints of the classic realist text.

Third, there has been attention to the nature of romance and GENDER relations in television SOAP OPERA, which, like some forms of cinema, is sometimes seen as a generic mixture of kitchen-sink drama and melodrama. The British continuous serial is seen as combining the naturalistic style of the 1950s realist movement in British culture with the focus on emotions and personal relationships of Melodrama (with a hint of music hall comedy thrown in). Prime-time and daytime American soaps were seen to possess melodramatic features to a greater extent and were also considered in the context of female experience and the pleasure derived from them emotionally by influential authors like IEN ANG.

SEE ALSO: **ideology; male gaze.**

rostrum camera A camera that is fixed in place.

rot (recorded off transmission) In radio the practice of recording a transmission, or part of a transmission, so that it can be used again in a subsequent programme.

Rothermere See: NORTHCLIFFE.

rough cut An edit of a film that is in the broadly envisioned final order, but is not the final version. Also known as an assembly edit.

royalty A payment made to the author on sales of a media text, normally a percentage of sales or receipts. Those who create a media text, whether they be the author of a book, a rock musician or a journalist, get paid in a variety of different ways. Some are salaried employees and some receive a fee on completion of the work. Still others receive a royalty. Royalty systems are most common in popular music and book publishing, where it is uncertain how extensive sales of a record or a book will be.

SEE ALSO: **advance; copyright; piracy**.

Ruge, Mari See: GALTUNG.

rumour Rumour is much assisted by the media. Newspapers and television not only start rumour but also add credibility to the rumours that circulate. In this, particular people in the community can be influential. As consumers of the media they pass on rumours supported by stories that they have got from the press, radio or television.

SEE ALSO: **moral panic; two-step flow**.

runner A person who acts as a general dogsbody in a media company, particularly in film crews or post-production companies. The post is often poorly paid and is regarded as a stepping stone to more prestigious and better-paid positions.

running order The basic list of the order that items or stories will be taken during broadcast radio or television.

SEE ALSO: **narrative**.

rushes The raw film or tape produced in a filming session for television or cinema production. Normally, these rushes will require editing to produce the final film or programme and, at that stage, a great deal of the raw material will be discarded.

SEE ALSO: **editor; offline editor**.

S

Said, Edward (1935–2003) A Palestinian intellectual who was Professor of Comparative Literature at Columbia University, New York. Said was an important commentator on the cultural politics of the Middle East. His best-known and most influential book was *Orientalism* (1978). He argued that images of the 'orient' had been constructed in a range of 'Western' texts to produce a DISCOURSE of orientalism, which was involved in processes of cultural, political and economic imperialism. He thus showed how texts were part of processes of global exploitation through the construction of the exotic other. This approach, which was influenced by the pioneering work of MICHEL FOUCAULT, remains of significance for media studies in showing how others are constructed by images and representations and hence demonized.

SEE ALSO: **difference; discourse; globalization; identity.**

salience The importance of a text, message or story to an individual or group. Thus certain stories or texts will have little significance to certain groups or individuals but will connect very directly to others. For fans, texts like *Star Trek* and *Doctor Who* have high salience, but they will not interest most audience members. Thus, in the classic audience study of the programme *Nationwide* Morley (1980) found that the programme was seen as irrelevant (or lacking in salience) for some black members of the audience, who then opposed the dominant meanings in the text. Salience is obviously of importance to commercial broadcasters, who will wish to know the salience of particular types of text when selling the slots in which those stories appear to advertisers, who will be interested in high attention levels from consumers.

SEE ALSO: **active audience.**

sampler A device used to take sounds from various sources, which can be reused in different musical contexts. For example, sampling might involve taking sections of a piece of music (such as a bass line, or part of a vocal) and combining them with other sounds.

SEE ALSO: **mixing.**

sans serif See: TYPEFACE.

satellite A variety of means of transmitting television signals have been developed including wireless broadcasting, cable and satellite. Broadcasting using towers has the disadvantage that the signals can only be received by those in line-of-sight. Small obstacles do not interfere with the signal but the curvature of the earth does. Satellites in a GEOSTATIONARY orbit above the earth overcome this problem in that they allow unobstructed transmission and, although they clearly have high initial costs, they can cover a wide geographical area.

SEE ALSO: **broadcasting; cable television**.

Saussure, Ferdinand de (1857–1913) A Swiss linguist, Saussure emphasized the collective, social nature of language. Language is a system of signs each of which has two dimensions, the SIGNIFIER and the SIGNIFIED. Saussure argued that the relationship between signifier and signified is arbitrary. There is no natural or intrinsic relationship between linguistic forms and their meanings.

SEE ALSO: **communication; semiology**.

scene This idea is much used to describe the way in which forms of popular music are located and developed in particular places. Examples would be the Manchester scene (based around bands like Joy Division, New Order and the Happy Mondays) and the Seattle scene (developed around Nirvana). This idea has been refined theoretically and empirically, to examine how place is important in the production and consumption of music. A classic and detailed study is of Austin, Texas (Shank, 1994). Shank examines in detail how the production and consumption of music in Austin has thrived on the interactions in the city over a significant period of time.

More recently, Peterson and Bennett (2004) have argued that there are three types of scene: 'local' (as in the main use identified above); 'translocal', where local scenes are in contact with each other through media and interpersonal links; and 'virtual', where participants are in contact through the internet or by other means.

SEE ALSO: **ethnography; youth culture**.

schedule In radio and TV the list of programmes to be aired during the course of the week.

SEE ALSO: **scheduling**.

scheduling The process of deciding the timetable of programmes on television or radio. While this looks a straightforward matter, it is not.

Schedulers have to decide who is likely to be watching or listening at particular times of day and then provide suitable programming. They need to try to maximize audiences for particular programmes and so they will put the most popular programmes on at times that they think the largest audience will be present. They need to think out the relationship between programmes throughout the day so that they can keep the audience watching and listening. All these decisions are compounded by the fact of competition between channels and stations. Schedulers will need to try to outguess the rival schedulers and place their programmes at times to maximize their competitive advantage. Competition of this kind can lead to 'ratings wars', which are much more common in the United States, where television stations are locked in a far more vicious struggle for audience share. British broadcast television and radio still effectively operate within the convention of PUBLIC SERVICE BROADCASTING, and the differences in funding methods which exist mean that audience share is not as important.

Scheduling is, however, likely to become more competitive (SEE: **television**) and there are indications of that even at the BBC. Thus, JOHN BIRT, a previous Director-General of the BBC, made his name by proclaiming the primacy of the schedule. According to this doctrine, the schedule should be decided and then programmes should be commissioned to fit particular kinds of audience and time-slots.

Scheduling is therefore part of the strategic planning process in television and radio. It involves balancing programming against finance against time-slots and is very much the province of senior management. Schedulers use a number of techniques for improving the likely audience for their programmes. For example, a programme that is likely to be less attractive will be placed between two programmes that do have substantial audiences (known as 'hammocking'). Alternatively, if a programme wins a large audience, the next programme can be expected to inherit a substantial proportion of the audience through audience inertia. Sometimes, through a process known as pre-echo, audiences will begin to watch a programme regularly simply because it precedes one that they particularly want to watch. There are also constraints that schedulers have to cope with. For example, the news is traditionally at a fixed time, and 'adult' drama cannot be shown on television before 9 p.m. Scheduling clearly involves the use of a model of audience behaviour in that schedulers have to make assumptions about who is watching at particular times of day. Traditionally these assumptions are concerned with family behaviour and they may very well be out of date.

SEE ALSO: **drive-time**.

scopophilia In psychoanalytic theory, the sexual pleasure derived from looking. The concept has been much used in FILM THEORY and in discussions of the MALE GAZE, where the male spectator is theorized as being constructed by the film through scopophilic pleasures of looking at the woman on the screen.

Screen theory An approach to the study of film and television associated with the British theoretical journal _Screen_, especially during the 1970s. While there were a number of dimensions to this, the most significant was the approach to the study of the relationship between text and audience, which emphasized how the spectator was constituted by the filmic experience. The theory was criticized for being theoretical rather than based in empirical research and for neglecting the social and personal factors that might affect the watching of a film. The journal was also particularly influential in developing psychoanalytical approaches to the study of film and in introducing much French film theory to the English-speaking world.

script The written document that is the basis for the construction of a television or radio programme or for a performance in the theatre, developed by a scriptwriter or scriptwriters.
SEE ALSO: **writer**.

search engine A piece of software designed to search out information on the WORLD WIDE WEB.
SEE ALSO: **google**.

secondary definer See: PRIMARY DEFINER.

secondary media See: PRIMARY MEDIA.

seg In radio, the broadcasting of more than one piece of music without comment from the DJ. Short for segue.

segmentation The process whereby a market is or becomes divided into parts. The music market in the USA is segmented by, for example, ethnicity, where different music is listened to by different ethnic groups or indeed different age, class and gender fractions of ethnic groups. The audience for television tends to become relatively more segmented over time in a society. For example, in the USA the market dominance of the big three networks has declined over time as more channels with a narrower appeal have been developed. The situation in the UK is similar, with the market increasingly segmenting due to the availability of cable and satellite technologies and the increasing number of channels.

SEE ALSO: **audience differentiation.**

segmented market See: SEGMENTATION.

segue See: SEG.

self identity See: IDENTITY.

self-regulation Media industries are quite extensively regulated (See: REGULATION). Where issues of invasion of PRIVACY or the moral content of the media are concerned, media organizations have typically argued that self-regulation by the industry is better than regulation by government. Their argument is that there are real dangers in statutory regulation in that the PRESS FREEDOM could be curtailed. The counter-argument is that media organizations are not effective at regulating themselves and tend to abuse their freedoms, especially in the way that they investigate individuals or infringe commonly accepted standards of taste and morality. At present, successive governments have tended to come down on the side of self-regulation.

SEE ALSO: **Advertising Standards Authority; censorship; government and the media; Press Complaints Commission.**

semiology The European name for the study or science of SIGNS, which is known as semiotics within North America. The key originator in Europe was the Swiss linguist FERDINAND DE SAUSSURE (1857–1913) and in North America, CHARLES SANDERS PIERCE (1839–1914). The sign is seen as made up of the SIGNIFIER and the SIGNIFIED. LANGUAGE is seen as made up of LANGUE and PAROLE. Signs relate to REFERENTS in an arbitrary way, as is shown by the fact that different signs (as in different languages) relate to the same referent. The distinction between different levels of meaning became a key aspect of STRUCTURALISM. Semiology was also influential beyond the academic study of language in other ways, especially through the literary and cultural analyses of ROLAND BARTHES (1915–80).

SEE ALSO: **binary opposition; code; myth.**

semiotics See: SEMIOLOGY.

sender/receiver In some ways it is useful to see the relationship between media institutions and their audiences as an act of communication of information from a sender to a receiver. It is very important, however, not to oversimplify. First, there are often intermediaries between sender and receiver (SEE: **personal influence**); second, the context – social, political or personal – critically affects how communications are received; third, the medium itself affects the relationship between sender and receiver (for example, some media, e.g. television and magazines, are low-involvement while others, e.g. films or books, are typically high-involvement); fourth, and most important of all, communications in the media have to be seen in terms of questions of meaning rather than the transmission of a message (SEE: **semiology**).

SEE ALSO: **communication; effects**.

sensitization The process by which people or groups become aware or further aware of events or ideas. While, on one hand, it has been argued that the media DESENSITIZE groups or individuals, perhaps leading to COMPASSION FATIGUE, there are contrary arguments that the media have played a significant role in the bringing to greater public awareness of a range of issues and events that would not have otherwise have been in such a position. The issue of poverty in Africa is a recent example.

serif See: TYPEFACE.

sewn binding See: BINDING.

sexuality The representation and communication of human desire. In this sense, sexuality is different from the human sex act as a physical practice. There can therefore be a range of representations of sex, which in turn might affect the sex act itself. Sexuality is a form of DISCOURSE, as most significantly analysed by MICHEL FOUCAULT (1979, 1987 and 1990). Within media studies sexuality has been much studied, especially by FEMINIST authors who have been concerned to contest negative representations of female sexuality as pandering to male tastes – as in the debates around PORNOGRAPHY. Music is often analysed in terms of the sexuality of both male and female performers. An important distinction was made between the aggressive male sexuality of the 'cock rocker' and the teeny-bop representation of romance (Frith and McRobbie, 1990).

SEE ALSO: **Butler; gender; male gaze**.

shock jock See: RADIO.

short messaging service (SMS) A method of sending short text messages to mobile phones and other portable devices. Although take-up of this service seemed slow to start, the bulk of traffic on mobile networks is now composed of text messages rather than voice.

SEE ALSO: **instant messaging; multimedia messaging service**.

shot The basic unit of a film. There are three broad types of shot: LONG, medium and CLOSE-UP. These, and their further sub-divisions, all convey different types of meaning and are recognized by the audience, which has built up understanding over a period of time.

SEE ALSO: **camera angle; 180 degree rule.**

sign In SEMIOLOGY and semiotics the sign is distinguished from the REFERENT. The sign 'dog' in the English language refers to a type of animal in the real world. The sign is made up of two parts – the SIGNIFIER (the sound or image) and the SIGNIFIED (the concept). For instance, the sign 'dog' refers to a real animal (the referent), using a particular combination of sounds (if spoken) or letters (if written) to communicate a concept, which may on one level denote the animal (it has a particular biological make-up) or may have further connotations (SEE: **denotation/connotation**) (such as 'man's best friend' of the producer of offensive waste material). However, the concept of dog does not bark.

SEE ALSO: **Barthes.**

signature In the printing industry, a large sheet of paper on which several FOLIOS or pages have been printed. When the book or magazine is finally made up, the signature is folded or cut and then bound.

signification The practice and process of sign construction and communication.

SEE ALSO: **sign.**

signified Within SEMIOLOGY and semiotics, one aspect of the SIGN, that is, the concept or meaning of the sign. It is normally analysed at two levels – see DENOTATION/CONNOTATION.

SEE ALSO: **signifier.**

signifier Within SEMIOLOGY and semiotics, one aspect of the SIGN, that is, the sound or the image.

SEE ALSO: **signified.**

signifying practice The social acts and discursive practices that produce SIGNIFICATION.

SEE ALSO: **sign.**

Silverstone, Roger (1945–2006) At the time of his death Professor of Media and Communications at the London School of Economics. Silverstone was an important figure in the development of the study of the media in Britain. His earlier work addressed such issues as how television programmes are made (Silverstone, 1985). He then played an important role in work that examined how media technologies are variously consumed in the home (Hirsch and Silverstone, 1992). His later work sought to address in primarily theoretical terms the place of television in everyday life (Silverstone, 1994). This led to consideration of the relationship between media (especially television) and suburban life (Silverstone, 1997).

simulacrum A copy of an original that does not exist any more, or never existed. The term has been developed by POSTMODERNIST writers such as JEAN BAUDRILLARD to characterize the general nature of contemporary culture in advanced Western societies. So, for example, it is argued that the ideal towns of Disneyland are copies of a crime-free and sanitized small-town America which has disappeared, assuming it ever existed. Thus, in producing such idealized copies, we are searching for a reality beyond current reality, which is often termed the HYPERREAL. The media are crucial to the construction of the simulacrum or the range of simulacra, as much representation offers images that seem to copy idealized or lost states of being.

SEE ALSO: **Disney; ideology**.

simulational culture The situation, which some commentators feel has been reached in advanced capitalist societies, where culture has lost contact with reality and become a series of images and simulations. The idea has been most associated with POSTMODERNIST commentators such as JEAN BAUDRILLARD, who have suggested that society has become HYPERREAL in its attempts to show a version of reality in images and media. While this idea may appear to be exaggerated when it seems to suggest that life is nothing but media images and simulations, it does capture something of the way in which culture is increasingly media- and image-saturated.

SEE ALSO: **Disney; simulacrum**.

simulcasting The process by which the same media event is broadcast on different media at the same time, most often on television and radio. This was partly because the sound quality of, say, a musical event would be much higher on FM radio than on TV. However, technological convergence (SEE: **media convergence**) would seem to be leading to less need for this sort of simulcasting as radio, television and other technologies converge through digital means.

situated culture A form of culture that is bounded by being situated in time and place. It suggests that forms of culture remain so located despite the increased globalization of contemporary media and culture. Indeed, it captures the way in which such culture can be formed in the context of such social and cultural mobility. For example, towns or regions may have distinctive cultures.

SEE ALSO: **globalization; localization**.

situation comedy A GENRE of television and radio, situation comedy is about the ordinary world rather than the extraordinary world of police series or thrillers (although sit coms can be set in a police station). Usually, though not invariably, they are set in domestic or work settings. Examples are *Porridge*, *Fawlty Towers* and *Only Fools and Horses*. Although typically taking up a half-hour slot in successive weeks, each episode follows the conventions of popular fiction (SEE: **narrative**). Because of the setting, situation comedy operates in a confined society, which therefore has a strongly marked contrast between the inside and the outside. Most plots are created by a tension between the characters of the people involved and the situation in which they find themselves, the characters frequently having aspirations and hopes that are unrealistic or pretentious. The tension is never finally resolved – though temporary relief is provided by laughter – and the audience knows perfectly well that it will resurface next week.

Sky TV See: BSKYB.

sleeper effect See: PERSUASION.

slow motion SPECIAL EFFECT produced by increasing the speed that film runs through a camera, so that when the film is projected at the standard rate of twenty-four frames per second the action appears to be slowed down.

slug In radio production, a term used to identify a particular story or item, which appears at the beginning of the script. It is also known as a catchline. The term comes from the days of printing when slugs were actual pieces of lead that were physically moved around the printers.

SMS See: SHORT MESSAGING SERVICE.

soap opera Soap operas developed on radio in the USA in the 1930s and derived their name from the fact that the series were designed around the advertising of soap powders. They are now a very popular TV GENRE. There are three broad types: prime-time (such as DALLAS and *Dynasty*, which were very popular in the 1980s); daytime soaps (such as *Neighbours*), which have been especially popular in the USA; and the British continuous serial (such as *Coronation Street* or *EastEnders*). There are also soap operas which have distinct characteristics that are popular in other parts of the world, such as the Brazilian series, which are also shown in Portugal.

Soaps revolve around the activities of a group of people who live in one place, and often the name of the programme signals that place. The characters live in close proximity to each other, and much of the narrative concerns their everyday interaction and the interpersonal conflicts and relationships that this involves (those from outside the community often cause problems for it). The key relationship is between men and women. Women are at the heart of the soap opera community, which is often led by an older woman (or women) shown ultimately to have moral authority. Men are often weak, devious or unreliable. They ultimately lack moral courage. Thus, even a series like *Dallas*, which had men at the centre, depicted the central male character as corrupt (J. R. Ewing).

The fact that soaps feature women so strongly led to much attention from more feminist media scholars, who sought to revalue the series in a number of ways. First, they showed that, in production terms, the supposed poor acting and wobbly sets were the product of low investment. Second, they argued that texts addressed issues that were significant to women and allowed a degree of openness in the resolution of narratives through the length of the series. Thus, with respect to the latter, the form of the soap allows an issue to be considered over a lengthy period of time and always allows for a storyline to be opened again at a later date. In this respect the soap opera was seen as a relatively OPEN TEXT. Third, the popularity of the texts with audiences was considered in terms of their fit with women's everyday lives and in terms of emotional attachment.

Much criticism of soaps has tended to focus on the effects of low production values and their emotionalism. Another area of debate has been around the theme of REALISM. For some critics, soaps are not realistic in that, for example, they do not accurately reflect the social composition of the area in which they are set – there are few black people in *Coronation Street*, for example – or they seem unrealistic in the sense that all the main characters meet in the same pub every night. A contrary argument is that the narratives deal with real issues, or address concerns that the audience connects to as emotionally real. There is also dispute about the precise definition of realism.

While soaps are often seen as old-fashioned (especially the British continuous serial) they do remain very popular. *Coronation Street* (which has been shown since 1960) and *EastEnders* (shown since 1984) regularly top the ratings in the UK.

SEE ALSO: **gender; ideology**.

soc See: STANDARD OUT CUE.

social constructionism The idea that things are not discovered as natural objects but are socially produced. All facts are necessarily social facts in that societies produce them. Social constructionism is radical in that it claims that society determines how we see the world. It is therefore at variance with models of inquiry in the social sciences that are derived from scientific method.

social control There is some debate as to whether the media act as agents of social control. There might be two ways in which they do that. First, they operate as one of the agents of SOCIALIZATION, instilling VALUES which incline people to compliant behaviour. There is little evidence that they do so, and, in fact, many public figures claim that they do the opposite, arguing, for example, that much film, television and rock music encourages anti-social behaviour (SEE: **domination; effects**). Second, the media act as a mechanism of constraint in that they encourage the authorities to be punitive towards particular behaviour and people. For example, the media identify particular groups of people as inclined to crime – black people or asylum-seekers – and, by this public exposure, persuade governments to act. There is evidence that this process occurs (SEE: **amplification of deviance**), though the effect is frequently to punish the innocent, to highlight some criminal activity but not other and more serious acts, or to STEREOTYPE sections of the population.

socialization The process whereby people learn to conform to social norms, a process that makes possible an enduring society and the transmission of culture between generations. Normally, socialization is divided into two phases. The first, primary socialization, takes place during infancy, and most of the learning occurs as the result of the interaction between the infant and surrounding adults. It is during this phase that we acquire the fundamentals of the culture and organization of the groups to which we belong. Secondary socialization is an adult, or near-adult, phase, and involves equals – playmates, brothers and sisters, friends and work colleagues. Clearly, socialization involving equals continues lifelong but the earlier years are the most significant in the acquisition of important values. The media are, potentially, a source of secondary socialization, and many people worry that they help to inculcate the wrong values. However, the evidence is that the media are actually a relatively inefficient agent of socialization.

SEE ALSO: **effects**.

soft sell See: HARD SELL.

solo A piece of music in which one instrument or voice takes a clear lead.

This may involve the instrument playing alone, but more usually will involve that instrument being very prominent while the others play the BACKING. The clearest case of this in popular music has been the lead and solo role of the electric guitar player, leading to concentration on the virtuosity of some players in the rock music that developed from the 1960s onwards. In popular music forms such as rock, but more especially jazz, the solo has been a key aspect of improvisation, which provides a central aspect of the definition of the music itself.

Sony Although primarily known as a manufacturer of electronic hardware, Sony has moved into media content as well. It now has interests in film, e.g. Columbia and Tri-Star, cinemas, music, e.g. Columbia and Epic, and broadcast television. The company, based in Japan, is also heavily involved in computer games, again producing both hardware and software.
SEE ALSO: **media companies**.

sound-bite See: NEWS CUT.

sound effects The use of sound to produce particular meanings in film, television or radio. Sound in this respect has often tended to be relatively neglected in the analysis of the media. However, sound effects are very important in conveying meaning to the audience in a very quick and economical way, as in the sound of a car crashing, which instantly conveys a sense that something significant has happened.

soundtrack The part of a film text that carries sound – the recorded sound of the action filmed as well as added items such as music, voice over and effects. The soundtrack has an important part to play in the generation of meaning. Certain sounds are conventionally understood to have particular connotations. For example, a horror film will use certain sounds to build up tension, the 'whoop, whoop' of helicopter blades has come to signify the Vietnam War, and so on. Soundtrack albums have increased in significance as objects of consumption in their own right, though soundtracks from MUSICALS have often been very successful in the past, especially from such films as *The King and I*, *South Pacific* and *The Sound of Music*.
SEE ALSO: **voice**.

space In general terms this refers to the distribution of culture and society physically. Thus, when we refer to going for a walk, we are referring to our ability to move through space through our own powers. We are obviously able to move through space in a number of technologically aided ways, such as the wheelchair, the bicycle, the car and the plane. All these have effects on the speed of our journeys and indeed our perception of what space is. When it first came along, train travel affected perceptions of space quite radically – imagine never having looked out of a train window before. Space is often contrasted with two other related terms: place and landscape. Place refers to specific locations. Thus, in going for a walk through space, we might move from place to place: home to school, for example. Landscape is often used to refer to representations of space and place: a landscape painted in oils is a depiction in a particular medium of space and place. It can be seen that technologies affect our sense of space (and indeed place and landscape), and media technologies have been crucially part of such processes. Thus, it has been held that television has shrunk space in that it makes events that are occurring at distant points of the globe immediately available to large numbers of people across the world. Moreover, it is also contended that media have helped create a situation where we have no sense of place, as forms of culture and places themselves become increasingly alike across the world: a shopping mall in the USA is similar to one in Germany or Scotland. Also, we have become increasingly familiar with places that we have never visited through the media representations of them.

SEE ALSO: **globalization; localization; mediascape**.

special effects Artificially created (trick) images (or sounds) in film, often to create the illusion that an action that cannot be performed naturally – for example, a man flying, a famous building being blown up – is actually happening. There are three broad categories of special effect: those done in camera (e.g. SLOW MOTION), those done on the set (e.g. rear screen projection) and those carried out in POST-PRODUCTION (e.g. adding filter effects) (Bernstein, 1994). It has been suggested that special effects have become so significant that they have become of key importance in the generation of meaning. While this area has always been of importance in the production of the SPECTACLE of cinema, in part due to the advance in computer techniques they have become one the key areas of pleasure in cinema.

SEE ALSO: **action**.

spectacle Visual display, or heightened visual importance in culture. It has increasingly been argued that contemporary societies have become more spectacular in a number of ways. Some POSTMODERNIST writers have suggested that EVERYDAY LIFE in advanced industrial societies is like a spectacle in that people perform in ways that draw attention to themselves and their distinctiveness. The modes of dress of youth subcultures are a good example of this process. In film, attention has been drawn to the way that more emphasis has been placed on the visual, partly due to the increased sophistication of the technological means so to do. The argument is that NARRATIVE has become less important as audience pleasure is derived from the sheer spectacle of what is displayed for them.

SEE ALSO: **action; Debord.**

spectator A member of a crowd looking in on an event, such as a football match. This commonsense meaning has been developed in media studies, and especially in film studies, to suggest a particular way of conceptualizing the AUDIENCE for a text. Thus, writers on film, being in the main text-centred, have argued that the film on the screen constructs a number of positions from which it can be viewed. The audience member, thought of as essentially passive, takes up one or several of these subject positions and therefore is a spectator of the film. These sorts of ideas have been much contested in media studies, especially by those approaches that have argued that audience members are not passive in this manner.

SEE ALSO: **active audience; male gaze.**

speech balloon The convention in COMICS where spoken words are printed in a (balloon-shaped) blank space joined by a line to the character uttering them. There is a similar convention for showing characters' thoughts – this is known as a thought balloon.

spin Most commonly a derogatory term which describes the attempts of governments to present to the media in the best possible light aspects of policy that are controversial. It carries with it the implication that such spinning is distorted, one-sided and dishonest. It furthermore suggests that governments will use underhand methods to control media presentation, such as unofficial briefing of journalists.

SEE ALSO: **news; public relations; spin doctor.**

spin doctor A person who is responsible for the origination and the distribution of SPIN, such as Alistair Campbell during the Blair administration in the UK.

spin-off In every branch of the media, a large number of individual items are produced – records, books, television programmes – most of which do not sell or reach large audiences. Companies tend to make their money from the few that do very well, but it is very difficult for them to predict which those will be. The result is that most media organizations try to reduce their risk by repeating or copying – spinning-off – products which have been successful. Best-selling authors are encouraged to write more books; actors for successful television shows appear in new vehicles; films will have endless sequels. Media companies will also try to capitalize on success by other kinds of spin-off – toys, clothes, the book of the film.

SEE ALSO: **adaptation; merchandising**.

splice editing In traditional film editing the film is physically cut; the sections are then stuck, or spliced, together in the desired sequence.

sponsorship When a company or other organization contributes to the cost of a public event in exchange for their name appearing at the event or for some other form of advertising associated with it. The media are clearly implicated in many sponsorship deals. For example, there is a great deal of advertising potential for a company in sponsoring a football match which is then televised so that the company's name is visible to millions of viewers.

SEE ALSO: **advertising ethics; product placement**.

spot colour The use of a small amount of colour to give emphasis to an item in a publication that is otherwise in black and white.

spot news An unexpected news event that had not been planned in the news diary.

SEE ALSO: **diary story; off-diary story**.

spread Loosely, a story that occupies a large area, one or two pages, of a newspaper or magazine. More precisely, an item taking up two facing pages.

standard out cue The closing statement used by a presenter, which conforms to a station or channel format. Now often used in this standardized form by news reporters on location on TV news in concluding their presentation.

SEE ALSO: **journalism; news**.

star A person who is of particular prominence or talent. In the media, the crucial characteristic of a star is that he or she is a skilful *performer* in a *public* setting. The term, therefore, is readily used for performers in film or popular music but hardly at all in television. The reason is that television is essentially a domestic medium. It is received in private spaces while both film and music are rather more public media. Print, on the other hand, does not involve performance in the same way.

Performance – or talented performance at any rate – gives the star aura or CHARISMA. The result is a considerable social distance between the star and his or her audience. To most people, stars are remote figures that one cannot hope to know personally. They remain enigmatic and incomplete (Dyer, 1979, 1987). At the same time, there is a great deal of interest in stars fostered by magazines and other branches of the media. Apparently, people want to know everything about their favourite stars from what colours they prefer to the details of their personal relationships.

The star system came into existence in something like its contemporary form with the advent of HOLLYWOOD. In this context, the star rapidly became a BRAND, associated with a particular GENRE of film (e.g. John Wayne in westerns or action films). From the point of view of the film industry, the star is a way of controlling demand, in that the consumer will want to see the latest Clint Eastwood or Julia Roberts film, or buy the latest REM or Madonna album.

The relationship between stars and members of their audience is often captured by the idea of identification. The research indicates, however, that there are different modes of identification (Stacey, 1994). A common-sense distinction is between identifications which are restricted solely to the context of film or music and those that spill over into the everyday lives of members of the audience. In the first mode, audiences may have fantasies about a star, perhaps wishing to escape from humdrum everyday life to the glamorous world of the star. In the second mode, identification may be more pronounced, extending to trying to resemble the star by talking, walking or dressing like him or her. Fan clubs provide a vehicle for identification of this kind, although it is probable that fans derive as much pleasure from the social contact with similarly engaged fellow fans as they do from immersion in the star's life.

SEE ALSO: **fan; personality; star system; star text**.

star system   The star system developed in the heyday of HOLLYWOOD and was a key way by which the production companies sought to organize audience taste so that they would visit the cinema consistently. So, for example, the audience would want to see the latest Judy Garland or John Wayne film because of their attachment to the star rather than necessarily to the genre or the individual film itself. The star system is still very significant in this respect, and the association of a star with a film can often determine whether a film is made at all. However, in itself this is not a guarantee of success of the film at the box office as there are many examples of films that have failed despite the presence of a big star.

SEE ALSO: **celebrity; star; star text**.

star text   The idea that the development of the star can be read as a text. Over a period of time the star text will take different directions, and different levels of meaning can be built up, which the audience can interpret in a range of ways. The star texts of popular figures such as Marilyn Monroe (McCann, 1988), Madonna (Schwichtenberg, 1993), George Michael (Goodwin, 1993) and Elvis Presley (Marcus, 1992; Rodman, 1996) have all been subject to extensive analysis.

SEE ALSO: **celebrity; Hollywood; star; star system**.

state See: GOVERNMENT AND THE MEDIA.

static shot As the name implies, when a camera is kept quite still and focused on an unmoving subject.

SEE ALSO: **panning; tilting; tracking**.

steadicam A harness, worn by a cameraman, to which the camera is attached. It keeps the camera steady while the cameraman moves, giving very smooth shots and avoiding jerky film.

SEE ALSO: **tracking**.

stereotype A one-sided, exaggerated and prejudicial view of a social group or set of individuals. Stereotypes can be dangerous because they appear to provide a justification for racist or other discriminatory behaviour. The media can be important in reinforcing stereotypes. For example, television drama used to cast black people in stereotypical roles as menial workers or criminals although, more recently, efforts have been made to vary the range of parts played by black actors. The way in which events in the Muslim world have been reported in the media from 2002 onwards contributes to a stereotype of Muslims as religious fanatics, potential terrorists and illegal immigrants, and such stereotypes have had a discernible effect on the way that Muslim communities in European countries have felt. Stereotyping by the media can put pressure on the authorities as well. For example, if the newspapers report disruptive or mildly criminal behaviour by young people and describe it in stereotypical terms (e.g. 'young thugs'), the police and the courts feel that they have to take strong action. Such action, in turn, is reported by the media and further reinforces the stereotype (SEE: **amplification of deviance**).

SEE ALSO: **gender**.

sting In radio, a short piece of music between other content.

storyboard A NARRATIVE in a film may be storyboarded in that draft representations of shots and scenes will be set out on paper before they are actually filmed.

SEE ALSO: **script**.

story-line The overall direction that a story, for example in a television SOAP OPERA, will take, leaving the precise detail, dialogue and action to be set out later by the scriptwriter.

strapline a short, pithy statement that sums up a story in a newspaper or magazine in a few words and may appear together with the main headline for the story.

strategies of containment A term invented by JOHN FISKE to describe the way in which news presentations in the media have to make sense of what happens in the world. Every day brings a welter of events, and the media have to have a strategy for containing them.

SEE ALSO: **news; objectivity**.

stringer A freelance reporter who covers an area for which no permanent employee is provided.

stripping Many television programmes are produced in long series, e.g. *Star Trek*. Stripping is the practice of broadcasting a programme in such a series once a day or even more frequently. The need to fill the schedules of an increasing number of television channels with cheap programming has meant that more television series are produced in bulk for stripping.

structuralism An intellectual approach and movement that was very influential in the humanities and social sciences in the 1960s and 1970s. The basic idea of structuralism is that individual social or cultural phenomena have common structures. The system and the relationships between them are more important than the individual elements that make up the system. Structuralism rests on a distinction between the surface appearance and the deeper (or hidden level) of structure and took its initial impetus from the work on SEMIOLOGY (science of signs) of SAUSSURE. Writers whose work (at some point of their career) was characterized by structuralism include ALTHUSSER, BARTHES, CHOMSKY, DERRIDA, FOUCAULT, KRISTEVA, Poulantzas and Lévi-Strauss. The movement also interpreted earlier writers such as Freud and Marx in a structuralist way. Examples of structuralist analysis of media include studies of the James Bond novels (Eco, 1982), the classic western film (Wright, 1975) and the romantic novel (Radway, 1987). Structuralism was extensively criticized by POSTSTRUCTURALISM in theoretical terms. However, many of the ideas associated with it (and semiology) continue to have great resonance in the study of media, especially the ideas of BINARY OPPOSITION and different levels of structured meaning.

SEE ALSO: **ideology; myth; sign**.

structure of feeling A term developed by RAYMOND WILLIAMS, who wanted to consider how texts and ideas could be seen to incorporate currents in society that were to do with feelings (rather than simply rational thought) and also coherent in the sense that they had structure. The idea of structure of feeling thus conveys how ideas and experience are diffuse in society but not random. Texts such as a novel or a television programme could manifest different structures of feeling, as well as more direct and formulated political and social ideas. At different points in his work Williams emphasized the way in which structures of feeling were related to classes to a variable extent. More generally, the idea also conveys the way in which Williams emphasized the importance of experience in culture and how it can be analysed. Since his death, the idea of structure of feeling has been an enduring part of Williams' legacy to the social sciences and humanities and it has been used to characterize the experience of living in different (parts of) cities (Taylor et al., 1996).

SEE ALSO: **discourse; ideology.**

studio In the most general sense, a space for cultural and media creativity, which results in a material product. The original use stems from the work of the individual artist in his/her studio. This has expanded to film, radio, television and music industries. The key distinction is between work in the studio, which now tends to be recorded (though in the early days of TV work went live from the studio to air without being recorded), and creative work that is carried out live outside the studio.

studio system The system set up in HOLLYWOOD that produced a small number of strong film production companies. The companies were powerful as they introduced an industrialized system of film production, kept movie actors under contract and controlled the exhibition of films.

SEE ALSO: **media mogul; movie mogul; star system.**

style A concept that has been used in cultural and media studies mainly with respect to youth subcultures to characterize dress, language, taste and so on. Borrowed from the common usage of the word, the argument is that the various elements of style form a coherent unity. For some writers, the style of such groups has been brought together in a creative way that shows how they (unconsciously) resist dominant modes of activity and dress (Hebdige, 1979). In this sense, style is oppositional to dominant groups. This argument has parallels with the way in which some writers conceptualize the media audience as resistant to dominant messages.

SEE ALSO: **youth culture.**

stylesheet The document which publishing (newspaper, book or magazine) organizations use to describe the style and design which their publications should adopt. This is increasingly important, as design is a means of differentiating BRANDS.

subculture See: FAN; YOUTH CULTURE.

sub-editor See: COPY EDITOR.

subject The way in which individual consciousness (as a subject) is constituted through the impact of the media. It is most often used by writers who have been influenced by psychoanalysis and MARXISM (especially in its more STRUCTURALIST variants). The individual is constituted as a subject through the operation of the IDEOLOGY that is part of the media text. The idea conveys the sense both that our subjectivity is thus constructed and that we are made the subjects of power (like being the subjects of the king or queen) through this process. For example, the repeated viewing of texts that only show women as performing domestic roles would lead to the constitution of a subjectivity which accepted that this was the proper or only work that women could do.

SEE ALSO: **Althusser; hegemony; interpellation.**

subliminal The aspect of a message or a text that may be picked up unconsciously by a viewer or reader. Thus, there has been concern in the past about the potential practice of subliminal advertising, where messages might be inserted into texts, unknown to the viewer since they flash by so quickly, which may then encourage the viewer to purchase a particular product. This sort of idea tends to rest on a very reductive and crude understanding of how the consumer operates which suggests that desires can almost be injected into the mind, without any conscious thought. AUDIENCE studies of the media has shown that people are far more reflective that this.

SEE ALSO: **propaganda.**

sub text A text that is implicit or hidden in a larger text. Commonsense understandings would tend to suggest that there are two basic levels within a text, that which is overt and explicit and that which is concealed or implicit. While this has influenced more theoretical understandings, such as the distinction within semiotics between denotation and connotation (SEE: **denotation/connotation**), texts can be seen to contain a number of levels of meaning or different competing DISCOURSES within them, which escape a relatively simple two-level model.

SEE ALSO: **semiology; structuralism.**

supply chain In order to make anything or to supply a service, organizations will require supplies or raw materials of various kinds. The organization of these supplies is referred to as the supply chain. It is a chain because each stage is connected with, and dependent on, others. For example, for a book to be bought, a book publisher will have to commission an author, who will eventually deliver a manuscript, which goes through a copy-editing process, which prepares it for a typesetter, who sets it ready for a printer. The printer prints the pages which are then bound together in a book. The publisher then arranges for the copies to go to a distributor who in turn sells the books to bookshops. Finally, the bookshop sells the book to a customer. Actually, the supply chain for book publishing is more complex than this description would imply. Furthermore, there are sub-chains which connect with the main chain. The books have to be advertised and marketed, for instance. All these steps in the supply chain could be carried out in separate organizations – a disaggregated supply chain – or some or all of them could be integrated into the one organization – an aggregated chain. More disaggregated chains tend to be more efficient through economics of scale, but they impose higher transaction costs – the steps have to be integrated together. Media firms go through cycles of aggregation and disaggregation in the search for lower costs.

SEE ALSO: **diagonal integration; economics of the media; horizontal integration; vertical integration.**

surveillance society The sort of society where surveillance has become a core aspect of how the society operates. For some writers, advanced capitalist societies such as Britain or the USA have become increasingly dependent on surveillance in this sense. Manifestations of this include the use of CCTV in a variety of situations, speed cameras on roads, identity cards and also the tracking of consumer spending through credit cards and store cards. Some commentators have argued that the development and popularity of formats like *Big Brother* exemplify aspects of the surveillance society. Thus, the participants in such programmes are kept locked in a building under constant camera surveillance, as if they are imprisoned. Such situations have become very popular viewing, allegedly showing how accepted such modes of behaviour and organization have become.

SEE ALSO: **panopticon.**

suture Process of drawing an audience member into a text. The idea derives from the literal meaning of the stitching up of a wound. It has been used in FILM THEORY and accounts of IDEOLOGY to examine how people are incorporated into the dominant message or discourse of a text.

SEE ALSO: **positioning**.

Sykes Committee Reporting in 1923, the Sykes Committee effectively set up the BBC as a PUBLIC SERVICE BROADCASTER. It argued that there was a substantial public interest in broadcasting which should be protected by the state. However, governments should not have direct control. Rather, the BBC should be required to operate by licence, the terms of which should be set by the government. In addition, the service offered by the BBC should be funded by the fees paid by the public for the licences that they bought to enable them to use their radios.

SEE ALSO: **Crawford Committee**.

symbol A word or a drawing that stands for something else, such as an idea, or an object or a feeling. Much textual analysis in media studies consists of the analysis of symbols and the different things that they represent. Deriving originally for anthropological approaches, analysis of this kind is also often carried out using the tools of SEMIOLOGY or semiotics. For example, toilet doors in public places will often use symbols of men or women to separate their gendered use. In an advertisement, a particular mode of dress may symbolize sophistication. The opening credits of British continuous serials such as *Coronation Street* symbolize a community of people living in a bounded area.

SEE ALSO: **structuralism**.

symbolism The process by which symbols are created as part of human social life, or a way of describing how symbols work together in a text in a systematic way.

SEE ALSO: **representation**.

synchronic Within SEMIOLOGY or semiotic analysis, the level of analysis which takes a 'snapshot' of meaning at any one point. It is contrasted with diachronic analysis, which is concerned with change in meaning. For example, a synchronic analysis of a film might involve the detailed analysis of how a scene or shot is framed or composed. The diachronic analysis will consider the progress of the narrative through the film.

SEE ALSO: **structuralism**.

syndication Originally used to describe the way that a newspaper writer's contributions would appear in more than one publication. The term is now also applied to a similar process in television, whereby a programme or series is syndicated over a number of television channels. Syndication is a way of lowering costs of production, particularly in television, or of attracting more readers or viewers to a particularly popular journalist, performer or programme.

synecdoche A figure of speech or language where a part of something may be used instead of a whole. For example, the word 'wheels' may be used to stand for the word 'car'.

SEE ALSO: **semiology**.

syntagm The combination of PARADIGMATIC elements to form a system of meaning. Thus the sentence 'the cat sat on the ground' is a syntagm. An alternative syntagm formed from different paradigmatic elements might be 'the dog lay on the earth'. In this example there are a number of different animals that form a paradigmatic group, such as a bird or a sheep, combining with the other paradigmatic groups to produce sentences like 'the bird perched on the twig' and 'sheep rested on the grass'. Thus, four different syntagms have been produced from the three paradigmatic groups: cat, dog, bird, sheep; sat, lay, perched, rested; and ground, earth, twig and grass.

tabloid Originally, the format in which a newspaper was printed, with a fairly small sheet size. The term is now used to refer to the content of newspapers rather than their physical appearance. Thus, tabloid newspapers are more interested in celebrities and crime than politics or international affairs, use photographs extensively, employ simple language and give more space to sport and relatively less to 'high culture'. The term has been extended to other forms of the media. Tabloid television, for example, relies on personalities, simple formats and a speedy style. The term – and its associated tabloidization – is often used in a derogatory way. The suggestion is that producers will adopt tabloid values in order to enhance market share, thereby leading to DUMBING DOWN, an emphasis on entertainment rather than 'serious' issues, and an intrusive and critical view of individuals. In this sense the tabloid is a particularly British phenomenon.

SEE ALSO: **broadsheet**.

take The attempt at filming a particular scene or portion of narrative. As is now well known from the popularity of OUT-TAKE programmes on TV, the production of the final take may involve many attempts.

SEE ALSO: **shot**.

talk show Much derided for their cheapness, exhibitionism and triviality, talk shows are a genre peculiar to television (and perhaps radio). Although formats vary, the typical talk show takes place in a studio filled with members of the public together with those able to offer a particular view, whether as expert or involved person. The group is invited to discuss a topic of current interest or an emotional or social problem faced by some of the participants. The discussion is moved along by a host who is, or becomes, a celebrity or PERSONALITY in his or her own right. Strong opinions are expressed and are, especially in American shows, positively encouraged.

Although criticized for allowing the unbridled public display of private emotion, some talk shows are engineering public debate of important issues. Unlike many DOCUMENTARIES, talk shows are relatively open in not coming to definite conclusions but allowing the free expression of different points of view – however extreme. Some research shows that the audience watching the shows on television at home are not involved merely as passive spectators but see themselves as participants in a debate (Livingstone and Lunt, 1995).

target audience   Magazines, newspapers, radio stations, television channels or programmes are usually devised with a particular – target – audience in mind. The more differentiated the audience becomes, the more important it is for producers to be clear what the audience is. Even for a mass medium like television, particular programmes are designed for specific audiences.

SEE ALSO: **audience differentiation; demographics**.

Target Group Index (TGI)   A large survey of consumer preferences, purchases and media habits conducted annually. Respondents are asked to answer a large number of questions in detail using a DIARY METHOD. TGI classifies people into lifestyle groupings, e.g. pleasure-seekers, trendies.

taste   The preferences for certain goods or cultural forms that are held by an individual or a group. While some think that taste is a purely individual matter, it is actually subject to complex social patterns and distributions. While one form of taste distinction is between high or popular, with often something akin to 'middle brow' inserted between, which has been used in both everyday and social science approaches to the study of taste (see for example, BOURDIEU, 1984), it has been argued that such distinctions are breaking down as the middle and upper classes become more omnivorous in taste in that they enjoy a wider range of cultural pursuits of high and popular types. However, while this may be the case, and the evidence is still to be collected and evaluated, it is clear that disputes around taste, be it high or popular, poor or good, are still as endemic in society as they have ever been.

SEE ALSO: **cultural capital; habitus; omnivore**.

taste public   A term used for a social group that shares a taste for certain goods or cultural forms. The group would be one that is not simply at the level of a household or a family (as this could be seen as the private domain), but would involve a large (or mass) group of people, who would not necessarily know each other.

SEE ALSO: **habitus**.

teasers   Words or information on the cover of a magazine that are used to attract the attention of the reader through conveying information about what is inside. Announcements of future programmes on radio and TV serve a similar function.

technological determinism The idea that social and cultural change is produced solely by changes in technology, such as the invention of the telegraph or of computers. It is difficult to deny that certain technologies do have profound social implications; it is impossible to conceive of modern society without the invention of print, for example. However, the idea that technology is all-powerful is misleading since it neglects the point that social changes are necessary for technological innovations to be made and applied. MARSHALL MCLUHAN carried the notion of technological determinism to extremes in believing that the media of communication themselves had powerful effects, and the content of the media were unimportant by comparison. For example, he held that the invention of the printing press and the subsequent widespread adoption of books and pamphlets led to the religious wars of the sixteenth century, not necessarily because of what the books contained but because print was a HOT MEDIUM. Most work in media studies has tended to reject strongly technologically determinist arguments in favour of attention to the interaction of a range of factors (see Williams, 1974).

SEE: **Medium is the Message**.

technology MacKenzie and Wajcman (1985) offer three different definitions of technology. First, technology can be defined as 'sets of physical objects'. Second technology is used to refer to these objects plus human activity. Third, technology is seen as the objects plus the human activity plus some knowledge. For example, an overhead projector is a physical object but it is of little practical use without a human being to switch it on, or the knowledge on the part of the human being about how to switch it on and place the slides on it correctly. The increased sophistication of technology has offered the opportunity for much increased sophistication of texts. One clear example is the development of computer graphics.

teletext A text-only service used to provide information of various kinds, including breaking news. Over half of the televisions sold in Britain have the capacity to receive teletext pages. Teletext is likely to be threatened by the increased use of computers to provide information from the INTERNET, although the television set will remain a very convenient source of information for many households for some time to come.

SEE ALSO: **ceefax**.

Televisa A media company based in Mexico but expanding into other markets globally, partly on the back of the importance of the Spanish language. It has interests in television, radio, music and magazine publishing.

SEE ALSO: **media companies**.

television It seems obvious that television is important in everyday life. About 98 per cent of the population in the UK have at least one television and over half own two or more. People also commit a substantial amount of time in watching the set or sets. The average daily hours of viewing varies over the year between 4.9 and 5.3 hours per household and between 3.0 and 3.8 for each individual in the UK. Television watching occupies more time than all other leisure pursuits put together. As a result, television functions as an important source of common experience for the British people, who are otherwise divided by class, ethnicity, gender or region.

One of the more obvious and important characteristics of television as a medium is that it is domestic in style and in the way in which it is received. Television is very concerned with the home, family and domestic life. A great deal of the action of many soap operas and situation comedies revolves around the domestic setting (SEE: **household**). Further, the style of television is very much like that of a conversation with the viewer (SEE: **directness of address**). Announcers, weathermen and -women, newsreaders, talk show hosts and many others face the camera directly and are therefore giving the illusion of having an intimate, direct, domestic conversation with the person watching. This is reinforced by the conversational language employed. Much television is conversation. Soap opera and situation comedy largely consist of conversation, often between people in private spaces. Other sorts of television consist of simulated conversation in which the participants pretend to be having the kind of conversation that viewers might have round the kitchen table.

Television is also largely received in homes – and in families. Television is integrated in the daily routine of families, and much domestic life may actually be organized around it. Broadcasters respond to this by organizing the programme schedules accordingly. They make assumptions about who is watching when, when mealtimes are taken, when children of a certain age will be in bed and so on. Much of this implies that families use television for their own purposes. In particular, it is misleading to concentrate on individuals looking at television without taking into account the social – family – context. Family members will refer to television programmes in their everyday conversation and use characters and events to illustrate what they want to say (SEE: **television talk**). More generally still, television may promote either affiliation or avoidance in families. Communal watching of programmes provides opportunities for displays of family warmth and affection. Studies have shown that families are more physically affectionate when watching the television. Or the medium can provide the means for withdrawal.

It is tempting to think that television is like cinema. In its early days, certainly, people did treat the experience of watching television rather like that of the cinema. In many ways, television is nothing like cinema, certainly as both the medium and its audiences have developed. First, film is designed to be a public event, and its characteristic mode is a complete performance. Television, on the other hand, is a procession of segments often arranged as a series or serial, and watched privately or domestically. Second, the intense photographic quality of film demands, and receives, sustained attention from the audience while television watching is more casual and episodic (SEE: **gaze; regimes of watching**). Third, cinema has STARS, while television has PERSONALITIES. Fourth, cinema operates with a different kind of NARRATIVE. Typically films start with a disordered narrative and then move through a series of ups and downs to a resolution of that disorder. Television presents itself as a set of repeated segments which do not form a unity of any kind. Lastly, television has a certain immediacy.

The first television broadcasts were made in Britain and the United States in the late 1920s and early 1930s. In these early experiments the quality was poor and the transmission range inadequate. Even so, systematic broadcasting began in both Britain and the United States by the middle of the 1930s. In 1936, there were 3,000 television sets in Britain and 50 in New York. Although further progress was interrupted by the Second World War, ownership of sets accelerated rapidly afterwards, and by 1980 almost every household had a set.

In its beginnings in Britain, television was heavily influenced by the way in which radio broadcasting had been set up in the early 1920s as PUBLIC SERVICE BROADCASTING. The government of the day argued that control over broadcasting should lie ultimately with the state, but that it should be an indirect control via a licence to broadcast which would put particular obligations on the broadcaster. At the time, the broadcasters, particularly in the person of JOHN REITH, the first Director-General of the BBC, had strong views about the kind of service broadcasting should be. It should educate, bring the nation together as a moral community, promote the highest standards of taste and, by the provision of information and argument, help to create a rational democracy. In order to fulfil this mission, broadcasting should be a monopoly able to ensure that standards were met.

Television broadcasting, located in the BBC, continued in the tradition of public service from its first broadcasts in 1936. However, its monopoly position was undermined in the mid-1950s by the introduction of COMMERCIAL TELEVISION, funded by advertising rather than the licence fee which provided the revenue for the BBC. This competition had a powerful effect on the BBC. Not only was there a change in the kinds of programme that were being made – they became more 'popular' – but the share of the audience commanded by the BBC plunged dramatically, at one point to as low as 20 per cent. Despite this element of commercial competition, however, the broadcasting of television remained roughly within the public service tradition. Commercial television was regulated by an independent body – the Independent Television Authority – which was charged with the same sort of public service aim as was the BBC. Many of the public service ideals survived the movement to greater pluralism in the late 1970s. This resulted in the formation of CHANNEL FOUR in 1980, which was charged with providing programming for minority audiences not served well by the existing providers. However, the 1980s saw a major collapse in the underpinnings of the ideals of public service broadcasting. The changes in television broadcasting begun in the 1980s are fundamental and far-reaching and are produced by a combination of political, social, financial, organizational and technological factors. As in so many other areas of social life, the government sought to deregulate – remove the controls over – the broadcasting industry and to bring in more competition, increasing the range of programming, all in the name of greater choice for the consumer of broadcasting. Many of these changes are enshrined in the Broadcasting Act of 1990, one of whose additional provisions was the creation of a third commercial channel, Channel Five. Channel Four pioneered a new form of television production modelled on the book publishing industry in which producers commissioned programmes from INDEPENDENT PRODUCTION COMPANIES. The boost to the independent sector given by the formation of Channel Four was further enhanced by the 1990 Act, which stipulated that one-quarter of BBC and ITV production had to be carried out by independent production companies. Employment in the BBC and commercial television declined, and many staff that remained were employed on short-term contracts (SEE: **casualization**).

Even greater changes were promoted by technological innovations. The traditional means of supplying television programmes is by broadcasting using the radio spectrum. The radio spectrum is a finite resource. If too many suppliers try to broadcast on it, the risk is that they will interfere with each other's transmissions. This traditional method of supply was challenged from the 1970s onwards by other means – CABLE and SATELLITE. Transmission via cable laid underground permits a much greater number of channels than is possible with broadcasting using the radio spectrum. Cable has proved fairly popular in the United States but less so in Europe. The technology that has attracted most attention, however, is satellite. Although satellites have high initial costs, they can cover a wide geographical area. The net effect of all these technological changes is that viewers have available to them a much larger number of channels. At the same time, the number of hours watched has not increased and, if anything, has declined. Competition between television providers has therefore increased, and it is still too early to say what effect this will have.

television audience We all make assumptions about what people are doing when they watch the television. For example, the couch potato is a familiar image – the person who will watch anything, at any time of day, without taking anything in, while eating crisps and drinking lager. Of course, such an image is always of other people; we ourselves could never be couch potatoes. The most important element in this image of the television audience is that it is seen as essentially passive.

There is some reason to hold that view. In Britain, almost everybody has a television set, and it is switched on for large amounts of time every day. Television is, by a long way, the most popular leisure pursuit, taking up almost twice as much time as all other leisure activities combined. Indeed, television occupies more of our time than *any* activity other than sleeping and working. The image of the passive viewer slumped in a chair for hours every day seems confirmed by the type of programme watched. Some two-thirds of material actually watched is apparently undemanding – soap opera, situation comedy, films, sport, game shows. Only one-third of the time is dedicated to documentaries, news or 'serious' drama. Intriguingly, this pattern of viewing is common to all social classes. The differences in patterns between men and women and between young and old are also very slight. Broadcast television is truly a mass medium. On the whole, viewers do not go to the BBC or the commercial channels in search of particular kinds of programmes; they treat the television as a generic leisure activity. These habits may well change as the provision of specialist digital channels increases and households have more television sets (SEE: **market segmentation/differentiation**). It is also worth noting that, if one asks what people want to watch rather than what they actually do watch, there is a much higher degree of programme preference. It is family negotiation that means that these preferences are not realized.

Is the television audience passive in this way? The most fundamental, if obvious, point about television is that it is a domestic medium and has become thoroughly integrated into domestic routines (SEE: **household**). Typically, it is watched at home in family settings while a lot else is going on. An implication of this is that the characteristic mode of viewing is a distracted one. For some of the time, viewers' attention is fully on the television set while at other times it is on something else. While the set is on, then, people can be found doing all sorts of other things. One study, which involved filming people while they were supposedly watching the television, discovered some slumped in front of the set while others were paying rapt attention. Still others were paying no attention at all and played the flute, wrote letters, engaged in animated conversation completely unrelated to what was on the set, did handstands and vacuumed the carpet – and left the room (SEE: **regimes of watching**). When television was a novelty, people drew the curtains, turned off the light, called for hush and concentrated fiercely on the set. They treated the television like the cinema but they have now learned to incorporate it into whatever else they are doing.

People talk about television. They will talk about programmes while they are on and afterwards with friends and family. Some of this talk may be trivial; much is not. There is now a substantial body of evidence that, in talking about television, people are actively using it to make sense of their lives. Characters and incidents in soap operas, for instance, will be related to real-life experiences and may help families to talk about isssues which would otherwise be difficult (SEE: **television talk**). The audience, in sum, is not composed of the passive creatures of mythology but relates more actively to television texts (SEE: **active audience**).

SEE ALSO: **audience; audience research; cultivation theory; effects; encoding/decoding; Peoplemeter; uses and gratifications.**

television franchise The right, granted by the INDEPENDENT TELEVISION COMMISSION and its predecessors, to broadcast television programmes within a particular area of the country for a particular period of time. The franchise system has been a cornerstone of the commercial, independent television sector since it was first introduced in the UK. It represents a compromise between a fully commercial, market system on the one hand and the principles of public service broadcasting on the other. It therefore allows this sector to be controlled to some extent while also allowing it to make a profit without any state funding. However, the balance between commercial demands and government regulation has shifted over time. Thus, as a result of the BROADCASTING ACT 1990, franchises were awarded partly on financial grounds in a bidding process, and a number of the independent companies lost their franchises. It is likely that the franchise system will come under further pressure as satellite and cable providers become more established still.

SEE ALSO: **Independent Television**.

television network A term that is used chiefly to describe the television broadcasting system in the United States which is made up of a few major competitive networks (SEE: **ABC; CBS; Fox Network; NBC**). Each network is composed of a set of locally based television stations which mix local material with common programming from the network. With the advent of CABLE and SATELLITE and reduced REGULATION, the costs of setting up a television network have fallen. As a result, the number of competing networks is increasing in the United States and across the world.

television news News programmes on television are important. They form a substantial proportion of television output and can attract substantial viewing figures (the BBC late-evening news, for instance, has an average of some 9 million viewers). Television news also has a high public visibility and so it attracts accusations of bias from many different quarters. As a source of international, regional and local news, television is more important than newspapers and radio. More than two-thirds of the population cite television as their main source of news. Furthermore, television is thought to be more reliable. Three-quarters of the population believe that television is the most complete, accurate, unbiased, quick and clear source of reporting of events of national and international importance. Even for events of regional or local significance, television is preferred to the local press, although the advantage is less clear.

In many respects, the issues that arise in television news are similar to those raised in any news presentation (SEE: **news**). However, television also has some distinctive features that make its presentation of news different (SEE: **television**). First, it borrows the conventions of REALISM. In television news programmes, events seem to come at us unselected and uninterpreted. This gives a certain authenticity and immediacy. This naturalness of television does not happen automatically. It is a style that has been evolved over the years. In its origins, television news owed more to the conventions of radio, the newsreel and, above all, print, all of which give older news programmes a stilted and unreal feel to audiences reared on modern televisual conventions. This distinctive convention is re-inforced by the MODE OF ADDRESS employed by television. An impression is created of a conversation which the television presenter is having with the audience. The newsreader looks directly into the camera and employs an informal style which creates the illusion of an exchange in the home.

It is also important to note that television news can only treat a small proportion of the stories that are dealt with in the press and cannot go into them in as much detail. One consequence is that events in television news are not explained. Lastly, and more obviously, television puts a premium on news that is visual rather than that which is abstract, a feature which may further contribute to the lack of background that television news programmes tend to have.

SEE ALSO: **Glasgow University Media Group**.

television ratings See: AUDIENCE RATINGS.

television talk A common idea of television watching is that it is a solitary and inactive pursuit. This is misleading. Actually, the television audience is typically involved in a social experience and actively interprets what it sees. One important feature of this social activity is that people talk about television, both at the time that they are watching it and afterwards. Television as a medium encourages this as, by contrast with film, which is very visual, it is essentially illustrated talk designed to be received in a domestic environment.

This is not to say that everybody talks about television to the same extent. Men claim not to talk about any television other than sport while women talk about a range of programming. Television talk is also used in different ways. Most importantly, people use it to relate television to their own lives and thus help them to make sense of both. Soap opera, for instance, can act as a resource of character or incident which makes it possible for people to talk about their own experiences and problems as the same or different from those depicted in the soap.

In a study of *Dallas*, Liebes and Katz (1993) refer to these uses of television talk as referential framings. When using them, viewers are essentially operating inside the programme, taking it on its own terms. Less commonly, though, viewers may adopt critical framings in which they stand outside the programme. When watching a soap, for example, viewers may comment on the quality of the acting, the themes of the episode or, even, the hidden message that they think that the producers are trying to get across. Critical framings, in other words, are treating the programme as a fictional construct, not as a slice of life. Some television watchers may operate much of the time with critical framings and others with referential ones. Typically, however, most audiences actually move between one and the other as they talk.

The connection between television talk and the impact of television on viewers' attitudes, beliefs and actions is not altogether clear. It seems plausible that the more that viewers adopt critical framings, the more they are resistant to any hidden message or bias that there might be in a programme.

One word of caution in interpreting research on television talk. Almost all this work is based on focus groups of viewers who are got together to talk about their television watching. There is very little research on talk in natural settings. As a result, we cannot be sure how television talk varies with the setting – home, work or playground – and there must be doubt about how good the experimental groups are at predicting the volume and nature of talk that happens naturally.

SEE ALSO: **dominant ideology/culture; effects; framing; preferred reading**.

terrestrial television From the early days of television, the signal was BROADCAST from radio transmitters. Transmission by CABLE is similarly terrestrial. These forms of transmission can be contrasted with that by SATELLITES in GEOSTATIONARY orbits above the earth.

terrorism The form of activity that seeks to further political or social aims through the use of some form of violence that is defined as illegitimate. There will always be debate over the definition of who or what is a terrorist, as some groups and organizations that are defined in this way will be seen as 'freedom fighters' by others. There has been debate over the representation of terrorism in the media in a number of ways. For example, it has been suggested that the media have turned terrorist acts into a spectacle, through the repeated use of footage such as the attack on the twin towers in New York City in 2001. In addition, there is debate over the extent to which so-called 'terrorist' groups can be given a voice or space in the media and whether this then accords them credibility and legitimacy. The Thatcher government in the UK introduced legislation on this issue in the 1980s with particular respect to Northern Ireland. This led to the situation where members of the Northern Irish political party Sinn Fein were appearing on television with an actor speaking their words because of restrictions on their real voices being heard.

SEE ALSO: **propaganda**.

text A concept used generally to describe a range of cultural objects such as books, television programmes, CDs, films. One of the important innovations made by media and cultural studies was to expand the range of cultural objects that could be analysed as texts, moving beyond the more familiar categorization of books and poems. In principle, similar approaches and concepts can be applied to the analysis of a text, be it a film, novel or TV programme. Of course, there will be differences due to the particularities of the media (whether it is visual or musical, for instance). Thus, the tools of SEMIOLOGY can be applied to different texts, as can the ideas of DISCOURSE analysis. Thinking of texts in this broadened way meant that many forms that would not have been thought of as legitimate objects of study in intellectual life have become so. Analysis is no longer restricted to 'high' culture, but can include Madonna as well as Mozart. This has been contentious. Some authors would argue that media studies has paid rather too much attention to textual analysis to the neglect of the manner in which texts are produced or consumed. However, it is increasingly recognized that textual analysis needs to be combined with study of production and audience processes.

SEE ALSO: **narrative**.

text message See: INSTANT MESSAGING; SHORT MESSAGING SERVICE.

textual studies Disciplines in the humanities such as history and English have primarily been concerned with the study of written texts. This has been influential on media studies in the sense that the discipline concerns itself with the analysis of media texts conceived in the broadest way. Thus, a text can be a television programme, an advertisement, a newspaper article or the newspaper itself, a cartoon, or a section of pop music and so on. It is commonly accepted that attention to texts alone will lead to the neglect of two sets of important issues, how the text is produced and how it is consumed by audiences.

thick description Any piece of research work in the media depends on the description of attitudes or conduct. Such a description is 'thick' in the sense that it depends on the multiple layers of meaning given by human beings to their actions. Every description given in an ethnographic account is actually based on descriptions provided by participants, which in turn are dependent on other descriptions – and so on.

Thompson, Edward Palmer (1924–93) An influential English Marxist historian, who is credited as being one of the key influences on the early development of CULTURAL STUDIES. Thompson was particularly influential through his discussion of how classes develop as cultural and social forms, rather than just as economic groups. Culture is thus important in how classes are made as social actors. This might involve attention to a range of cultural forms including the role of media such as newspapers in the ongoing development of social classes.

SEE ALSO: **Hoggart; Williams**.

thought balloon See: SPEECH BALLOON.

three par cue In news the way that a story is written in three paragraphs. The paragraphs may vary in length but will show the significance of the story or event at the beginning, develop it in the second paragraph and then conclude in the third.

SEE ALSO: **narrative**.

tilting In film and television when the camera lens moves up and down while the camera itself does not move horizontally.

SEE ALSO: **panning**; **static shot**; **tracking**.

timbre In music the variations in tonal quality between different voices and instruments.

time-shift The way in which video-recorders are used to record television programmes that can then be viewed at a different time. Studies of video-recorder use suggest that this is the most important way in which the technology is used, rather than in the viewing of pre-purchased tapes or rented tapes.

SEE ALSO: **active audience**.

Time Warner Now the name for a company formed in 2000 by a merger between America Online and Time Warner and then called AOL TIME WARNER. It had sales in 2004 of more than £20 billion. Time Warner has interests in every field of the media – magazines, e.g. *Time* and UK titles formerly published by the International Publishing Corporation; books, e.g. Little, Brown; music, e.g. Atlantic; film, e.g. Warner Brothers; television, e.g. CNN and Home Box Office; and internet service provision and online publishing, e.g. AOL. It also owns shops, theme parks and sports teams. Time Warner is itself a company built up by merger and acquisition of well-known media companies over a long period of time. In particular, the two halves, Time Inc. as a newspaper and book publisher and Warner Brothers as a film producer and distributor, came together in 1989, and the combined group then acquired the Turner empire, including CNN, in 1996.

SEE ALSO: **media companies**.

TIVO A digital recording system for television. It will allow for a large volume of recording, simultaneous playback and recording, recording of particular kinds of programme, e.g. by favourite actors, or every episode of the programme.

SEE ALSO: **digital revolution**.

Todorov, Tzvetan (b. 1939) Bulgarian-born philosopher and literary analyst who is resident in France. He was an important influence in the propagation of STRUCTURALIST ideas and has written a number of books which have developed further understanding of the work of BAKHTIN in the western world and have been centrally involved in the furtherance of DIALOGIC methods of analysis.

tone 1 The nature of sound both of the voice and of an instrument.
2 The quality of a picture, especially with respect to shade.
SEE ALSO: **voice**.

Toronto School The grouping of those media scholars such as HAROLD INNIS and MARSHALL MCLUHAN who worked at the University of Toronto. A common theme in the work of these writers is some form of TECHNO-LOGICAL DETERMINISM, where technology and technical change are held to determine the development of texts and ways of consuming them. The approach had much influence during the 1960s and then rather waned in importance. The work of McLuhan in particular regained currency from the 1990s on, especially in the light of the influence of those forms of POSTMODERNISM that place a degree of importance on the effects of technology.
SEE ALSO: **political economy**.

tracking In film or television any shot in which the camera itself is moved. Traditionally this was done on a wheeled device called a DOLLY, though modern technology allows the camera to be carried in a harness by the cameraman (SEE: **steadicam**).
SEE ALSO: **panning; static shot; tilting**.

tracking study A form of research that follows a group or number of people over time to see how their views or practices may change over a period. Thus, a study of how people change their television viewing habits over time in the UK, sponsored by the British Film Institute, has led to a number of important insights about television audiences (see Gauntlett and Hill, 1999).
SEE ALSO: **attitude; audience measurement**.

track laying The process of fitting sounds to images in a film. Often sound may not have come across clearly in the original film, or extra sound needs to be inserted.

trademark A legal control on the use of a term, brand name or logo. Once a trademark is registered by an organization, it then has exclusive use of it.
SEE ALSO: **intellectual property**.

trailer A text that advertises another text. For example, in the cinema a film will be prefaced by shorter films that display information about forthcoming productions, and a significant part of television scheduling consists of promotions for programmes to be screened at a later time or date.

SEE ALSO: **advertisement**.

transculture A global culture that transcends any specific place. This idea suggests that certain aspects of culture, such as pop music, are now instantly recognizable across the world. Commonly, transculturation is thought of as an aspect of CULTURAL IMPERIALISM, chiefly on the part of the United States. However, the idea of transculture has also been developed to take account of the interaction between cultures, which produce new hybrids rather than the simple imposition of one upon another. The term GLOBALIZATION has similar connotations.

SEE ALSO: **global media; glocalization; localization**.

transgression Process by which certain forms of culture or media can cross over or break acceptable or common understandings, ethics, practices or forms of representation. Running naked along the pitch at a football match transgresses the norms of acceptable forms of behaviour in such a situation. In media, this process is sometimes carried out through the relocation of a well-known form into a different context. For example, in the 1960s, some authors associated with the radical counter culture used the American comic- book form to convey ideas concerning sexual freedom and drug-taking. More recently, Madonna became famous for using the symbolism and representations of PORNOGRAPHY in the videos for very successful pop songs. The incorporation of these previously marginal and hidden activities and images transgressed what had previously been acceptable in broadcast media.

transmission area The geographical area to which a radio signal is sent by a station.

SEE ALSO: **footprint**.

Trinity Mirror See: MIRROR GROUP NEWSPAPERS.

truth The media in all countries are frequently accused by governments or different sections of the public of distorting the truth. Actually, absolute truth is unattainable (SEE: **objectivity**). While the media have to avoid bias, they can only pursue truth by engaging in processes which permit constant debate and subsequent revision to accepted accounts. It is not a case, in other words, of seeking to present a completely truthful account at any one time, but of engaging in a process which guarantees open scrutiny.

SEE ALSO: **bias; news.**

two-page spread See: SPREAD.

two shot In film-making, a shot with two subjects in frame.

two-step flow In studying the effects that media messages have on the audience, it is sometimes assumed that ideas flow directly from the producers of the message to the receivers (SEE: **sender/receiver**). Actually, the flow is likely to be more complicated than that and is mediated by agencies between sender and receiver. For example, there may be a two-step flow whereby particularly influential people pass on to others in their personal network ideas that they have derived from the media.

SEE ALSO: **effects; mass media; personal influence.**

two-way In radio and television, discussion through questions and answers between a presenter or newsreader and a reporter or journalist.

type-casting The process whereby an actor becomes associated with an individual character or particular type of part. For example, the actor William Roach has become synonymous with the character of Ken Barlow in the long-running British continuous serial *Coronation Street*, having played the part since 1960, so much so that the actor sued a national newspaper when it ascribed Ken's characteristics to him. Certain actors become associated with types of role. For instance, there are a number of male actors who often play action heroes. The actors often wish to break out of this mould. Sometimes they will be cast against type to upset audience expectations. For example, in *Once Upon a Time in the West* (dir. Sergio Leone, 1968), Henry Fonda, who often played humane men, was cast as a ruthless killer.

typeface A set of print characters, all of which clearly have the same design features. Well-known examples are Times Roman and Century Schoolbook, but there are now many thousands of typefaces adapted to different purposes. A set almost always consists of the alphabet, numbers, punctuation marks and other symbols. Particularly in the nineteenth and twentieth centuries the aesthetics of typeface design became important, and significant artists, e.g. Eric Gill, were involved in their production.

Typefaces – or FONTS as they are more commonly known now – will incorporate characters of different sizes (SEE: **point size**), different weights, e.g. bold, and different characteristics e.g. italic. There are differences between typefaces, which may determine their use in particular design contexts. For example, typefaces can be either non-proportional or proportional. In non-proportional typefaces, each character will occupy the same space. Proportional typefaces, on the other hand, vary the space taken up by the characteristics of each letter. The letter 'i', for example, occupies a relatively narrow space, while the letter 'm' is relatively wider. Proportional typefaces are thought to be easier to read for large blocks of print, as in newspapers and books, while non-proportional examples tend to be used in specific design environments. Again, there is a significant difference between serif and sans serif fonts. The former have decorative features at the end of each stroke of individual letters. Serif typefaces are often thought to be easier on the eye and tend to be used for large blocks of text.

typesetter In the days when books and newspapers were printed by LETTERPRESS, the typesetter was the person who set up the printing plates by inserting individual letters cast from metal. The term survived the transition from letterpress to computer typesetting, in which pages are set on computer using software like a sophisticated word-processing programme. The trade has become less skilled over time, first as computers replaced earlier technologies, and then as typesetting software improved. Now many book authors and, certainly, print journalists effectively do much of the typesetter's work in composing their material on computers.

SEE ALSO: **print**.

typography The appearance of the printed page, especially the choice of FONT, but also the line and paragraph spacing and use of white space, is usually referred to as the typography.

U

ubiquitous computing Systems of computing that are integrated into everyday life and everyday objects rather than being restricted to boxes on desks. Many people have speculated on a future in which houses, domestic appliances or cars will effectively be operated as computers of a kind. However, at present, the most obvious applications of ubiquitous computing, certainly as far as the media are concerned, lie in those devices that people can carry around with them, such as mobile phones, computers or MP3 players.

SEE ALSO: **new media; personal media**.

underground press Newspapers or magazines that express minority moral, personal or political views. They are likely to have a relatively small readership, and, because of this, and their content, will not be handled by traditional newsagents. They therefore have to look for informal or unconventional methods of distribution. It is uncommon for such publications to be started in the hope of making money. It is more likely that their publishers simply want to express themselves or to influence others. However, some magazines, such as *Private Eye* in the UK, may have started in this way but have gone on to commercial success. It is relatively cheap to start an underground publication, especially if contributors are not paid. Internet publication is even cheaper, and there has been a proliferation of material published in this way.

SEE ALSO: **fanzine; radical media/radical press**.

unique selling proposition (USP) A form of advertising offering to the buyer benefits of the product that cannot be found elsewhere. A popular doctrine in the advertising industry in the 1960s and 1970s, and still influential today, was that the marketing of every product should emphasize its distinctiveness from other competitive products. The USP could be found in any aspect of the product, from its ingredients to the way that it is packaged or sold.

United Newspapers A group previously associated with LORD BEAVER-BROOK and which used to publish the *Daily Express*, *Star* and *Sunday Express*, which were, controversially, sold to RICHARD DESMOND'S Northern and Shell Group in 2000. Renamed United News and Media, the group has concentrated on business services and magazine publishing.

URL (Uniform Resource Locator) A set of characters that identifies a website or, more generally, any resource on the internet, so that that resource can be located by a computer. For example, http://www.bbc.co.uk is a URL.

uses and gratifications A common view of audiences for the media is that they are essentially passive. Such a view implies that audience members simply take up media messages uncritically. The evidence is, however, that audiences are active (SEE: **active audience; effects**). One aspect of this is that audiences are selective. There may be some doubt as to how much selectivity is exercised, but it is clear, for example, that different sections of the audience choose different television programmes to watch. Women prefer soap opera while men select sport. Uses and gratifications theory proposes that people actively use the media to gratify their aspirations, needs and wants.

Needs can be identified and classified in many different ways. Different accounts will stress the use of the media in personal relationships – to serve as a topic of conversation, to provide models of personal behaviour or to act as a means of retreat from family interaction; or in the formation of personal identity – as when young people model themselves on stars or people use the events in soap operas to think about issues in their own lives; or simply as diversion or escape.

An influential formulation of the theory runs as follows. Social background and psychological dispositions jointly influence general habits of media use and the expectations about the benefits offered by the media. These in turn form particular choices of media (e.g. what programme to watch on television). Assessment of the benefits derived from those choices then follows, and those benefits may be applied in other areas of audience members' lives.

SEE ALSO: **audience**.

USP See: UNIQUE SELLING PROPOSITION.

utopia The original meaning of this term is 'no place', but it is more generally used within fiction to refer to a place that is better than the society from which the fiction springs. The depiction of utopias therefore necessarily implies criticism of existing societies. Dystopian fictions are those that show a vision of a terrifying future. Examples are George Orwell's *Nineteen Eighty-Four* (1949) or Aldous Huxley's *Brave New World* (1932).

V

values There is a conventional distinction between values, which are held more or less life-long, and are important and fundamental beliefs, and ATTITUDES, which are more specific, often situational, and fleeting. So, for example, a person may believe in being charitable to others who are worse off but, at the same time, have varying attitudes to beggars in the street, travellers and gypsies or the victims of earthquakes abroad. While the media may well influence attitudes there is little evidence that they are formative of values.

SEE ALSO: **effects; socialization.**

vertical integration When a company acquires or starts up other companies earlier or later in its SUPPLY CHAIN. For example, if a book publisher moves into typesetting, printing and bookselling and directly employs its authors, it would be pursuing a strategy of growth through vertical integration. Advantages of such a strategy include a lowering of costs by integrating the transactions involved and greater control over supply. Despite these advantages, media companies are, if anything, less vertically integrated than they were. Television companies are turning to INDEPENDENT PRODUCTION COMPANIES for much of their programming, and book publishing companies have long since divested themselves of print works and are looking for other means of OUTSOURCING their supply (SEE: **book publishing**).

SEE ALSO: **concentration of ownership; diagonal integration; horizontal integration.**

Viacom A very large global media group with sales in 2004 of over £11 billion and with interests in book publishing, e.g. Simon and Schuster and Prentice-Hall; film, e.g. Paramount; broadcast and cable television, e.g. CBS and MTV; radio; advertising; theme parks; cinemas; and video rental, e.g. Blockbuster.

SEE ALSO: **media companies.**

video A format for recording sound and image, based on the magnetic recording of images, that was developed in succession to film. Video technology has led to new modes of artistic creation in both AVANT-GARDE and popular culture. Within the latter, the creation of the new form of MUSIC VIDEO (or promo) was of particular importance. Video also meant that films and television programmes could be produced for sale for the home market (now increasingly replaced by digital technology in the DVD) and with the advent of the video cassette recorder (VCR) that households could also record and TIME-SHIFT programmes.

SEE ALSO: **MTV**.

video-conferencing A type of communication that uses visual images as well as sound and therefore lends itself to small meetings or conferences where not everybody has to be physically present. Because the transmission of images requires substantial BANDWIDTH, there have been technical problems with the satisfactory development of video-conferencing systems.

video games See: COMPUTER GAMES.

video nasty A GENRE of video that depicts forms of violence and/or sexual activity in an explicit way. While there is a long history of social concern about the representation of such aspects of human life, the debate took a particular turn with the development of the term 'video nasty'. That such videos could be viewed in the home led to concerns that they would be available to children in ways that were not regulated by the state. The claim was that videos of this kind could have an effect on suggestible or young people, and proof was alleged to have been found in the 1993 murder of James Bulger by two older children, who, it was thought (actually wrongly), had watched a video nasty beforehand. There are two problems with claims of this kind. First, there is actually very little analysis of the nature of the texts of the so-called 'video nasty'. Second, it is thought that they act in a very direct way to influence behaviour. A potentially unfortunate effect of any such simplistic understanding is to curtail adequate and informed discussion of the limits of representation and the rights of citizens in a democracy to watch whatever they want to.

SEE ALSO: **censorship; effects; moral panic; violence**.

video-on-demand A method of distributing films (or other video material) so that customers can download the film over a computer network and watch it in REAL TIME. The method requires powerful computers and a BROADBAND connection. As yet, as a result, take-up of the technology has been fairly limited to areas with good cable services, but it is likely

to be a more popular way of watching films at home in the future.
    SEE ALSO: **media streaming**.

video-recorder The commercial introduction of the video-recorder in the early 1970s signalled an important change in television watching. For the first time, people could influence what they watched and when they watched it. As a result, they proved very popular and became the most rapidly accepted item of domestic technology there has been. Video-recorders work using an electromagnetic head which records by magnetizing a tape, which is then rewound past the same head, reproducing the original material. Video-recorders became famous because it rapidly became clear that many people did not know how to use them effectively. One survey, for example, found that almost three-quarters of owners could not operate the timer. Video-recording is gradually giving way to DVD recording and devices which give even more control to the viewer (SEE: **TIVO**). These more recent machines use digital technology, which permits a much greater range of functions.

video-stream See: MEDIA STREAMING.

viewer See: AUDIENCE.

violence There is persistent public concern that exposure to the media, especially film and television, can make some individuals violent. There have been a number of well-publicized cases in which claims have been made that particular films have had a decisive effect in inducing violent acts. For example, one of the two young boys who abducted and subsequently murdered the child James Bulger in 1993 was alleged to have been influenced by watching a video of the film *Chucky 3*. Actually, there is no evidence at all that he saw this film. Similar claims were made about the Columbine school shootings in the United States in 1999.

This claim is essentially that people – or perhaps particularly susceptible individuals – imitate what they see or hear. There have been many attempts to test this claim. Most of these are laboratory experiments in which people are exposed to violent material, and then their subsequent behaviour is observed by comparison with a control group which has not been exposed to the violent material. There have been many variants of the experimental design, but no firm conclusions have emerged. Some studies do appear to show that children imitate what they see on television or that university students become more violent if they see violent material and then are made angry. However, other studies conclude that many very different kinds of material, not only violent, seem to produce effects of this kind. The evidence, in other words, is very inconclusive. In any case, laboratory studies of this kind will only measure short-term behaviour. In addition, they of necessity create unreal circumstances, and it may well be fallacious to project from the laboratory to the real world. Actually, most people, children included, know perfectly well that there is a difference between screen violence and real violence.

In response to these defects in purely laboratory-based research, attention has turned to longer-term effects and real-world situations. So, for example, there have been studies of communities before and after they were able to receive television. Groups of people have been followed for some years to investigate the effects of long-term exposure to television. Young offenders have had their viewing history studied to see if they were any different from comparable young people who were not offenders. Unfortunately, these studies also contradict one another. At best, therefore, the evidence is inconclusive, and it is likely that the causal patterns are so complex that exposure to film and television that some people find violent will only have a small part to play – if indeed it has any part at all.

SEE ALSO: **children and the media; effects**.

viral marketing A form of marketing in which news of a product or service is passed from person to person rather as a virus is transmitted. The media message may be passed on simply by word of mouth but is more effective when people use the internet, especially email, when it is possible for any one person to reach several others with one message. Viral marketing is therefore relying on customers to do the promotion and only works well if the rate at which the message is passed on is high, which typically only happens if the product is innovatory in some respect.

virtual community Communities of people formed by those who communicate with each other by the INTERNET and share some common interest, whether it is work, voluntary activity or play, and do so over a period of time. They may never meet physically but maintain a sense of common interest via email, by participation in a newsgroup or by membership of a mailing list. Of course, there have been communities rather like this that are sustained by telephone, or letter writing or even imagination (SEE: **imagined community**). Internet-enabled virtual communities, however, not only enable far faster, even REAL-TIME, communication, they also encourage interaction between several people at once. Virtual communities have proved critical in sustaining modern political and social movements from environmental protests to presidential primary elections in the US to FAN groups. Examples of a different kind may be found in the COMPUTER GAMES that can be played on the internet that allow people to take on different personalities. Over time the players get to know each other through their AVATARS and can form fairly strong relationships with each other without ever meeting.

Many people argue that the use of computers and the internet is an essentially solitary activity. Actually, it clearly has a social dimension, as is indicated above. One current area of controversy is the claim that websites such as MYSPACE and LIVEJOURNAL can facilitate the development of friendships online. There is currently not enough research in this area which would indicate whether, and in what ways, online friendship differs from face-to-face relationships.

SEE ALSO: **electronic commons**.

virtual reality 1 The way that people using the internet construct an online space or world for their daily interactions (SEE: **virtual community**). This virtual reality is essentially a text-based world.

2 The capacity of the computer, through sophisticated graphics software, to create life-like images which can themselves form whole worlds. This is essentially a visual experience. There are, in turn, several levels of visual virtual reality. At its simplest, the term is applied to contemporary films which use COMPUTER-GENERATED IMAGES to simulate worlds (the later *Star Wars* films, for example). These are simple because the viewer's perspective does not vary, and hence there is no interaction between viewer and the created world. Many computer games, however, will alter the character of the virtual world depending on what the game player does. Similar effects are used in architectural or engineering simulations to see how changes in one part of a structure will have effects on the whole. A third level permits even greater interactivity. There have been various experiments with devices, headsets or gloves, for example, that enable the wearer to immerse herself in a virtual reality and to change her viewpoint or even to touch and hold virtual objects.

SEE ALSO: **internet; virtual world**.

virtual world An invented environment complete with animals, plants, physical structures and social organization, usually simulated on a computer. Such worlds may be very different from that existing on the planet Earth, as in many COMPUTER GAMES. It may, on the other hand, closely approximate to the world we know, as in VIRTUAL REALITY simulators intended, for example, to model new architectural structures.

visual culture Describes ways in which human beings relate towards the visual aspects of the world. This can encompass texts which are predominantly visual, such as photographs or oil paintings, or aspects of everyday life that predominantly depend upon sight, such as how we look at and thus understand the countryside or buildings in a city.

visual imperative The sense that the visual is becoming increasingly important in culture. For example, the visual aspect of a film in the sense of SPECTACLE may be becoming more important than NARRATIVE.

SEE ALSO: **action**.

VJ (video jockey) A term derived from 'disc jockey' to refer to the presenter of video clips on music satellite and cable TV channels.

SEE ALSO: **DJ; MTV**.

vlog A BLOG that incorporates a significant amount of video material. A good deal of media attention has concentrated on blogs which consist of video diaries.

voice In the study of popular music, attention has sometimes been paid to the voice of a singer rather than the words that are sung. Voice is thus a particular way of manipulating sound to produce meaning. There are obviously techniques and methods of instruction to teach singing and the 'correct' use of the voice. However, one of the most difficult phenomena to analyse is the texture of a voice, which can have great significance for audiences. This was in some ways captured through the concept of the 'grain of the voice' developed by the French cultural analyst ROLAND BARTHES (1990). While this grain or texture may be connected with particular words, it may simply be to do with sound itself. This can produce a physical reaction, as is caught by the everyday idea that a certain voice sends a shiver down the spine. In this sense the grain of the voice can be seen as more important than the lyrical content or other aspects of the music.

SEE ALSO: **lyrics**.

voicer A report, written by someone else, that is read by a presenter, or a piece of journalism contained within a radio news report. It may be done live or be pre-recorded.

voicetrack Term used to refer to the part of an animated film recorded by the actors, which is then synchronized with the ANIMATION.

vox pop From *vox populi*, Latin for 'voice of the people', vox pop is most commonly used to describe radio or television programmes which seek the opinions of ordinary people on some topic, usually obtained by interviews in the street. It can also be used more contemptuously to refer to media products of all kinds that are thought to be undemanding and lowbrow.

voyeur A member of a cinema audience who is disengaged and uninvolved in the film, but derives sexual pleasure from observation of it. In some respects the experience of all cinema is voyeuristic in that the film spectator is physically separated from the film that is played in front of him or her. However, the film in many ways seeks to engage us, through getting us involved in the narrative of the film often through a process of identification with a hero. At certain moments, though, film remains intensely voyeuristic, especially where bodies are displayed to be looked at.

SEE ALSO: **gender; male gaze; Mulvey; pornography.**

walk-through In television and film-making, a rehearsal with actors used to confirm camera placement and so on.

Wapping During much of the post-war period, the trade unions active in the newspaper industry enjoyed considerable power based on their pivotal role in the production process. They operated closed shops, obtained very favourable working conditions and kept wages high. They were also able to resist the introduction of new technology (SEE: **electronic publishing**), which would lower costs of production but would also reduce the number of jobs. NEWS INTERNATIONAL, publishers of the *Sun* and *The Times*, decided to take the unions on and transferred production to a new facility at Wapping. A bitter industrial dispute ensued which the unions lost through a combination of new industrial relations legislation and the fact that the new technology made their position in production much less pivotal.

SEE ALSO: **newspaper**.

Warner Brothers Network Founded by the Warner Brothers film studio in the mid-1990s, this US television network is best known for television for children, although its best-known creation is *Buffy the Vampire Slayer*.

SEE ALSO: **television network**.

watchdog The media, and the press in particular, are sometimes referred to as watchdogs in that they will warn the public of government or corporate misdemeanours. Though this undoubtedly happens in some cases, there are anxieties that media watchdogs do not bark very loudly.

SEE ALSO: **government and the media**.

watershed The time of day, usually set at 9 p.m., before which television programmes deemed unsuitable for children cannot be shown.

web See: WORLD WIDE WEB.

webcam A video-camera connected to a computer. The camera provides live (current) film to a website running on the computer and can therefore potentially give access to the video-stream (SEE: **media streaming**) to a large number of people.

weblog See: BLOG.

website A set of documents and images collected together in one virtual location on the WORLD WIDE WEB. Most commonly, there are not only links within a website, there are also links between sites. Websites vary enormously in their purpose and content. Some are promotional and designed to sell goods and services. Others simply provide information. Still others are personal and can be more or less revealing.

western One of the most popular GENRES of cinema. The western has been a part of cinema more or less from its inception and has been seen as a key American form. It has been much analysed as a form or genre of cinema and sociologically in its social context, especially with respect to American society. A particularly sophisticated discussion that integrates these two approaches can be found in the work of Wright (1975). Wright analysed the plots of popular westerns during their most popular period (c.1930–70) and sought to understand why they were so popular during this period. He suggests that westerns function as MYTHS, in the sense that they deal with deep-seated issues in the society that produced them and try to resolve the problems of that society. Wright argues (p. 15) that there are four main western plots: (1) the classical (c.1930–55), where a lone hero 'saves the town, or the farmers from the gamblers, or the ranchers', which corresponds 'to the individualist conception of a society, underlying a market economy'; (2) the vengeance variation (overlaps the end of the classical and carries on until c.1960), where 'the plot concerns an ill-used hero who can find no justice in society and therefore becomes a gun fighter seeking vengeance', which reflects a society where changes are occurring in the market society; (3) the transition theme, which occurs in the early to mid-1950s, where the plot centres on 'a hero and a heroine who, while defending justice, are rejected by society'; (4) the professional plot, which develops from 1958 onwards, which revolves around 'a group of heroes who are professional fighters taking jobs for money' – for Wright this plot reflects the development of a corporate society. Wright develops his analysis of the plots of the western by using STRUCTURALIST methods derived from the work of the anthropologist Claude Lévi-Strauss and VLADIMIR PROPP. While in many respects enormously illuminating, his work has been criticized. Some of the most important points are: (1) that he oversimplifies the plots and characterization in westerns; (2) that the plot types overlap in time, which makes the straightforward connection to different stages of society difficult to sustain; (3) that the plots are linked to a very broad characterization of society rather than to changes in specific parts of it – such as the HOLLYWOOD STUDIO system; (4) that it is doubtful whether this scheme can be applied to other genres of film; (5) that he neglects the study of the audience and what the audience actually make of the film; (6) that he is selective in the films that he discusses. One can also add that the western was also popular in societies outside the United States, and that some of the most popular examples (especially so-called 'spaghetti westerns') were made in Europe by European film-makers. However, the broad methods and approach, if not the social connections posed by Wright, can still be applied to contemporary westerns in an illuminating way.

SEE ALSO: **action; ideology**.

white space Those parts of the printed page not occupied by text or illustration.

widescreen Cinema with an ASPECT RATIO which produces a wider image than the standard of 4:3 (width to height) The proportions of width to height in contemporary cinema include 2.2:1 and 1.66:1. Contemporary HDTV is 1.76:1. Cinema began to experiment with widescreen in the 1950s, with formats like Cinerama, in the face of competition from television. As home television has become more cinema-like it has also moved to more widescreen formats (SEE: **convergence**).

SEE ALSO: **anamorphic; Cinemascope; IMAX**.

widow The last line on a printed page which contains only one word or part of a word. In printing, traditionally, widows are regarded as unsightly and are removed. At times, however, they are put in for effect, precisely because they draw the attention.

wifi Also written WiFi. The technology and standards that underpin the connectivity of wireless devices in a wireless local area network. An increasingly large number of pieces of equipment – e.g. computers, mobile phones, PDAs – are now connected to each other wirelessly. The most important advantage of this technology is that it allows for mobile communication without the necessity of connection via a cable. In order to achieve this, the user has to be relatively near to access points in a wireless local area network.

wiki A kind of website that permits visitors to the site to alter the content of the site easily and quickly. The technology is used for collaborative writing, and the best-known example is the online encyclopedia Wikipedia.

Williams, Raymond (1921–88)   At the time of his death, Williams was Professor of Drama at Cambridge. He was a Welsh-born cultural analyst, literary critical and media scholar. His attention to 'ordinary culture' was a key influence on the development of cultural studies, and he carried out some of the first systematic analyses of media.

Williams' early work can be seen as reasonably conventional literary criticism. His reputation was made by two key works published at the end of the 1950s and beginning of the 1960s. *Culture and Society* (1958) reconsidered a variety of authors, to examine the reconstitution of culture in response to industrialism. *The Long Revolution* (1961) discussed the democratic possibilities of cultural change. Williams was keen to distinguish his commitment to a democratic socialism from conservative criticisms of cultural decline (as in the work of T. S. Eliot and F. R. Leavis) and more mechanical forms of MARXISM.

Williams' arguments for social and cultural democracy fed into his short but very influential book on *Communications* (1962), which can be seen as a founding text of media studies, in paying attention to textual analyses and institutional contexts. Williams' best-known contribution to the study of media came in his book *Television: Technology and Cultural Form* (1974), which criticized TECHNOLOGICAL DETERMINISM, and introduced the concept of 'flow'. This idea that television programmes flow into each other and that the viewer thus watches television as an ongoing narrative which contextualizes the distinct narratives of each programme has caused much debate. From the 1960s onwards, Williams' work became more influenced by Marxism, as he developed the ideas that became known as CULTURAL MATERIALISM. Another key conceptual development came with the idea of STRUCTURE OF FEELING.

Windows   See: GRAPHICAL USER INTERFACE.

wipe   A technique in film and video editing whereby one image is replaced by another, typically by a line moving across the screen.
  SEE ALSO: **dissolve**.

wireless   An everyday term used in earlier times to describe radio and also used in computer technology to refer to new technologies that do not require cables and wires to connect them.

women's magazines   Magazines targeted at a largely female readership have a long history and form a significant part of the magazine market.

In 2006, one of the highest-selling women's weekly magazines, *Take a Break*, for example, had sales exceeded only by a television guide; of the ten top-selling weeklies, six are women's magazines and three are TV guides. In the monthly magazine sector, women's magazines are less dominant, taking four of the top ten slots. As with the media industry in general, magazine ownership has become progressively more concentrated. In 2006, four magazine groups in the UK – Condé Nast, EMAP, IPC and the National Magazine Company – took more than 90 per cent of the market, and those groups are themselves part of diversified media companies.

The interests of women's magazines are closely tied to those of the advertising industry. The magazines depend for their survival on revenue from advertising and, therefore, try to sell to those women readers that the advertisers also want to reach. In particular, advertisers are most interested in middle-class women because they have more to spend, and it is important, therefore, for magazine editors to aim at this audience. A great deal of effort is therefore expended on finding out – or guessing – what women want from their magazines. Since the ending of the Second World War, there have been several changes in the way that the magazines conceive of their readership. In the 1950s, 1960s and first part of the 1970s, they aimed at the traditional image of the woman as housewife and mother with distinctively feminine interests. By the 1980s women's magazines – and the advertising industry – had discovered the 'New Woman', who had a career and, although she had traditional female concerns, was also interested in more conventionally masculine pursuits, such as financial services or career management. In the 1990s, however, editors evidently believed that a different kind of woman was emerging who was more interested in sex, shopping and celebrity, and magazines began concentrating on these areas rather more.

Academic analysis has largely concentrated on the role of women's magazines in forming feminine identities (Ferguson, 1983; Winship, 1987), often focusing on the visual aspects of the magazines and especially on the advertisements that they contain. Public disquiet has also taken up the notion that the magazines have a decided effect on their readers. There has been rather less work on the organization of the magazines themselves (though see Gough-Yates, 2003) or on the way in which the magazines are actually read by women. One important study on the latter aspect (Hermes, 1995) concludes that women's reading of magazines is simply a part of everyday life, an apparently obvious judgement that is actually at variance with earlier academic work on magazines and women's identities.

SEE ALSO: **magazine**.

world music A genre of popular music that gained currency in the 1990s. Like many genres of popular music, 'world' is as much a marketing label as reflective of common and clear musical features. Thus, world music can include acoustic guitars from Britain, brass bands from South America, Bhangra from the Indian subcontinent and so on. It has been argued that the audience for world music is mostly in those sections of the middle class displaying OMNIVORE-type characteristics.

SEE ALSO: **globalization**.

world wide web Often used interchangeably, but mistakenly, with the INTERNET, the world wide web is a set of protocols that enables the publication of documents (SEE: **website**) which can be read by anyone with access to the internet. The web depends for its working on a method of marking up pages in the documents called HTML (Hypertext Markup Language), a web browser which can present HTML pages on a computer and a protocol which enables the browser to send and receive pages from across the internet. In the early days of the web in the 1990s, web documents were text only, but now they can be multimedia, and websites not only use sounds and visual images of all kinds but also whole films. The world wide web is actually not unlike conventional print media. It is designed to be read, and most people still use it as a source of information. What makes it different, however, is the system of links – hypertext links – which enables a connection with any other page in any other website. If the world wide web is not unlike more conventional media, the question is whether audiences act in the same way. In one respect, at least, there seems to be a more ACTIVE AUDIENCE in that people are setting up their own personal websites, which are relatively cheap to construct and run, yet potentially can reach a large number of people.

In common with other media, the web raises the question of REGU-LATION. Indeed, many of the same issues arise, though often in an accentuated form because of the decentralized nature of the web. On the one hand, there are those who argue for an unfettered freedom of speech and of use of the web. For this camp, the web has a great democratic potential in encouraging free and well-informed debate (SEE: **public sphere**). On the other side, there are arguments about morality, the dangers of untrammelled free speech, copyright, sedition and the use of the web for commercial purposes. So, the free availability of pornography is an offence to some people as are the violent opinions expressed in some websites. Because copying is so very easy, authors' rights, whether in text or music, are in danger of being ignored (SEE: **copyright; Napster**). Some governments are worried about the use of the web by their opponents (SEE:

government and the media). Lastly, even the most radical advocates of freedom on the web are becoming concerned by the risk that the system may become overwhelmed by commercial organizations attracted by its possibilities for selling goods and services. Although some of the business opportunities promised by the internet and the world wide web have evaporated, it remains a very cheap marketing tool.

SEE ALSO: **new information and communication technology; new media**.

wrap In radio, when a news journalist joins an interview with other content, thus 'wrapping' an extract up.

writer Writing of one kind or another is clearly central to the media industries. Whether they occur in songs as lyrics, in television as scripts, or in newspapers and books, words are the critical, though often hidden, element. There is a natural temptation, for example, to see television as an essentially visual medium. Actually, it is really a writer's medium. In many ways this is scarcely surprising. Writers, after all, do not just produce the dialogue, they also effectively provide the structure of the programme. This is especially significant in the case of soap opera. It is often said that what makes any particular soap opera is not the quality of the acting or lavish production values, but rather the story and the characters, and it is the writer who is responsible for those. In addition, television is peculiarly dependent on writers because the medium is very verbal. It is about talk, and the pictures essentially illustrate the talk. In turn this is related to the fact that television is a domestic medium. Television is addressed to everyday life and, as such, is more about talk than it is about dramatic events.

SEE ALSO: **household**.

yellow journalism Originally used in the United States towards the end of the nineteenth century to describe the appearance of sensationalist journalism. It has been revived in recent years in the UK as tabloid newspapers, increasingly competitive with one another, and led by RUPERT MURDOCH'S purchase of the *News of the World* in 1968, became much more interested in celebrities, prying into people's private lives, disasters, and, above all, sex.

youth culture The culture of young people. At one point in the 1960s it was suggested that a global youth culture was emerging. However, this idea was quickly subject to criticism as it neglected the way in which the cultures of young people were divided and fragmented in a number of ways, such as by gender, race, class and locality. The idea of youth subculture came to prominence to capture these modes of division. A subculture is a distinct form of culture, but is contextualized by the wider cultures of society. The most significant development of the idea came at the Birmingham CENTRE FOR CONTEMPORARY CULTURAL STUDIES in the 1960s and 1970s. The key ideas here are that youth subcultures are developed in response to social and cultural changes such as housing redevelopment, market shifts and increased affluence, where young people's lives are being changed in ways that the cultures they were born into cannot help them to cope with. Thus, for young working-class people in London in the 1950s and 1960s, patterns of employment were changing in ways that produced cultural change and subcultures (P. Cohen, 1980). The spectacular subcultures that emerged at this point were understood in such contexts, but also as representing a form of opposition or resistance to dominant culture. Thus, Willis (1977) studied the oppositional culture of young white men in a school in the English Midlands and showed how this form of resistance prepared the young men for factory labour and its male culture. In addition, Hebdige (1979) analysed subcultural style as an indirect mode of opposition to dominant culture. This idea fed into studies of the television audience, which was seen as active and resistant to dominant meanings (See: FISKE).

The role of media in the everyday lives of subcultures was explored in much of this writing. This was especially the case with popular music (Willis, 1978; Hebdige, 1979) and with magazines and GENDER (McRobbie, 1991). The place of media in the lives of young people was then looked at through the idea of subculture and style. More recently, these ideas have been significantly revised through attention to the way in which media figure in the lives of all young people rather than those who can be seen as part of distinct subcultures. For example, the work of Willis et al. (1990) examined young people's creative relationship to, for example, television and popular music, showing its significance in their day-to-day activities. This theme has also been taken up in studies of young people and the media within the tradition of audience studies (Laughey, 2006).

The idea of youth culture is perhaps due for revival in the context of discussions of GLOBALIZATION and TRANSCULTURE. In this light, it can again be suggested that there are important common patterns in the ways in which media are located in the lives of young people. While this has continued to be a matter of concern on the part of those commentators who suggest that too much engagement with television is in itself a bad thing (which tends to neglect the finding that young people are relatively light viewers of television compared with older adults), for media studies the issue should be the further understanding of the specific ways in which media figure centrally in young people's experiences and imaginations.

SEE ALSO: **children and the media.**

Z

zapping The process, much helped by remote control devices, of moving rapidly between television channels. About one-fifth of households can be classified as heavy zappers, changing channels more than once every two minutes.

SEE ALSO: **channel loyalty**.

zipping Television viewers can use VIDEO-RECORDERS to disregard television schedules and watch what they want when they want. Zipping refers to the practice of using the fast-forward to bypass unwanted material, often advertisements.

SEE ALSO: **audience**.

zoo format See: RADIO.

zoom lens A lens of variable focal length, which can move between CLOSE-UP and wide-angle.

Abercrombie, N. (1996), *Television and Society*, Cambridge: Polity Press

Abercrombie, N., Lash, S. and Longhurst, B. (1992), 'Popular Representation: Recasting Realism', in S. Lash and J. Friedman (eds.), *Modernity and Identity*, Oxford: Blackwell

Abercrombie, N. and Longhurst, B. (1991), *Individualism, Collectivism and Gender in Popular Culture*, Salford Papers in Sociology, 12, Salford: Institute for Social Research

Abercrombie, N. and Longhurst, B. (1998), *Audiences: A Sociological Theory of Performance and Imagination*, London: Sage

Anderson, B. (1991), *Imagined Communities: Reflections on the Origins and Spread of Nationalism*, London: Verso

Anderson, C. (2006), *The Long Tail*, London: Random House

Ang, I. (1985), *Watching 'Dallas': Soap Opera and the Melodramatic Imagination*, London: Methuen

Appadurai, A. (1993), 'Disjuncture and Difference in the Global Cultural Economy', in B. Robins (ed.), *The Phantom Public Sphere*, Minneapolis and London: University of Minnesota Press

Appadurai, A. (1996), *Modernity at Large*, Minneapolis and London: University of Minnesota Press

Bacon-Smith, C. (1992), *Enterprising Women: Television Fandom and the Creation of Popular Myth*, Philadelphia: University of Pennsylvania Press

Bakhtin, M. M. (1981), *The Dialogic Imagination*, Austin: University of Texas Press

Bakhtin, M. M. (1984), *Rabelais and His World*, Bloomington: Indiana University Press (originally 1968)

Baldwin, E., Longhurst, B., McCracken, S., Ogborn, M. and Smith, G. (1999), *Introducing Cultural Studies*, Harlow: Prentice Hall

Ball, M. S. and Smith, G. W. H. (1992), *Analyzing Visual Data*, London: Sage

Banker, A. (2001), *The Pocket Essential Bollywood*, Harpenden: Pocket Essentials

Barnard, Stephen (2000), *Studying Radio*, London: Arnold

Barthes, R. (1973), *Mythologies*, St Albans: Paladin

Barthes, R. (1977), 'The Death of the Author', in R. Barthes *Image-Music-Text*, Glasgow: Fontana/Collins

Barthes, R. (1990), 'The Grain of the Voice', in S. Frith and A. Goodwin (eds.), *On Record: Rock, Pop and the Written Word*, London: Routledge

Baudrillard, J. (1988), *Selected Writings*, ed. M. Poster, Cambridge: Polity Press

Becker, H. (1963), *Outsiders: Studies in the Sociology of Deviance*, New York: The Free Press

Benjamin, W. (1970), 'The Work of Art in the Age of Mechanical Reproduction', in W. Benjamin, *Illuminations*, Glasgow: Fontana/Collins

Bennett, A. and Peterson, R. A. (eds.) (2004), *Music Scenes: Local, Translocal, and Virtual*, Nashville: Vanderbilt University Press

Bennett, H. S. (1980), *On Becoming a Rock Musician*, Amherst: University of Massachusetts Press

Berger, J. (1972), *Ways of Seeing*, London: British Broadcasting Corporation, and Harmondsworth: Penguin

Bernstein, B. (1971, 1973, 1975), *Class, Codes and Control*, vols. 1–3, London: Routledge and Kegan Paul

Bernstein, S. (1994), *Film Production*, 2nd edn, Oxford: Focal Press

Billig, M. (1995), *Banal Nationalism*, London: Sage

Bird, S. E. (2003), *The Audience in Everyday Life: Living in a Material World*, London: Routledge

Bishop, J. and Hoggett, P. (1986), *Organizing Around Enthusiasms: Mutual Aid in Leisure*, London: Comedia

Bordwell, D. and Thompson, K. (2005), *Film Art: An Introduction*, 7th edn, New York: McGraw Hill (originally 1979)

Bourdieu, P. (1984), *Distinction: A Social Critique of the Judgement of Taste*, London: Routledge and Kegan Paul

Brown, D. (2004), *The Da Vinci Code*, London: Corgi

Brunsdon, C. and Morley, D. (1978), *Everyday Television: 'Nationwide'*, London: British Film Institute

Bryce, J. (1987), 'Family Time and Television Use', in T. R. Lindlof (ed.), *Natural Audiences*, Norwood: Ablex

Bryson, B. (1997), 'What About the Univores? Musical Dislikes and Group-based Identity Construction among Americans with Low Levels of Education', *Poetics*, 25

Butler, J. (1990), *Gender Trouble: Feminism and the Subversion of Identity*, London: Routledge

Carr, D., Buckingham, D., Burn, A. and Schott, G. (2006), *Computer Games; Text, Narrative and Play*, Cambridge: Polity Press

Castells, M. (1996), *The Rise of Network Society*, Oxford: Blackwell

Centre for Contemporary Cultural Studies (1977), *Working Papers in Cultural Studies 10: On Ideology*, Birmingham: Centre for Contemporary Cultural Studies

Centre for Contemporary Cultural Studies (1982), *The Empire Strikes Back: Race and Racism in 70s Britain*, London: Hutchinson

Clarke, J., Critcher, C. and Johnson, R. (eds.) (1979), *Working Class Culture: Studies in History and Theory*, London: Hutchinson

Cohen, P. (1980), 'Subcultural Conflict and Working-class Community', in S. Hall et al., *Culture, Media, Language: Working Papers in Cultural Studies, 1972–79*, London: Hutchinson

Cohen, Sara (1991), *Rock Culture in Liverpool: Popular Music in the Making*, Oxford: Clarendon

Cohen, Stanley (1973), *Folk Devils and Moral Panics: The Creation of Mods and Rockers*, St Albans: Paladin

Connor, S. (1989), *Postmodernist Culture*, Oxford: Blackwell

Cook, P. and Bernink, M. (eds.) (1999), *The Cinema Book*, 2nd edn, London: British Film Institute

Corner, J. (2002), 'Performing the Real', *Television and New Media* 3(3)

Couldry, N. (2000), *Inside Culture: Re-imagining the Method of Cultural Studies*, London: Sage

Cultural Trends (1993), no. 19, London: Policy Studies Institute

Debord, G. (1994), *The Society of the Spectacle*, New York: Zone Books

de Certeau, M. (1984), *The Practice of Everyday Life*, Berkeley: University of California Press

Derrida, J. (1976), *Of Grammatology*, London and Baltimore: Johns Hopkins University Press

Derrida, J. (1978), *Writing and Difference*, London: Routledge

Dyer, R. (1979), *Stars*, London: British Film Institute

Dyer, R. (1987), *Heavenly Bodies: Film Stars and Society*, Basingstoke: Macmillan

Dyer, R. (1997), *White*, London: Routledge

Eco, U. (1982), 'The Narrative Structure in Fleming', in B. Waites, T. Bennett and G. Martin (eds.), *Popular Culture: Past and Present*, London: Croom Helm in association with The Open University Press

Ferguson, M. (1983), *Forever Feminine*, London: Heinemann

Finnegan, R. (1989), *The Hidden Musicians: Music-making in an English Town*, Cambridge: Cambridge University Press

Fish, S. (1980), *Is There a Text in this Class? The Authority of Interpretive Communities*, Cambridge, MA: Harvard University Press

Fiske, J. (1987), *Television Culture*, London: Methuen

Fiske, J. (1989a), *Reading the Popular*, London: Unwin Hyman

Fiske, J. (1989b), *Understanding Popular Culture*, London: Unwin Hyman

Fiske, J. and Hartley, J. (1978), *Reading Television*, London: Methuen

Fleming, C. (2002), *The Radio Handbook*, 2nd edn, London: Routledge

Foucault, M. (1971), *Madness and Civilisation*, London: Tavistock

Foucault, M. (1973), *The Birth of the Clinic*, London: Tavistock

Foucault, M. (1974a), *The Order of Things: An Archaeology of the Human Sciences*, London: Tavistock

Foucault, M. (1974b), *The Archaeology of Knowledge*, London: Tavistock

Foucault, M. (1977a), *Discipline and Punish*, London: Tavistock

Foucault, M. (1977b), 'What Is an Author?', in *Language, Counter-Memory, Practice*, Oxford: Blackwell

Foucault, M. (1979), *The History of Sexuality*, London: Tavistock

Foucault, M. (1987), *The Use of Pleasure: The History of Sexuality, vol. 2*, Harmondsworth: Penguin

Foucault, M. (1990), *The Care of the Self: The History of Sexuality, vol. 3*, Harmondsworth: Penguin

Freud, S. (1930), *Civilization and its Discontents*, London: Hogarth Press

Freud, S. (1962), *Five Lectures on Psychoanalysis*, Harmondsworth: Penguin Press (originally 1910)

Freud, S. (1976), *Jokes and Their Relation to the Unconscious*, Harmondsworth: Penguin Press (originally 1905)

Freud, S. (1984a), *The Interpretation of Dreams*, London: Hogarth Press (originally 1900)

Freud, S. (1984b), *Leonardo da Vinci*, London: ARK (originally 1910)

Frith, S. (1978), *The Sociology of Rock*, London: Constable

Frith, S. (1983), *Sound Effects: Youth, Leisure and the Politics of Rock*, London: Constable

Frith, S. (1988), 'Why Do Songs Have Words?', in S. Frith, *Music for Pleasure: Essays in the Sociology of Pop*, Cambridge: Polity Press

Frith, S. (1996), *Performing Rites: Evaluating Popular Music*, Oxford: Oxford University Press

Frith, S. and Goodwin, A. (eds.) (1990), *On Record: Rock, Pop and the Written Word*, London: Routledge

Frith, S. and McRobbie, A. (1990), 'Rock and Sexuality', in S. Frith and

A. Goodwin, *On Record: Rock, Pop and the Written Word*, London: Routledge

Galtung, J. and Ruge, M. (1973), 'Structuring and Selecting News', in S. Cohen and J. Young (eds.), *The Manufacture of News*, London: Constable

Garafalo, R. (1992), *Rockin' the Boat: Mass Music and Mass Movements*, Boston: South End Press

Gauntlett, D. and Hill, A. (1999), *TV Living: Television, Culture and Everyday Life*, London: Routledge

Gibson, W. (1984), *Neuromancer*, London: Gollancz

Gilbert, P. (2005), *Passion Is a Fashion: The Real Story of The Clash*, London: Aurum

Gillett, C. (1983), *The Sound of the City: The Rise of Rock and Roll*, London: Souvenir

Gilroy, P. (1987), *'There Ain't No Black in the Union Jack': The Cultural Politics of Race and Nation*, London: Hutchinson

Gilroy, P. (1993), *The Black Atlantic: Modernity and Double Consciousness*, London: Verso

Gitlin, T. (1983), *Inside Prime Time*, New York: Pantheon

Gitlin, T. (ed.) (1987), *Watching Television: A Pantheon Guide to Popular Culture*, New York: Pantheon

Glasgow University Media Group (1976), *Bad News*, London: Routledge and Kegan Paul

Glasgow University Media Group (1980), *More Bad News*, London: Routledge and Kegan Paul

Glasgow University Media Group (1982), *Really Bad News*, London, Writers and Readers Publishing Cooperative Society

Glasgow University Media Group (1985), *War and Peace News*, Milton Keynes: Open University Press

Glasgow University Media Group (1993), *Getting the Message*, London: Routledge

Gledhill, C. (1980), 'Klute 1: a Contemporary Film Noir and Feminist Criticism', in E. Ann Kaplan (ed.), *Women in Film Noir*, London: British Film Institute

Gledhill, C. (1987), 'The Melodramatic Field: An Investigation', in C. Gledhill (ed.), *Home Is Where the Heart Is: Studies in Melodrama and the Woman's Film*, London: British Film Institute

Goffman, E. (1959), *The Presentation of Self in Everyday Life*, Garden City, New York: Doubleday

Goffman, E. (1979), *Gender Advertisements*, Basingstoke: Macmillan

Goodwin, A. (1993), *Dancing in the Distraction Factory: Music Television and Popular Culture*, London: Routledge

Gough-Yates, A. (2003), *Understanding Women's Magazines*, London: Routledge

Greenberg, B. S. (1965), 'Diffusion of News of the Kennedy and Oswald Deaths', in B. S. Greenberg and E. B. Parker (eds.), *The Kennedy Assassination and the American Public: Social Communication in Crisis*, Stanford, CA: Stanford University Press

Gripsrud, J. (1995), *The 'Dynasty' Years: Hollywood Television and Critical Media Studies*, London: Routledge

Gross, L. (1989), 'Out of the Mainstream: Sexual Minorities and the Mass Media', in E. Seiter, H. Borchers, G. Kreutzner and E.-M. Warth (eds.), *Remote Control: Television, Audiences and Cultural Power*, London: Routledge

Grossberg, L. (1992), *We Gotta Get Out of This Place*, London: Routledge

Habermas, J. (1989), *The Structural Transformation of the Public Sphere*, Cambridge: Polity Press

Hall, S. (1992), 'The Question of Cultural Identity', in S. Hall, D. Held and T. McGrew (eds.), *Modernity and Its Futures*, Cambridge: Polity Press in association with Blackwell Publishers and the Open University

Hall, S., Critcher, C., Jefferson, T., Clarke, J. and Roberts, B. (1978), *Policing the Crisis: Mugging, the State and Law and Order*, London: Macmillan

Hall, S. and Jefferson, T. (eds.) (1976), *Resistance Through Rituals: Youth Subcultures in Post-war Britain*, London: Hutchinson

Hall, S. and Whannel, P. (1964), *The Popular Arts*, London: Hutchinson

Haraway, D. (1989), *Primate Visions: Gender, Race and Nature in the World of Modern Science*, London: Routledge

Haraway, D. (1991), *Simians, Cyborgs and Women: The Reinvention of Nature*, London: Free Association Books

Hatch, D. and Millward, S. (1987), *From Blues to Rock: An Analytical History of Pop Music*, Manchester: Manchester University Press

Hebdige, D. (1979), *Subculture: The Meaning of Style*, London: Methuen

Herman, E. S. and Chomsky, N. (1994), *Manufacturing Consent: The Political Economy of the Mass Media*, London: Vintage

Hermes, J. (1995), *Reading Women's Magazines*, Cambridge: Polity Press

Heylin, C. (1993), *From the Velvets to the Voidoids: A Pre-Punk History for a Post-Punk World*, London: Penguin

Hills, M. (2002), *Fan Cultures*, London: Routledge

Hirsch, E. and Silverstone, R. (eds.) (1992), *Consuming Technologies: Media and Information in Domestic Spaces*, London: Routledge

Hoggart, R. (1957), *The Uses of Literacy*, London: Chatto and Windus hooks, bell (1983), *Ain't I a Woman*, London: Pluto

hooks, bell (1992), *Black Looks: Race and Representation*, Boston: South End Press

hooks, bell (1996), *Reel to Real: Race, Sex and Class at the Movies*, London: Routledge

Hornby, N. (1992), *Fever Pitch*, London: Gollancz

Hornby, N. (1994), 'Sparing the Rod', in C. Roberts (ed.), *Idle Worship: How Pop Empowers the Weak, Rewards the Faithful and Succours the Needy*, London: HarperCollins

Hornby, N. (1995), *High Fidelity*, London: Gollancz

Hornby, N. (2003), *31 Songs*, London: Penguin

Horton, D. and Wohl, R. (1956), 'Mass Communications and Para-social Interaction', *Psychiatry*, vol. 19

James, C. L. R. (1980), *The Black Jacobins*, London: Allison and Busby

Jenkins, H. (1992), *Textual Poachers: Television Fans and Participatory Culture*, London: Routledge

Jenson, J. (1992), 'Fandom as Pathology: The Consequences of Characterization', in L. Lewis (ed.), *The Adoring Audience: Fan Culture and Popular Media*, London: Routledge

Kaplan, E. A. (1987), *Rocking Around the Clock: Music Television, Postmodernism and Consumer Culture*, London: Routledge

Kuhn, A. (2002), *An Everyday Magic: Cinema and Cultural Memory*, London: I. B. Tauris

Laing, D. (1985), *One Chord Wonders: Power and Meaning in Punk Rock*, Milton Keynes: Open University Press

Laing, D. (2004), 'World Record Sales 1992–2002', *Popular Music*, 23 (1)

Laughey, D. (2006), *Music and Youth Culture*, Edinburgh: Edinburgh University Press

Liebes, T. and Katz, E. (1993), *The Export of Meaning*, Oxford: Oxford University Press

Livingstone, S. M. and Lunt, P. (1995), *Talk on Television*, London: Routledge

Longhurst, B. (2007), *Popular Music and Society*, 2nd edn, Cambridge: Polity Press

Lull, J. (1988), *World Families Watch Television*, London: Sage

Lull, J. (1990), *Inside Family Viewing*, London: Routledge

Lum, C. M. K. (1998), 'The Karaoke Dilemma: On the Interaction between Collectivism and Individualism in the Karaoke Space', in T. Mitsui and S. Hosokawa (eds.), *Karaoke Around the World*, London: Routledge

Lyotard, J.-F. (1984), *The Postmodern Condition*, Manchester: Manchester University Press

McCann, G. (1988), *Marilyn Monroe: The Body in the Library*, Cambridge: Polity Press

McCloud, S. (1994), *Understanding Comics: The Invisible Art*, New York: HarperCollins

McGuigan, J. (1992), *Cultural Populism*, London: Routledge

MacKenzie, D. and Wajcman, J. (1985), 'Introduction' to D. MacKenzie and J. Wajcman, *The Social Shaping of Technology: How the Refrigerator Got Its Hum*, Milton Keynes: Open University Press

McLuhan, M. (1964), *Understanding Media: the Extensions of Man*, London: Routledge and Kegan Paul

McLuhan, M. and Fiore, Q. (1967), *The Medium Is the Massage*, Harmondsworth: Penguin

McQuail, D. (1997), *Audience Analysis*, London: Sage

McQuail, D. (2003), *Media Accountability and Freedom of Information*, Oxford: Oxford University Press

McQuail, D. (2005), *McQuail's Mass Communication Theory*, 5th edn, London: Sage

McRobbie, A. (1984), 'Dance and Social Fantasy', in A. McRobbie and M. Nava (eds.), *Gender and Generation*, Basingstoke: Macmillan

McRobbie, A. (1991), *Feminism and Youth Culture*, Basingstoke: Macmillan

McRobbie, A. (1993), 'Shut Up and Dance: Youth Culture and Changing Modes of Femininity', *Cultural Studies*, 7

McRobbie, A. (1994), *Postmodernism and Popular Culture*, London: Routledge

Marcus, G. (1992), *Dead Elvis: A Chronicle of a Cultural Expression*, London: Penguin

Marshall, L. (2005), *Bootlegging: Romanticism and Copyright in the Music Industry*, London: Sage

Martin, B. (1981), *A Sociology of Contemporary Cultural Change*, Oxford: Blackwell

Mathieson, T. (1997), 'The Viewer Society: Michel Foucault's Panopticon Revisited', *Theoretical Criminology*, 1 (2)

Middleton, R. (1990), *Studying Popular Music*, Milton Keynes: Open University Press

Miller, F. with K. Janson and L. Varley (2002), *Batman: The Dark Knight Returns*, New York: DC Comics

Millington, B. and Nelson, R. (1986), *'Boys from the Blackstuff': The Making of TV Drama*, London: Comedia

Mitsui, T. (1998), 'The Genesis of Karaoke: How the Combination of Technology and Music Evolved', in T. Mitsui and S. Hosokawa (eds.), *Karaoke Around the World*, London: Routledge

Mitsui, T. and Hosokawa, S. (1998), 'Introduction' to T. Mitsui and S. Hosokawa (eds.), *Karaoke Around the World*, London: Routledge

Morgan, M. and Signorelli, N. (1990), 'Cultivation Analysis: Conceptualization and Methodology', in N. Signorelli and M. Morgan (eds.), *Cultivation Analysis: New Directions in Media Effects Research*, London: Sage

Morley, D. (1980), *The 'Nationwide' Audience*, London: British Film Institute

Morley, D. (1986), *Family Television: Cultural Power and Domestic Leisure*, London: Comedia

Morley, D. (2000), *Home Territories: Media, Mobility and Migrancy*, London: Routledge

Mulvey, L. (1981), 'Visual Pleasure and Narrative Cinema', in T. Bennett et al. (eds.), *Popular Television and Film*, London: British Film Institute

Negus, K. (1992), *Producing Pop: Culture and Conflict in the Popular Music Industry*, London: Edward Arnold

Negus, K. (1996), *Popular Music in Theory*, Cambridge: Polity Press

Pearson, R. E. and Uricchio, W. (eds.) (1991), *The Many Lives of the Batman: Critical Approaches to a Superhero and His Media*, London: Routledge

Penley, C. (1992), 'Feminism, Psychoanalysis and the Study of Popular Culture', in L. Grossberg, C. Nelson and P. Treichler (eds.), *Cultural Studies*, London: Routledge

Peterson, R. (1997), *Creating Country Music: Fabricating Authenticity*, Chicago: University of Chicago Press

Peterson, R. and Anand, N. (2004), 'The Production of Culture Perspective', *Annual Review of Sociology*, 30

Peterson, R. and Bennett, A. (2004), 'Introducing Music Scenes', in A. Bennett and R. A. Peterson (eds.), *Music Scenes: Local, Translocal and Virtual*, Nashville: Vanderbilt University Press

Peterson, R. and Berger, D. G. (1990), 'Cycles in Symbol Production: The Case of Popular Music', in S. Frith and A. Goodwin (eds.), *On Record: Rock, Pop and the Written Word*, London: Routledge

Peterson, R. and Kern, R. M. (1996), 'Changing Highbrow Taste: From Snob to Omnivore', *American Sociological Review*, 61

Philo, P. (1990), *Seeing and Believing*, London: Routledge

Propp, V. (1968), *The Morphology of the Folk Tale*, Austin and London: University of Texas Press

Radway, J. (1987), *Reading the Romance: Women, Patriarchy and Popular Literature*, London: Verso

Reynolds, S. (2005), *Rip it Up and Start Again: Post Punk 1978–1984*, London: Faber and Faber

Ritzer, G. (1993), *The McDonaldization of Society: An Investigation into the*

Changing Character of Contemporary Social Life, Thousand Oaks: Pine Forge Press

Robertson, R. (1995), 'Glocalization: Time-Space and Homogeneity-Heterogeneity', in M. Featherstone, S. Lash and R. Robertson (eds.), *Global Modernities*, London: Sage

Rodman, G. B. (1996), *Elvis after Elvis: The Posthumous Career of a Living Legend*, London: Routledge

Rojek, C. (2001), *Celebrity*, London: Reaktion

Said, E. (1978), *Orientalism*, Harmondsworth: Penguin

Sandvoss, C. (2005), *Fans: The Mirror of Consumption*, Cambridge: Polity Press

Savage, J. (1991), *England's Dreaming: Sex Pistols and Punk Rock*, London: Faber and Faber

Schlesinger, P. (1978), *Putting 'Reality' Together: BBC News*, London: Constable

Schloss, J. (2004), *Making Beats: The Art of Sample-Based Hip-Hop*, Middletown, CT: Wesleyan University Press

Schwichtenberg, C. (ed.) (1993), *The Madonna Connection: Representational Politics, Subcultural Identities and Cultural Theory*, Oxford: Westview Press

Shank, B. (1994), *Dissonant Identities: The Rock 'n' Roll Scene in Austin, Texas*, Hanover, NH: Wesleyan University Press/University Press of New England

Shelley, M. (1985), *Frankenstein or The Modern Prometheus*, London: Penguin (originally 1818)

Shuker, R. (2001), *Understanding Popular Music*, London: Routledge

Silverstone, R. (1985), *Framing Science: The Making of a BBC Documentary*, London: British Film Institute

Silverstone, R. (1994), *Television and Everyday Life*, London: Routledge

Silverstone, R. (ed.) (1997), *Visions of Suburbia*, London: Routledge

Stacey, J. (1994), *Stargazing: Hollywood Cinema and Female Spectatorship*, London: Routledge

Staiger, J. (2005), *Media Reception Studies*, New York: New York University Press

Tagg, P. (1989), 'Open Letter: "Black Music", "Afro-American Music" and "European Music"', *Popular Music*, 8

Taylor, I., Evans, K. and Fraser, P. (1996), *A Tale of Two Cities*, London: Routledge

Thornton, S. (1995), *Club Cultures: Music, Media and Subcultural Capital*, Cambridge: Polity Press

Toynbee, J. (2000), *Making Popular Music: Musicians, Creativity and Institutions*, London: Arnold

Tudor, A. (1989), *Monsters and Mad Scientists*, Oxford: Blackwell

Wicke, P. (1992), 'The Role of Rock Music in the Political Disintegration of East Germany', in J. Lull (ed.), *Popular Music and Communication*, Newbury Park: Sage

Williams, R. (1958), *Culture and Society: 1780–1950*, London: Chatto and Windus

Williams, R. (1961), *The Long Revolution*, London: Chatto and Windus

Williams, R. (1962), *Communications*, Harmondsworth: Penguin

Williams, R. (1973), *Drama from Ibsen to Brecht*, Harmondsworth: Penguin

Williams, R. (1974), *Television: Technology and Cultural Form*, Glasgow: Fontana/Collins

Williams, R. (1975), *Drama in a Dramatised Society: An Inaugural Lecture*, Cambridge: Cambridge University Press

Willis, P. (1977), *Learning to Labour: How Working Class Kids Get Working Class Jobs*, Farnborough: Saxon House

Willis, P. (1978), *Profane Culture*, London: Routledge and Kegan Paul

Willis, P. et al. (1990), *Common Culture: Symbolic Work at Play in the Everyday Cultures of the Young*, Milton Keynes: Open University Press

Winship, J. (1987), *Inside Women's Magazines*, London: Pandora

Women's Studies Group, Centre for Contemporary Cultural Studies, University of Birmingham (1978), *Women Take Issue: Aspects of Women's Subordination*, London: Hutchinson in association with the Centre for Contemporary Cultural Studies, University of Birmingham

Wright, W. (1975), *Sixguns and Society*, Berkeley, CA: University of California Press